Praise for *Essential LINQ*

"*Essential LINQ* is the most comprehensive book I have read so far on LINQ technology. Both Charlie and Dinesh have done an excellent job bringing their internal expertise to developers through this book. The book starts with the basics of LINQ and delves deep into the LINQ Ocean. If you would like to learn the internals of LINQ technology and master it, this book is for you."

—*Mahesh Chand, MVP, MCP, author and founder of C# Corner*

"LINQ is one of the most transformational technologies of .NET and will have a profound impact on how developers architect and code applications going forward. *Essential LINQ* is an excellent book that will help you learn and understand LINQ, and enable you to immediately start applying it with your projects."

—*Scott Guthrie, Corporate Vice President, .NET Developer Platform, Microsoft*

"Essential LINQ provides an excellent and cohesive overview of LINQ with emphasis on LINQ to Objects, LINQ to SQL, and LINQ to XML."

—*Pat Helland, Partner Architect, Microsoft Corporation*

"Self-effacing, Charlie Calvert will tell you he is just lucky to hang around smart guys that let him explain things to others, but his straightforward, clear, and precise explanations will make LINQ one of your new best friends."

—*Paul Kimmel, Microsoft MVP and author of* LINQ Unleashed for C#

"Something wonderful is happening. Developers are discovering the newly integrated ability to query in-memory collections such as arrays and lists, Datasets, XML, and relational databases directly from their .Net code. These collective capabilities, typically referred to as a paradigm shift, have already begun to shake foundations and open developers' eyes to new possibilities. As the initial waves of this shift take place, there exists a parallel need for understanding essential fundamentals and principles. "Essential LINQ" is the best written, most concise source from which to build your fundamental understanding of LINQ. Read this book!"

—*Ron Landers, Senior Technical Consultant, Right-Click Consulting, LLC*

Essential LINQ

Microsoft .NET Development Series

John Montgomery, *Series Advisor*
Don Box, *Series Advisor*
Brad Abrams, *Series Advisor*

The award-winning Microsoft .NET Development Series was established in 2002 to provide professional developers with the most comprehensive and practical coverage of the latest .NET technologies. It is supported and developed by the leaders and experts of Microsoft development technologies, including Microsoft architects, MVPs, and leading industry luminaries. Books in this series provide a core resource of information and understanding every developer needs to write effective applications.

Titles in the Series

Brad Abrams, *.NET Framework Standard Library Annotated Reference Volume 1: Base Class Library and Extended Numerics Library*, 978-0-321-15489-7

Brad Abrams and Tamara Abrams, *.NET Framework Standard Library Annotated Reference, Volume 2: Networking Library, Reflection Library, and XML Library*, 978-0-321-19445-9

Chris Anderson, *Essential Windows Presentation Foundation (WPF)*, 978-0-321-37447-9

Bob Beauchemin and Dan Sullivan, *A Developer's Guide to SQL Server 2005*, 978-0-321-38218-4

Adam Calderon, Joel Rumerman, *Advanced ASP.NET AJAX Server Controls: For .NET Framework 3.5*, 978-0-321-51444-8

Eric Carter and Eric Lippert, *Visual Studio Tools for Office: Using C# with Excel, Word, Outlook, and InfoPath*, 978-0-321-33488-6

Eric Carter and Eric Lippert, *Visual Studio Tools for Office: Using Visual Basic 2005 with Excel, Word, Outlook, and InfoPath*, 978-0-321-41175-4

Steve Cook, Gareth Jones, Stuart Kent, Alan Cameron Wills, *Domain-Specific Development with Visual Studio DSL Tools*, 978-0-321-39820-8

Krzysztof Cwalina and Brad Abrams, *Framework Design Guidelines: Conventions, Idioms, and Patterns for Reusable .NET Libraries*, Second Edition, 978-0-321-54561-9

Joe Duffy, *Concurrent Programming on Windows*, 978-0-321-43482-1

Sam Guckenheimer and Juan J. Perez, *Software Engineering with Microsoft Visual Studio Team System*, 978-0-321-27872-2

Anders Hejlsberg, Mads Torgersen, Scott Wiltamuth, Peter Golde, *The C# Programming Language*, Third Edition, 978-0-321-56299-9

Alex Homer and Dave Sussman, *ASP.NET 2.0 Illustrated*, 978-0-321-41834-0

Joe Kaplan and Ryan Dunn, *The .NET Developer's Guide to Directory Services Programming*, 978-0-321-35017-6

Mark Michaelis, *Essential C# 3.0: For .NET Framework 3.5*, 978-0-321-53392-0

James S. Miller and Susann Ragsdale, *The Common Language Infrastructure Annotated Standard*, 978-0-321-15493-4

Christian Nagel, *Enterprise Services with the .NET Framework: Developing Distributed Business Solutions with .NET Enterprise Services*, 978-0-321-24673-8

Brian Noyes, *Data Binding with Windows Forms 2.0: Programming Smart Client Data Applications with .NET*, 978-0-321-26892-1

Brian Noyes, *Smart Client Deployment with ClickOnce: Deploying Windows Forms Applications with ClickOnce*, 978-0-321-19769-6

Fritz Onion with Keith Brown, *Essential ASP.NET 2.0*, 978-0-321-23770-5

Steve Resnick, Richard Crane, Chris Bowen, *Essential Windows Communication Foundation: For .NET Framework 3.5*, 978-0-321-44006-8

Scott Roberts and Hagen Green, *Designing Forms for Microsoft Office InfoPath and Forms Services 2007*, 978-0-321-41059-7

Neil Roodyn, *eXtreme .NET: Introducing eXtreme Programming Techniques to .NET Developers*, 978-0-321-30363-9

Chris Sells and Michael Weinhardt, *Windows Forms 2.0 Programming*, 978-0-321-26796-2

Dharma Shukla and Bob Schmidt, *Essential Windows Workflow Foundation*, 978-0-321-39983-0

Guy Smith-Ferrier, *.NET Internationalization: The Developer's Guide to Building Global Windows and Web Applications*, 978-0-321-34138-9

Will Stott and James Newkirk, *Visual Studio Team System: Better Software Development for Agile Teams*, 978-0-321-41850-0

Paul Yao and David Durant, *.NET Compact Framework Programming with C#*, 978-0-321-17403-1

Paul Yao and David Durant, *.NET Compact Framework Programming with Visual Basic .NET*, 978-0-321-17404-8

For more information go to informit.com/msdotnetseries/

Essential LINQ

Charlie Calvert
Dinesh Kulkarni

✦✦ Addison-Wesley

Upper Saddle River, NJ • Boston • Indianapolis • San Francisco
New York • Toronto • Montreal • London • Munich • Paris • Madrid
Capetown • Sydney • Tokyo • Singapore • Mexico City

U.S. Corporate and Government Sales
(800) 382-3419
corpsales@pearsontechgroup.com

For sales outside the United States please contact:

International Sales
international@pearson.com

Visit us on the Web: www.informit.com/msdotnetseries

Library of Congress Cataloging-in-Publication Data:

Calvert, Charles
  Essential LINQ / Charlie Calvert, Dinesh Kulkarni. — 1st ed.
    p. cm.
  ISBN 0-321-56416-2 (pbk. : alk. paper) 1. Microsoft LINQ. 2. C# (Computer program language) 3. Query languages (Computer science) 4. Microsoft .NET Framework.
I. Kulkarni, Dinesh, 1968- II. Title.

  QA76.7.C35 2009
  006.7'882—dc22

                              2008052508

ISBN-13: 978-0-321-56416-0
ISBN-10: 0-321-56416-2
Text printed in the United States on recycled paper at RR Donnelley in Crawfordsville, Indiana.
First printing March 2009

This book is dedicated to my wife Margie. When authors dedicate their books to their wife or parents, I perhaps unfairly suspect them of a failure of imagination or paucity of emotional range. I would have no problem coming up with other worthies to whom I could dedicate this book. My good friends, such as David Intersimone, Lino Tadros, John Kaster, and Steve Teixeira, have been a joy to me for many years. I'm blessed with a wonderful father, and I would be happy to dedicate another book to him. My siblings, nieces, nephews, and other relatives are deserving of a dedication. So are my godparents, George and MaryAnn Kephart. I've recently been reintroduced to the Pacific Northwest, and I undoubtedly could never have written a word of this text were it not for the regular support I get from the mountains, forests, and waterways of this wonderful land. My many spiritual mentors—Christian, Buddhist, and Hindu—have been the very air I breathe for many years, and I could do nothing without them. I also lucked into—through no skill of my own, and despite all my best efforts to deny myself the privilege—a wonderful wife to whom I can never sufficiently offer enough thanks. Margie, I once again find myself dedicating a book to you, wishing only that this simple dedication were worthy of even some small portion of all that you have done for me.

—Charlie Calvert

Dedicated to the Lord for all he has given and continues to give.
—Dinesh Kulkarni

Contents at a Glance

Contents

Foreword

For years I have been fascinated with the differences between general-purpose programming languages and databases. Practically every enterprise application built today is coded in a general-purpose programming language and talks to a database, yet the two ecosystems are amazingly different and quite poorly integrated—the impedance mismatch between object-oriented programming and the relational model is the gift that keeps on giving when it comes to application complexity.

But the thing I find particularly puzzling is the lack of query capabilities in general-purpose programming languages. Why is it you can query database tables but not in-memory objects? Why are XPath and XQuery so arbitrarily different from SQL? Why is it so hard to transform data between the object, relational, and XML domains? These are the kinds of questions that launched us on the Language Integrated Query (LINQ) journey. Along the way we got wise to the wonders of functional programming, lambda expressions, type inference, monads, O/R mapping, and all sorts of fascinating computer science. Fortunately, we managed to boil our learnings down to a set of pragmatic language features and APIs that are useful in practically any .NET application.

LINQ extends the .NET Framework and programming languages with a uniform model for querying and transforming in-memory collections, relational data, and XML documents. With LINQ, C# 3.0 and VB 9.0 gain the expressive power of SQL and XQuery to become the first general-purpose programming languages to natively support queries and transformations over all classes of data.

LINQ was a very interesting and unique project to work on. One reason is that it wasn't just about language features. In order to gain experience with the query capabilities we were developing, we needed to validate them against the important data domains—objects, relational, and XML. That led us to create the LINQ to Objects, LINQ to SQL, and LINQ to XML APIs, all of which were built alongside the language features. The synergy and agility we got from having a joint team working on both language and APIs was just amazing—and loads of fun!

Also, LINQ isn't just a single monolithic language feature, but rather a collection of several smaller and individually useful features—such as lambda expressions, extension methods, expression trees, object initializers, and anonymous types—that all come together to form the concept of Language Integrated Query. This made our work much more relevant and leveraged.

Finally, LINQ is big step toward a more declarative style of programming. This may be subtle, but it is really important. Programs written in today's imperative programming languages are too much about the "how" and too little about the "what." We tend to over-specify the solutions to our programming problems—for example, by deconstructing queries into for loops, if statements, manipulation of temporary collections, and so on. By the time such programs run, it is all but impossible for the execution environment to "understand" what they do. The higher level semantic meaning has been lost in a sea of imperative, low-level instructions that must be blindly executed in exact sequence. This contrasts with LINQ queries, which preserve the programmer's exact intent and allows the execution infrastructure to be much smarter. A great example here is the Parallel LINQ (PLINQ) API that parallelizes query execution on concurrent hardware with practically no changes required to the source code.

Of course, the creation of a new technology such as LINQ is really only the first part of our job. The next step is to find ways to explain our new technology to the world of developers.

Essential LINQ is an important book because it provides a clear, easy-to-understand explanation of what LINQ does, how it does it, and the many practical ways you can use this technology to make your daily programming life easier and more productive.

Both authors of this text bring an important set of skills to this project. Throughout the development of LINQ, I worked daily with Dinesh Kulkarni in this role as Program Manager for the LINQ to SQL project. Few understand LINQ to SQL better than Dinesh, and the many insights he provides into LINQ will prove to be an invaluable tool for any reader of this book. The chapters Dinesh contributed to this book will be a resource that developers will frequently mine for their rich, well-thought-out content.

I've known Charlie Calvert since we worked together on Turbo Pascal and Delphi at Borland International. Charlie is an accomplished author with a gift for finding the key threads in a technology and explaining them to readers in a clear, easy-to-understand prose style. He is also one of nicest people I've met.

Charlie and Dinesh each bring important skills to this project that have enabled them to create an excellent book that shows how LINQ works and the many practical ways you can use it in your daily development process.

Anders Hejlsberg
Redmond, WA
February 2009

Acknowledgments

Charlie Calvert:

Like most authors, I feel a deep and true gratitude to those who helped me complete this text. Many of them made major contributions to the finished product and deserve much more acclaim than the conventions of book publishing allow them to receive. I'm very grateful to everyone who has helped me, and I hope that everyone mentioned here and those who I unintentionally left out understand that my gratitude extends beyond what can be expressed in these few paragraphs.

I want to thank Nick Paldino, Christophe Nazarre, and Ron Landers for their excellent technical review. All three did a fine job, and I learned much from each of them. Although each reviewer had his own set of valuable contributions, I should perhaps add that Christophe did an unusually excellent job, providing one of the best reviews of a technical document I've ever seen. It's interesting to trace the arc that a writer's reaction to reviews swings through over the years. When I was in grade school, I took the marks on my paper by teachers as the word of God and never thought to question them. Later I learned to plumb the depths of ingratitude by learning to resent the numerous and well-deserved red scratchings that showed up on college papers and early professional manuscripts. At last I learned to endure the criticism with feigned good will, knowing that the medicine might taste badly but ultimately would be beneficial. And now, after all these years, my only reaction is wonder and amazement that anyone is willing to take the time to help me clean up what I have written. Ron,

Christophe, and Nick: Your review of this text saved me from numerous egregious blunders and made many worthwhile contributions to the pages of this book. Thank you for your excellent and thoughtful review of my writing, and thank you to my publishers for assembling this excellent team! Whatever merit there may be in the chapters I contributed to this book owes much of its value to your efforts.

At one time or another, nearly every engineer on the teams I work with has given me valuable help. However, four people have consistently come to my aid with excellent explanations of some of the trickiest and most interesting parts of the C# language. In no particular order, I want to thank Eric Lippert, Luke Hoban, Alex Turner, and Mads Torgersen for the support they have so generously given me. These are four of the most talented engineers I've ever spoken with, but I value them even more for their ability to take complex ideas and put them in language that anyone can understand.

Other folks at work who deserve thanks include Damien Watkins, Dustin Campbell, Kirill Osenkov, DJ Park, Marcelo Guerra Hahn, David Sterling, Matteo Taveggia, Anders Hejlsberg, Eric Maino, Mary Deyo, Lisa Feigenbaum, Beth Massi, Jomo Fisher, Sam Ng, Tim Ng, Kevin Pilch-Bisson, Wes Dyer, Esen Tuna, Luca Bolognese, Scott Nonnenberg, and Karen Liu. Lists like this always leave out nearly as many people as they include. I hope that those who are deserving of mention, but don't see their names here, will forgive me the omission.

I also want to thank my coauthor, Dinesh Kulkarni, for giving me the chance to work with him on this book. That Dinesh is an excellent engineer and manager goes without saying. My special privilege has been to get to know him so well. In the rarified technical atmosphere where Dinesh dwells, one encounters many extraordinary professionals. Dinesh's special gift is to combine his technical talent with the warmth, wit, and generosity of a first-class human being. If there were more people like Dinesh, this would be a better world.

My editors at Addison Wesley, most particularly the redoubtable Joan Murray and the ever-helpful Olivia Basegio, were both patient and supportive. I have to confess that I was completely outclassed by them nearly every step of the way, and I feel very privileged to have had the chance to work with such extraordinary professionals. Joan, Olivia, and the others at

Addison Wesley give me something to aspire to: They demonstrate how it ought to be done. What a joy it has been to work with you all!

I have to thank my wife Margie for her otherworldly patience and an understanding beyond the capacity of mere mortals. Margie is an angel, and the support she gave me while I wrote this book is but one of the many, many things for which I owe her my undying gratitude and love.

Dinesh Kulkarni:

For me, this book is the culmination of an incubation project I joined almost four years ago. Although my name appears as one of the two authors, the book is a record of the work done by a large number of people inside and outside Microsoft. I am fortunate to have had a chance to write about the work, and I acknowledge their contributions here.

I would like to start with Erik Meijer, who introduced and urged me to join the Language-Integrated Query incubation project headed by Anders Hejlsberg in the small but elite C# Product Unit at Microsoft. There, the design of LINQ was carried out primarily in the grueling but delightful language design meetings attended by a small group of dedicated people. There I had the privilege of joining Anders Hejlsberg, Matt Warren, Erik Meijer, Peter Hallam, and later, Mads Torgersen, for some intense design discussions about all aspects of LINQ. That is where I learned the essence of language and API design with LINQ as a working example. It was as much a work of art as a product of engineering practices.

The response of the .NET community to our LINQ previews in Fall 2005 and Spring 2006 was phenomenal. Their continued encouragement, support, and criticisms throughout the process helped shape LINQ. They have had a significant impact on the subject of this book.

The C# product unit was a perfect place for turning the incubation and previews into a shippable product. That is where C# 3.0, LINQ to Objects, and LINQ to SQL morphed from preview into products. Matt Warren built most of the LINQ preview components and was the architect and super developer for the LINQ to SQL component that I ended up driving as the program manager. He is one of the best developers I have ever had a chance to work with. Likewise, the development team lead by Terry Adams and the QA team lead by Daigo Hamura provided great examples of engineering and innovation required to go from a preview to a product under very challenging conditions. A partner team led by Antoine Cote, Jay Hickerson, and Young Joo provided a great designer experience for our run-time work and also provided a foundation for the Entity Framework designer. Thank you for building a wonderful product and for being so supportive throughout the process. From that team, Mathew Charles and Vijay Upadya continue to inspire me as colleagues on our new project to build a multitier application framework using LINQ. Overall, the heroic efforts of the team really motivated me to tell the story of LINQ through this book.

My management chain—especially Luca Bolognese, Raj Pai, and Drew Fletcher—struck a great balance between being demanding and nurturing. Alex Turner, who joined as an intern and developed more than 300 samples (with $1/sample bounty) for the preview, perfectly rounded out the team.

I was fortunate to find an experienced and well-known coauthor—Charlie Calvert. He set an example for making the most complex topics simple through his writing. Charlie's empathy for the common developer and his understanding of the developer community are truly exceptional, and I feel privileged to have had a chance to learn from him about the process of writing a book. His constant encouragement and calm approach were essential for me to get to the finish line. His exemplary dedication and professionalism will continue to inspire me well into the future.

I would like to thank Nick Paldino, Christophe Nazarre, and Ron Landers for their detailed reviews that have significantly improved the clarity and accuracy. Each of them had a unique perspective that nicely complemented the other. Nick has been a reviewer of LINQ and C# since the early previews and continues to be an advocate for clarity and precision. Ron's insistence on better explanation has hopefully made the book more accessible. Christophe in particular did such a wonderful job finding subtle errors that I would not want to write again without having him as a reviewer.

The patience and sacrifice of my family enabled me to complete the book. My children, Siddharth and Shruti, and my wife, Devaki, put up with my regular absence as I kept writing and revising chapters for twice as long as expected. Devaki also helped with preliminary reviews of my early drafts. I am thankful to them for being the silent and patient contributors.

About the Authors

Charlie Calvert is the Community Program Manager for the Microsoft C# team. While working on outreach and bridge building to both external and internal teams through the Web and live events, Charlie focuses his technical energies on LINQ and core C# language scenarios such as generics. He has degrees in Journalism and Computer Science from the Evergreen State College. The author of ten technical books that have sold more than 100,000 copies, Charlie currently lives in the Seattle area where he enjoys outdoor activities such as hiking, sailing, and skiing in the mountains.

Dinesh Kulkarni is a Senior Program Manager in the Microsoft .NET Developer Platform team working on framework support for multitier applications. Before that he worked on the LINQ project in the C# team from the incubation phase through the shipping of the first release with Visual Studio 2008. He received his Ph.D. in Computer Science from the University of Notre Dame, Indiana, and B.Tech. from IIT Bombay, India. He has published extensively in technical journals and filed more than a dozen patents. He lives in the Seattle area and enjoys outdoor activities with his family.

■ 1 ■
Introduction

WELCOME TO *ESSENTIAL LINQ*. This book was written by two managers from the Microsoft C# team. One is the Program Manager who guided the design and development of LINQ to SQL, and the other worked daily with the engineers, testers, and designers who built LINQ to SQL and LINQ to Objects. All the key ideas in this book were vetted with the designers of LINQ and reflect the current best practices for LINQ development.

LINQ is an acronym for Language Integrated Query. It is pronounced "link." You may sometimes hear it pronounced "lin-queue," but that is incorrect.

LINQ introduces querying into the C# language as a first-class citizen. The compiler type checks LINQ queries. Inside Visual Studio LINQ queries are syntax-highlighted and IntelliSense-aware. They provide developers with a strongly typed, logically structured syntax for querying data.

Before LINQ there was no single native syntax for querying data in the C# language. There were tools for branching and looping, tools for writing object-oriented code, even tools for creating delegates or serializing data. But there was no single, standardized way to query multiple data sources.

You can use LINQ's SQL-like syntax to query SQL databases, XML files, or generic data structures such as lists and queues. LINQ can also be extended to allow developers to access virtually any other data source.

Developers have always been able to query databases, XML files, and other data sources. LINQ's contribution is to provide a single, unified syntax for performing these queries. In the past, developers used one syntax to query SQL data, another to query XML, a third to query a collection, and so on. Now we have a single syntax for performing all these tasks. Just as `if` statements provide an integrated way to branch, and `for` and `while` statements provide a technique for looping over data, LINQ provides a single, integrated syntax for querying data.

The introduction of LINQ is one of the biggest changes in the C# world since the inception of the language. The only other change of comparable magnitude was the introduction of generics, but even that change probably does not have as many long-term implications.

This book is designed to introduce you to LINQ and to explain the most important of its advanced features. When you finish reading this book, you will have received a thorough introduction to the LINQ syntax. You will know how to query all the major LINQ data sources, such as SQL databases and XML files. The text also provides sections on best practices for LINQ development and provides tips on how to integrate the technology into your projects.

The Varied Uses of the LINQ Syntax

The introduction of LINQ into C# has broad implications. Although LINQ's primary purpose is to allow you to query data, the syntax that enables this technology also allows developers to write a new style of code.

New syntactical features include *lambdas* and *extension methods*. Developers will find these useful even when they are not writing LINQ queries. Other LINQ-related concepts, such as deferred execution and composition, also have far-reaching implications. These features give the language new flexibility that can be invaluable in some scenarios.

LINQ does more than simply add new features to the language. It introduces a declarative style of programming into the C# language. The declarative programming model allows developers to craft code that succinctly captures their intent, without forcing them to worry about the order in which events take place, or their precise implementation. It allows developers to state what they want to do, rather than how it will be done.

LINQ is flexible enough that you can apply new syntax features, and the declarative style of programming, to domains other than querying data. Creating programs that run on multiple threads has proven to be one of the most difficult hurdles for modern developers to cross. LINQ is a particularly efficient tool for creating threads that run concurrently. By developing an understanding of the LINQ syntax, you will be able to take advantage of PLINQ, or Parallel LINQ, a technology that was being developed as this book was written.

LINQ Is a Practical Technology

You might find this talk of declarative programming and composition a bit abstract. However, this book is a practical text designed primarily to give you the information you need to use LINQ to get work done quickly, easily, and in a style that is easy to maintain. When more abstract ideas are introduced, they are explained slowly and carefully, making it easy to understand exactly how they work and why they are important.

You will find that LINQ introduces a number of exciting new concepts into the life of the average C# developer, but none of them are particularly difficult to understand if they are properly introduced. The goal of this book is to ease you into these technologies so that you will become conversant with LINQ queries and LINQ syntax sooner and more easily than you might expect.

LINQ is designed to help you get your work done quickly and to write code that can be easily maintained. New ideas are useless if they don't have practical implications. LINQ's syntax may be exciting, but developers will love this technology because it helps them get a lot of work done in a short period of time. The primary goal of this book is to help you learn how to use LINQ to get practical work done in as short a period of time as possible.

Audience and Subject Matter

This book is designed to present LINQ to the average developer. In simple terms it explains why LINQ is important and how to use it. You are expected to have an intermediate-level understanding of C#.

This book is designed as a general introduction to LINQ, but it can be especially helpful if you

- Want to focus on practical solutions rather than abstract theory.
- Prefer high-performance tools that are lightweight and highly scalable.
- Have an interest in understanding the C# language and how to use it to solve problems quickly and efficiently.

LINQ is a useful tool designed for use by typical C# developers. You might have to do some work to understand how to use LINQ, but it is not an advanced tool for use only by the most sophisticated developers. It is a general-purpose tool that any competent C# developer can easily incorporate into his or her daily development cycle.

Read this book to obtain a comprehensive overview of all the major features of LINQ, including advanced features such as deferred execution, lambdas, and expression trees. However, make sure that you never lose sight of LINQ's primary goal, which is to make it easy for you to quickly query data from multiple sources. Understanding the advanced features is valuable, but not if it diverts you from LINQ's primary purpose as a practical tool.

This book is divided into 18 chapters:

- Chapter 1, "Introduction": This chapter.
- Chapter 2, "Getting Started": Here you find a few simple examples of the major features of LINQ. Use these examples to help get started with this new technology.
- Chapter 3, "The Essence of LINQ": An overview of the LINQ technology from a theoretical perspective. Here you read about the main ideas around which the LINQ architecture is organized.
- Chapter 4, "C# 3.0 Technical Overview": In this chapter you learn about the various features of C# 3.0 and C# 2.0 that come together to make LINQ possible. Lambdas, extension methods, and deferred execution are a few of the features outlined in this chapter.

- Chapter 5, "Writing Query Expressions": Most LINQ developers spend the majority of their time writing expressions. This is the primary syntax for writing LINQ queries. If you become an expert at writing query expressions, you will be an expert at LINQ.

- Chapter 6, "Query Operators": The LINQ query operators give LINQ its power and flexibility. These operators are a set of tools built into the LINQ language that allow you to accomplish a wide range of tasks.

- Chapter 7, "A Quick Tour of LINQ to SQL": You might be reading this book primarily to learn about LINQ to SQL. The first six chapters of this book give you the background you need to understand how LINQ works. Now at last you can begin learning how to query a SQL database with LINQ.

- Chapter 8, "Reading Objects with LINQ to SQL": You can use LINQ to SQL to populate the objects in your program with relational data. This chapter explains the nuances of how to write LINQ to SQL queries.

- Chapter 9, "Modifying Objects with LINQ to SQL": No API for querying relational data would be complete without the ability to post changes back to the database. This chapter explains how to proceed.

- Chapter 10, "Using Stored Procedures and Database Functions with LINQ to SQL": Modern database development relies on the developer's ability to work with stored procedures and table and scalar functions. You also read about how to use stored procedures when performing inserts, updates, and deletes.

- Chapter 11, "Customizing Entity Persistence and Adding Business Logic": LINQ provides developers with many opportunities to customize their code. This chapter shows you how to take control of LINQ so that you can bend it to your specific needs and the needs of your business.

- Chapter 12, "LINQ to Entities Overview": Like LINQ to SQL, the Entity Framework allows developers to use LINQ to access relational databases. This chapter explains how to use LINQ to Entities and how it differs from LINQ to SQL. Entity Framework is a large component that is evolving substantially, and it includes many concepts beyond LINQ. Hence, we have scoped the discussion to an overview of LINQ to Entities.

- Chapter 13, "LINQ to XML: Creation": Shows you how to create XML files with LINQ.

- Chapter 14, "Querying and Editing XML": Shows you how to query XML data with LINQ.

- Chapter 15, "XML Namespaces, Transformations, and Schema Validation": Shows you how to transform XML data. This chapter focuses primarily on transforming SQL data into XML and XML into relational data. It also explains the general principles behind transforming one LINQ data source into another.

- Chapter 16, "Introduction to LINQ Patterns and Practices": LINQ is a new technology, and developers will have many questions about how best to use it. This chapter lays out some best practices and common patterns that LINQ developers can use to help them write robust code that is easy to maintain.

- Chapter 17, "LINQ Everywhere": Microsoft or third-party developers can extend LINQ by writing providers that give developers access to new data sources or to new functionality. Three LINQ providers currently under development are reviewed in this chapter. Perhaps the most important is Parallel LINQ (PLINQ), which enables you to write LINQ queries that automatically execute simultaneously on multiple processors.

- Chapter 18, "Conclusion": This chapter reviews the book's main themes.

The Essence of LINQ

Seven key themes, outlined in Chapter 3, recur throughout this text. I'll outline them here briefly to give you an easy-to-find reference to these central and very important concepts. These seven foundational principles state that LINQ is

- **Integrated**: LINQ is a first-class citizen of .NET languages such as C# and VB and as such is fully type-checked. Inside Visual Studio it is syntax-highlighted and IntelliSense-aware.
- **Unitive**: LINQ provides a single syntax for querying multiple data sources, including relational data found in a SQL database, XML data, and the objects in a program.
- **Extensible**: LINQ can be adapted to work with multiple languages and to query multiple data sources. LINQ to XML, LINQ to SQL, and LINQ to Objects are only three possible forms of LINQ. Developers can extend the language to query almost any arbitrary data source, such as a file system, web service, or network protocol.
- **Declarative**: A LINQ developer tells the compiler what to do, without focusing on how to perform a task or in what order tasks must be performed.
- **Hierarchical**: LINQ provides a rich, object-oriented view of data. A more rigorous or mathematical view of this same theme would focus on LINQ's capability to generate and manipulate graphs.
- **Composable**: The results of one query can be used by a second query, and one query can be a subclause of another query. In many cases, this can be done without forcing the execution of any one query until the developer wants that execution to take place. Thus, you can write three separate but related queries. LINQ automatically notes the connections between them and combines them into a

single, efficient query that executes only once. This allows you to "divide and conquer" by breaking up the logic of your query just as you divide the logic of your program across multiple classes and methods.

- **Transformative**: The results of a LINQ query against one data source can be transformed into a second data source. For instance, a query against a SQL database can produce an XML file as output.

These ideas represent the heart of LINQ, and they reappear in many different forms throughout this book. They are the exclusive focus of Chapter 3. That chapter is one of the cornerstones of this book, so you might want to refer to it while reading other chapters. Chapter 15 also is one of the key parts of the book.

Comparing LINQ to SQL and LINQ to Objects

We know that many, but by no means all, of the readers of this book are very interested in learning how to query a relational database using LINQ to SQL. Nevertheless, the book begins by studying LINQ to Objects. An in-depth exploration of LINQ to SQL does not begin until nearly halfway through the book, in Chapter 7. Why did we wait so long to introduce such an important topic?

LINQ to SQL is not innately more difficult to understand than LINQ to Objects. In many cases, it is not even possible to distinguish a LINQ to SQL query from a LINQ to Objects query without seeing the context in which the two queries occur. So the delay in introducing LINQ to SQL has nothing to do with its complexity.

The great advantage of LINQ to Objects over LINQ to SQL is that it does not require a connection to a database. Most of the examples in the first six chapters are designed to be run quickly and easily by anyone with an up-to-date C# compiler. With a few brief exceptions, there is no need to have a SQL database available, or to worry about connection strings and data access rights. This ease of use is perhaps the primary reason why LINQ to Objects is introduced before LINQ to SQL.

If you are eager to get to the material on LINQ to SQL, please keep in mind that in many cases the syntax of a LINQ to SQL query is nearly identical to the syntax for a LINQ to Objects query. Every topic in the first six chapters, and every sample that is shown, contains information that LINQ to SQL developers need to know. Each query shown in these opening chapters contains information directly applicable to LINQ to SQL.

However, there's another very important reason to begin with LINQ to Objects. When many developers hear that LINQ is a tool for querying data, they begin thinking about querying relational databases. That is an important part of LINQ development, but it is not the only or even the primary reason to write LINQ code.

In later chapters you learn that many `for` and `while` loops—particularly nested `for` and `while` loops—can be more easily, and more intuitively, expressed as LINQ statements. Just as developers new to generics are encouraged to consider converting their old-style collections into generic collections, so should you consider translating `for` and `while` loops into LINQ statements.

LINQ is not just a tool for querying databases. It is true that LINQ to SQL is a powerful, intuitive, and time-saving way to query a database, but that is only one facet of LINQ. Anytime you find yourself working with collections of data, you should look for ways to introduce LINQ queries into your project. A great deal of the development that we do involves working with lists, queues, collections, and other data structures. All of this code lends itself to LINQ development, and in many cases we can improve our code by judiciously introducing LINQ queries into all parts of our programs.

A Few Words About Generics

Generics play a key role in LINQ. To read this book, you need to know a few basic facts about generics, none of which are particularly difficult to grasp. This book assumes that you understand the basics of generics. Particularly during the discussion of lambdas, it will become important for you to understand generic methods. This is not a widely understood topic, so this text explores it in enough depth to make sure that you can follow the discussion.

Even if you're familiar with generic syntax, you might not know how to pronounce the elements of that syntax. Consider the following code fragment:

```
List<string>
```

This should be read as "list of string." You are about to read an entire book that uses this kind of generic syntax often. When most of us read, we tend to hear the sound of the words we encounter. It would be painful for you to go through this entire book seeing syntax like this and pronouncing it "list open bracket string close bracket." It would be worse to say something like "list, some funny-looking stuff with the word string in it." Your comfort level will increase considerably if you read `List<string>` as "list of string."

Another type that you will see frequently in this book is `IEnumerable<T>`. You should pronounce this type as "I enumerable of T."

Both `List<T>` and `IEnumerable<T>` are collections: they are containers for elements of a similar type. `IEnumerable<T>` is an interface that is implemented by `List<T>`.

Source for the Samples and Troubleshooting Resources

Appendix A contains information about downloading and installing the samples that accompany this book. It also has additional information in case you're new to C#.

Many of the programs in this book are console applications. If you run a console application by pressing F5, the output often disappears before you have a chance to read it. Some developers solve this problem by placing a call to `Console.ReadLine()` at the end of their program. If you are working in Visual Studio, that is not necessary. Instead, press Ctrl-F5 (Debug | Start Without Debugging) to run the program. A console window appears as usual, but it pauses and waits for a keystroke before it closes.

Additional information about this book is available on the web. Charlie Calvert maintains a blog and a web site:

http://blogs.msdn.com/charlie

http://www.elvenware.com

You can find Dinesh Kulkarni's blog here:

http://blogs.msdn.com/dinesh.kulkarni/

Information about LINQ and C# often can be found at the C# Development Center:

http://csharp.net

The publisher's web site for this book is located here:

http://www.informit.com/register

Summary

LINQ is a practical technology. As you read this text, your primary goal should be to learn how to write LINQ queries. If you have a confident and thorough knowledge of how to write a LINQ query, you will be able to use LINQ to reliably and speedily complete your day's work. The bottom line is efficiency, and LINQ is designed to help you become a more efficient developer.

All the ideas and technologies presented in this text are designed to help you become a better developer. Absorb these technologies as best you can, but always remember that these are practical tools designed to make your life easier and your work more robust. If the subject matter occasionally becomes too abstract for your tastes, absorb it as best you can, and rest assured that more practical subject matter is usually no more than a page or two away.

As always, do everything you can to enjoy both this book and your journey into the exciting and exotic land of LINQ development. Writing code is not easy. No one should try programming in C# unless they enjoy it. I find development rewarding because I frequently get excited about the technologies behind the C# language. Do everything you can to cultivate that sense of excitement and to explore LINQ with a sense of adventure. All the great developers I've met get excited about the art of programming. They pursue it with passion and obviously derive great joy from the work. Partake of that spirit as best you can, knowing that one part of the path to excellence is learning how to enjoy your work.

2
Getting Started

M ANY DEVELOPERS PREFER to use a new technology rather than simply read about it. Practical experience provides a foundation on which to construct the theoretical understanding needed when mastering a new skill.

This chapter helps you understand LINQ by showing several simple programs that illustrate

- LINQ to Objects
- LINQ to SQL
- LINQ to XML

These examples demonstrate three themes that recur frequently in this book:

- The usefulness of query expressions
- The significance of deferred execution
- The primacy of IEnumerable<T>

The examples shown in this chapter also illustrate how to write *query expressions*, the key syntactic construct used by LINQ developers to query a data source. When executing even these simple LINQ queries, you will encounter *deferred execution,* a characteristic of LINQ that developers must comprehend if they want to claim a thorough knowledge of the subject. Finally, you will be introduced to `IEnumerable<T>`, the data source for LINQ to Objects and LINQ to XML queries. These queries usually also return a variable of this type. A thorough understanding of LINQ is impossible without first becoming acquainted with `IEnumerable<T>`.

This chapter also introduces several new features of C# 3.0 that are not LINQ-specific:

- Type inference
- Collection initializers
- Object initializers
- Automatic properties

These features are discussed in more depth in Chapter 4, "C# 3.0 Technical Overview." That chapter also covers other important features, such as lambdas and extension methods.

Querying a Collection of Integers

Our first query will be run against a collection of integers. Listing 2.1 shows a complete program demonstrating how to write a LINQ query against a collection that contains the numbers 1, 2, and 3. The query selects the numbers in the collection that are smaller than 3 and prints them to the screen.

LISTING 2.1   When Compiled, the Source for the SimpleNumericQuery Program Returns the Values 1 and 2

```
using System;
using System.Collections.Generic;
using System.Linq;

namespace NumericQuery
{
    class Program
    {
        static void Main(string[] args)
        {
            List<int> list = new List<int>() { 1, 2, 3 };
```

```
        var query = from number in list
                    where number < 3
                    select number;

        foreach (var number in query)
        {
            Console.WriteLine(number);
        }

    }
  }
}
```

There are two simple ways to compile and run this program:

- Method 1:
    1. Enter the program directly into a default console application in Visual Studio 2008 or later.
    2. Press F5 to run it. (If you press Ctrl-F5, it will run and the console window will stay open so that you can view the results. Alternatively, you could add a `Console.Readline()` statement to the end of the listing.)
- Method 2:
    1. Open a text editor and enter Listing 2.1.
    2. Save the text file as SimpleNumericQuery.cs.
    3. Compile and run the program by entering the following at the command prompt:

```
PATH=%PATH%;%windir%\Microsoft.NET\Framework\v3.5\
csc.exe SimpleNumericQuery.cs
SimpleNumericQuery.exe
```

The first line sets the path to give you access to the .NET Framework. The second line compiles the program. The third line executes it. When run, the program's output displays the numbers 1 and 2. I should add that two assemblies, `System` and `System.Core`, are implicitly included in your application when you compile it. Appendix A contains more information on compiling and running C# programs.

Collection Initializers

The first line of code in the body of the SimpleNumericQuery program uses a new feature of C# 3.0 called *collection initializers*. This feature helps you populate a collection using a concise and easy-to-read syntax.

Consider this single line of code that initializes a collection with three integers:

```
List<int> list = new List<int>() { 1, 2, 3 };
```

This single line of code is called a collection initializer. It is a shorthand way of writing the following code:

```
List<int> list = new List<int>();
            list.Add(1);
            list.Add(2);
            list.Add(3);
```

Although collection initializers are not part of LINQ proper, they are written in the spirit of LINQ in that they allow you to concisely declare your intentions in code that is easy to understand.

Query Expressions

The centerpiece of Listing 2.1 resides in three lines of code called a LINQ query expression:

```
var query = from number in list
            where number < 3
            select number;
```

Query expressions will be analyzed in more depth in later chapters; for now we will only take a quick look at their most salient features.

On the right side of the = operator, you see the body of the query:

```
from number in list
where number < 3
select number;
```

All query expressions begin with the keyword from and end with a line that begins with the select or group by contextual keywords. It is important that you fully understand these keywords or the query operators that underlie them. It is also important to know that query expressions always begin with a `from` clause and usually end with a `select` clause.

The `where` clause in the second line of the query expression shown in Listing 2.1 instructs the compiler to filter the numbers in the list, returning only those that are smaller than 3. Chapter 6, "Query Operators," describes 49 different operators, such as `where` and `select`, that are available in LINQ to Objects. However, the pattern shown here, with a `from`, `where`, and `select` clause, is the most commonly used.

■ Contextual Keywords

Contextual keywords are not reserved words in any traditional sense. They are words that have a significant meaning only when used in a particular setting. For instance, the words `from`, `where`, and `select`, when used in a query expression with the pattern just shown, have specific and important significance. Some contextual keywords may have more than one meaning, depending on their context. For instance, `where` can also be used as a contextual keyword to define a generic constraint. The following are the contextual keywords used in C# 3.0:

- LINQ contextual keywords found in query expressions: `from`, `where`, `join`, `on`, `equals`, `into`, `let`, `orderby`, `ascending`, `descending`, `select`, `group`, and `by`
- Property-based contextual keywords: `get`, `set`, `value`
- Other contextual keywords: `partial`, `var`, `yield`

The `select` clause in a query expression comes on the last line. This might seem counterintuitive if you're not used to SQL queries. Here is why the `select` clause appears on the last line of a LINQ query:

- Query expressions in LINQ are fully type-checked and IntelliSense-aware.
- If the `select` clause came first, the IDE and the compiler would not immediately know the type of data you wanted to query. As a result, they could not provide type checking or IntelliSense while you were composing your query.

- If you place the from clause first, the compiler is immediately informed of the type of data you want to query, and it can begin giving you feedback as you type. In strongly typed languages such as C#, you always establish the type as quickly as possible, and LINQ simply follows that well-established pattern by beginning query expressions with a from clause.

Although it may seem strange at first, I've found that the logic that led the team to begin query expressions with a from clause is so compelling that it quickly became second nature to me. I've been told that in Microsoft SQL Server, the from clause of a T-SQL query is actually executed first, and then the joins, and then the where clause. The select clause is actually the *last* part of the query to be evaluated.

Type Inference

On the left of the = operator, you see the words var query. The new contextual keyword var tells the compiler to rely on *type inference* to infer the type of the identifier query. The type is determined by an analysis of the expression on the right of the operator.

> ### ▪ Quick Insight into Type Inference
>
> In Visual Studio, if you hover the mouse over the word var, a window appears showing its underlying type.

This query, like most LINQ to Objects queries, returns a variable of type IEnumerable<T>. In this case, T is of type int. Therefore, you could have declared the query expression as follows:

```
IEnumerable<int> query = from number in list
                         where number < 3
                         select number;
```

Although this code is valid, the preferred style is to use the contextual keyword var. Type inference provides several benefits. It ensures that strong typing is enforced, and it also

- Eliminates the need to guess the type of the data returned from a LINQ query.
- Eliminates verbose and repetitive code in some circumstances.
- Makes possible the use of a new feature of C# 3.0 called *anonymous types* when you're writing query expressions.
- Allows you to easily use a powerful feature of LINQ called composability.

All these features of type inference are discussed in more depth later in this book. Anonymous types are discussed in this chapter, and composability in the next.

Our sample uses a `foreach` loop to iterate over the results of the query. As mentioned, this loop prints the numbers 1 and 2.

Introduction to IEnumerable<T>

A `foreach` loop can iterate over the results of this query because it is of type `IEnumerable<T>`. Objects that implement `IEnumerable<T>` have access to the methods and properties `MoveNext()`, `Current`, and `Reset()`. They can all be enumerated like this:

```
List<int>.Enumerator e = list.GetEnumerator();

while (e.MoveNext())
{
    Console.WriteLine(e.Current);
}
```

A `foreach` loop is simply the preferred shorthand way of writing the preceding code:

```
foreach (var number in query)
{
  Console.WriteLine(number);
}
```

The `foreach` loop is preferable because it expands into a `try/catch/finally` construct that calls the `Dispose` method of `IEnumerable<T>`. The example shown here does not.

Let's take a moment to review and emphasize the central role of IEnumerable<T> in LINQ to Objects. Here are the key points:

- LINQ to Objects queries are run against variables that support the IEnumerable<T> interface.
- They also usually return a variable of type IEnumerable<T>. To see the return type, hover the mouse over the word var, as described earlier in this chapter.

This simple program has introduced four key concepts:

- Collection initializers
- Type inference
- Query expressions
- IEnumerable<T>

All these technologies are important, but the latter three are central, recurring themes of this text.

Querying a Collection of Objects

The previous example showed how to query a collection of the simple Integer type. This next example demonstrates how to query a collection of objects. The objects are of a custom type called Customer:

```
class Customer
{
  public string CustomerID { get; set; }
  public string ContactName { get; set; }
  public string City { get; set; }
}
```

The declaration for this class uses a new C# 3.0 feature called automatic properties that is designed to help you easily declare properties in a concise style.

Introducing Automatic Properties

The original C# syntax for properties involved using get and set methods to access data. For instance, the City property shown previously would look like this in C# 2.0:

```
private string city;

public string City
{
   get
   {
      return city;
   }

   set
   {
      city = value;
   }
}
```

This syntax still works in C# 3.0, but now you can also use this simple short-hand to produce semantically equivalent code.

The code produced when you use automatic properties includes an inaccessible private backing store. One way to see this is to use the free program available on the Internet called Red Gate's .NET Reflector. If you right-click the Customer class and choose Disassemble, that program produces the following code:

```
internal class Customer
{
    // Fields
    [CompilerGenerated]
    private string <City>k__BackingField;
    [CompilerGenerated]
    private string <ContactName>k__BackingField;
    [CompilerGenerated]
    private string <CustomerID>k__BackingField;

    // Methods
    public Customer();
```

```
  // Properties
  public string City { [CompilerGenerated] get; [CompilerGenerated]
  set; }
  public string ContactName { [CompilerGenerated] get;
    [CompilerGenerated] set; }
  public string CustomerID { [CompilerGenerated] get;
    [CompilerGenerated] set; }
}
```

Three backing fields are declared with oddly shaped identifiers such as
<CustomerID>k__BackingField. They would never compile in C#, although
they are valid Intermediate Language (IL) identifiers. Code similar to what
is shown here is generated for you in the background whenever you use
automatic properties.

■ Intermediate Language (IL)

The C# compiler translates the code that we write into Intermediate
Language (IL). IL is executed at runtime by the .NET Common Language Runtime (CLR).

If you want to access the backing fields of a property, you must declare
them using the traditional property style. Automatic properties are useful
only as a means of doing less typing and keeping your code short and
precise.

Introducing Object Initializers

In the preceding section, you saw how to initialize a collection of integers
in C# 3.0. Here is how to use similar syntax to initialize a collection of
objects:

```
private static List<Customer> GetCustomers()
{
  return new List<Customer>
  {
    new Customer { CustomerID = "ALFKI", ContactName = "Maria Anders",
        City = "Berlin" },
    new Customer { CustomerID = "ANATR", ContactName = "Ana Trujillo",
```

```
            City = "Mexico D.F." },
        new Customer { CustomerID = "ANTON", ContactName = "Antonio Moreno",
            City = "Mexico D.F." }
    };
}
```

The lines beginning with the word new are examples of *object initializers*. They instantiate an instance of the object Customer and initialize all three of its public properties. You can also initialize fields with this same syntax.

Like collection initializers, object initializers are a shorthand way of performing a common task. In particular, the first new statement in the GetCustomers method looks like this in C# 2.0 syntax:

```
Customer customer1 = new Customer();

customer1.CustomerID = "ALFKI";
customer1.City = "Berlin";
customer1.ContactName = "Maria Anders";
```

This code still compiles, but the new syntax is clearly more concise.

The entire body of the GetCustomers method is a collection initializer. This time, instead of initializing a collection of integers, three objects are placed in the collection. I won't waste space in this text showing how much code it would take to perform the same task using C# 2.0 syntax. It should be obvious that the new syntax is both shorter and easier to read.

The code in Listing 2.2 is a complete program demonstrating how to use LINQ to Objects to query a collection of Customer objects.

LISTING 2.2 A Simple LINQ to Objects Query Against a Collection of Customer **Objects**

```
using System;
using System.Collections.Generic;
using System.Linq;

namespace SimpleLinqToObjects
{
  class Customer
  {
      public string CustomerID { get; set; }
      public string ContactName { get; set; }
      public string City { get; set; }
  }
```

continues

LISTING 2.2 *(continued)*

```
class Program
{

  private static List<Customer> GetCustomers()
  {
    return new List<Customer>
    {
      new Customer { ContactName = "Maria Anders", City = "Berlin" },
      new Customer { ContactName = "Ana Trujillo", City =
                     "Mexico D.F." },
      new Customer { ContactName="Antonio Moreno", City="Mexico D.F." }
    };
  }

  static void Main(string[] args)
  {
    var query = from c in GetCustomers()
                where c.City == "Mexico D.F."
                select new { City = c.City, ContactName =
                             c.ContactName };

    foreach (var cityAndContact in query)
    {
       Console.WriteLine(cityAndContact);
    }
  }
}
}
```

As in the previous example, the query expression in this program is three lines long:

```
var query = from c in GetCustomers()
            where c.City == "Mexico D.F."
            select new { City = c.City, ContactName = c.ContactName };
```

It takes each of the three customers and filters out those in which the City field is not set to Mexico D.F.

Introducing Anonymous Types

Notice the last line of the preceding query:

```
select new { City = c.City, ContactName = c.ContactName };
```

This line creates an anonymous type. Behind the scenes, at compile time, a very simple class is generated automatically. In this particular case, two properties, `City` and `ContactName`, are added to the class.

In this case the names of these properties are explicitly called out:

```
City = c.City, ContactName = c.ContactName
```

However, you could allow the compiler to derive the names from the fields themselves:

```
select new { c.City, c.ContactName };
```

This code would again create two properties called `City` and `ContactName`. In many cases, you can use either syntax, depending on your preference. In some cases you might choose to change the name of one or more fields:

```
select new { Town = c.City, Contact = c.ContactName };
```

In later chapters, you will see cases in which the compiler forces you to create names to distinguish fields from two objects that have the same name.

The `foreach` loop at the end of the program implicitly calls the automatically implemented `ToString()` method for this anonymous object to format the program's output:

```
{ City = Mexico D.F., ContactName = Ana Trujillo }
{ City = Mexico D.F., ContactName = Antonio Moreno }
```

Here you see output based on the two fields of our very simple anonymous class.

The example shown in this section demonstrated how to write a simple LINQ query that retrieves data from a collection of objects. You might still have questions about the three technologies introduced here:

- Object initializers
- Automatic properties
- Anonymous types

These subjects are covered in more depth in Chapter 4.

A Simple LINQ to SQL Example

Listing 2.3 illustrates the technology on which LINQ to SQL is built. To keep this example as concise as possible, much of the machinery that makes this technology powerful and flexible has been stripped away. All that is left is the minimum code required to query a database with LINQ to SQL.

LISTING 2.3　The LinqToSqlWithoutDesigner Sample Demonstrates How to Use LINQ to SQL to Query a Database

```csharp
using System;
using System.Data.Linq;
using System.Data.Linq.Mapping;
using System.Linq;

namespace LinqToSqlWithoutDesigner
{

    [Table(Name = "Customers")]
    class Customer
    {
        [Column]
        public string CustomerID;
        [Column]
        public string City;
    }

    class Program
    {
        static void Main(string[] args)
        {

            DataContext db = new DataContext(@"c:\data\northwnd.mdf");

            var query = from c in db.GetTable<Customer>()
                        where c.City == "London"
                        select new { CustId = c.CustomerID, City =
                                        c.City };

            foreach (var cust in query)
            {
                Console.WriteLine(cust);
            }
        }
    }
}
```

This code assumes the presence of SQL Server Express on your development system. You also need a copy of the Northwind database. It is available as a free download over the web. It also ships with the official C# samples found in the MSDN Code Gallery. See Appendix A for additional information on obtaining and setting up the Northwind database. In this example, I have stored the database in a directory on the C drive called Data. You can change the path if you want to, but you must have a copy of the database to run this sample. If you meet these prerequisites, you should be able to compile and run the program using the same commands you used in the previous examples. If you need help meeting these requirements, or if you are having trouble connecting to the database, see Appendix A.

> **■ User Instances Enabled**
>
> To compile this program, you need to include a reference to System.Data.Linq.dll. If you are working in Visual Studio, bring up the Solution Explorer, open the References node, and right-click to add this assembly from the .NET page.
>
> To get this sample to run correctly, you may also have to run these commands in a query window in SQL Server Management Studio Express:
>
> ```
> exec sp_configure 'user instances enabled', 1.
> Reconfigure
> ```

The preceding code has two interesting sections. The first is the declaration of the class called Customer. In LINQ, classes like this are called *entities*.

Entity classes are designed to map directly to a table in a database. The compiler knows to perform this mapping because of the Table attribute above the declaration of the class:

```
[Table(Name = "Customers")]
class Customer
```

This simple attribute tells the LINQ runtime that this class is designed to mirror a table in the database. As soon as LINQ knows to link the table to the class, it can automatically populate instances of the class with the data from the database.

Before LINQ can correctly map the `Customer` table to the `Customer` class, it must know how the fields in the database table map to the fields in the C# class. The two `Column` attributes shown in the declaration of the `Customer` class map the properties of the class in your program to the fields of the table in the database:

```
[Column]
public string CustomerID;
```

LINQ uses this information when it maps data pulled from the database to instances of the `Customer` class.

Let's now consider the initialization of the `DataContext`. This class performs several tasks for developers including:

- It automatically sets up a connection to the database.
- It maps the rows of data retrieved from the database to instances of the `Customer` class.

To set up the connection, we only need to pass the location of the database that we want to query to one of the `DataContext`'s constructors:

```
DataContext db = new DataContext(@"c:\data\northwnd.mdf");
```

The `DataContext` also plays a role in the query expression run against the data in the database:

```
var query = from c in db.GetTable<Customer>()
            where c.City == "Mexico D.F."
            select new { CustId = c.CustomerID, City = c.City };
```

The query expression shown here looks very much like those that we wrote in the previous LINQ to Objects example. The only difference between the two queries is in the last part of the `from` clause:

```
var query = from c in GetCustomers()              // LINQ to Objects
            where c.City == "Mexico D.F."
            select new { City = c.City, ContactName = c.ContactName };

var query = from c in db.GetTable<Customer>()   // LINQ to SQL
            where c.City == "Mexico D.F."
            select new { City = c.City, ContactName = c.ContactName };
```

Other than the from clause, the entire query expression—including the where clause, the select clause, and the anonymous type—is identical. This fact is emphasized again in the next chapter, which discusses the *unitive* principle of LINQ development.

Despite the similar syntax, the LINQ to SQL example is, in fact, very different from the LINQ to Objects example. In LINQ to Objects, the data is pulled from a collection in your program. In LINQ to SQL, the entire query expression is converted into a SQL statement, and the statement is executed against a database that resides in a different process. Finally, the data returned from the query is ferried between processes and is converted into instances of the Customer object.

One of this book's primary goals is to explain exactly how LINQ to SQL works. To fully understand that subject, you need to study lambdas, expression trees, and extension methods. You also need to understand how IEnumerable<T> and IQueryable<T> are implemented, and why they were implemented. All of that lies before us.

This chapter's purpose, however, is simply to give you a working example of LINQ to SQL and to point out some of its most salient features. If you now also find yourself anticipating the unveiling of some of the secrets behind this fascinating technology, all the better.

I'd like to close this section by showing you a simple program that I do not expect you to compile. In Listing 2.3, you saw the declaration for the Customer entity class and learned how it was mapped to a class in the database. The average database in a line-of-business application might have more than 100 tables, and many of those tables might have as many as 20 or more fields. Clearly, it would be a major undertaking to map each of those tables to handmade C# classes.

Fortunately, LINQ ships with Object Relational Mapping (ORM) tools that automatically create classes that map to the tables in your database. These tools relieve you of the need to manage the entity classes in your program. As a result, you will be able to write programs like the one shown in Listing 2.4. This program, has no declaration for the Customer entity class. Instead, it was created behind the scenes by the ORM tools that ship with Visual Studio or the .NET Framework 3.5. All of this will be described in some depth in Chapters 7 through 10.

LISTING 2.4   A Simple Example of Using LINQ to SQL to Query a Database After Running the Object Relational Designer

```
using System;
using System.IO;
using System.Linq;
using System.Windows.Forms;

namespace GettingStartedWithLinqToSql
{
    class Program
    {
        static void Main(string[] args)
        {
            Northwind db = new Northwind(@"C:\Data\Northwnd.mdf");

            var query = from c in db.Customers
                        where c.City == "Nantes"
                        select new { c.City, c.CompanyName };

            foreach (var q in query)
            {
                Console.WriteLine(q);
            }
        }
    }
}
```

LINQ to XML

LINQ to XML makes it easy for you to create, parse, and transform XML files. In this section you see two programs. The first, shown in Listings 2.5 and 2.6, reads in a simple XML file and runs a query against it. The second, shown in Listing 2.7, demonstrates how to create the XML file used in the first program.

Parsing XML

Let's begin by studying the code shown in Listing 2.5. This program reads in a simple XML file and queries the data in the file to retrieve only the rows where the City attribute is set to Mexico D.F. To run this program, you need to reference the System.Xml.Linq.dll assembly, which is included by default when you create a console application in Visual Studio.

LISTING 2.5   A Simple LINQ to XML Program That Parses a Small XML File and Finds Customers Who Live in Mexico D.F.

```csharp
using System;
using System.Linq;
using System.Xml.Linq;

namespace SimpleXmlCustomers
{
    class Program
    {
        static void Main(string[] args)
        {
            XDocument customers = XDocument.Load(@"Customers.xml");

            var xml = from x in customers.Descendants("Customer")
                      where x.Attribute("City").Value == "Mexico D.F."
                      select x;

            foreach (var x in xml)
            {
                Console.WriteLine(x);
            }
        }
    }
}
```

LISTING 2.6   The Data Stored in the Customers.xml File Used in the SimpleXmlCustomers Program

```xml
<?xml version="1.0" encoding="utf-8" ?>
<Customers>
 <Customer ContactName="Maria Anders" City="Berlin" />
 <Customer ContactName="Ana Trujillo" City="Mexico D.F." />
 <Customer ContactName="Antonio Moreno" City="Mexico D.F." />
</Customers>
```

In Listing 2.5, notice the `using` statement that introduces the `System.Xml.Linq` namespace. All the key types you will use in LINQ to XML are found in this namespace. Each one is discussed in depth in Chapter 13, "LINQ to XML: Creation."

Listing 2.6 contains a short XML file that you can easily type in by hand. If you download the samples, you can find longer copies of this file that you can use when composing more complex queries.

The code for loading this XML file is very simple:

```
XDocument customers = XDocument.Load(@"Customers.xml");
```

The `XDocument` class is declared in the `System.Xml.Linq` namespace. The static `Load` method of this class is used to transfer the XML file from disk into memory. After its execution, the `customers` object contains a fully parsed XML file.

The following code shows how to write a query against the XML that has been loaded into memory:

```
var xml = from x in customers.Descendants("Customer")
          where x.Attribute("City").Value == "Mexico D.F."
          select x;
```

This query looks very much like the LINQ to SQL query, which, in turn, looked much like the LINQ to Objects query. The overall pattern of the three queries is essentially identical:

```
from x in XXX
where x == YYY
select x
```

In this case, however, the details are quite different from what you saw in the LINQ to Objects and LINQ to SQL examples. Why is this?

- Both CSharp collections and SQL databases contain discrete types and rigid structures that are easily mapped to C# objects. Although XML schemas can help you pin down the types in an XML file, currently there is no way to directly map a C# object to a row in an XML file.

- The "rows" of data in an XML file can contain elements, attributes, comments, or other XML types such as CDATA. As a result, we need to have classes with names such as XElement, XAttribute, and XComment to work with these different types. There was no inherent need for this kind of complexity when working with LINQ to SQL or LINQ to Objects.

For both of these reasons, LINQ to XML queries differ substantially from the queries shown earlier in this chapter. An entire lengthy section of this book is dedicated to explaining how LINQ to XML works. In this chapter, however, I'll just say a few simple words to help walk you through the most obvious sections of our LINQ to XML sample.

Take a look at the from clause in the query expression. The Descendants operator of the XDocument class locates all the descendants of the XML document, starting at a specified depth. In particular, the code is designed to search only the "Customer" elements in our document:

```
from x in customers.Descendants("Customer")
```

Here are those nodes as they appear in the XML document itself:

```
<Customer ContactName="Maria Anders" City="Berlin" />
<Customer ContactName="Ana Trujillo" City="Mexico D.F." />
<Customer ContactName="Antonio Moreno" City="Mexico D.F." />
```

As you can see, these customer nodes correspond, roughly, to rows in a database.

When iterating over the data at runtime, the range variable x in the from clause of this query contains a single XML customer node and its Contact-Name and City attributes:

```
<Customer ContactName="Maria Anders" City="Berlin" />
```

A LINQ to XML type called XElement is used to store this data. Inside each XElement you will find the attributes called ContactName and City. This data is stored in instances of a type called XAttribute. To get started using LINQ to XML, you only need to know that these types are wrappers around their respective node types in the XML file. For instance, in this case an `XElement` wraps a single `Customer` node, and an `XAttribute` type wraps the `ContactName` and `City` attributes of that node.

A filter also is specified in our query:

```
where x.Attribute("City").Value == "Mexico D.F."
```

The `where` operator is used here to filter out all the `Customer` nodes that do not have their city set to `Mexico D.F.` The `Attribute` method of the range variable x returns a variable of type `XAttribute`.

The final line in the query projects the result returned to the user. In this case, we are simply selecting the `Customer` nodes that have their `City` attribute set to `Mexico D.F.` As a result, the program prints the following:

```
<Customer CustomerID="ANATR" ContactName="Ana Trujillo" City=
   "Mexico D.F." />
<Customer CustomerID="ANTON" ContactName="Antonio More" City=
   "Mexico D.F." />
```

Although there is no need to do so in this case, you could create an anonymous object in the `select` statement:

```
select new { ContactName = x.Attribute("ContactName").Value,
   City = x.Attribute("City").Value } ;
```

Creating XML

Now that you have learned a little about querying an XML file, the next step is to learn how to create an XML file. Listing 2.7 shows the code for building the XML shown in Listing 2.6.

LISTING 2.7   Creating the Simple XML File Shown in Listing 2.6

```
using System;
using System.Xml.Linq;

namespace CreateXmlCustomers
{
    class Program
    {
        static void Main(string[] args)
        {
```

```
XDocument doc = new XDocument(new XDeclaration("1.0",
                                "utf-8", "yes"),
    new XElement("Customers",
        new XElement("Customer",
            new XAttribute("ContactName", "Maria Anders"),
            new XAttribute("City", "Berlin")),
        new XElement("Customer",
            new XAttribute("ContactName", "Ana Trujillo"),
            new XAttribute("City", "Mexico D.F.")),
        new XElement("Customer",
            new XAttribute("ContactName", "Antonio Moreno"),
            new XAttribute("City", "Mexico D.F."))
));

Console.WriteLine(doc.Declaration);
Console.WriteLine(doc);
doc.Save(@"Customers.xml");
        }
    }
}
```

The document is created in a single statement that is written in the functional style. Many other XML tools have you create the various attributes and elements one at a time and then add them to the document individually. LINQ to XML also supports that syntax, but the preferred technique is to create a single statement, as shown here, that reflects the document's structure.

This program uses four types, two of which you saw in the previous example. For now, I will be content to describe the roles they play in this example:

- XDocument: A wrapper for an XML tree that contains XElements, XAttributes, XDeclarations, and other types such as XComment.

- XDeclaration: An optional type used to specify the XML version, the encoding, and whether the XML document is stand-alone.

- XElement: This type represents an XML element. Like an XDocument, it can be used to construct XML trees. It typically contains a name and some content. It can contain other types such as XAttributes and XComments.

- XAttribute: Represents an XML attribute. Each XAttribute contains a name-value pair.

If you wanted to create a single XElement, you could write code like this:

```
XElement xml = new XElement("Node", "Content");
```

This code creates a valid XML element. When written to the console, the output of the variable xml would look like this:

```
<Node>Content</Node>
```

If you wanted to add an attribute to your node, you could write the following code:

```
xml = new XElement("ElementName",
    new XAttribute("AttributeName", "value"));
```

When written to the console with a WriteLine statement, this code produces the following simple XML tree:

```
<ElementName AttributeName="value" />
```

If you wanted to use an XDocument, you could write the following code:

```
XDocument document = new XDocument(
    new XElement("ElementName",
        new XAttribute("AttributeName", "value")));
```

This document, when written to the console, produces exactly the same output as the previous example. The XDocument type adds something of value to your code only when you want to use a type, such as XDeclaration, that is specific to the XDocument type.

Listing 2.7 shows an example of using the XDeclaration type with an XDocument. You should now be able to go back to Listing 2.7 and apply the principles shown in the sample examples we have been studying. You should be able to see how XDocument, XDeclaration, XElement, and XAttribute types were combined to create an XML document.

The simple examples in this subsection aim to initiate you into the world of LINQ to XML. Designed to pique your curiosity, they have almost certainly raised as many questions as they have answered. More in-depth coverage of this subject will be included in Chapter 13.

Summary

This chapter contained several fairly short programs designed to introduce you to the most common forms of LINQ programs: LINQ to Objects, LINQ to SQL, and LINQ to XML. All the programs were simple, and many important details were covered only in passing. This is an important chapter nevertheless, because it gave you an opportunity to work with real LINQ code. Technologies often become real to you only when you actually start to use them. This chapter gave you a chance to run real LINQ programs that you can easily create by hand in just a few minutes.

Several technologies were introduced that will be touched on repeatedly in this book. They include two LINQ technologies:

- Query expressions
- Deferred execution

and four new features of C# 3.0:

- Object initializers
- Collection initializers
- Automatic properties
- Type inference

You also learned that all the generic collections in C# support `IEnumerable<T>`. Thus, the `List<int>` collection used in the first query in this chapter supports that interface. If it did not, we could not use that type in a `from` clause:

```
from number in list
```

All LINQ to Objects queries follow this pattern:

```
from x in SomeVariableThatSupportsIEnumerable<T>
```

LINQ to Objects revolves around `IEnumerable<T>`. It is the alpha and omega of LINQ to Objects. Each query consumes this type, and they usually return it.

LINQ to SQL is the subject of several weighty chapters at the heart of this book. Using LINQ to write SQL queries is a very important subject, and one that will be explored in considerable depth. This chapter includes only the minimum code necessary to introduce you to the topic.

You also had a quick look at LINQ to XML. You saw that the XDocument class contains a method called Descendants that can be used to discover a particular node type in a document. When converted into LINQ to XML, these nodes typically are of type XElement, and they frequently contain subnodes of type XAttribute. In Chapter 13, you will learn more about these types and how to use them when you parse, transform, and create XML documents.

This chapter gave you just enough information to help you understand the basics of LINQ. In the next chapter, you will learn about the theoretical foundation on which LINQ is built. The practical knowledge in this chapter, and the theoretical knowledge found in the next chapter, will give you a strong foundation on which to begin an in-depth study of how to use LINQ to query data.

3
The Essence of LINQ

N OW THAT YOU'VE SEEN several practical examples of LINQ's syntax, it is time to view the technology from a more theoretical perspective. This chapter covers the seven foundations on which an understanding of LINQ can be built. LINQ is

- Integrated
- Unitive
- Extensible
- Declarative
- Hierarchical
- Composable
- Transformative ·

These ideas may sound esoteric at first, but I believe you will find them quite easy to understand. LINQ has a fundamental simplicity and elegance. In this chapter and the next, we explore LINQ's architecture, giving you a chance to understand how it was built and why it was built that way. This chapter explains goals that LINQ aims to achieve. The next chapter explains each of the pieces of the LINQ architecture and shows how they come together to achieve those goals.

Integrated

LINQ stands for Language Integrated Query. One of the central, and most important, features of LINQ is its integration of a flexible query syntax into the C# language.

Developers have many tools that have been crafted to neatly solve difficult tasks. Yet there are still dark corners in the development landscape. Querying data is one area in which developers frequently encounter problems with no clear resolution. LINQ aims to remove that uncertainty and to show a clearly defined path that is well-lit and easy to follow.

In Visual Studio 2005, attempts to query data in a SQL database from a C# program revealed an impedance mismatch between code and data. SQL is native to neither .NET nor C#. As a result, SQL code embedded in a C# program is neither type-checked nor IntelliSense-aware. From the perspective of a C# developer, SQL is shrouded in darkness.

Here is an example of one of several different techniques developers used in the past when querying data:

```
SqlConnection sqlConnection = new SqlConnection(connectString);
sqlConnection.Open();
System.Data.SqlClient.SqlCommand sqlCommand = new SqlCommand();
sqlCommand.Connection = sqlConnection;
sqlCommand.CommandText = "Select * from Customer";
return sqlCommand.ExecuteReader(CommandBehavior.CloseConnection)
```

Of these six lines of code, only the last two directly define a query. The rest of the lines involve setup code that allows developers to connect and call objects in the database. The query string shown in the next-to-last line is neither type-checked nor IntelliSense-aware.

After these six lines of code execute, the developers may have more work to do, because the data returned from the query is not readily addressable by an object-oriented programmer. You might have to write more lines of code to access this data, or convert it into a format that is easier to use.

The LINQ version of this same query is shorter, easier to read, color-coded, fully type-checked, and IntelliSense-aware. The result set is cleanly converted into a well-defined object-oriented format:

```
Northwind db = new Northwind(@"C:\Data\Northwnd.mdf");

var query = from c in db.Customers
            select c;
```

By fully integrating the syntax for querying data into .NET languages such as C# and VB, LINQ resolves a problem that has long plagued the development world. Queries become first-class citizens of our primary languages; they are both type-checked and supported by the powerful IntelliSense technology provided inside the Visual Studio IDE. LINQ brings the experience of writing queries into the well-lit world of the 21st century.

A few benefits accrue automatically as a result of integrating querying into the C# language:

- The syntax highlighting and IntelliSense support allow you to get more work done in less time. The Visual Studio editor automatically shows you the tables in your database, the correctly spelled names and types of your fields, and the operators you can use when querying data. This helps you save time and avoid careless mistakes.
- LINQ code is shorter and cleaner than traditional techniques for querying data and, therefore, is much easier to maintain.
- LINQ allows you to fully harness the power of your C# debugger while writing and maintaining queries. You can step through your queries and related code in your LINQ projects.

If language integration were the only feature that LINQ offered, that alone would have been a significant accomplishment. But we are only one-seventh of the way through our description of the foundations of LINQ. Many of the best and most important features are still to be covered.

Unitive

Before LINQ, developers who queried data frequently needed to master multiple technologies. They needed to learn the following:

- SQL to query a database
- XPath, Dom, XSLT, or XQuery to query and transform XML data

- Web services to access some forms of remote data
- Looping and branching to query the collections in their own programs

These diverse APIs and technologies forced developers to frantically juggle their tight schedules while struggling to run similar queries against dissimilar data sources. Projects often encountered unexpected delays simply because it was easier to talk about querying XML, SQL, and other data than it was to actually implement the queries against these diverse data sources. If you have to juggle too many technologies, eventually something important will break.

LINQ simplifies these tasks by providing a single, unified method for querying diverse types of data. Developers don't have to master a new technology simply because they want to query a new data source. They can call on their knowledge of querying local collections when they query relational data, and vice versa.

This point was illustrated in the preceding chapter, where you saw three very similar queries that drew data from three different data sources: objects, an SQL database, and XML:

```
var query = from c in GetCustomers()
            where c.City == "Mexico D.F."
            select new { City = c.City, ContactName = c.ContactName };

var query = from c in db.Customers
            where c.City == "Mexico D.F."
            select new { City = c.City, ContactName = c.ContactName };

var query = from x in customers.Descendants("Customer")
            where x.Attribute("City").Value == "Mexico D.F."
            select x;
```

As you can see, the syntax for each of these queries is not identical, but it is very similar. This illustrates one of LINQ's core strengths: a single, unitive syntax can be used to query diverse types of data. It is not that you never have to scale a learning curve when approaching a new data source, but only that the principles, overall syntax, and theory are the same even if some of the details differ.

You enjoy two primary benefits because LINQ is unitive:

* The similar syntax used in all LINQ queries helps you quickly get up to speed when querying new data sources.
* Your code is easier to maintain, because you are using the same syntax regardless of the type of data you query.

Although it arises naturally from this discussion, it is worth noting that SQL and other query languages do not have this capability to access multiple data sources with a single syntax. Those who advocate using SQL or the DOM instead of LINQ often forget that their decision forces their team to invest additional time in learning these diverse technologies.

Extensible Provider Model

In this text I have tended to define LINQ as a tool for querying SQL, XML, and the collections in a program. Strictly speaking, this is not an accurate description of LINQ. Although such a view is useful when you first encounter LINQ, it needs to be abandoned if you want to gain deeper insight. LINQ is not designed to query any particular data source; rather, it is a technology for defining *providers* that can be used to access any arbitrary data source. LINQ happens to ship with providers for querying SQL, XML, and objects, but this was simply a practical decision, not a preordained necessity.

LINQ provides developers with a syntax for querying data. This syntax is enabled by a series of C# 3.0 and C# 2.0 features. These include lambdas, iterator blocks, expression trees, anonymous types, type inference, query expressions, and extension methods. All of these features are covered in this book. For now you need only understand that they make LINQ possible.

When Visual Studio 2008 shipped, Microsoft employees frequently showed the image shown in Figure 3.1. Although people tend to think of LINQ as a means of enabling access to these data sources, this diagram actually depicts nothing more than the set of LINQ providers that were implemented by Microsoft at the time Visual Studio shipped. Granted, the team carefully planned which providers they wanted to ship, but their decisions were based on strategic, rather than technical, criteria.

FIGURE 3.1   VB and C# ship with LINQ providers for databases, XML, and data structures found in a typical program.

Using the LINQ provider model, developers can extend LINQ to query other data sources besides those shown in Figure 3.1. The following are a few of the data sources currently enabled by third-party LINQ providers:

LINQ Extender	LINQ to Google
LINQ over C# project	LINQ to Indexes
LINQ to Active Directory	LINQ to `IQueryable`
LINQ to Amazon	LINQ to JavaScript
LINQ to Bindable Sources	LINQ to JSON
LINQ to CRM	LINQ to LDAP
LINQ to Excel	LINQ to LLBLGen Pro
LINQ to Expressions	LINQ to Lucene
LINQ to Flickr	LINQ to Metaweb
LINQ to Geo	LINQ to MySQL

LINQ to NCover	LINQ to Sharepoint
LINQ to NHibernate	LINQ to SimpleDB
LINQ to Opf3	LINQ to Streams
LINQ to Parallel (PLINQ)	LINQ to WebQueries
LINQ to RDF Files	LINQ to WMI

These projects are of varying quality. Some, such as the LINQ Extender and LINQ to `IQueryable`, are merely tools for helping developers create providers. Nevertheless, you can see that an active community is interested in creating LINQ providers, and this community is producing some interesting products. By the time you read this, I'm sure the list of providers will be longer. See Appendix A for information on how to get updated information on existing providers.

One easily available provider called LinqToTerraServer can be found among the downloadable samples that ship with Visual Studio 2008. You can download the VS samples from the release tab found at http://code. msdn.microsoft.com/csharpsamples.

After unzipping the download, if you look in the ...\LinqSamples\ WebServiceLinqProvider directory, you will find a sample called Linq-ToTerraServer. The TerraServer web site, http://terraserver-usa.com, is a vast repository of pictures and information about geographic information. The LinqToTerraServer example shows you how to create a LINQ provider that queries the web services provided on the TerraServer site. For example, the following query returns all U.S. cities and towns named Portland:

```
var query1 = from place in terraPlaces
             where place.Name == "Portland"
             select new { place.Name, place.State };
```

This query returns a number of locations, but here are a few of the more prominent:

```
{ Name = Portland, State = Indiana }
{ Name = Portland, State = Maine }
{ Name = Portland, State = Michigan }
{ Name = Portland, State = Oregon }
{ Name = Portland, State = Texas }
```

```
{ Name = Portland, State = Alabama }
{ Name = Portland, State = Arkansas }
{ Name = Portland, State = Colorado }
```

In Chapter 17, "LINQ Everywhere," you will see examples of several other providers, including LINQ to Flickr and LINQ to SharePoint. It is not easy to create a provider.. After the code is written, however, it is easy to use the provider. In fact, you should already have enough familiarity with LINQ to see that it would be easy to modify the preceding query to suit your own purposes.

The LINQ provider model has hidden benefits that might not be evident at first glance:

- It is relatively open to examination and modification. As you read the next few chapters, you will find that most of the LINQ query pipeline is accessible to developers.
- It allows developers to be intelligent about how queries execute. You can get a surprising degree of control over the execution of a query. If you care about optimizing a query, in many cases you can optimize it, because you can see how it works.
- You can create a provider to publicize a data source that you have created. For instance, if you have a web service that you want C# developers to access, you can create a provider to give them a simple, extensible way to access your data.

I will return to the subject of LINQ providers later in the book. In this chapter, my goal is simply to make it clear that LINQ is extensible, and that its provider model is the basis on which each LINQ query model is built.

Query Operators

You don't always need to use a LINQ provider to run queries against what might—at least at first—appear to be nontraditional data sources. By using the LINQ to Objects provider, and a set of built-in LINQ operators, you can run queries against a data source that does not look at all like XML or SQL data. For instance, LINQ to Objects gives you access to the reflection model that is built into C#.

The following query retrieves all the methods of the string class that are static:

```
var query = from m in typeof(string).GetMethods()
            where m.IsStatic == true
            select m;
```

The following are a few of the many results that this query returns:

```
System.String Join(System.String, System.String[])
System.String Join(System.String, System.String[], Int32, Int32)
Boolean Equals(System.String, System.String)
Boolean Equals(System.String, System.String, System.StringComparison)
Boolean op_Equality(System.String, System.String)
Boolean op_Inequality(System.String, System.String)
Boolean IsNullOrEmpty(System.String)
Int32 Compare(System.String, System.String)
Int32 Compare(System.String, System.String, Boolean)
Int32 Compare(System.String, System.String, System.StringComparison)
```

Using the power of LINQ, it is easy to drill into these methods to find out more about them. In particular, LINQ uses the extension methods mentioned in the preceding section to define a set of methods that can perform specific query operations such as ordering and grouping data. For instance, the following query retrieves the methods of the string class that are static, finds out how many overloads each method has, and then orders them first by the number of overloads and then alphabetically:

```
var query = from m in typeof(string).GetMethods()
            where m.IsStatic == true
            orderby m.Name
            group m by m.Name into g
            orderby g.Count()
            select new { Name = g.Key, Overloads = g.Count() };

foreach (var item in query)
{
    Console.WriteLine(item);
}
```

The results of this query look like this:

```
{ Overloads = 1, Name = Copy }
{ Overloads = 1, Name = Intern }
{ Overloads = 1, Name = IsInterned }
{ Overloads = 1, Name = IsNullOrEmpty }
```

```
{ Overloads = 1, Name = op_Equality }
{ Overloads = 1, Name = op_Inequality }
{ Overloads = 2, Name = CompareOrdinal }
{ Overloads = 2, Name = Equals }
{ Overloads = 2, Name = Join }
{ Overloads = 5, Name = Format }
{ Overloads = 9, Name = Concat }
{ Overloads = 10, Name = Compare }
```

This makes it obvious that `Format`, `Compare`, and `Concat` are the most frequently overloaded methods of the `string` class, and it presents all the
methods with the same number of overloads in alphabetical order.

You can run this code in your own copy of Visual Studio because the
LINQ to Objects provider ships with C# 3.0. Other third-party extensions to
LINQ, such as LINQ to Amazon, are not included with Visual Studio. If you
want to run a sample based on LINQ to Amazon or some other provider
that does not ship with Visual Studio, you must download and install the
provider before you can use it.

Declarative: Not How, But What

LINQ is declarative, not imperative. It allows developers to simply state
what they want to do without worrying about how it is done.

Imperative programming requires developers to define step by step
how code should be executed. To give directions in an imperative fashion,
you say, "Go to 1st Street, turn left onto Main, drive two blocks, turn right
onto Maple, and stop at the third house on the left." The declarative version
might sound something like this: "Drive to Sue's house." One says *how* to
do something; the other says *what* needs to be done.

The declarative style has two advantages over the imperative style:

- It does not force the traveler to memorize a long set of instructions.
- It allows the traveler to optimize the route when possible.

It should be obvious that there is little opportunity to optimize the first
set of instructions for getting to Sue's house: You simply have to follow
them by rote. The second set, however, allows the traveler to use his or her
knowledge of the neighborhood to find a shortcut. For instance, a bike

might be the best way to travel at rush hour, whereas a car might be best at night. On occasion, going on foot and cutting through the local park might be the best solution.

Here is another example of the difference between declarative and imperative code:

```
// imperative style
List<int> imperativeList = new List<int>();
imperativeList.Add(1);
imperativeList.Add(2);
imperativeList.Add(3);

// declarative style
List<int> declaractiveList = new List<int> { 1, 2, 3 };
```

The first example details exactly how to add items to a list. The second example states what you want to do and allows the compiler to figure out the best way to do it. As you will learn in the next chapter, both styles are valid C# 3.0 syntax. The declarative form of this code, however, is shorter, easier to understand, easier to maintain, and, at least in theory, leaves the compiler free to optimize how a task is performed.

These two styles differ in both the amount of detail they require a developer to master and the amount of freedom that each affords the compiler. Detailed instructions not only place a burden on the developer, but also restrict the compiler's capability to optimize code.

Let's consider another example of the imperative style of programming. As developers, we frequently end up in a situation where we are dealing with a list of lists:

```
List<int> list01 = new List<int> { 1, 2, 3 };
List<int> list02 = new List<int> { 4, 5, 6 };
List<int> list03 = new List<int> { 7, 8, 9 };

List<List<int>> lists = new List<List<int>> { list01, list02, list03 };
```

Here is imperative code for accessing the members of this list:

```
List<int> newList = new List<int>();

foreach (var item in lists)
{
    foreach (var number in item)
```

```
        {
            newList.Add(number);
        }
    }
```

This code produces a single list containing all the data from the three nested lists:

```
1
2
3
4
5
6
7
8
9
```

Notice that we have to write nested for loops to allow access to our data. In a simple case like this, nested loops are not terribly complicated to use, but they can become very cumbersome in more complex problem domains.

Contrast this code with the declarative style used in a LINQ program:

```
var newList = from list in lists
              from num in list
              select num;
```

You can access the results of these two "query techniques" in the same way:

```
foreach (var item in newList)
{
    Console.WriteLine(item);
}
```

This code writes the results of either query, producing identical results, regardless of whether you used the imperative or declarative technique to query the data:

```
1
2
3
4
5
6
7
8
9
```

The difference here is not in the query's results, or in how we access the results, but in how we compose our query against our nested list. The imperative style can sometimes be verbose and hard to read. The declarative code is usually short and easy to read and scales more easily to complex cases. For instance, you can add an orderby clause to reverse the order of the integers in your result set:

```
var query = from list in lists
            from num in list
            orderby num descending
            select num;
```

You probably know how to achieve the same results using the imperative style. But it was knowledge that you had to struggle to learn, and it is knowledge that applies only to working with sequences of numbers stored in a List<T>. The LINQ code for reordering results, however, is easy to understand. It can be used to reorder not only nested collections, but also SQL data, XML data, or the many other data sources we query using LINQ.

To get the even numbers from our nested lists, we need only do this:

```
var query = from list in lists
            from num in list
            where num % 2 == 0
            orderby num descending
            select num;
```

Contrast this code with the imperative equivalent:

```
List<int> newList = new List<int>();

foreach (var item in lists)
{
    foreach (var number in item)
    {
        if (number % 2 == 0)
        {
            newList.Add(number);
        }
    }
}

newList.Reverse();
```

This imperative style of programming now has an `if` block nested inside the nested `foreach` loops. This is not only verbose and applicable to only a specific type of data, it also can be like a straight jacket for both the compiler and the developer. Commands must be issued and followed in a rote fashion, leaving little room for optimizations.

The equivalent LINQ query expression does not describe in a step-by-step fashion how to query our list of lists. It simply lets the developer state what he wants to do and lets the compiler determine the best path to the destination.

After nearly 50 years of steady development, the possibilities inherent in imperative programming have been extensively explored. Innovations in the field are now rare. Declarative programming, on the other hand, offers opportunities for growth. Although it is not a new field of study, it is still rich in possibilities.

■ Use the Right Tool for the Job

In extolling the virtues of LINQ's declarative syntax, I should be careful not to overstate my case. For instance, the LINQ operator called `ToList` is provided to allow developers to easily translate the sequence of results returned by a LINQ query into a traditional `List<T>`. This functionality is useful because some operations, such as randomly accessing items in a list (`myList[2]`), are more easily performed using the imperative syntax. One of the great virtues of C# 3.0 is that it allows you to easily move between imperative and declarative syntax, allowing you to choose the best tool for the job. My job right now is to help you understand the value of LINQ and the declarative style of programming. LINQ is indeed a very powerful and useful tool, but it is not the solution to all your problems.

Because LINQ is a new technology from Microsoft, you might find it a bit jarring to see me write that declarative programming is not new. In fact, declarative code has been with us nearly as long as imperative code. Some older languages such as LISP (which was first specified in 1958) make heavy use of the declarative style of programming. Haskel and F# are examples of other languages that use it extensively. One reason LINQ and SQL look so much alike is that they are both forms of declarative programming.

The point of LINQ is not that it will replace SQL, but that it will bring the benefits of SQL to C# developers. LINQ is a technology for enabling a SQL-like declarative programming style inside a native C# program. It brings you the benefits of SQL but adds declarative syntax, as well as syntax highlighting, IntelliSense support, type checking, debugging support, the ability to query multiple data sources with the same syntax, and much more.

Hierarchical

Complex relationships can be expressed in a relational database, but the results of a SQL query can take only one shape: a rectangular grid. LINQ has no such restrictions. Built into its very foundation is the idea that data is hierarchical (see Figure 3.2). If you want to, you can write LINQ queries that return flat, SQL-like datasets, but this is an option, not a necessity.

Grid versus Hierarchies

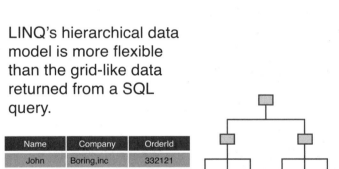

LINQ's hierarchical data model is more flexible than the grid-like data returned from a SQL query.

Name	Company	OrderId
John	Boring,inc	332121
Mary	RidgeCo, A.E.	322336

FIGURE 3.2   Both object-oriented languages and the developers who use them have a natural tendency to think in terms of hierarchies. SQL data is arranged in a simple grid.

Consider a simple relational database that has tables called Customers, Orders, and OrderDetails. It is possible to capture the relationship between these tables in a SQL database, but you cannot directly depict the relationship in the results of a single query. Instead, you are forced to show the result as a join that binds the tables into a single array of columns and rows.

LINQ, on the other hand, can return a set of `Customer` objects, each of which owns a set of 0-to-*n* `Orders`. Each `Order` can be associated with a set of `OrderDetails`. This is a classic hierarchical relationship that can be perfectly expressed with a set of objects:

Customer

    Orders

        OrderDetails

Consider the following simple hierarchical query that captures the relationship between two objects:

```
var query = from c in db.Customers
            select new { City = c.City,
                         orders = from o in c.Orders
                         select new { o.OrderID }
                 };
```

This query asks for the city in which a customer lives and a list of the orders the person has made. Rather than returning a rectangular dataset as a SQL query would, this query returns hierarchical data that lists the city associated with each customer and the ID associated with each order:

```
City=Helsinki    orders=...
  orders: OrderID=10615
  orders: OrderID=10673
  orders: OrderID=10695
  orders: OrderID=10873
  orders: OrderID=10879
  orders: OrderID=10910
  orders: OrderID=11005
City=Warszawa    orders=...
  orders: OrderID=10374
  orders: OrderID=10611
  orders: OrderID=10792
  orders: OrderID=10870
  orders: OrderID=10906
  orders: OrderID=10998
```

This result set is multidimensional, nesting one set of columns and rows inside another set of columns and rows.

Look again at the query, and notice how we gain access to the Orders table:

```
orders = from o in c.Orders
```

The identifier c is an instance of a Customer object. As you will learn later in the book, LINQ to SQL has tools for automatically generating Customer objects given the presence of the Customer table in the database. Here you can see that the Customer object is not flat; instead, it contains a set of nested Order objects.

Listing 3.1 shows a simplified version of the Customer object that is automatically generated by the LINQ to SQL designer. Notice how LINQ to SQL wraps the fields of the Customer table. Later in this book, you will learn how to automatically generate Customer objects that wrap the fields of a Customer table.

LISTING 3.1   A Simplified Version of the Customer Object That the LINQ to SQL Designer Generates Automatically

```
public partial class Customer
{
    ... // Code omitted here
    private string _CustomerID;
    private string _CompanyName;
    private string _ContactName;
    private string _ContactTitle;
    private string _Address;
    private string _City;
    private string _Region;
    private string _PostalCode;
    private string _Country;
    private string _Phone;
    private string _Fax;
    private EntitySet<Order> _Orders;
    ... // Code omitted here
}
```

The first 11 private fields of the Customer object simply reference the fields of the Customer table in the database. Taken together, they provide a location to store the data from a single row of the Customer table. Notice, however, the last item, which is a collection of Order objects. Because it is bound to the Orders table in a one-to-many relationship, each customer has from 0-to-*n* orders associated with it, and LINQ to SQL stores those orders in this field. This automatically gives you a hierarchical view of your data.

The same thing is true of the Order table, only it shows not a one-to-many relationship with the Customer table, but a one-to-one relationship:

```
public partial class Order
{
    ... // Code omitted here
    private int _OrderID;
    private string _CustomerID;
    private System.Nullable<int> _EmployeeID;
    private System.Nullable<System.DateTime> _OrderDate;
    private System.Nullable<System.DateTime> _RequiredDate;
    private System.Nullable<System.DateTime> _ShippedDate;
    private System.Nullable<int> _ShipVia;
    private System.Nullable<decimal> _Freight;
    private string _ShipName;
    private string _ShipAddress;
    private string _ShipCity;
    private string _ShipRegion;
    private string _ShipPostalCode;
    private string _ShipCountry;
    private EntityRef<Customer> _Customer;
    ... // Code omitted here
}
```

Again we see all the fields of the Orders table, their types, and whether they can be set to Null. The difference here is that the last field points back to the Customer table not with an `EntitySet<T>`, but an `EntityRef<T>`. This is not the proper place to delve into the `EntitySet` and `EntityRef` classes. However, it should be obvious to you that an `EntitySet` refers to a set of objects, and an `EntityRef` references a single object. Thus, an `EntitySet` captures a one-to-many relationship, and an `EntityRef` captures a one-to-one relationship.

The point to take away from this discussion is that LINQ to SQL captures not a flat view of your data, but a hierarchical view. A `Customer` class is connected to a set of orders in a clearly defined hierarchical relationship, and each order is related to the customer who owns it. LINQ gives you a hierarchical view of your data.

In a simple case like this, such a hierarchical relationship has obvious utility, but it is possible to imagine getting along without it. More complex queries, however, are obviously greatly simplified by this architecture. Consider the following LINQ to SQL query:

```
var query = from c in db.Customers
            where c.CompanyName == companyName
            from o in c.Orders
            from x in o.Order_Details
            where x.Product.Category.CategoryName == "Confections"
            orderby x.Product.ProductName
            group x by x.Product.ProductName into g
            orderby g.Count()
            select new { Count = g.Count(), Product = g.Key };
```

Here we use LINQ's hierarchical structure to move from the Customers table to the Orders table to the Order_Details table without breaking a sweat:

```
var query = from c in db.Customers
            from o in c.Orders
            from x in o.Order_Details
```

The next line really helps show the power of LINQ hierarchies:

```
where x.Product.Category.CategoryName == "Confections"
```

The identifier x represents an instance of a class containing the data from a row of the Order_Details table. Order_Details has a relationship with the Product table, which has a relationship with the Category table, which has a field called CategoryName. We can slice right through that complex relationship by simply writing this:

```
x.Product.Category.CategoryName
```

LINQ's hierarchical structure shines a clarifying light on the relational data in your programs. Even complex relational models become intuitive and easy to manipulate.

We can then order and group the results of our query with a few simple LINQ operators:

```
orderby x.Product.ProductName
group x by x.Product.ProductName into g
orderby g.Count()
```

Trying to write the equivalent code using a more conventional C# style of programming is an exercise that might take two or three pages of convoluted code and involve a number of nested loops and if statements. Even writing the same query in standard SQL would be a challenge for many developers. Here we perform the whole operation in nine easy-to-read lines of code.

In this section, I have introduced you to the power of LINQ's hierarchical style of programming without delving into the details of how such queries work. Later in this book you will learn how easy it is to compose your own hierarchical queries. For now you only need to understand two simple points:

- There is a big difference between LINQ's hierarchical structure and the flat, rectangular columns and rows returned by an SQL query.
- Many benefits arise from this more powerful structure. These include the intuitive structure of the data and the ease with which you can write queries against this model.

Composable

The last two foundations of LINQ shed light on its flexibility and power. If you understand these two features and how to use them, you will be able to tap into some very powerful technology. Of course, this chapter only introduces these features; they are discussed in more detail in the rest of the book.

LINQ queries are composable: You can combine them in multiple ways, and one query can be used as the building block for yet another query. To see how this works, let's look at a simple query:

```
var query = from customer in db.Customers
            where customer.City == "Paris"
            select customer;
```

The variable that is returned from the query is sometimes called a computation. If you write a foreach loop and display the address field from the customers returned by this computation, you see the following output:

```
265, boulevard Charonne
25, rue Lauriston
```

You can now write a second query against the results of this query:

```
query2 = from customer in query
         where customer.Address.StartsWith("25")
         select customer;
```

Notice that the last word in the first line of this query is the computation returned from the previous query. This second query produces the following output:

```
25, rue Lauriston
```

LINQ to Objects queries are composable because they operate on and usually return variables of type `IEnumerable<T>`. In other words, LINQ queries typically follow this pattern:

```
IEnumerable<T> query = from x in IEnumerable<T>
                       select x;
```

This is a simple mechanism to understand, but it yields powerful results. It allows you to take complex problems, break them into manageable pieces, and solve them with code that is easy to understand and easy to maintain. You will hear much more about `IEnumerable<T>` in the next chapter.

The next chapter also details a feature called deferred execution. Although it can be confusing to newcomers, one of the benefits of deferred execution is that it allows you to compose multiple queries and string them together without necessarily needing to have each query entail an expensive hit against the server. Instead, three or four queries can "execute" without ever sending a query across the wire to your database. Then, when you need to access the result from your query, a SQL statement is written that combines the results of all your queries and sends it across the wire only once. Deferred execution is a powerful feature, but you need to wait until the next chapter for a full explanation of how and why it works. The key point to grasp now is that it enables you to compose multiple queries as shown here, without having to take an expensive hit each time one "executes."

> ### ■ Discreet Computations and PLINQ
>
> LINQ queries are not only composable, but also discreet. In other words, the computation returned by a query is a single self-contained expression with only a single entry point. This has important consequences for a field of study called Parallel LINQ (PLINQ). Because each computation returned by a query is discreet, it can easily be run concurrently on its own thread. PLINQ is discussed briefly in Chapter 17, "LINQ Everywhere."

Transformative

SQL is poor at transformations, so we are unaccustomed to thinking about query languages as a tool for converting data from one format to another. Instead, we usually use specialized tools such as XSLT or brute-force techniques to transform data.

LINQ, however, has transformational powers built directly into its syntax. We can compose a LINQ query against a SQL database that effortlessly performs a variety of transforms. For instance, with LINQ it is easy to transform the result of a SQL query into a hierarchical XML document. You can also easily transform one XML document into another with a different structure. SQL data is transformed into a hierarchical set of objects automatically when you use LINQ to SQL. In short, LINQ is very good at transforming data, and this adds a new dimension to our conception of what we can do with a query language.

Listing 3.2 shows code that takes the results of a query against relational data and transforms it into XML.

LISTING 3.2   A Simple Query That Transforms the Results of a LINQ to SQL Query into XML

```
var query = new XElement("Orders", from c in db.Customers
            where c.City == "Paris"
            select new XElement("Order",
                new XAttribute("Address", c.Address),
                new XAttribute("City", c.City)));
```

Embedded in this query is a simple LINQ to SQL query that returns the Address and City fields from all the customers who live in Paris. In Listing 3.3 I've stripped away the LINQ to XML code from Listing 3.2 to show you the underlying LINQ to SQL query.

LISTING 3.3   The Simple LINQ to SQL Query Found at the Heart of Listing 3.2

```
var query = from c in db.Customers
            where c.City == "Paris"
            select new { c.Address, c.City };
```

Here is the output from Listing 3.3:

```
265, boulevard Charonne
25, rue Lauriston
```

Here is the output from Listing 3.2:

```
<Orders>
  <Order Address="265, boulevard Charonne" City="Paris" />
  <Order Address="25, rue Lauriston" City="Paris" />
</Orders>
```

As you can see, the code in Listing 3.2 performs a transform on the results of the LINQ to SQL query, converting it into XML data.

Because LINQ is composable, the following query could then be used to run a second transform on this data:

```
var query1 = new XElement("Orders", new XAttribute("City", "Paris"),
    from x in query.Descendants("Order")
    where x.Attribute("City").Value == "Paris"
    select new XElement("Address", x.Attribute("Address").Value));
```

This query takes the XML results of the first query and transforms that XML into the following format:

```
<Orders City="Paris">
  <Address>265, boulevard Charonne</Address>
  <Address>25, rue Lauriston</Address>
</Orders>
```

LINQ is constantly transforming one type of data into another type. It takes relational data and transforms it into objects; it takes XML and transforms it into relational data. Because LINQ is extensible, it is at least theoretically possible to use it to tear down the walls that separate any two arbitrary data domains.

Because LINQ is both composable and transformative, you can use it in a number of unexpected ways:

- You can compose multiple queries, linking them in discrete chunks. This often allows you to write code that is easier to understand and maintain than traditional nested SQL queries.

- You can easily transform data from one data source into some other type. For instance, you can transform SQL data into XML.

- Even if you do not switch data sources, you can still transform the shape of data. For instance, you can transform one XML format into another format. If you look back at the section "Declarative: Not How, But What," you will see that we transformed data that was stored in nested lists into data that was stored in a single list. These kinds of transformations are easy with LINQ.

Summary

In this chapter you have read about the foundations of LINQ. These foundations represent the core architectural ideas on which LINQ is built. Taken together, they form the essence of LINQ. We can summarize these foundations by saying the following about LINQ:

- It is a technique for querying data that is *integrated* into .NET languages such as C# and VB. As such, it is both strongly typed and IntelliSense-aware.

- It has a single *unitive* syntax for querying multiple data sources such as relational data and XML data.

- It is *extensible*; talented developers can write providers that allow LINQ to query any arbitrary data source.

- It uses a *declarative* syntax that allows developers to tell the compiler or provider what to do, not how to do it.

- It is *hierarchical*, in that it provides a rich, object-oriented view of data.

- It is *composable*, in that the results of one query can be used by a second query, and one query can be a subclause of another query. In many cases, this can be done without forcing the execution of any one query until the developer wants that execution to take place.

- It is *transformative*, in that the results of a LINQ query against one data source can be morphed into a second format. For instance, a query against a SQL database can produce an XML file as output.

Scattered throughout this chapter are references to some of the important benefits of LINQ that emerge from these building blocks. Although these benefits were mentioned throughout this chapter, I'll bring them together here in one place as a way of reviewing and summarizing the material discussed in this chapter:

- Because LINQ is integrated into the C# language, it provides syntax highlighting and IntelliSense. These features make it easy to write accurate queries and to discover mistakes at design time.
- Because LINQ queries are integrated into the C# language, it is possible for you to write code much faster than if you were writing old-style queries. In some cases, developers have seen their development time cut in half.
- The integration of queries into the C# language also makes it easy for you to step through your queries with the integrated debugger.
- The hierarchical feature of LINQ allows you to easily see the relationship between tables, thereby making it easy to quickly compose queries that join multiple tables.
- The unitive foundation of LINQ allows you to use a single LINQ syntax when querying multiple data sources. This allows you to get up to speed on new technologies much more quickly. If you know how to use LINQ to Objects, it is not hard to learn how to use LINQ to SQL, and it is relatively easy to master LINQ to XML.
- Because LINQ is extensible, you can use your knowledge of LINQ to make new types of data sources queriable.
- After creating or discovering a new LINQ provider, you can leverage your knowledge of LINQ to quickly understand how to write queries against these new data sources.
- Because LINQ is composable, you can easily join multiple data sources in a single query, or in a series of related queries.

- The composable feature of LINQ also makes it easy to break complex problems into a series of short, comprehensible queries that are easy to debug.

- The transformational features of LINQ make it easy to convert data of one type into a second type. For instance, you can easily transform SQL data into XML data using LINQ.

- Because LINQ is declarative, it usually allows you to write concise code that is easy to understand and maintain.

- The compiler and provider translate declarative code into the code that is actually executed. As a rule, LINQ knows more than the average developer about how to write highly optimized, efficient code. For instance, the provider might optimize or reduce nested queries.

- LINQ is a transparent process, not a black box. If you are concerned about how a particular query executes, you usually have a way to examine what is taking place and to introduce optimizations into your query.

This chapter touched on many other benefits of LINQ. These are described throughout this book. This entire text is designed to make you aware of the benefits that LINQ can bring to your development process. It also shows you how to write code that makes those benefits available to you and the other developers on your team.

The more you understand LINQ, the more useful it will be to you. As I have dug more deeply into this technology, I have found myself integrating LINQ into many different parts of my development process. When I use LINQ, I can get more work done in less time. The more I use it, the more completely these benefits accrue.

4

C# 3.0 Technical Overview

L INQ IS BUILT on a set of language features included in C# 3.0 and C# 2.0. Each feature was carefully crafted to fulfill a vision. The purpose of this chapter is to describe all these key features and to show exactly how they align to make LINQ possible.

LINQ to Objects can be used to query the collections found in the `System.Collections.Generic` namespace. These include `List<T>`, `Stack<T>`, `LinkedList<T>`, `Queue<T>`, `HashSet<T>`, and `Dictionary<TKey, Value>`. One particular C# type, `IEnumerable<T>`, is implemented by all these classes and plays an especially important role in LINQ to Objects. One of the purposes of this chapter is to explain how `IEnumerable<T>` and iterators contribute to the LINQ architecture.

Although LINQ to Objects has pride of place in this chapter, the lessons you learn also apply to LINQ to SQL and LINQ to XML. In truth, the changes you can run on `IEnumerable<T>` and the other features covered in this chapter apply to any version of LINQ.

Toward the end of the chapter, I relax the focus a bit and allow the text to zoom out far enough to encompass LINQ to SQL and expression trees. With the inclusion of this final subject, this chapter can stand on its own as a complete description of the LINQ architecture.

C# 2.0 and 3.0 Features Related to LINQ

The following technologies are covered in this chapter:

- Partial methods
- Automatically implemented properties
- Collection initializers
- Object initializers
- Type inference
- Anonymous types
- Generic methods, delegates, and lambda expressions
- Extension methods
- Scoping issues
- `IEnumerable<T>` and iterator blocks
- Deferred execution
- Overriding LINQ operators
- Expression trees

The first four features are only tangentially related to LINQ, but they are new to C# 3.0 and are used throughout this book and in much of the LINQ code you encounter. Because they are easy to explain and easy to understand, I've decided to include a brief description of them in this chapter for the sake of completeness. These features help you write code that is both concise and easy to understand.

Partial Methods

Partial methods are a C# 3.0 feature that help developers modify autogenerated code without fearing that their changes will be overwritten if the code is regenerated. In Visual Studio 2008, they are used by the Object Relational Designer and SqlMetal, two tools that play an important role in LINQ to SQL development. Although code generation is the primary scenario for partial methods, they are now a standard feature of the C# language, and developers can use them when and where they want.

Partial methods allow developers to reserve a name for a method that can optionally be implemented by consumers of their code. They are declared inside partial classes, as shown in Listing 4.1.

LISTING 4.1   A Simple Example of a Partial Method

```csharp
using System;
using System.IO;

namespace AbstractMethod
{
    public partial class MyPartialClass
    {
        partial void MyPartialMethod();

        public void WriteFile(string fileName, string contents)
        {
            using (TextWriter textWriter = new StreamWriter(fileName))
            {
                textWriter.Write(contents);
            }

            MyPartialMethod();
        }
    }

    public partial class MyPartialClass
    {
        partial void MyPartialMethod()
        {
            Console.WriteLine("File written");
        }
    }

    class Program
    {
        static void Main(string[] args)
        {
            MyPartialClass m = new MyPartialClass();
            m.WriteFile(@".\data.txt", "passaddhi");
        }
    }
}
```

Notice that `MyPartialClass` is declared as `partial`, as is `MyPartial-Method`:

```csharp
partial void MyPartialMethod();
```

In the first declaration of `MyPartialClass`, `MyPartialMethod` appears as a header and as a call in the method called `WriteFile`. Note, however, that `MyPartialMethod` is not implemented in this first declaration for `MyPartialClass`. In effect, this is an invitation to the developer to implement this method if desired in a second declaration for `MyPartialClass`. In our case, the invitation provides consumers of this class with the opportunity to extend the method called `WriteFile`. The invitation is called a *defining partial method declaration*.

If the developer accepts the invitation and creates the second half of `MyPartialClass` and includes an implementation of `MyPartialMethod`, the implementation is compiled into the code. At runtime, it is called by the `WriteFile` method in the first part of this partial class. The implementation of the method is called an *implementing partial method declaration*.

If the developer decides to decline the invitation, the declaration of `MyPartialMethod` and the code to call it are optimized out of the program by the compiler, causing all traces of `MyPartialMethod` to disappear. This ensures that no unnecessary overhead results when partial methods are used.

Suppose the first of the two partial classes shown in Listing 4.1 were autogenerated. The developer would be free to rerun the designer that created the first part of `MyPartialClass` without fear that this action would overwrite the code in the developers' implementation of the second half of `MyPartialClass`. It also allows the developer to work with a relatively small implementation of `MyPartialClass` that contains only a few methods, without needing to wrestle with the potentially long and complex listings that are often found in autogenerated code.

Although partial methods are easy to use, a number of rules govern their use. Partial methods

- Must be declared inside a partial class.
- Must not return a type. Their declarations contain the keyword `partial` followed by the keyword void. `partial` is a contextual keyword and can be used as a regular variable if it is not followed by `void`.
- Cannot be marked as `extern`.

- Can be marked `static` or `unsafe`.
- Can be generic.
- Can have `ref` parameters, but not out parameters.
- Cannot be referenced as a delegate until they are implemented.
- Cannot have access modifiers such as `public`, `private`, or `internal`. Partial methods are implicitly marked as `private`. This means that they cannot be called from outside the partial class and cannot be declared as `virtual`.
- Can be implemented in the same half of a partial class in which it is defined, although this is not a common practice.

Although partial methods are primarily designed as a tool for use with autogenerated code, there may be occasions when you would want to use this technology in your own code, giving consumers of your objects a place where they can hook into events in your class. For instance, in Listing 4.1 the `WriteText` method uses a partial method as a means of broadcasting a notification that a text file is being written. Although there are other ways to perform this same task, this is a useful technique whether or not code is autogenerated.

Automatically Implemented Properties

Automatic properties were touched on briefly in Chapter 2, "Getting Started." Here the subject is explored in more depth.

Automatically implemented properties are a convenience. They are valuable because their syntax is concise. Consider the simple class shown in Listing 4.2, which contains two properties declared with the new syntax.

LISTING 4.2   Using the C# 3.0 Feature Called Automatic Properties

```
class Operator
{
   public int OperatorId { get; set; }
   public string OperatorName { get; set; }
}
```

Both `OperatorId` and `OperatorName` are automatic properties. They are a shorthand way of telling the compiler that you want it to automatically generate the most obvious, default implementation for your property. Notice that their getters and setters have no explicit implementation. When you declare properties in this manner, the C# compiler automatically generates backing fields and fully implemented accessors behind the scenes. You never see the getters and setters, and you cannot see or access the backing fields.

■ Using the prop Snippet

You can use the prop snippet to help you quickly declare an automatic property. Just type prop and then press Tab twice.

The `Operator` class just shown is roughly semantically equivalent to the C# 2.0 code shown in Listing 4.3. Automatic properties are an alternative to the C# 2.0 syntax; they do not eclipse or replace it.

LISTING 4.3   C# 2.0-Style Properties Have Fully Implemented Getters and Setters and an Explicitly Declared Backing Field

```
class Operator
{
   private int operatorId;
   private string operatorName;

   public int OperatorId
   {
      get
      {
         return operatorId;
      }

      set
      {
         operatorId = value;
      }
   }

   public string OperatorName
   {
      get
```

```
    {
        return operatorName;
    }

    set
    {
        operatorName = value;
    }
  }
}
```

The patterns followed in Listing 4.3 are repeated often in production C# code. This syntax is valuable because it allows developers to add validation code, or side effects, to their getters and setters. Nevertheless, they frequently use the default implementation shown a moment ago. Automatic properties are simply a shorthand means of writing the default implementation. They make your code more concise and, hence, easier to read and maintain.

To get a deeper understanding of automatic properties, focus for a moment on just the declaration for `OperatorId`:

```
public int OperatorId { get; set; }
```

Reflector shows that the compiler generates the code shown in Listing 4.4 behind the scenes when you create the `OperatorId` property.

■ Reflector

Reflector is a free third-party tool you can download from http://www.aisto.com/roeder/dotnet/. It can sometimes be used to translate IL into standard C# code, thus giving you a peek behind the scenes in a C# program.

LISTING 4.4 The Code Generated by Reflector for an Automatic Property

```
[CompilerGenerated]
private int <OperatorId>k__BackingField;

public int OperatorId
{
  [CompilerGenerated]
  get
```

```
  {
    return this.<OperatorId>k__BackingField;
  }

  [CompilerGenerated]
  set
  {
    this.<OperatorId>k__BackingField = value;
  }
}
```

This code is similar to a C# 2.0-style property. The big difference is the presence of the [CompilerGenerated] attribute and the funny-looking name of the backing field: <OperatorId>k__BackingField. This name is not a valid C# identifier, but it is a valid CLR identifier. Because these are not valid C# names, you are unable to access these fields in your own C# code. This was an intentional decision, but it is not inconceivable that the team may provide access to these backing fields in some future version of C#.

■ About the Code Generated by Reflector

The [CompilerGenerated] attribute simply marks code so that certain tools can choose to ignore it.

The use of invalid C# identifiers for variable names is a theme that will recur throughout this chapter. I'll show you the Reflector code for them in only this one case, but that tool can be useful when working with the code seen in several sections of this chapter.

You must keep in mind a few caveats when working with automatic properties:

- You must declare both a getter and setter.
- Because you do not have access to the backing field, read-only and write-only properties would not be useful, so they are not allowed. You can, however, place the public or private modifiers before one of the two accessors.

- You should not use automatic properties as an excuse not to include validation code or other safety checks in your program. If you need getters and setters, you should implement them.

Here is an example of placing the modifier `private` before your setter:

```
public int Data { get; private set; }
```

Technically there is a difference between having a private setter and creating a read-only property, but in practice the difference is not significant.

The following code will not compile because both accessors have modifiers:

```
public int Data { protected get; private set; }
```

This code will not compile because it does not contain both a setter and a getter:

```
public int Data { get; }
```

The following property would be a poor candidate for an automatic property because it contains validation code that could not be easily implemented with automatic properties:

```
private int data;
public int Data
{
    get
    {
        if (data <= -5)
        {
            throw new Exception("Data has an invalid range");
        }
        return data;
    }
    set
    {
        data = value;
    }
}
```

In general, automatic properties are a simple feature, designed to help you get more work done with less code. Use them with care, but use them.

Initializers

C# 3.0 includes two new ways to initialize the elements of a collection or the fields and properties of an object. These techniques, called *collection initializers* and *object initializers*, are designed to help you write a more declarative style of code that is more succinct, easier to read, and easier to maintain. Again, you were introduced to these topics earlier in the book, but they are covered in more depth here. Later in this chapter, you will read about *anonymous types*, which use a technology closely related to object initializers.

Collection Initializers

Collection initializers save typing and make code more readable. They provide a means of quickly initializing any collection that implements `System.Collections.IEnumerable` and includes an `Add` method. Consider this code fragment that creates and initializes a simple collection:

```
List<string> list = new List<string>();
list.Add("LINQ");
list.Add("query");
list.Add("adventure");
```

Because `List<T>` implements `IEnumerable` and has an `Add` method, you can use collection initializers to condense these four lines into one:

```
List<string> list = new List<string> { "LINQ", "query", "adventure" };
```

The same simple technique can be used to initialize an array of integers:

```
List<int> list1 = new List<int> { 1, 2, 3, 4 };
```

In either case, you can optionally include parentheses for a call to the default constructor:

```
List<int> list2 = new List<int>() { 1, 2, 3, 4 };
```

Of course, other types have elements that can be initialized with this syntax. Here is how to use collection initializers with the `Dictionary` class:

```
var myDictionary = new Dictionary<string, string>()
{
```

```
    { "var", "type inference" },
    { "range variable", "Found in query expression after the word from" }
};

if (myDictionary.ContainsKey("range variable"))
{
    Console.WriteLine(myDictionary["range variable"]);
}
```

A `SortedList` works almost exactly the same way. Only the name of the object to be created differs:

```
SortedList<string, string> sortedList = new SortedList<string, string>();
```

The rest of the code is identical.

Here is how to initialize and use `HashSets`:

```
HashSet<int> hash1 = new HashSet<int> { 1, 2, 3 };
HashSet<int> hash2 = new HashSet<int> { 3, 4, 5 };

hash1.IntersectWith(hash2);

foreach (var item in hash1)
{
    Console.WriteLine(item); // Write the number 3
}
```

You would not be able to use collection initializers with a `Queue<T>`, `LinkedList<T>`, or `Stack<T>`, because they have no `Add` methods. Here, for instance, is an attempt to use collection initializers with a `Stack`:

```
Stack<int> stack = new Stack<int>() { 1, 2, 3 };
```

This code fails with the following error:

```
System.Collections.Generic.Stack<int>' does not contain a definition
for 'Add.'
```

The important case of initializing a collection with a set of objects is shown in the next section.

In general, collection initializers are useful, easy to implement, and without significant drawbacks. It is recommended that you use them whenever possible.

Object Initializers

C# 3.0 also provides a concise way to initialize one or more of the properties or fields of an object. Consider the `Operator` class declared in the section called Automatically Implemented Properties:

```
class Operator
{
    public int OperatorId { get; set; }
    public string OperatorName { get; set; }
}
```

Regardless of whether you used automatic properties, you can now initialize an instance of the `Operator` class with this simple syntax:

```
Operator o = new Operator() { OperatorId = 1, OperatorName = "Where" };
```

Compare this with the old style of object initialization:

```
Operator o = new Operator();
o.OperatorId = 1;
o.OperatorName = "Where";
```

Clearly the new style is more succinct.

You may combine object and collection initializers in a single statement:

```
private List<Operator> OperatorList;

private void CreateLists()
{
    // Collection initializer
    OperatorList = new List<Operator>
    {
        new Operator() { OperatorId = 1, OperatorName = "Where" },
        new Operator() { OperatorId = 2, OperatorName = "Select" },
        new Operator() { OperatorId = 3, OperatorName = "SelectMany" }
    };
    Console.WriteLine(OperatorList[1].OperatorName);
}
```

This code folds three object initializers inside a collection initializer. Declarative syntax of this kind is both orderly and concise.

You can pass in parameters to the constructor of an object when using object initializers, and you can omit any properties you don't want to initialize:

```
class Operator
{
    public Operator() { }
    public Operator(int i) { OperatorId = i; }
    public int OperatorId { get; set; }
    public string OperatorName { get; set; }

    public override string ToString()
    {
        return (string.Format("Id = {0}, Op = {1}",
            OperatorId, OperatorName));
    }

}

class Program
{
    static void Main(string[] args)
    {
        Operator o = new Operator(1) { OperatorName = "Where" };

        System.Console.WriteLine(o);
    }
}
```

The initialization code in the Main method explicitly uses the OperatorName property. The same line of code calls a constructor of class Operator that takes the integer value 1 to initialize the OperatorId. I've also added an optional ToString method that is used in the call to WriteLine. I've added it simply in the hopes that it will better help those who type in the code to understand what is happening. Try changing the call to the constructor to pass in the number 2, and then check the result:

```
Operator o = new Operator(2) { OperatorName = "Where" };
```

Types in C# 3.0

C# 3.0 introduced two major changes to the type system. One is type inference, which allows the compiler to automatically infer the type of a variable. The other is anonymous types, which allows you to declare a new type without explicitly giving it a name. Both of these features play a significant role in LINQ.

Type Inference

The var keyword tells the compiler to use type inference to determine the type of a variable. The developer never explicitly states the type of these variables; instead, it is up to the compiler to infer their type based on their context.

Consider the following simple statements:

```
var i = 2;
i = "LINQ is strongly typed."; // An error is generated by this line.
```

The first line uses type inference to determine the type of the variable i. The literal value 2 is of type System.Int32, so the compiler infers that i is an integer.

C# has always been a strongly typed language, and type inference does nothing to change this state of affairs. The second line of code shown here illustrates this fact. In the first line, the compiler infers that the type of i must be an int. C# does not allow assigning a string to an int. As a result, the second line of code creates a compile-time error stating that the compiler cannot implicitly convert type string to int. The lesson: *Inferred types are strongly typed.*

Do not use type inference unless you have a need for it, or if a developer reading the code could not possibly be confused about its type. As you will see later in this chapter, LINQ query expressions are one place where type inference is needed. However, on other occasions you can safely choose to use it. Consider the following code:

```
List<int> list = new List<int> { 1, 2, 3 };
```

This code repeats the declaration for List<string>. Use type inference to remove the repetition:

```
var list = new List<int> { 1, 2, 3 };
```

This code is arguably cleaner and easier to read.

The following code compiles cleanly but is probably not a good candidate for type inference:

```
public static List<int> GetList()
{
```

```
        return new List<int> {1, 2, 3};
    }

    static void Main(string[] args)
    {
        var list = GetList();
    }
```

The compiler will have no problem determining that `list` is of type `List<int>`, but a developer browsing the code might become confused, particularly in a large, complex program. As a result, it is probably best to explicitly declare the type of the list returned by the call to `GetList`:

```
List<int> list = GetList();
```

You cannot use type inference in the parameters of a method or in the return type of a method:

```
public var MyMethod(var myParameter) // generates two errors
{
}
```

In the cases shown here, the compiler complains, stating:

```
The contextual keyword 'var' may only appear within a local variable
declaration.
```

Because `var` is a contextual keyword, the following compiles cleanly, and the word `var` is treated as a standard identifier, not as a keyword:

```
string var = "Sam";
Console.WriteLine(var);
```

The subjects of type inference and anonymous types are interrelated. As a result, you will read more about type inference in the next section. In particular, you will see that in the case of anonymous types, type inference is not just useful, but a necessity.

Anonymous Types

Anonymous types provide a shorthand means of creating read-only classes with a few simple properties. They are both a new type and a form of initializer. Anonymous types play an important role in LINQ.

Consider the following statement, which declares and initializes an anonymous type:

```
var mountain = new { Name = "Rainier", Height = 4392, State = "WA" };
```

This statement has three parts:

- On the right is an object initializer.
- In the middle is the keyword new.
- On the left, type inference is used to determine the type of the identifier mountain.

Note that there is no type declaration between the word new and the opening curly brace:

```
var mountain = new [No Type Name Appears Here]{ Name = ... };
```

Anonymous types get their name because they are never explicitly named.

In the preceding section, you saw cases when type inference is useful. Here is a case when it is a necessity. It is not possible to declare the variable mountain without using type inference, because we do not, and cannot, know or write the name of its type at compile time. From the point of view of a C# developer, anonymous types have no name, just as we cannot know the name of a backing field for an automatic property. In the background, a "funny-looking" name is generated like those we saw in the backing fields for automatic properties. But this name is not valid C# code and cannot be known by C# developers at design time.

You can, however, learn the name of an anonymous class by calling getType at runtime:

```
foreach (var CityAndContact in query)
{
    Console.WriteLine(CityAndContact.GetType().ToString());
}
```

You can also view the type name in Reflector. However, very little can be gained by learning the name, because it is not valid C# code. It is primarily of academic interest.

When it creates an anonymous class like the one shown here, the C# compiler fully and properly implements the ToString(), Equals(), GetHashCode(), and GetType() methods. You will never see this class, but the pseudocode in Listing 4.5 gives you a very general sense of what it looks like. (You can use Reflector to learn more details.)

LISTING 4.5   The Compiler Generates Code for Your Anonymous Classes That Looks Something Like the Pseudocode Shown in This Listing

```
class SomeUnknownFunnyLookingNameNotValidInCSharp
{
  public string Name { get;}
  public int Height { get; }
  public string State { get; }

  public override string ToString()...
  public int GetHashCode() ...
  public Type GetType() ...
  bool Equals(object obj) ...
}
```

Note that the properties are read-only. I include GetType in this pseudocode because it is properly implemented even though it is not really overridden. Finally, remember that you can't use var in the parameter list or the return type of a method, so you can use this class only within the scope of the current method. There is usually no way to pass it to another method or give it broader scope.

Every Rule Has an Exception

In his review of this text, Nick Paldino found exceptions to the rule I just stated. His comments on the subject are clear, so I'll include them almost exactly as he presented them to me: You can pass an anonymous type out of a method by passing it as type Object, and Reflection will be able to parse it. Anders Hejlsberg gave a presentation at the MVP summit in 2007 that bound the output of an anonymous type to a DataGridView; he could do that because the DataGridView uses reflection to get the information on the type. Also, the extension methods that LINQ uses actually are outside of the method. When anonymous types are used, they are passed to the Select<T> extension method on the Enumerable class. Technically, that is a means of passing an anonymous type out of a method.

Anonymous types are also used in LINQ queries. Consider this LINQ to Objects code fragment borrowed from one of the samples in Chapter 2:

```
var query = from c in Customers
            where c.City == "London"
            select new { c.City, c.CompanyName };
```

The select clause contains an anonymous type. You could create your own type and use it instead, but it is a common and useful practice to write code like that shown here.

Because this LINQ query uses an anonymous type, developers must use type inference to declare its return type. In the section "Composable" in the preceding chapter, you learned that query expressions both return and operate on instances of IEnumerable<T>. In this case T is some anonymous type with two fields of type string. This means that again we must use type inference to declare the identifier query. Without type inference, code of this type would not be possible.

Consider this code fragment, which operates on the variable returned from the query we are studying:

```
foreach (var x in query)
{
  Console.WriteLine(x);
}
```

In the current context, x is an anonymous type, so again it would be impossible to declare it explicitly. This is yet another case where we could not go forward if type inference did not exist.

Even if we could explicitly declare the type used in this foreach statement, it would probably cause us more trouble than it would be worth. The problem is that the type of x could easily change if we made small changes to the query expression from which it is derived. In complex LINQ queries, especially those that use composability, this could cause a cascading series of changes. All of this is avoided by using the keyword var and type inference.

In this section you have learned about anonymous types and type inference. You have seen that these subjects are inextricably linked, because only rarely can you make use of anonymous types without also needing to use type inference.

Generic Methods, Delegates, and Lambdas

Lambdas are important both as a stand-alone C# 3.0 feature and as a significant part of the LINQ architecture. The C# 2.0 technologies called delegates and generic methods serve as stepping-stones and building blocks for lambdas. Thus, I will cover them first and then focus on lambdas. I will also briefly mention a C# 2.0 technology called anonymous methods that has been eclipsed by lambdas.

Delegates

Delegates provide a means of declaring a variable that references an individual method. Developers can invoke the delegate, and the delegate, in turn, calls the method it references. Because the delegate is just a variable, you can pass it to other methods and perform similar tricks with it that would otherwise be impossible.

In many other languages, delegates are called and implemented as function pointers. In C#, however, a delegate is implemented as a class, rather than as a pointer. The advantage of this system is that you can fully type-check a class, whereas a pointer is less type-safe.

Consider the code shown in Listing 4.6. It shows a simple delegate type called `MyDelegate`, used to reference the `Add` method.

LISTING 4.6   A Simple Delegate

```
using System;

namespace SimpleLambda
{
    class Program
    {
        public delegate int MyDelegate(int a, int b);

        public static int Add(int a, int b)
        {
            return a + b;
        }

        public static void CallDelegate(MyDelegate func)
        {
```

```
            Console.WriteLine(func(272, 153));
        }

        static void Main(string[] args)
        {
            MyDelegate myDelegate = Add;

            Console.WriteLine(myDelegate(271, 152));

            CallDelegate(myDelegate);
        }
    }
}
```

Before we examine this code in depth, let's take a moment to simply describe what it does. The code defines a delegate type that has the same signature as the Add method. An instance of this delegate type is used to call the Add method. The same instance is then passed to another method that, in turn, calls the Add method.

Now let's step back and examine the code in more depth. We first need to declare a type that is compatible with the Add method:

```
public delegate int MyDelegate(int a, int b);
```

Notice that this type has the same signature as the Add method:

```
public static int Add(int a, int b)
```

Both declarations are for a type that takes two integers and returns an integer. This is why it is possible to assign the Add method to an instance of MyDelegate:

```
MyDelegate myDelegate = Add;
```

After this assignment is made, a call to the myDelegate variable translates into a call to the Add method. For instance, the following call returns the sum of 271 and 152, which is 423:

```
myDelegate(271, 152);
```

> ## More on Assigning Delegates
>
> The code I've shown here is valid shorthand for the following syntax, which is actually generated behind the scenes:
>
> ```
> MyDelegate myDelegate = new MyDelegate(Add);
> ```
>
> I believe, however, that it is easier to read and understand delegates if you use the shorthand without calling new.

To pass around delegate instances, we must first declare a method that takes our delegate as a parameter:

```
public static void CallDelegate(MyDelegate myDelegate)
{
    myDelegate(272, 153);
}
```

As you would expect, calls to the MyDelegate instance resolve to calls to the Add method and thus return the value 425 in this case. Here is how you call this method:

```
MyDelegate myDelegate = Add;
CallDelegate(myDelegate);
```

We will use delegates in LINQ, but you should understand that they existed before LINQ and have value in their own right. In particular, a commonly used pattern for sorting data uses delegates. When implementing this pattern, consumers of a hypothetical sort routine pass in a delegate, which a user defines to compare two items and decide which is "larger":

```
public void Sort<T>(CompareDelegate compare, List<T> items);
```

Users of this method define their own implementation of compare, which, in turn, is called by the Sort routine. Please recall that I'm providing this example simply to illustrate that delegates have practical uses outside of LINQ. It is not really that important that you understand the particular example I show here.

In this section you saw that delegates consist of two parts—a delegate type and a delegate instance. You learned how to declare delegates and how to use them to call a method and pass a reference to a method. This is just enough information to ensure that you can understand the role they will play in LINQ. I have not, however, covered other aspects of delegates, such as their role in C#'s event processing.

Generic Delegates

Before we cover lambdas, you need to understand one other C# 2.0 technology. Generic methods are one of the most powerful features of the C# language, and they play a key role in LINQ. Let's take a moment to be sure you know how they work.

As things stand, our `MyDelegate` type can work with any routine that takes two integers and returns an integer:

```
public delegate int MyDelegate(int a, int b);
```

This delegate would be considerably more flexible if it worked with all routines that took two parameters of any type and returned a parameter of any type. If we had that ability, this delegate would no longer be confined to use with methods that accepted and returned integers. It could, for instance, be used with methods that accepted and returned `doubles`, or that accepted `integers` and returned a `long`.

Here is how to declare a generic delegate that does exactly that:

```
public delegate TResult MyDelegate<T1, T2, TResult>(T1 a, T2 b);
```

To understand this code, we need to break it into two parts. Look at the following pseudo-declaration, and you will see that it still has the same general signature as the `Add` method: it takes two parameters and returns a parameter:

```
public delegate TResult MyDelegate(T1 a, T2 b);
```

The problem here is that we don't know the type of `T1`, `T2`, and `TResult`. C# solves that problem by providing a place where you can declare the types of the parameters used by this delegate:

```
public delegate TResult MyDelegate<T1, T2, TResult>(T1 a, T2 b);
```

Notice the funny-looking syntax after the word `MyDelegate`: `<T1, T2, TResult>`. This is a place where you can pass in type parameters that define what types you want to work with when you declare an instance of this type:

```
MyDelegate<int, int, int> myDelegate = Add;
```

This declaration declares the types of `T1`, `T2`, and `TResult` as integers, thus resolving the ambiguity that is inherent in the generic declaration of `MyDelegate`. In particular, it states that `T1` maps to an integer, `T2` to an integer, and `TResult` to an integer. In effect, it transforms, through substitution, our generic declaration for `MyDelegate` back into a standard method declaration. We start with this declaration:

```
public delegate TResult MyDelegate<T1, T2, TResult>(T1 a, T2 b);
```

`T1`, `T2`, and `TResult` are mapped to the type `int`, and somewhere behind the scenes we end up with this declaration:

```
public delegate int MyDelegate(int a, int b);
```

A delegate of this type is compatible with our `Add` method.

Let me show a second example to help further illustrate how this works. Instead of working with integers, we could have used doubles:

```
public static double AddDoubles(double a, double b)
{
    return a + b;
}

MyDelegate<double, double, double> myDelegate = AddDoubles();
```

In this case the delegate would be transformed behind the scenes as follows:

```
public delegate double MyDelegate(double a, double b);
```

These substitutions take place at compile time and have no effect on the run-time performance of your code. Note also that I had to create a new standard method called `AddDoubles` that was compatible with our new delegate.

A generic declaration for a delegate is so flexible that you can easily imagine a small set of such declarations that would cover nearly every function any reasonable developer would be likely to declare. This is an excellent opportunity to employ the 80 percent rule: Most functions that return a value take between zero and four parameters. Stick with those five cases, and safely ignore the rare method that takes more than four parameters. Or rather, you can leave it for the developer to declare any such declaration should he or she need it.

The developers of C# have done exactly that—they have declared two sets of delegates in the System namespace. One set called Func returns a value, and another set called Action does not. Here are the ones that do return a value:

```
public delegate TResult Func<TResult>();
public delegate TResult Func<T, TResult>(T a);
public delegate TResult Func<T1, T2, TResult>(T1 a, T2 b);
public delegate TResult Func<T1, T2, T3, TResult>(T1 a, T2 b, T3 c);
public delegate TResult Func<T1, T2, T3, T4, TResult>(T1 a, T2 b, T3 c,
                                                       T4 d);
```

Here are the declarations for the type that do not return a value:

```
public delegate void Action();
public delegate void Action<T>(T a);
public delegate void Action<T1, T2>(T1 a, T2 b);
public delegate void Action<T1, T2, T3>(T1 a, T2 b, T3 c);
public delegate void Action<T1, T2, T3, T4>(T1 a, T2 b, T3 c, T4 d);
```

Given the presence of these declarations in the System namespace, we can modify our program as shown in Listing 4.7.

LISTING 4.7   Using the Predeclared Func Delegates

```
using System;

namespace SimpleLambda
{
    class Program
    {
        public static int Add(int a, int b)
        {
            return a + b;
        }
```

```
public static void CallDelegate(Func<int, int, int> func)
{
    Console.WriteLine(func(271, 152));
}

static void Main(string[] args)
{
    Func<int, int, int> myDelegate = Add;

    Console.WriteLine(myDelegate(271, 152));

    CallDelegate(myDelegate);
}
}
}
```

The declaration of our delegate has been deleted and replaced with the Func<T1, T2, TResult> declaration from the System namespace. Otherwise, the code is the same as that found in Listing 4.7.

The last two sections have focused only on the features of generic methods and generic delegates that are directly applicable to LINQ. More could be said about this subject, but that information would be outside the scope of this book.

Lambdas

Lambdas are a simple technology with an intimidating name. They sound like they will be difficult to understand, but in practice they are relatively trivial.

For reasons that will become clear later in this chapter, LINQ has an almost inordinate need for its users to declare a large number of small, simple delegates. The architects of C# decided that forcing the users of LINQ to declare delegates using the syntax shown in the previous two sections was too verbose. They wanted to find a shorter, more concise way to accomplish the same task.

The syntax they settled on looks like this:

```
Func<int, int, int> myLambda = (a, b) => (a + b);
```

This is a shorthand way of writing code that is roughly semantically equivalent to the following:

```csharp
public static int Add(int a, int b)
{
    return a + b;
}
```

```csharp
Func<int, int, int> myDelegate = Add;
```

In the next few paragraphs I will compare these two ways of creating a delegate instance and explain how they map back and forth.

It is obvious that the left sides of the following two code fragments have the same meaning:

```csharp
Func<int, int, int> myLambda = (a, b) => (a + b);
Func<int, int, int> myDelegate = Add;
```

But how can the right sides be the same?

The expression on the right side of the first statement is a shorthand way of writing a method that is semantically equivalent to the Add method. Just to be clear, a lambda is not a reference to the Add method; it is second method that does the same thing as the Add method.

Here is the lambda:

```csharp
(a, b) => (a + b);
```

And here is the Add method:

```csharp
public static int Add(int a, int b)
{
    return a + b;
}
```

Here is the place in the Add method where we define the parameters it will take:

```csharp
(int a, int b)
```

Here is the place in the lambda where we define the parameters it will take:

```csharp
(a, b)
```

Here is the place in the Add method where we define what it will return:

```csharp
return a + b;
```

Here is the place in the lambda where we define what it will return:

```
(a + b)
```

As you can see, a lambda and a method do the same thing: They define a set of parameters and an executable body of code.

The type declarations for a lambda are resolved using a technique very similar to the one we employ for generic methods and generic delegates. To see how this works, look again at the full declaration for the lambda:

```
Func<int, int, int> myLambda = (a, b) => (a + b);
```

The generic delegate Func says that the method being implemented takes two integers as parameters and returns an integer. The compiler takes this information and applies it to the lambda. Behind the scenes it resolves (a, b) to (int a, int b) and defines the function such that the body of the lambda (a + b) returns an integer. Thus, we give the compiler enough information to convert our lambda into a method that performs the same action as the Add method.

The => symbol is called a lambda operator and is usually pronounced "goes to." Thus, the lambda just shown can be read as "a comma b goes to a plus b" or "a and b goes to a plus b."

Although you will rarely need to do so, you can explicitly declare the type of parameters to a lambda expression:

```
Func<int, int, int> f = (int a, int b) => (a + b);
```

For void functions that do not return a value, just use an empty set of parentheses:

```
() => Console.WriteLine();
```

Lambdas have access to local variables:

```
public static void UseLocal()
{
    int n;
    Func<int> func = () => { n = 6; return n; };
    n = func();
    Console.WriteLine(n); // Outputs the number 6
}
```

■ Lambdas and Anonymous Methods

You might be familiar with anonymous methods from C# 2.0. Semantically, anonymous methods and lambdas are identical, but the lambda syntax is easier to use. As a result, there is probably no reason for you to use anonymous methods in the future unless you find that their syntax makes your code pleasing or easier to read. Here are a lambda and anonymous method side by side:

```
Func<int, int, int> myLambda = (a, b) => (a + b);
Func<int, int, int> myAnonMethod = delegate(int a, int b)
{
    return a + b;
};
```

Both methods take two integers, add them together, and return the result. Commenting further on anonymous methods at this point would serve no purpose, because lambdas create the same result with less work.

You saw earlier that the compiler generates "funny-looking" names that we never see for the backing fields of automatic properties, and for the classes created when we declare an anonymous type. A similar process is employed for lambdas. Behind the scenes, the compiler generates code that looks much like the Add method, but it gives the method a "funny-looking" name that is valid in the CLR but illegal—hence, by necessity, invisible—to the C# programmer.

Exercises

In the beginning of this section, I said that lambdas are easy to understand. To help reinforce that point, I've included a few quick exercises. When you have had an "aha!" moment when the idea behind lambdas becomes clear, you should find these exercises, and lambdas in general, very simple. Appendix A contains the answers.

1. As you have seen, the following lambda and method are semantically equivalent:

```
(a, b) => (a + b);
public int Add(int a, int b)
{
    return a + b;
}
```

Given that this is the case, what is the lambda equivalent of the following method?

```
public int Subtract(int a, int b)
{
    return a - b;
}
```

2. What lambda is semantically equivalent to this method?

```
public int Multiply(int a)
{
    return a * 5;
}
```

3. What lambda is semantically equivalent to this method?

```
public void Display(string value)
{
    Console.WriteLine(value);
}
```

4. What is the lambda equivalent of this method?

```
public void DisplayWarning()
{
    Console.WriteLine("Warning");
}
```

5. What is the lambda equivalent of this method?

```
public decimal SimpleMath(int a, int b, int c)
{
    return (a + b) / c;
}
```

6. What lambda is equivalent to this method?

```
public static long Add(int a, int b)
{
    return a + (long)b;
}
```

Here is the declaration for a lambda and a statement that calls it:

```
Func<string, int, int, string> showMe =
    (a, b, c) => string.Format(a, b, c, (b + c));
Console.WriteLine(showMe("{0} + {1} = {2}", 3, 5));
```

Lambdas provide you with a concise syntax for writing a method. They are valuable in large part because they are so short. This concision helps make possible the functional style of programming used in LINQ query expressions, where each expression is composed into a single, discreet entity with no external references. If this latter point does not yet make sense to you, simply focus on the fact that lambdas are useful because they are concise and short.

Extension Methods

Extension methods allow you to add optional functionality to an existing class or interface without modifying the class itself. Added in C# 3.0, extension methods appear to be instance methods of an object, but they are actually declared as static methods in a separate class.

Suppose you have an easy-to-use class with three methods. Much of the time, those three methods would provide all the power a developer needs from your class. But under certain circumstances, you might want the class to have more functionality. Before extension methods, there were three ways to solve this problem, each with its own drawbacks:

- Add the new methods to the existing class.
- Use inheritance to add the methods in a derived class.
- Use static methods.

Suppose you are working on a program that needs to test whether strings are valid abbreviations for a state. In this case, you can't use option 1 for two reasons:

- You don't have access to the source of class `string`.
- Even if you did have access to it, you might not want to add the weight and overhead of this feature to all strings—only to a subset of all `strings`.

Option 2, inheritance, might also be a bad choice:

- It would force developers who wanted your added functionality to use your type instead of normal `strings`.
- Even if they were willing to do that, it is not possible, because class `string` is sealed.

Because options 1 and 2 are unavailable, this leaves only option 3, which I have implemented in Listing 4.8.

LISTING 4.8   Using a Static Method to Add the Functionality of the `string` Class

```
using System;

namespace ConsoleApplication1
{
    public static class SpecialString
    {
        public static bool IsState(string source)
        {
            string[] stateCodes =
                {"AL","AK","AZ","AR","CA","CO","CT","DE","DC",
                 "FL","GA","HI","ID","IL","IN","IA","KS","KY",
                 "LA","ME","MD","MA","MI","MN","MS","MO","MT",
                 "NE","NV","NH","NJ","NM","NY","NC","ND","OH",
                 "OK","OR","PA","RI","SC","SD","TN","TX","UT",
                 "VT","VA","WA","WV","WI","WY"};

            if (source == null) return false;
            source = source.ToUpper();

            foreach (var item in stateCodes)
            {
                if (source == item)
                {
                    return true;
                }
            }
```

continues

LISTING 4.8   Continued

```
            }
            return false;
        }
    }

    class Program
    {
        public static void ShowTest(string state)
        {
            string format = "You entered: {0}. It is a state: {1}";
            Console.WriteLine(format, state,
                            SpecialString.IsState(state));
        }

        static void Main(string[] args)
        {
            ShowTest("co");
            ShowTest("WA");
            ShowTest("AW");
            ShowTest("AL");
            ShowTest("NV");
            ShowTest("NB");
            ShowTest("MI");
        }
    }
}
```

The class `SpecialString` implements a static method named `IsState`. We access that class and our new method in the following line:

```
Console.WriteLine(format, state, SpecialString.IsState(state));
```

This is not such a bad solution, but it could be improved if we could write the following:

```
Console.WriteLine(format, state, state.IsState());
```

When placed side by side, it should be obvious that the second solution is more succinct than the first:

```
SpecialString.IsState(state)
state.IsState()
```

To enable the second syntax in C# 3.0, you need to make only one small change to your code. Here is the original declaration for the `IsState` method:

```
public static bool IsState(string source)
```

And here is the same code converted into an extension method:

```
public static bool IsState(this string source)
```

Simply add the keyword `this` to the method declaration to make the `IsState` method an extension of the `string` class. You can now write `myString.IsState()`. It's that simple.

You can use IntelliSense to discover the `IsState` method, just as if it were a real instance method of `SpecialString`, as shown in Figure 4.1.

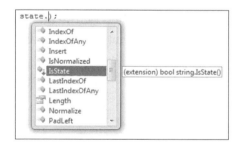

Figure 4.1   The variable state, which is of type `string`, appears to the developer to support an instance method called `IsState`.

It should come as no surprise to learn that behind the scenes the compiler converts the call into a static method call: `SpecialString.IsState (myString)`. From the developer's perspective, it appears to be like an instance method of type `string`, but behind the scenes it is a static method call. This is another place where the compiler takes code that you write and transforms it behind the scenes.

The `SpecialString` class has several traits that must be true if you want to use extension methods:

- The class must be declared to be static.
- The extension method must also be static.
- The first parameter of an extension method must include the this modifier, and it cannot be a pointer type.
- Extension methods cannot appear in generic classes.

Follow these guidelines, and you will find it easy to create extension methods.

Scoping Issues

You must keep in mind a few scoping rules when using extension methods. Problems with scoping and extension methods are rare, but when you encounter them, they are quite vexing.

An instance method is always called before an extension method. The compiler looks first for an instance method. If it finds an instance method with the right name and signature, it executes it and never looks for your extension method. The following code illustrates this problem:

```
using System;
namespace ConsoleApplication1
{
    public class MyClass
    {
        public void DoThis()
        {
            Console.WriteLine("MyClass.DoThis");
        }
    }


    public static class MyExtensions01
    {
        // Can never be called as if it were an instance method
        // of MyClass.
        public static void DoThis(this MyClass myClass)
        {
            Console.WriteLine("MyExtensions01.DoThis");
        }
    }
```

```
        class Program
        {
            static void Main(string[] args)
            {
                MyClass myClass = new MyClass();
                myClass.DoThis();                  // Calls MyClass.DoThis
                MyExtensions01.DoThis(myClass);  // Calls
                                                   // MyExtensions01.DoThis
            }
        }
}
```

`MyExtensions01.DoThis` is a valid extension method for `MyClass`. However, it will never be called, because `MyClass.DoThis` always takes precedence over it unless you explicitly call it as a static method of `MyExtensions01`.

In cases where you have two extension methods with the same name, an extension method in the current namespace wins out over one in another namespace. Ambiguity becomes an issue, however, when you try to call two extension methods with the same name and signature in the same namespace, or in two different namespaces that are both used by the current namespace. Listing 4.9 gives an example of this problem.

LISTING 4.9   **This Code Does Not Compile Because the Compiler Finds the Call to** DoThat **Ambiguous**

```
using System;
using System.Collections.Generic;
using System.Linq;

namespace ExtensionScope
{
    public class MyClass
    {
        public void DoThis()
        {
            Console.WriteLine("Do this");
        }
    }
}

namespace Extensions01
{
    using ExtensionScope;
```

continues

LISTING 4.9   Continued

```csharp
    public static class MyExtensions01
    {
        // Can never be called
        public static void DoThis(this MyClass myClass)
        {
            Console.WriteLine("Do this");
        }

        public static void DoThat(this MyClass myClass)
        {
            Console.WriteLine("Do bop");
        }
    }
}

namespace Extensions02
{
    using ExtensionScope;

    public static class MyExtensions02
    {
        // Can never be called
        public static void DoThis(this MyClass myClass)
        {
            Console.WriteLine("Do this");
        }

        public static void DoThat(this MyClass myClass)
        {
            Console.WriteLine("Do bang");
        }
    }
}

namespace ExtensionScope
{
    using Extensions01;
    using Extensions02;

    class Program
    {
        static void Main(string[] args)
        {
            MyClass m = new MyClass();
            m.DoThat();
        }
    }
}
```

This program throws a compile-time error because the compiler does not know if you want `MyExtensions01.DoThat()` or `MyExtensions02. DoThat()`. There are three ways to resolve this error:

- You could remove the `using` directive for either `Extensions01` or `Extensions02`. In this case, that would be a fine resolution. But if there were other methods or classes in both `Extensions01` and `Extensions02` that you wanted to use, this could become a painful, or even unacceptable, choice.
- You could explicitly state which method you want to call using standard static syntax: `MyExtensions01.DoThat(m)`.
- You could move either `MyExtensions02` or `MyExtensions01` into the `ExtensionScope` namespace:

```
namespace ExtensionScope
{
    public static class MyExtensions02
    {
        public static void DoThat(this MyClass myClass)
        {
            Console.WriteLine("MyExtensions02.DoThat");
        }
    }
}
```

This solution works so long as you have access to the source.

It should be clear that some of the issues discussed here can lead to trouble if you are not careful. In particular, you don't want to end up in a situation where forcing someone to remove a namespace results in his losing access to important functionality. Nor do you want to force him to choose between functionality he wants and using your extensions.

It can also be a serious nuisance if you muddy a namespace with what many developers might consider superfluous methods. If you added 50 extension methods to the C# `string` class, developers who just want to access the base functionality of that object would always have to contend with your methods, particularly when using IntelliSense.

To avoid or at least mitigate the seriousness of these problems, you should always place your extension methods in a unique namespace separate from the rest of your code. That way, you can easily include the extension methods in or exclude them from a program. Listings 4.10 and 4.11 illustrate this technique.

LISTING 4.10   Place Your Extensions in a Separate File, and Give Them a Unique Namespace

```csharp
namespace MyCode
{
    ... Code omitted here
}

namespace MyCode.Extensions
{
    public static class SpecialString
    {
        private static string[] stateCodes =
            {"AL","AK","AZ","AR","CA","CO","CT","DE","FL",
             "GA","HI","ID","IL","IN","IA","KS","KY","LA",
             "ME","MD","MA","MI","MN","MS","MO","MT","NE",
             "NV","NH","NJ","NM","NY","NC","ND","OH","OK",
             "OR","PA","RI","SC","SD","TN","TX","UT","VT",
             "VA","WA","WV","WI","WY"};

        public static bool IsState01(this string source)
        {
            if (source == null) return false;
            source = source.ToUpper();
            foreach (var item in stateCodes)
            {
                if (source == item)
                {
                    return true;
                }
            }
            return false;
        }
    }
}
```

LISTING 4.11   Accessing Extension Methods in a Namespace

```csharp
using System;
using MyCode;
using MyCode.Extensions;

namespace ConsoleApplication1
{
    class Program
    {
```

```
        static void Main(string[] args)
        {
            MyCode myCode = new MyCode();
            ... // Use My Code here.
            string test = "WA";
            if (test.IsState())
            {
                Console.WriteLine("{0} is a state", test);
            }
        }
    }
}
```

In Listing 4.11 your extension method is available, and the code compiles. If you were to comment out the third using directive, your extension method would be unavailable, and the code would not compile. The developer would, however, still have access to the functionality found in the MyCode namespace. You could perhaps improve this technology by putting your extensions in their own assembly with its own namespace. You could then be sure that developers could choose to include or exclude the extra weight of your extension methods when they ship their code.

Listing 4.10 shows you two alternative ways to implement the IsState extension method. The second, which uses the LINQ Contains operator, is probably easier to maintain. The Contains operator is discussed in the next chapter.

The primary reason for the inclusion of extension methods in C# 3.0 is to enable LINQ. It is unlikely that this feature would have been added to the language had LINQ not existed. They are, however, now a part of the language, and, if used with caution, they can be useful. Placing them in their own namespace is a best practice that should help you get the most from this feature. Near the end of this chapter we will revisit extension methods, and you will see the crucial role they play in LINQ development.

IEnumerable<T>

As mentioned at the beginning of this chapter, each of the collections in the System.Collections.Generic namespace supports the IEnumerable<T> interface. For instance, here is part of the declaration for List<T>:

```
public class List<T> : IList<T>, ICollection<T>, IEnumerable<T> ...
```

As you can see, the `List<T>` class supports `IEnumerable<T>`. This fact, and this fact alone, makes it possible to write a LINQ to Objects query against this variable, or any variable of this type.

As you learned in the preceding chapter in the section "Composable," LINQ to Objects queries always interrogate and usually return an instance of `IEnumerable<T>`. Consider the following code fragment:

```
List<int> list = new List<int> { 1, 3, 2 };

var query = from num in list
            where num < 3
            select num;

foreach (var item in query)
{
    Console.WriteLine(item);
}
```

The type `IEnumerable<T>` plays two key roles in this code:

- The query expression has a data source called `list` that implements `IEnumerable<T>`. The data source produces a sequence of elements.
- The query expression returns an instance of a type that implements `IEnumerable<T>`.

Every LINQ to Objects query expression, including the one just shown, begins with a line of this type:

```
var w = from X in y
```

In each case, the data source represented by the variable y must support the `IEnumerable<T>` interface, and the variable w usually supports it. As you have already seen, the list of integers shown in this example supports that interface.

The same query shown here could also be written as follows:

```
IEnumerable<int> query = from num in list
                         where num < 3
                         select num;
```

This code makes explicit the type of the variable returned by this query.

In practice, you will find that most LINQ to Objects queries return IEnumerable<T>, for some type T. The only exceptions are those that call a LINQ query operator that returns a simple type, such as Count():

```
int number = (from num in list
              where num < 3
              select num).Count();
```

In this case the query returns an integer specifying the number of items in the list created by this query. LINQ queries that return a simple type like this are an exception to the rule that LINQ to Objects queries operate on classes that implement IEnumerable<T> and return an instance that supports IEnumerable<T>.

Although it might not be immediately obvious, simple arrays in C# 3.0 implement IEnumerable<T>. As a result, the following code compiles and runs as expected:

```
int[] array = new int[] { 1, 2, 3 };

var query = from i in array
            where i < 3
            select i;

foreach (var item in query)
{
    Console.WriteLine(item);
}
```

▪ Differences Between LINQ to Objects and LINQ to SQL

LINQ to SQL queries both operate on and return types that implement an interface called IQueryable<T>. It, in turn, implements the IEnumerable<T> interface. As a result, LINQ to SQL queries still provide the functionality found in LINQ to Objects, plus they use features of IQueryable<T> to enable the generation of SQL strings and calls to a SQL server. Exactly how this works is covered in section "Expression Trees" and is explained in more depth in Chapters 7 through 10.

Understanding Sequences

The `IEnumerable<T>` interface gives developers access to a sequence of items. For instance, a collection contains a sequence of some instances of type `T` arranged in a particular order. Here, for instance, is a sequence of integers that could be stored in a `List<int>`:

```
1, 3, 2
```

It is important to understand the differences between a sequence and a set:

- In a set, order is not important, and there is always a finite number of items.
- In a sequence, order is important, and there is not always a limit on the number of items.
- Re-enumeration is not built into sequences. If you ask to enumerate the values returned by a LINQ query a second time, it is not guaranteed that this will yield the same sequence of items in the same order.

It is important to understand that the data source found in the `from` clause at the beginning of a query expression provides a sequence of elements. A sequence has no defined limit. For instance, there is no limit on the number of items in the Fibonacci sequence, and it's possible to use such a sequence as the data source for a LINQ query. That sort of sequence may not be a typical LINQ data source, but it is nonetheless a possible data source. The next two sections help explain the theory behind that type of query and provide an example of a data source that produces an infinite sequence. I should add that set theory also encompasses the idea of infinite sets. For instance, the set of all integers is infinite. You will see, however, that implementing an infinite sequence in LINQ is fairly trivial, whereas implementing an infinite set in computer programming is rare.

Enumeration

All generic collections provide the ability to ask for the first item in the sequence, and then for the next item, and the next item, until either the sequence or the need for new elements is exhausted. This is called enumerating over a sequence of elements, and it is an ability granted to us by the IEnumerable<T> interface.

The IEnumerable<T> interface looks like this:

```
public interface IEnumerable<T> : IEnumerable
{
   IEnumerator<T> GetEnumerator();
}
```

The GetEnumerator method returns an implementation of the IEnumerator<T> interface, which, in turn, supports the following interface, called IEnumerator:

```
public interface IEnumerator
{
   object Current { get; }
   bool MoveNext();
   void Reset();
}
```

You can use this interface to iterate over a collection, as shown in Listing 4.12.

LISTING 4.12   Enumerating the Items in a List with the IEnumerator<T> Interface

```
using System;
using System.Collections.Generic;

namespace ConsoleApplication1
{
    class Program
    {
        static void Main(string[] args)
        {
            var list = new List<int> { 1, 2, 3 };

            IEnumerator<int> e = list.GetEnumerator();

            while (e.MoveNext())
            {
                Console.WriteLine(e.Current);
            }
        }
    }
}
```

The code in Listing 4.12 uses MoveNext() and Current from IEnumerator to enumerate the values in a list. It is worth pointing out that because we are working with generic types, e.Current is strongly typed. In this case, for instance, Current is of type int. This means that you do not need to worry about typecasts.

As you know, the same effect can be achieved by writing the following code:

```
foreach (var item in list)
{
    Console.WriteLine(item);
}
```

The C# foreach syntax is just a shorthand way of writing out the enumeration code shown in Listing 4.12. This syntax exists only because it is easier and cleaner for you to write. Behind the scenes the compiler actually executes a while loop on the MoveNext() method.

Iterators

Because a foreach loop is a shorthand way to use the IEnumerator interface, it should not be a surprise to learn that there is a shorthand way to implement it. Rather than forcing you to create a class that explicitly implements MoveNext(), Current, and Reset(), C# 2.0 lets you implement that interface by using yield return. Listing 4.13 shows how this works.

LISTING 4.13   Using the Power of yield return to Implement IEnumerable<T>

```
using System;
using System.Collections.Generic;

namespace IteratorTests
{
    class Program
    {

        public static IEnumerable<int> GetList()
        {
            var length = 3;

            for (int i = 1; i <= length; i++)
            {
                yield return i;
            }
```

```
        }

        static void Main(string[] args)
        {
            var list = GetList();

            // Iterate over a list with an Enumerator
            IEnumerator<int> e = list.GetEnumerator();

            while (e.MoveNext())
            {
                Console.WriteLine(e.Current);
            }

            // Now do the same thing with foreach
            foreach (var item in list)
            {
                Console.WriteLine(item);
            }
        }
    }
}
```

Listing 4.13 is much like Listing 4.12, except that the implementation of a list is now found in a method that returns IEnumerable<T> rather than in a simple List<T>. But as you can see, both sets of code work the same way.

The call to yield return sets in motion quite a bit of hand waving and compiler magic. Behind the scenes the code we write is changed almost beyond recognition. Nevertheless, the end result is as follows:

1. The first time you call GetList(), it returns the first item produced by the for loop, which it implements.
2. The second time you call GetList(), it returns the second item from the for loop, and so on.
3. The process ends when it runs out of items to iterate over.

The compiler actually transforms our simple call to yield return into an autogenerated class that contains a state machine for keeping track of the items yielded up to the user. The series of case statements and calls to goto that populate this autogenerated class are perhaps more utilitarian than elegant. Nevertheless, something is compelling about these kinds of

transformations. If you are curious to learn more, I recommend Raymond
Chen's summation of the subject, because it is relatively succinct:

http://blogs.msdn.com/oldnewthing/archive/2008/08/12/
8849519.aspx

One interesting implication of this system is that you could use a technique like this to implement an endless loop that never stopped returning
values. Consider the following implementation of IEnumerable<T>:

```csharp
public static IEnumerable<int> GetList()
{
    int i = 2;

    while (true)
    {
        i = i * 2;

        if ((i <= 0) || (i > int.MaxValue))
        {
            i = 2;
            Console.WriteLine("Enter to continue, CTRL-C to break.");
            Console.ReadLine();
        }
        else
        {
            yield return i;
        }
    }
}
```

The preceding code, plugged into the code shown in Listing 4.13, produces
the following sequence in an endless loop:

```
4
8
16
32
64
128
256
512
1,024
2,048
4,096
8,192
16,384
```

```
32,768
65,536
131,072
262,144
524,288
1,048,576
2,097,152
4,194,304
8,388,608
16,777,216
33,554,432
67,108,864
134,217,728
268,435,456
536,870,912
1,073,741,824
4
8
16
Etc...
```

Deferred Execution

For newcomers to LINQ, deferred execution is a mysterious feature. But now that you understand iterators and `yield return`, deferred execution should be easy to understand, even immediately intuitive. Consider the code shown in Listing 4.14.

LISTING 4.14   A Simple LINQ Query with a Sequence Provided by an Iterator

```csharp
using System;
using System.Collections.Generic;
using System.Linq;

namespace DeferredTests
{
    class Program
    {

        public static IEnumerable<int> GetSequence()
        {
            var length = 3;

            for (int i = 1; i <= length; i++)
            {
                yield return i;
```

continues

LISTING 4.14   Continued

```
            }
        }

        static void Main(string[] args)
        {
            var list = GetSequence();

            var query = from num in list
                        where num < 3
                        select num;

            foreach (var item in query)
            {
                Console.WriteLine(item);
            }
        }
    }
}
```

Listing 4.14 is very much like Listing 4.13, only it uses the System.Linq namespace and includes a simple LINQ query expression.

If you stepped through the code in Listing 4.14 with a debugger, it would be natural to assume that you would see the LINQ query execute when the debugger stepped over this statement:

```
var query = from num in list
            where num < 3
            select num;
```

To the surprise of nearly every newcomer to LINQ, this is not what happens. The query actually executes when you reach the foreach statement.

▪ Use the Debugger to Help You Understand LINQ

If you have the tools available, consider running this program in Visual Studio and stepping through it with the debugger. It will help drive home this point if you see it for yourself. The C# and Debugger teams worked very hard to integrate LINQ and the Debugger. I've found it instructive to allow the Debugger to illuminate my LINQ code. Alternatively, try inserting a WriteLine statement into the for loop found in the call to GetSequence(), as shown in the sample program (available on this book's web site) called DeferredExecution.

Execution of a query expression is deferred until the moment when you ask for the first item in the result sequence. Until that time, the value returned from a query expression is simply a computation; it is not a result set. As you learned in the section "Composable" in the preceding chapter, you can use these computations in additional queries, but even then execution is deferred until something forces LINQ to ask for the first element in the result sequence.

I'll provide two different explanations of what happens when the `foreach` code executes. My first explanation will be entirely utilitarian; it will explain the practical, visible results of a call to `foreach`. I will then revisit the subject and explain what is happening behind the scenes. The difference between the explanations is somewhat like the difference between saying that the sun rises in the east, and explaining what really happens when you know that the Earth is a spinning ball revolving around the sun. There is nothing misleading or dangerous about thinking that the sun rises in the east. In fact, the sun doesn't rise at all: the Earth spins. Nevertheless, you can make reliable plans based on the assumption that the sun rises in the east. From the point of view of an observer out in space, that is an incorrect explanation of what happens. But practically speaking, from the point of view of a person on Earth, the sun rises in the east.

So I will explain this business from two points of view—one utilitarian, and the other more theoretical. The theoretical explanation will be more rigorously correct, but when you are writing code, you can easily make do with the more practical explanation. In fact, you might find it preferable to use the practical explanation, just as we find it simpler to state that the sun rises in the east.

When thinking about the solar system, we say that from a practical perspective, it appears that the sun rises in the east. When thinking about the code in Listing 4.14, we can make the practical observation that a method called `GetSequence` yields a series of values. When you loop through `foreach` the first time, it appears that `GetSequence` is called and yields the value 1. This is the first number produced by the `for` loop found inside `GetSequence`. (Step through the code with the debugger, and you will see what I mean.) After this value is retrieved, *then* the LINQ query is executed. The `where` clause in the query expression tests if 1 is smaller than 3, and if it is, it returns the value, which is printed to the console. Now we are back up at the top of the foreach loop, and GetSequence is "called" a second time. This time it returns the number 2, which is again passed through the Where clause in the query expression and returned for printing to the console. The foreach loop begins again, and this time the number 3 is retrieved. The Where clause tests if 3 is smaller than 3. It is not, so the query expression does not return this value, and nothing is printed to the console. The loop requests the next number from the sequence, and GetSequence returns false, so the loop ends and the program exits. For all practical purposes, that is what happens. You will never go astray by living with this interpretation of events, just as you will never go astray believing that the sun rises in the east.

However, in a book of this kind, I need to dig beneath the surface and explain what is really happening. Behind the scenes, the method called GetSequence is called only once. It does not really return values one at a time. Instead, it returns an instance of an autogenerated object with a name such as GetListEnumerator that implements a state machine. Again, this is a case where the compiler radically transforms your code into something very different from what you originally wrote.

I've worked with a developer on the C# team named Eric Lippert to produce the following code, which approximates the code produced by the compiler when it sees our call to GetSequence:

```csharp
public static IEnumerable<int> GetSequence()
{
    return new GetListEnumerable();
}

private class GetListEnumerable : IEnumerable<int>
{
    public IEnumerator<int> GetEnumerator()
    {
        return new GetListEnumerator();
    }
}

private class GetListEnumerator : IEnumerator<int>
{

    public int Current { get; private set; }
    private int i;
    private int length;
```

```
    private int state = 0;
    public bool MoveNext()
    {
        if (state == 0) goto State0;
        if (state == 1) goto State1;
        if (state == 2) goto State2;

        State0:
        this.length = 3;
        for (this.i = 1; this.i <= this.length; this.i++)
        {
            this.State = 1;
            this.Current = this.i;
            return true;
        State1:
        }
        State2:
        this.state = 2;
        return false;
    }
}
```

Ultimately, the call to GetSequence yields a class that we call GetListEnumerator, which contains a single method called MoveNext. A state machine is implemented in the class such that calls to MoveNext mimic what would happen if we called the simple for loop in the original GetSequence method. The difference is that the results from the for loop are retrieved one at a time, so that the first call to MoveNext returns the first value from the loop, the next call to MoveNext returns the next value, and so on, until the items generated by the loop are exhausted.

The actual location of the MoveNext loop can differ, depending on the type of query you write. In our case, it is actually called from inside the implementation of Where, as shown in the next section.

Deferred execution ensures that LINQ never wastes time performing calculations you don't actually need. This is made possible by LINQ's reliance on sequences of numbers that are retrieved from a class that implements the IEnumerator interface. This is true even if we declare a list like this:

```
var list = new List<int> { 1, 2, 3 };
```

Even with a seemingly static list like this, behind the scenes the C# compiler uses the IEnumerator pattern and pulls the numbers from a MoveNext() loop, grabbing each current item one at a time.

Consider the following variation of the code from Listing 4.14:

```
static void Main(string[] args)
{
    var list = GetList();

    int bound = 3;

    var query = from num in list
                where num < bound
                select num;

    bound = 4;

    foreach (var item in query)
    {
        Console.WriteLine(item);
    }
}
```

A newcomer to LINQ might suppose that this method prints the numbers 1 and 2, because bound is equal to 3 when the query expression is "executed." However, the code actually prints the values 1, 2, and 3. The variable bound is equal to 4 when the code reaches the foreach loop, and that is when the query expression is executed.

Why is execution of the query deferred? A primary reason is because it enables composition to work as expected. You can link two, three, four, or more queries using the compositional style of development, and none of the queries will execute until you begin to iterate over the results. This means that each query can be combined into a single "computation" that is executed only once.

When you are using query expression syntax, execution is always deferred. Only operators that must be called using query method syntax might execute immediately. For instance, when you call First() or ToList(), execution is immediate:

```
var query = (from m in typeof(Enumerable).GetMethods()
             orderby method.Name
             where m.DeclaringType == typeof(Enumerable)
             select m).First();
```

The orderby, where, and select methods are all called using query expression syntax and are all deferred. The First operator is called using query method syntax and is not deferred.

Overriding LINQ Operators

We are now deep inside the implementation of LINQ to Objects and near the end of our journey. Just one piece is missing: How are LINQ operators, such as where, actually implemented?

This chapter has told you several times that code that appears to say one thing is actually translated by the compiler into something else. The compiler translates automatic properties into standard properties with funny names. Anonymous types are translated into real classes that have funny names. Behind the scenes foreach loops actually call the IEnumerator interface with its MoveNext() method. Most surprising of all, the compiler translates yield iterators into classes that implement the IEnumerator interface.

Given this background, it should come as no surprise that the compiler translates query expressions into something else. Consider the following query, which you have seen several times:

```
var query = from num in list
            where num < value
            select num;
```

Behind the scenes, at compile time, this query is translated into the following code:

```
var query = list
            .Where<int>(num => num < value)
            .Select<int, int>(num => num);
```

Or if you prefer, the compiler is smart enough to work with this shortened version of the statement:

```
var query = list.Where<int>(num => num < value);
```

These three statements are semantically quite similar, even if they differ syntactically. The second and third statements are valid C# code and can be used in lieu of the first implementation. They are said to use query method syntax, whereas the first statement is a query expression.

■ Why Query Expressions?

Why are query expressions translated into query methods? Why didn't the developers of LINQ ask developers to write query methods?

The original implementation of LINQ had no such thing as a query expression. You could use only query method syntax. The team ran a series of usability tests on this syntax and found that many developers found it confusing, especially as queries grew more complex. This feedback forced them to return to the whiteboard, where they scratched their heads for a bit before inventing query expressions. This proved a more viable solution, because developers picked it up with relative ease.

■ Query Expressions and Lambdas

You are now in a position to appreciate the role that lambdas play in query expressions. Of the three examples just shown, it is obvious that the second and third contain lambdas. It is less obvious, however, that the first example, the query expression, also contains a shortened form of a lambda. The `where` clause contains the body of a lambda. The designers of LINQ decided that it was not necessary for developers to include a complete lambda expression, because the type of the variable num is inferred in the first line, where it appears as a range variable.

We can now see that the `Where` and `Select` operators appear to be normal methods. In fact, a little experimentation will reveal that they are methods that can be called on any implementation of `IEnumerable<T>`. This fact is actually a bit puzzling when you consider that the implementation for `IEnumerable<T>` looks like this:

```
public interface IEnumerable<T> : IEnumerable
{
    IEnumerator<T> GetEnumerator();
}
```

This simple interface has no place for an implementation of the `Where` and `Select` methods, nor for any of the approximately 50 other operators supported by LINQ and their numerous overloads.

By now you have probably guessed that `Where`, `Select`, and all the other LINQ operators are really extension methods. It turns out that they are declared in the `System.Linq` namespace, in a class called `Enumerable`, which is a variation on the `SpecialString` class shown earlier. In other words, it is a static class that contains a long list of extension methods, one for each of the LINQ operators, plus numerous overloads of these methods.

> ## ■ `IEnumerable<T>` Supports All the LINQ Operators
>
> `IEnumerable<T>` is a lightweight interface with one method, which you can implement with a simple `yield` iterator. This means that it is easy for you to support `IEnumerable<T>` on any list-like structure you create. If you then add a `System.Linq` directive, you can query your list using LINQ and its broad range of operators. Nothing else needs to be done. The other two options that the C# team could have used to provide this functionality would have been to force you to inherit your list from a class that implemented all the extensions methods that support the LINQ operators, or to put all 50 operators and their numerous overloads in the `IEnumerable<T>` interface and force you to implement them. Neither option is very appealing. The fact that `IEnumerable<T>` can use extensions methods to support all the LINQ operators is a very nice trick that makes your life as a developer much simpler.

Let's create our own version of the `Where` method. By placing it nearer in scope to our code than the `Where` method that ships with LINQ, we will be able to watch it execute and get some insight into how LINQ works. To get started, take a look at Listing 4.15.

LISTING 4.15   Implementing the `Where` Operator to See How It Works

```
using System;
using System.Collections.Generic;
using System.Linq;

namespace WhereTests
{
```

continues

LISTING 4.15   Continued

```csharp
public static class MyExtensions
{
    public static IEnumerable<T> Where<T>(this IEnumerable<T> source,
        Func<T, bool> predicate)
    {
        foreach (var item in source)
        {
            if (predicate(item))
            {
                yield return item;
            }
        }
    }
}

class Program
{
    public static IEnumerable<int> GetList()
    {
        var length = 6;

        for (int i = 1; i <= length; i++)
        {
            yield return i;
        }
    }

    static void Main(string[] args)
    {
        var list = GetList();

        var query = list.Where(num => num < 3).Select(num => num);

        foreach (var item in query)
        {
            Console.WriteLine(item);
        }
    }
}
```

This code differs from our previous implementations of this query only in the fact that we can explicitly see the implementation of the Where operator. The header for the Where method shows that it is an extension method that works with the IEnumerable<T> interface. It is also passed a simple delegate that takes a value of type T and returns a bool:

```
static IEnumerable<T> Where<T>(this IEnumerable<T> source,
                       Func<T, bool> predicate)
```

> ### ■ Finding the Where Metadata Declaration
>
> Our Where method has the same declaration as the Where method in the LINQ source code. To see that declaration, type in a query with a Where operator. Use query method syntax, as shown in Listing 4.15. Place the mouse cursor over the word Where, right-click, and select Go to definition. You are taken to the declaration for Where, and you also see the declaration for all the other LINQ operators.

Looking at our query, we see that the delegate is passed the following lambda expression:

```
num => num < 3
```

The loop in the Where method iterates over our collection of numbers, pulling them out one at a time, just as we showed in the section "Deferred Execution." It pulls the number 1 first and passes it to the predicate:

```
foreach (var item in source)
{
    if (predicate(item))
    {
        yield return item;
    }
}
```

The predicate compares the number 1 to the number 3, sees that it is smaller, and returns true. The code in the Where method then yield returns this value, and it is printed to the Console in the foreach loop found in the Main method. Then Where is called again, and this time the number 2 is pulled from our GetList() method. It is run through the predicate, returns true, is passed back to the foreach loop and printed to the screen, and so on. Each item is passed to the predicate, and, if true is returned, the item is yield returned. Otherwise, the foreach loop simply iterates the next item until the last item in source has been tested through predicate, just as before. You are now seeing the entire scope of the LINQ query, witnessing exactly how each portion of it is implemented.

At this stage, you know almost everything there is to know about LINQ to Objects. You have seen how extension methods, lambdas, and iterators come together to form a query language that works with collections. This background knowledge will act as a foundation on which you can build a deep understanding of LINQ to Objects.

Expression Trees

After getting a close look at LINQ to Objects, you might think that this tour through the LINQ architecture would be complete. Yet one more key feature is left to explore. This feature is not part of LINQ to Objects, but it does play a key role in other technologies, such as LINQ to SQL.

In LINQ to Objects, the data that is being queried is local and is stored in objects that support the `IEnumerable<T>` interface. That is not the case, however, in LINQ to SQL. In that scenario, the data is stored in a different process, which is likely to be running on a different machine. And, of course, the data structures in a relational database know nothing about `IEnumerable<T>`.

The technology for calling a database from a C# program already exists, so at least that part of the problem is solved. Two issues, however, still need to be resolved:

- How do we translate a query expression into a SQL statement that can be sent to a server?
- How do we convert the data we get back from the SQL server into objects that LINQ can query?

The answer to the second question is covered later in this book, in Chapters 7 through 10. The first question, however, is one that you need to come to terms with if you want to understand the LINQ architecture.

Expression trees allow you to convert code into data. In particular, they make it possible to convert a query expression into a data structure. A LINQ provider can then parse that data structure, determine what data the developer wants, and then retrieve it. For instance, an expression tree can convert a LINQ to SQL query expression into a data structure, parse that data structure, and compose a SQL statement based on its contents. It can then use conventional techniques to execute that SQL statement and return the results to the developer. In this chapter, I'll explain the basics of this process, and then in Chapter 17, "LINQ Everywhere," you will be introduced to providers that parse entire expression trees and convert them into useful code.

Let's begin by creating a simple expression tree based on a lambda. As you can see from Listing 4.16, the first step is to use the System.Linq. Expressions namespace. After you have included the namespace, you can create an expression.

LISTING 4.16   Creating an Expression Tree Based on a Lambda

```
using System;
using System.Linq.Expressions;

namespace SimpleExpressions
{
    class Program
    {
        static void Main(string[] args)
        {
            Expression<Func<int, int, int>> expression = (a, b) =>
                                         (a + b);
        }
    }
}
```

Each expression is of a particular type. In this case, the type is our old friend: a delegate that takes two integers and returns an integer. By setting an instance of this type equal to a lambda expression, we are creating not code that can be executed, but a data structure that can be parsed. Here is another way to think about what is happening: The Expression type is a generic type parameterized by the type of the delegate that it is supposed to wrap. Our old friend Func fits perfectly for this job. In this particular example, the lambda takes two integers' parameters and returns an integer.

Listing 4.17 shows how to parse this data structure to discover a few basic facts about it. Listing 4.18 shows the output.

LISTING 4.17   Code to Perform Basic Parsing Operations on an Expression Tree

```
Expression<Func<int, int, int>> expression = (a, b) => (a + b);

Console.WriteLine("Expression Type: {0}", expression.NodeType);

foreach (var item in expression.Parameters)
{
    Console.WriteLine("Parameter: {0}; Type: {1}", item, item.Type);
}
BinaryExpression body = (BinaryExpression)expression.Body;
ParameterExpression left = (ParameterExpression)body.Left;
ParameterExpression right = (ParameterExpression)body.Right;
ExpressionType nodeType = body.NodeType;

Console.WriteLine("Body: {0} = Analysis of body: {1} {2} {3}",
    body, left, nodeType, right);
```

LISTING 4.18   The Output from Listing 4.17

```
Expression Type: Lambda
Parameter: a; Type: System.Int32
Parameter: b; Type: System.Int32
Body: (a + b) = Analysis of body: a Add b
```

The code in Listing 4.17 begins by discovering the type of the expression, which is a lambda:

```
Console.WriteLine("Expression Type: {0}", expression.NodeType);
```

It then looks at the parameters to the lambda and discovers that they are called a and b and are of type Int32:

```
foreach (var item in expression.Parameters)
{
    Console.WriteLine("Parameter: {0}; Type: {1}", item, item.Type);
}
```

The next step is to examine the body of the lambda. We look at the expression on the left and see that it is our friend a, and the expression on the right and see that it is b. The NodeType of the expression is Add:

```
BinaryExpression body = (BinaryExpression)expression.Body;
ParameterExpression left = (ParameterExpression)body.Left;
ParameterExpression right = (ParameterExpression)body.Right;
ExpressionType nodeType = body.NodeType;
```

```
Console.WriteLine("Body: {0} = Analysis of body: {1} {2} {3}",
    body, left, nodeType, right);
```

Although there is considerably more information in the expression tree, we have harvested enough information to see that our lambda takes two parameters of type integer and adds them together.

There is, of course, a difference between parsing a simple lambda like this and parsing a complex query expression. Nevertheless, you should now understand enough to grasp the basic principles involved. To help drive home the point, let's use a tool called the Expression Tree Visualizer that ships with the Visual CSharp samples.

The Expression Tree Visualizer is an add-on that lets Visual Studio display an expression tree. To use it, first you need to obtain a copy of the sample. You can do this by choosing Help, Samples from Visual Studio. You are taken to an HTML page, where you find a set of instructions for downloading the CSharp samples. After you have unzipped the samples, open the ExpressionTreeVisualizer project and build it. Go to following directory, and locate the file called ExpressionTreeVisualizer.dll:

...\ExpressionTreeVisualizer\ExpressionTreeVisualizer\bin\Debug

Copy the DLL into a directory called Visualizers that is located at the root of the Visual Studio 2008 folder in your Documents directory. If the Visualizers directory does not already exist, create it. Create a default console application, and type in and run the program found in Listing 4.17, or open the SimpleExpression project sample that accompanies this book. Set a break point after this line:

```
Expression<Func<int, int, int>> expression = (a, b) => (a + b);
```

Right-click the word expression. A ToolTip pops up with a magnifying class icon, as shown in Figure 4.2. Click the down arrow next to the magnifying glass, and then click the popup menu to open the Expression Tree Visualizer. You see a window like the one shown in Figure 4.3.

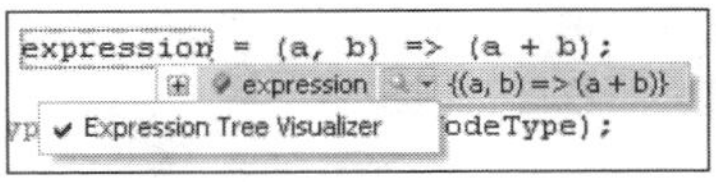

FIGURE 4.2 Opening the Expression Tree Visualizer.

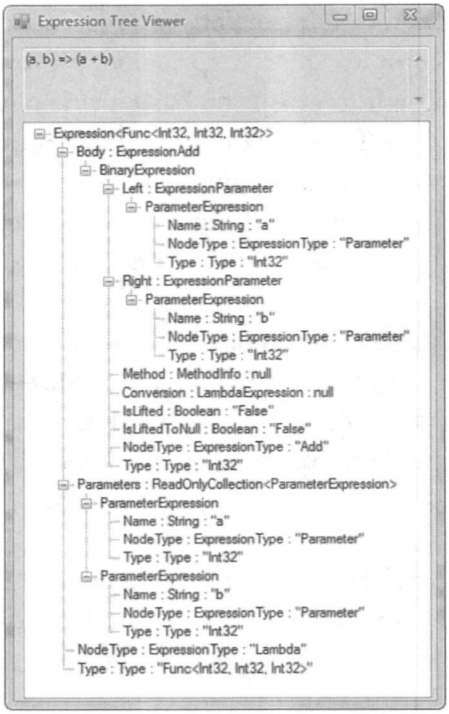

FIGURE 4.3 Parsing the expression for a simple lambda with the Expression Tree Visualizer.

Looking at Figure 4.3, you can see the four main nodes of the expression tree:

- Body
- Parameters
- NodeType
- Type

The parameters are called a and b, are of type Int32, and are of NodeType parameter. The body also has two parameters and a NodeType of Add. The return type of the body is Int32, and so on. All the information you need to work with this expression is available to you. Studying the code for the Expression Tree Visualizer would obviously be a good way to learn more about parsing these objects.

You can also use the Expression Tree Visualizer to parse the code from the LINQ to SQL program. The tree generated from that query is too long to show here, but the principles involved are similar to those shown in parsing the simple lambda just shown.

To get started, open the sample run to a point right after the query expression:

```
var query = from c in db.Customers
            where c.City == "London"
            select c;
```

At runtime, hold the mouse cursor over the variable query to bring up the Data tip window. Click the plus symbol to open the Data Tip, and explore the Non-Public members. Look for the field called queryExpression. This is the variable containing the expression tree that represents your query. Notice that on the right is a magnifying glass, as shown in Figure 4.4. Click the down arrow next to it, which brings up the Expression Tree Visualizer. You see a completely parsed image of the tree for your program.

FIGURE 4.4   The popup menu item for the Expression Tree Visualizer in an IntelliSense fly-by window.

In this section you have seen that expressions allow you to convert code into data. If you parse that data, you can extract the semantic meaning of that code, and use that information to call into another process. This is the only way that LINQ can execute a query expression when it needs to work with a data source that does not implement IEnumerable<T>. In general, LINQ must use expression trees if it wants to query a data source that resides in another process.

Summary

This chapter has covered all the major features of C# 2.0 and C# 3.0 that make LINQ possible. The text began by covering general-purpose features such as collection and object initializers. The middle portions of the chapter covered type inference, lambdas, and extension methods, all of which play key roles in the LINQ syntax. Near the end of the chapter you learned about the type IEnumerable<T>, the central axis around which LINQ to SQL revolves. Finally, at the end of the chapter you learned about expression trees, a feature that is very important to developers who want to create providers.

The interesting thing about the LINQ syntax is that it is built from a set of fairly simple features. Lambdas, extension methods, and iterators are all quite simple ideas. When brought together in LINQ, however, they form a very powerful query syntax that can change how developers write code. In the next chapter, you will learn more about the power of query expressions, and you'll finally get a chance to begin exploring the ways to use this syntax in real programs.

∎ 5 ∎
Writing Query Expressions

T HIS CHAPTER EXPLORES the various rules and syntactical elements that define the structure of LINQ query expressions. It covers the seven types of query expression clauses and explains the four ways in which they introduce range variables. In the next chapter, you will read about the 49 different LINQ operators that can play 12 different roles in a query expression.

This chapter analyzes the structure of query expressions. It is divided into five main sections and various subsections:

- Syntactical analysis
    - Nomenclature
    - Clauses
    - Range variables
- Composing queries
    - `Group-by` clauses
    - The `into` keyword
    - Let clauses
- Joins
    - Inner joins
    - Group joins

Several important concepts from the preceding chapter are referenced in this chapter, including deferred execution and extension methods. If you feel you don't fully understand those concepts, you might want to review them before reading this chapter.

Query expressions are both the topic of this chapter and a central theme in LINQ. They are the most common, the easiest, and the recommended way to write LINQ queries. They provide us with an easy way to write query methods. Behind the scenes they are always translated back into query method syntax.

Query expressions are simply a machine for creating query methods. When we write a query expression, the compiler applies simple rules to it and converts it into code that follows the query method syntax.

Syntactical Analysis

In this section you will learn the names of the parts of a query expression, how to identify the clauses in a query expression, and the role of range variables.

Nomenclature

To begin exploring query expressions, we must find a common language for describing our key terms. As shown in Figure 5.1, even a simple query expression has several key elements.

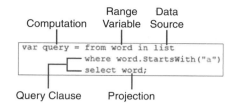

FIGURE 5.1   The key parts of a query expression.

The following are the key elements shown in Figure 5.1:

- The `var` keyword tells the compiler to infer the type returned by a query. When a LINQ to Objects query is deferred, the sequence returned from a query expression is of type `IEnumerable<T>` and is called a *computation* or *result sequence*.
- The individual lines in a properly formatted query are called clauses. Figure 5.1 shows a `from` clause, `where` clause, and `select` clause.
- The `select` clause at the end of the query helps define the type returned by the query. A select clause is said to *project* a result.

Clauses

Each line in a properly formatted query is called a *clause*. Nothing forces you to arrange a query with one clause per line, but your code will be easier to maintain if it is formatted that way.

Here is a simple query expression.

```
var query = from word in list
            where word.StartsWith("a")
            select word;
```

Note that it starts with a `from` clause, ends with a `select` clause, and has a `where` clause in the middle. This is a classic pattern that you will see often in LINQ.

Seven different types of clauses are used in query expressions: `from`, `let`, `where`, `orderby`, `join`, `select`, and `group-by`. They can be legally arranged only in the ways shown in Table 5.1.

TABLE 5.1 The Structure of a Query Expression

First line	`from` clause with a range variable and data source
Middle lines	`from`, `where`, `orderby`, `join`, `let` clauses
Last line	`select` or `group-by` clause

Query expressions begin with a `from` clause and end with a `select` or `group-by` clause. The body of a LINQ query may consist of many different combinations of zero or more `from`, `where`, `orderby`, `join`, or `let` clauses.

The `where`, `orderby`, `join`, `select`, and `group-by` clauses can be immediately translated into calls to LINQ operators. This relationship between the clauses and the operators can be a bit confusing at times. In the example found at the beginning of this section, the identifiers `from`, `where`, and `select` are all keywords. The identifiers `where` and `select`, however, can be immediately translated into operators:

```
var query = list.Where(word => word.StartsWith("a"))
                .Select(word => word);
```

In practice, the distinction between a `where` clause and a call to the `Where` operator is somewhat academic. However, you should understand the distinction sufficiently to be able to make the differentiation when necessary. The `Where` operator is a method, and a `where` clause is a bit of syntactic sugar that is transformed at compile time into a call to the `Where` operator.

This section has shown you only the most basic clauses—`from`, `where`, and `select`. The section "Composing Queries" provides examples showing how to use all the other clauses. The next chapter provides examples of using most of the 49LINQ operators. For now, however, I want to stay focused on the basics so that I can introduce topics one at a time in an orderly fashion, without passing everything to you in one indigestible heap. Next up is a discussion of range variables.

Range Variables

Four elements make up the clauses in a query expression:

- LINQ operators
- Keywords
- Variables from your program that are currently in scope
- Range variables

Consider this simple query expression:

```
List<string> list = new List<string> { "LINQ", "query", "adventure" };

var query = from word in list
            where word.StartsWith("a")
            select word;
```

In this query, `from`, `in`, `where`, and `select` are all LINQ keywords. Both `where` and `select`, however, can be translated immediately into LINQ operators. The identifier `list` is a local variable. That leaves only one element unexplained: the identifier `word`, which is a *range variable*.

There is nothing unusual about range variables. They are simply a read-only subset of ordinary variables. Nevertheless, range variables seem odd at first because they are introduced inside a query expression and need not be formally declared:

```
string word;
```

Instead of being formally declared, `word` is said to be *introduced* by the `from` clause. The compiler determines its type through type inference. In this case the compiler knows `word` is a `string` because it is derived from a `List<string>`.

The variable `word` goes out of scope when one of two things happens:

- The query expression ends.
- The `into` keyword is encountered. The contextual keyword `into` is frequently used to splice two queries. It is discussed later in the chapter in the sections on the `group-by` and `join` operators.

There may be cases where you need to explicitly state the type of a range variable. For instance, the following code will not compile because of a type mismatch:

```
object[] ints = new object[] { 1, 2, 3 };

var query = from num in ints
            where num < 3
            select num;
```

While processing the `where` clause, the compiler complains that the

```
operator '<' cannot be applied to operands of type 'int' and 'object'.
```

To resolve this problem, explicitly declare the type of the range variable:

```
var query = from int num in ints
            where num < 3
            select num;
```

Here we tell the compiler that num should be treated as an `int`. Because the cast will succeed, the code compiles and runs as expected.

■■ Avoid Explicitly Declaring the Type of a Range Variable

It is best not to explicitly declare the type of a range variable unless absolutely necessary. For instance, the following code compiles cleanly, but the type could have been inferred by the compiler without a formal declaration:

```
List<string> list = new List<string> { "LINQ", "query",
                                        "adventure" };
var query = from string word in list
        where word.Contains("r")
        orderby word ascending
        select word;
```

Explicitly declaring the type of a range variable forces a behind-the-scenes call to the LINQ `Cast<T>` operator. This call may have unintended consequences and may hurt performance. If you encounter performance problems with a LINQ query, a cast like the one shown here is one possible place to begin looking for the culprit. (The one exception to this rule is when you are working with a nongeneric `Enumerable`, in which case you should use the cast.)

Like any other variable, a range variable must be a unique identifier within the current scope. The following code, therefore, is illegal because the variable word is declared twice:

```
string word = "ahimsa";

var query = from word in list
            where word.StartsWith("a")
            select word;
```

After being exposed to this code, the compiler grows irritable and complains that the

```
Range variable 'word' conflicts with a previous declaration of 'word'.
```

You have seen that the from keyword introduces a range variable. The let and into keywords also allow developers to introduce a range variable, as does the join operator. Again, I don't want to precipitously expose you to illustrations of these clauses until I've had more time to lay preparatory groundwork. For now I will provide Table 5.2, which neatly encapsulates the settings in which range variables appear. The next section shows working examples of each of these ways of introducing range variables.

TABLE 5.2   The Variables word, theType, instrument, and myGroup in the Following Code Fragments Are All Range Variables

from	`var query = from word in list`
let	`let theType = typeof(Enumerable)`
join	`join instrument in instruments on p.InstrumentId equals instrument.InstrumentId`
into	`group method by method.Name into myGroup`

Composing Queries

In the previous sections I promised that I would give you a chance to see all seven types of query clauses and the four different ways you can introduce a range variable. It is time to make good on that promise. In particular, this section shows working examples of how to

- Compose `from`, `let`, `where`, `orderby`, `join`, `select`, and `group-by` clauses.
- Use `from`, `let`, `join`, and `into` to introduce range variables.

The text is broken into three subsections:

- group-by clauses at the end of a query expression
- group-by clauses and the `into` keyword
- `let` clauses

Because Join clauses play such an important role in queries, I have dedicated a full section of the chapter to that subject. It begins after the section on Let clauses.

Group-by Clauses at the End of a Query Expression

Although most queries end with a `select` clause, they can also end with a group-by clause. The following query, which uses reflection to iterate over all the LINQ query methods, shows how it works:

```
var query = from method in typeof(System.Linq.Enumerable).GetMethods()
            where method.DeclaringType == typeof(Enumerable)
            orderby method.Name
            group method by method.Name;

foreach (var item in query)
{
    Console.WriteLine(item.Key);
}
```

This code prints all the LINQ operators and three associated utilities. To save space, I'll show only the first few results:

```
Aggregate
All
Any
AsEnumerable
Average
Cast
Concat
```

The data source for this query is a C# reflection call to `GetMethods` on the `Enumerable` type. The `Enumerable` type has only one purpose: It is the class that contains all the extension methods that define the LINQ to Objects operators. It also contains three simple utilities that support those operators. The call to `GetMethods` returns an array of the type `System.Reflection.MethodInfo[]`, where each `MethodInfo` object defines one LINQ operator or utility.

The code contains a `where` clause that strips out all the methods not declared in the `Enumerable` class. This simple filter ensures that we don't see any of the methods inherited from class `object`, such as `ToString` or `GetHashCode`:

```
where method.DeclaringType == typeof(Enumerable)
```

The `orderby` clause arranges the names returned from `GetMethods` in alphabetical order:

```
orderby method.Name
```

Just as a where clause filters data, an orderby clause sorts data.

The only line remaining in this query is the last one: the `group-by` clause. LINQ uses `group-by` clauses to arrange elements into a set of keys, and a set of elements that belong to the keys. The type of the object returned by a call to `group-by` is `System.Linq.IGrouping<TKey, TElement>`. This object implements `IEnumerable<TElement>` and provides a `Key` property of type `TKey`.

To understand how this works, let's begin by examining the problem the `group-by` operator solves in this query. There are 49 different LINQ query operators. Some of these operators are overloaded many times. For instance, there are 22 overloads of the `Min` and `Max` operators. Printing the same word 22 times can be confusing. To help bring some organization to our query result, the `group-by` operator allows us to organize these 22 repeated return values into a single group.

Take a second look at the `group-by` clause from our query:

```
group method by method.Name;
```

This line asks LINQ to create one group and one key for each unique method name returned by the query. Operator names such as `Aggregate`,

All, Any, Min, or Max become the Keys for our groups. Arranged under each Key are the overloads for that particular operator. In the case of Min or Max, 22 different overloads are grouped. Here is the explicit declaration for the type returned by this group-by clause:

```
System.Linq.IGrouping<string, System.Reflection.MethodInfo>
```

This shows that the Key in each group, which is the name of the method, is of type string and that the elements associated with it are of type MethodInfo. This latter type is declared in the C# Reflection namespace.

This pattern is followed every time you use the group-by operator. There is always a Key, and under that key are arranged from zero to *n* elements that belong to the Key.

You can print the elements that belong to a Key by simply writing a nested foreach loop, as shown in this excerpt from the SimpleReflection program found with the samples that accompany this book:

```
foreach (var items in query.Take(3))
{
    int i = 0;
    Console.WriteLine("============================");
    Console.WriteLine("Method Name: {0}", items.Key);
    Console.WriteLine("============================");
    foreach (var item in items)
    {
        Console.WriteLine("Parameters in Overload {0} of {1}",
            ++i, item.Name);
        foreach (var param in item.GetParameters())
        {
            Console.WriteLine("--{0}", param.Name);
        }
    }
}
```

This foreach loop pulls out the following data:

```
============================
Method Name: Aggregate
============================
Parameters in Overload 1 of Aggregate
--source
--func
```

```
Parameters in Overload 2 of Aggregate
--source
--seed
--func
Parameters in Overload 3 of Aggregate
--source
--seed
--func
--resultSelector
===========================
Method Name: All
===========================
Parameters in Overload 1 of All
--source
--predicate
===========================
Method Name: Any
===========================
Parameters in Overload 1 of Any
--source
Parameters in Overload 2 of Any
--source
--predicate
```

Our code prints the Key, which in this case is a method name, followed by the names of the parameters of each overload. These names are retrieved from the ParameterInfo field of the MethodInfo object. For instance, Aggregate is the name of the first operator. It has three overloads, and the first overload takes two parameters called source and func.

Group-by Clauses and the into Keyword

group-by clauses can also be used in the middle lines of a properly formatted query expression. In this scenario, you always combine group-by clauses with the into keyword. Listing 5.1 shows an example.

LISTING 5.1   This Query Is Found in the GroupByOperators Program That Accompanies This Chapter

```
var query = from method in typeof(System.Linq.Enumerable).GetMethods()
            where method.DeclaringType == typeof(Enumerable)
            orderby method.Name
            group method by method.Name into g
            select new { Name = g.Key, Overloads = g.Count() };
```

If you `foreach` over the computation returned by this deferred query, you will find that the first few items in the result sequence look like this:

```
{ Name = Aggregate, Overloads = 3 }
{ Name = All, Overloads = 1 }
{ Name = Any, Overloads = 2 }
{ Name = AsEnumerable, Overloads = 1 }
{ Name = Average, Overloads = 20 }
```

This query shows examples of using `from`, `where`, `orderby`, `group-by`, and `select` clauses. That's five of the seven possible types of LINQ clauses.

Here is a line-by-line description of the clauses in this query:

- The `from` clause defines a range variable called `method` of type `MethodInfo` and a data source that can enumerate all the methods in the `Enumerable` class.
- The `where` clause filters out all the inherited methods that are not declared inside class `Enumerable`. This ensures that we are dealing with only the 49 LINQ operators including the three utility methods.
- The `orderby` clause sorts the sequence alphabetically on the name of each method.
- The `group-by` clause folds all the overloads into groups. One group has a `Key` called `Aggregate` and contains a sequence of `MethodInfos` that describe the overloads for the `Aggregate` operator. The next group has a key called `All` and a series of `MethodInfo` objects that define the overloads for the `All` operator, and so on.
- The `select` clause defines a projection that consists of an anonymous class with two fields. The `Count()` extension method is used to get the number of overloads because `IGrouping<>` does not expose this information.

These are the five most commonly used LINQ clauses, along with the things they do best:

- `from` clauses introduce a range variable and a data source.
- `where` clauses filter data.
- `orderby` clauses sort data.

- group-by clauses set up a set of keys and an associated list of items.
- select clauses project a result based on the range variables that are still in scope.

You've just seen that group-by clauses can be used to end a query. Here, the group-by clause does not end the query, but it nevertheless forms a divide in the middle of this query. In many cases the range variables on one side of this divide cannot be mixed with the range variables on the other side.

The into keyword that is part of this group-by clause is used to link or splice the two halves of this query. As such, it marks the boundary in the midst of the query over which range variables typically cannot climb. The range variables above the into keyword go out of scope in the last part of this query. For instance, the range variable called method cannot be used in the select clause.

As the old range variables go out of scope, a new range variable called g is introduced. It holds the results of the first half of this query. Nevertheless, this query is still deferred, and neither half is enumerated until code is written to iterate over the elements in the computation. Typically, the code that performs that task is some type of foreach loop similar to the ones you have seen in previous chapters.

The into contextual keyword feeds the results of the first part of the query into the second part of the query. This is called a *continuation*, and it is a form of composability. The into keyword is most commonly used with the group-by operator, but I will also show you how it can be used with the join operator.

Let Clauses

let clauses allow you to introduce a range variable into your program. They play a role in a query expression that is very similar to that played by variable declarations in a standard C# method. In fact, they are the functional programming equivalent of a type declaration in imperative code.

Listing 5.2 shows a modification of the reflection query we've been working with in the past few sections. A range variable called theType is introduced in a let clause and is reused in two subsequent portions of the expression. This version of the query ends with a group-by clause rather than a select clause.

LISTING 5.2   A Query from the GroupByOperators Sample Program

```
var query = from method in typeof(System.Linq.Enumerable).GetMethods()
            let theType = typeof(Enumerable)
            where method.DeclaringType == theType
            orderby method.Name
            group method by theType + "." + method.Name;
```

Run through a foreach loop that lists the Key property of each retrieved IGrouping<>, the computation returned from this query prints the following:

```
System.Linq.Enumerable.Aggregate
System.Linq.Enumerable.All
System.Linq.Enumerable.Any
System.Linq.Enumerable.AsEnumerable
System.Linq.Enumerable.Average
Etc...
```

I could have written this same query like this:

```
var query = from method in typeof(System.Linq.Enumerable).GetMethods()
            where method.DeclaringType == typeof(Enumerable)
            orderby method.Name
            group method by typeof(Enumerable) + "." + method.Name;
```

Although it's shorter, this query is more difficult to maintain than the previous version. The problem is that the call to typeof(Enumerable) is repeated. When modifying the code, we could easily think to update one instance but forget the second instance. This danger is eliminated when we use the let clause just shown.

Here is another case when you might find a let clause useful:

```
var list = new List<int> { 1, 2, 3, 4, 5, 6, 7, 8, 9 };

var query = from n in list
            where (n > 3) & (n < 8)
            let g = n * 2
            where g % 2 == 0
            let newList = new List<int> { 2, 3 }
            from l in newList
            select new { l, r = g * l };
```

Although egregiously contrived, this example nevertheless illustrates how you can use `let` clauses to manipulate the items in a query or introduce new items. The output from the program looks like this, where we create a sequence where numbers alternately increase by 4 and 6:

```
==================
AnotherSample
==================
{ l = 2, r = 16 }
{ l = 3, r = 24 }
{ l = 2, r = 20 }
{ l = 3, r = 30 }
{ l = 2, r = 24 }
{ l = 3, r = 36 }
{ l = 2, r = 28 }
{ l = 3, r = 42 }
```

The sequence of r numbers produced here has a satisfying and very regular pattern.

Joins

You have learned about `from`, `let`, `group-by`, `orderby`, `where`, and `select` clauses. The only clause left unexplored is the `join` clause.

Inner Joins

Listing 5.3 shows a simple join in LINQ. This query from the SimpleJoin program that accompanies this text uses a `join` clause to wed the `Musician` and `Instrument` classes.

LISTING 5.3   A Query from the SimpleJoin Program

```
class Instrument
{
    public int InstrumentId { get; set; }
    public string Name { get; set; }
}

class Musician
{
    public int MusicianId { get; set; }
    public string Name { get; set; }
}
```

continues

LISTING 5.3   Continued

```
class Order
{
    public int OrderId { get; set; }
    public int MusicianId { get; set; }
    public int InstrumentId { get; set; }
}

public void Test()
{
    List<Musician> people = new List<Musician>
    {
        new Musician { MusicianId = 1, Name = "Sonny Rollings" },
        new Musician { MusicianId = 2, Name = "Miles Davis"},
        new Musician { MusicianId = 3, Name = "John Coltrane" },
        new Musician { MusicianId = 4, Name = "Charlie Parker" },
        new Musician { MusicianId = 5, Name = "Bela Fleck" }
    };


    List<Instrument> instruments = new List<Instrument>
    {
        new Instrument { InstrumentId = 1, Name = "Soprano Saxophone" },
        new Instrument { InstrumentId = 2, Name = "Tenor Saxophone" },
        new Instrument { InstrumentId = 3, Name = "Trumpet" },
        new Instrument { InstrumentId = 4, Name = "Keyboards" }
    };

    List<Order> orders = new List<Order>
    {
        new Order { OrderId = 1, MusicianId = 1, InstrumentId = 2 },
        new Order { OrderId = 2, MusicianId = 2, InstrumentId = 3 },
        new Order { OrderId = 3, MusicianId = 3, InstrumentId = 1 },
        new Order { OrderId = 4, MusicianId = 3, InstrumentId = 2 },
        new Order { OrderId = 5, MusicianId = 4, InstrumentId = 2 },
        new Order { OrderId = 6, MusicianId = 2, InstrumentId = 4 }
    };

    var query = from p in people
                join o in orders on p.MusicianId equals o.MusicianId
                select new { Musician = p.Name, OrderId = o.OrderId };

    foreach (var item in query)
    {
        Console.WriteLine(item);
    }
}
```

Most of the code shown in Listing 5.3 is setup code. You see the declarations for the classes, the initializers that create some data for us to work with, and then finally the query, which asks a question and returns a result sequence. The tables are linked by a series of ID numbers. The `Musician` and `Order` classes each have an ID field, and the `Order` class uses the `MusicianId` field as a "foreign key" that defines which `Musician` is associated with which `Order`.

In this first query, we work with two of the three classes, `Musician` and `Order`. For now we will ignore the `Instrument` class. Our goal is to join the `Musician` and `Order` classes to show which musicians are associated with which orders. When iterated with a `foreach` loop, the output from our query looks like this:

```
{ Musician = Sonny Rollings, OrderId = 1 }
{ Musician = Miles Davis, OrderId = 2 }
{ Musician = Miles Davis, OrderId = 6 }
{ Musician = John Coltrane, OrderId = 3 }
{ Musician = John Coltrane, OrderId = 4 }
{ Musician = Charlie Parker, OrderId = 5 }
```

We see that Sonny Rollins made order 1, Miles made orders 2 and 6, Trane made orders 3 and 4, and Bird made the fifth order.

Here are the first two lines of the query:

```
var query = from p in people
            join o in orders on p.MusicianId equals o.MusicianId
```

This `join` clause creates a range variable called `o` of type `Order` and then uses the `equals` operator to join the tables on the `MusicianId` field. Note that this is not the == operator, but the `equals` operator. All LINQ joins are *equijoins*. That is, they use the `equals` operator and cannot use the "greater than" or "not equal to" operators. By using the `equals` operator rather than the == operator, the developers of LINQ are hoping to remind you that only equijoins are supported.

Also note that the order in which items are introduced into the `join` statement matters. You must place the class or table to be joined on the left side of the `equals` operator and the joining class or table on the right side:

```
p.MusicianId equals o.MusicianId
```

In this case people is the class to be joined, and orders is the joining class. Thus, p.MusicianId is on the left, and o.MusicianId is on the right.

The development team did some work to ensure that the compiler catches errors with the ordering of these elements. If you put items on the wrong side, you get an error. In this particular case, were we to mix up the order of the parameters in the join clause, the error would look like this:

```
The name 'o' is not in scope on the left side of 'equals'.
Consider swapping the expressions on either side of 'equals'.
```

This error makes it impossible for you to accidentally misplace the parameters in a join clause.

Now that you understand how join clauses work, let's introduce the Instrument table into the query:

```
var query1 = from p in people
            join o in orders on p.MusicianId equals o.MusicianId
            join i in instruments on o.InstrumentId equals i.InstrumentId
            select new { Musician = p.Name, OrderId = o.OrderId,
                Instrument = i.Name };
```

The query contains a second join:

```
join i in instruments on o.InstrumentId equals i.InstrumentId
```

This time the range variable called i is of type Instrument, and the join is made on the InstrumentId field. It is now a simple matter to project a result based on the range variables:

```
select new { Musician = p.Name, OrderId = o.OrderId, Instrument =
            i.Name };
```

Again, this is just a standard inner join between three tables. It produces the expected results:

```
{ Musician = Sonny Rollings, OrderId = 1, Instrument = Tenor Saxophone }
{ Musician = Miles Davis, OrderId = 2, Instrument = Trumpet }
{ Musician = Miles Davis, OrderId = 6, Instrument = Keyboard }
{ Musician = John Coltrane, OrderId = 3, Instrument = Soprano Saxophone }
{ Musician = John Coltrane, OrderId = 4, Instrument = Tenor Saxophone }
{ Musician = Charlie Parker, OrderId = 5, Instrument = Tenor Saxophone }
```

Group Joins

A group join uses the `into` keyword and creates an outer join-like group of associated records, keyed to the one-to-many values on which the join pivots. This is not entirely dissimilar to the set of `Key` and `IGrouping<>` results returned by a `group-by` clause. Result sequences of this kind have a hierarchical or graph-like structure and, hence, are not traditional left outer joins with a flat, or relational, structure. There is no corresponding SQL query that produces a similar result, because left outer joins in SQL have flat result sets with a rectangular structure of rows and columns.

Using the same data shown in Listing 5.3, here is a simple group join:

```
var query = from p in people
            join o in orders on p.MusicianId equals o.MusicianId
               into orderGroups
            select new { Musician = p.Name, Orders = orderGroups };
```

You could write this `join` clause on a single line, but I have broken it into two lines here because of line-width restrictions. It could be argued that breaking into two lines like this is valuable because it draws attention to the range variable rather than pushing out to an obscure position at the end of a long line of code.

The anonymous class returned by this query contains a name and group. The group contains a `Key` and its associated records, so we need nested `foreach` loops to iterate over the result set:

```
foreach (var items in query)
{
    Console.WriteLine(items.Musician);
    foreach (var item in items.Orders)
    {
        Console.WriteLine("..OrderId: {0}", item.OrderId);
    }
}
```

The output from this code looks like this:

```
Sonny Rollings
..OrderId: 1
Miles Davis
..OrderId: 2
..OrderId: 6
John Coltrane
```

```
..OrderId: 3
..OrderId: 4
Charlie Parker
..OrderId: 5
Bela Fleck
```

Here we see the classic hierarchical view of data that is so often found in a LINQ computation.

Quite often you will want to nest a second query to run against the results of a group join:

```
var query1 = from p in people
            join o in orders on p.MusicianId equals o.MusicianId
                into orderGroups
            select new
            {
                Musician = p.Name,
                Orders = from o in orderGroups
                        join i in instruments on o.InstrumentId
                            equals i.InstrumentId
                        select i.Name
            };
```

In this query I needed to wrap both joins because of line-width limitations. In your code, you could write both join statements on a single line, or keep the syntax I've shown here if you find it easier to read.

Take a look at the nested query expression:

```
Orders = from o in orderGroups
        join i in instruments on o.InstrumentId equals i.InstrumentId
        select i.Name
```

This code iterates over the result of our first join. The from clause introduces a range variable called o of type Order. The join statement associates the Instrument class with the Order class by linking them on the InstrumentId field. This allows us to project the name of the instrument in the select clause, rather than simply printing an order number, as we did in the first group join example.

Here is the code we can use to display the result sequence from this query:

```
foreach (var items in query1)
{
    Console.WriteLine(items.Musician);
    foreach (var item in items.Orders)
    {
        Console.WriteLine("..{0}", item);
    }
}
```

The output looks like this:

```
Sonny Rollins
..Tenor Saxophone
Miles Davis
..Trumpet
..Keyboards
John Coltrane
..Soprano Saxophone
..Tenor Saxophone
Charlie Parker
..Tenor Saxophone
Bela Fleck
```

Left Outer Joins

In the result sets we have been looking at, the artist Bela Fleck has no instrument associated with him, but he still is listed in the result set. This is very much what we'd expect when performing a left outer join, though of course traditional SQL developers would expect to see a flat, relational dataset returned from the query. There are also times when you want to see the name and some kind of record associated with even those customers who do not post any orders. Listing 5.4 shows how to proceed.

LISTING 5.4   This Case Is Similar to Listing 5.3, but This Time We Get a Flat Result Set and Include a Blank Order Associated with the Musician Bela Fleck

```
public void Tester()
{
    // Omitting object initializers, which are the same as Listing 5.3

    var query0 = from o in orders
                 join i in instruments
                     on o.InstrumentId equals i.InstrumentId
                 select new { o.OrderId, o.MusicianId, i.Name };
```

continues

LISTING 5.4   Continued

```
    var query = from p in people
                join o in query0
                    on p.MusicianId equals o.MusicianId into m
                from x in m.DefaultIfEmpty()
                select new { p, x };

    foreach (var items in query)
    {
        Console.WriteLine("{0} {1}", items.p.Name, items.x);
    }
}
```

In this listing I use composition to link two queries. Nevertheless, I want you to focus on the second query. The first query simply joins the Order and Instrument classes to create a new anonymous class that includes the name of each instrument:

```
1 1 Tenor Saxophone
2 2 Trumpet
3 3 Soprano Saxophone
4 3 Tenor Saxophone
5 4 Tenor Saxophone
6 2 Keyboard
```

The second query in this series joins the Musicians in the people collection with the anonymous class returned by the first query in this series. The into operator is used just as in a group join. The key of this join is a musician, and the associated data is the anonymous class returned by the first query.

The distinguishing trait of a left outer join in LINQ is the from clause that uses DefaultIfEmpty as a data source. We have an artist, Bela Fleck, with no associated orders. If we asked for the first order associated with Bela Fleck, we would get a range error on the empty collection of orders associated with this artist. DefaultIfEmpty resolves this error by returning the default value for this anonymous reference type, which is null. (Recall that the default value for any reference type is null.) In our foreach loop, when it comes time to print the orders associated with Bela Fleck, C# handles our null value smoothly, and prints nothing to the screen.

Most importantly, it returns a flat relational table rather than hierarchical data:

```
Sonny Rollings { OrderId = 1, MusicianId = 1, Name = Tenor Saxophone }
Miles Davis { OrderId = 2, MusicianId = 2, Name = Trumpet }
Miles Davis { OrderId = 6, MusicianId = 2, Name = Keyboard }
John Coltrane { OrderId = 3, MusicianId = 3, Name = Soprano Saxophone }
John Coltrane { OrderId = 4, MusicianId = 3, Name = Tenor Saxophone }
Charlie Parker { OrderId = 5, MusicianId = 4, Name = Tenor Saxophone }
Bela Fleck
```

The point here is not that flat datasets are better or worse than the hierarchical data seen in the group join from the previous section. The point is merely that you should use `DefaultIfEmpty` if you want to return a traditional, SQL-like flat dataset.

If we wanted to, we could use an override of `DefaultIfEmpty` to send back custom data:

```
var query03 = from p in people
              join o in query0
                  on p.MusicianId equals o.MusicianId into m
              from x in m.DefaultIfEmpty(
                  new { OrderId = 0, MusicianId = 0, Name = "Nothing" })
              select new { p, x };
```

This call to `DefaultIfEmpty` is fairly interesting. The method is expecting an instance of our anonymous type. How can we create an instance of a type if we don't know its name? It would seem impossible, but there is a solution. LINQ knows the fields of our anonymous type, and if we create another anonymous object with the same fields, in the same order, the compiler is smart enough to match it up with our anonymous type and create the proper instance!

Here is the output "flat" result set returned by running this computation through a `foreach` loop:

```
Sonny Rollings { OrderId = 1, MusicianId = 1, Name = Tenor Saxophone }
Miles Davis { OrderId = 2, MusicianId = 2, Name = Trumpet }
Miles Davis { OrderId = 6, MusicianId = 2, Name = Keyboard }
John Coltrane { OrderId = 3, MusicianId = 3, Name = Soprano Saxophone }
John Coltrane { OrderId = 4, MusicianId = 3, Name = Tenor Saxophone }
Charlie Parker { OrderId = 5, MusicianId = 4, Name = Tenor Saxophone }
Bela Fleck { OrderId = 0, MusicianId = 0, Name = Nothing }
```

Using the Object Model to "Join" Classes

I've spent quite a bit of time showing you how to write join clauses. There is no doubt that join clauses play an important role in LINQ, but they do not take center stage as often as they do in SQL. That is because object-oriented developers have a better way of showing the relationship between classes: They simply establish an association. Consider the code shown in Listing 5.5.

LISTING 5.5   Working with the Simple Association Between the Instrument and Musician Classes

```csharp
class Instrument
{
    public int InstrumentId { get; set; }
    public string Name { get; set; }
}

class Musician
{
    public int MusicianId { get; set; }
    public string Name { get; set; }
    public Instrument instrument;
}

public void RunTest03()
{
    List<Musician> people = new List<Musician>
    {
        new Musician { MusicianId = 1, Name = "Charlie Parker",
            instrument = new Instrument {
                InstrumentId = 1, Name = "Saxophone" } },
        new Musician { MusicianId = 1, Name = "Sonny Rollings",
            instrument = new Instrument {
                InstrumentId = 1, Name = "Saxophone"} },
        new Musician { MusicianId = 2, Name = "Miles Davis",
            instrument = new Instrument {
                InstrumentId = 2, Name = "Trumpet" } }
    };

    var query = from p in people
                where p.instrument.InstrumentId == 1
                select new { Musician=p.Name,
                             Intrument=p.instrument.Name };

}
```

In this example, the `Musician` and `Instrument` tables are associated by a field in the `Musician` table called `Instrument`. In a real-world program, this would probably be declared as an array of `Instruments`, but I have simplified matters here to keep the code short and easy to read.

After declaring the types, this code fragment creates a list of musicians and the instruments they use. Given these declarations, we can now move from the `Musician` class to the `Instrument` class using dot notation: `p.instrument.Name`.

It is obviously much easier to use this syntax than it is to create a `join` clause, as we did in the previous listings. As a result, the syntax I've shown here is the preferred way to handle joins in LINQ.

However, many times there is no direct relationship in the object model between classes. The kind of association needed to use this dot notation requires that one object, or a collection of objects, be declared as a field of a second object. If that relationship does not exist, you must use the `join` clauses shown earlier to link two tables.

Associations in LINQ to SQL

Join syntax plays a big role in SQL queries. As a result, you would probably expect that LINQ to SQL would make heavy use of `join` clauses. In practice, however, that is usually not the case. In Chapters 7 through 10, you will see that whenever you have a true relationship between tables based on key, you can use dot notation to perform joins. As a result, join syntax is something that you use infrequently in LINQ.

That is all I'll say about creating joins at this time. However, if you keep reading, you will find sections on the `SelectMany` operator that describe how to use multiple `from` clauses in a single query. Those sections reveal yet another very important way to perform a join between two classes.

Projections

Although some details have been omitted, by this point in the chapter you have had a chance to look at all the major features of query expressions except for the return sequence, or computation, that they produce. This section is designed to give you a close look at that subject. It covers the following topics:

- An overview of projections
- Projections and deferred execution
- Using Select, SelectMany, and two from clauses to project a result from a query

Overview of Projections

A select or group-by clause usually determines the type returned, or *projected*, by a deferred query expression. In this sense, it plays much the same role in a query expression as the keyword return plays in a method. But a query expression is said to project a type, whereas a function is said to return a type. Furthermore, a deferred query expression does not execute until you begin asking for the individual members of the result sequence.

As you've seen in previous chapters, a query expression can use anonymous types to project a new class in a select clause. The code shown in Listing 5.6 provides a quick review of this subject.

LISTING 5.6   This Program Uses a List of Customers as a Data Source and Returns an IEnumerable<T>, Where T is an Anonymous Class

```
class Customer
{
    public string CustomerID { get; set; }
    public string ContactName { get; set; }
    public string City { get; set; }
}

class Program
{
    private static List<Customer> GetCustomers()
    {
        return new List<Customer>
        {
            new Customer { CustomerID = "ALFKI",
                        ContactName = "Maria Anders", City = "Berlin" },
            new Customer { CustomerID = "ANATR",
                        ContactName = "Ana Trujillo", City = "Mexico D.F." },
            new Customer { CustomerID="ANTON",
```

```
                    ContactName="Antonio Moreno", City="Mexico D.F." }
        };
    }

static void Main(string[] args)
{
    var query = from c in GetCustomers()
                where c.City == "Mexico D.F."
                select new { City = c.City, ContactName = c.ContactName };
}
```

The data source for this query is a collection of `Customers`, but it returns a collection of some anonymous class defined in the `select` clause of the query.

Projects in SQL

SQL queries also project a new type. Assume the existence of a table called `Customer` that contains five fields: `Id`, `Name`, `Address`, `Zip`, and `Phone`. If you write `select Name, Address from Customer`, you are projecting a new type that contains two fields called `Name` and `Address`. LINQ does much the same thing, but it uses an anonymous class to encapsulate the data that is returned from the query.

The projection found in a `select` clause can also play a role in determining the transformational properties of a LINQ query. You've already read about transformations, and they will surface frequently in subsequent chapters. So for now I'll simply include Listing 5.7, taken from the Linq-Transform sample that accompanies this book, as a reminder of how a `select` clause can help transform object-oriented data into XML.

LISTING 5.7   Using a LINQ Query to Transform Objects into XML

```
class Mountain
{
    public string Name { get; set; }
    public int Height { get; set; }
    public string State { get; set; }
}

static void Main(string[] args)
{
```

continues

LISTING 5.7   Continued

```
    var Mountains = new List<Mountain>() {
        new Mountain { Name = "Rainier", Height = 4392, State = "WA" },
        new Mountain { Name = "Baker", Height = 3286, State = "WA" },
        new Mountain { Name = "Adams", Height = 3742, State = "WA" }
    };

    var xml = new XElement("Mountains",
            from mountain in Mountains
            orderby mountain.Name
            where mountain.Name.EndsWith("r")
            select new XElement("Mountain",
                new XAttribute("Name", mountain.Name),
                new XAttribute("Height", mountain.Height)));

    Console.WriteLine(xml);
}
```

The code shown in Listing 5.7 transforms data stored in C# classes into XML that looks like this:

```
<Mountains>
  <Mountain Name="Baker" Height="3286" />
  <Mountain Name="Rainier" Height="4392" />
</Mountains>
```

Projections and Deferred Execution

The code placed in a projection usually defines whether a query is deferred. The general rule to follow is fairly simple: *If a LINQ to Objects query returns a type that supports the* IEnumerable<T> *interface, at least some portion of the query is deferred. Otherwise, it executes immediately.*

Consider again the query shown in Listing 5.7. It is not deferred because it returns an XElement. By contrast, the following query would be deferred because it returns an IEnumerable<XElement>:

```
    var query = from mountain in Mountains
            orderby mountain.Name
            where mountain.Name.EndsWith("r")
            select new XElement("Mountain",
                new XAttribute("Name", mountain.Name),
                new XAttribute("Height", mountain.Height));
```

This second query returns the following data:

```
<Mountain Name="Baker" Height="3286" />
<Mountain Name="Rainier" Height="4392" />
```

There are two ways to tell whether a LINQ to Objects query returns IEnumerable<T>, and hence whether it is at least partially deferred. To use the first technique, you must be inside the Visual Studio IDE. Hover the mouse cursor over the var keyword used to declare the computation returned by the query. If it displays the type IEnumerable<T>, the query is deferred; otherwise, it is not deferred.

Figure 5.2 shows our first query, which returns an XElement. This query is not deferred because XElement is not IEnumerable<T>. Figure 5.3 shows our second query, which returns an IEnumerable<T>, where T is an XElement. This query is deferred. These figures include an image of the cursor, which you can see is placed directly over the keyword var.

FIGURE 5.2   You can tell that this query executes immediately because it does not return IEnumerable<T>.

FIGURE 5.3   You can tell that this query is deferred because it returns IEnumerable<T>.

A second way to tell if a query is deferred is simply to try to iterate over its return value with foreach. If you get back an error stating that foreach cannot iterate over your variable because it does not support GetEnumerator, you know that the query is not deferred.

If you see a query expression that contains a bit of query method syntax, that might be a hint that the query is not deferred. An example of this is shown in Listing 5.8, where a call is made to the Count operator.

LISTING 5.8   In This Query the Count Operator Is Explicitly Called Using Method Syntax

```
public void WordQuery2()
{
  List<string> list = new List<string> { "LINQ", "query", "adventure" };

  var query = (from word in list
               where word.Contains("r")
               orderby word ascending
               select word).Count();

  Console.WriteLine("There are {0} results in this query", query);
}
```

This query uses a mixture of the standard query expression syntax and query method syntax. As you saw in the preceding chapter, it is possible to compose any LINQ query exclusively using query method syntax. For instance, the body of this query, absent the call to Count, would look like this in query method syntax:

```
list.Where(word => word.Contains("r")).OrderBy(word => word)
```

This code uses query method syntax, but it is still entirely deferred. It is only when you have to use query method syntax that you should consider the possibility that your query might not be deferred.

The query shown in Listing 5.8 does not return IEnumerable<T>. Instead, the Count() operator returns a single integer. Because integers do not support IEnumerable<T>, you can be sure that this query is not deferred. Note also that the Count method requires iteration over the elements, and that causes the query to be executed immediately. As soon as the query has been executed, it is, by definition, no longer deferred.

It is important to understand that seeing a call to a query method is just a hint that a method might be executed immediately. It is not a hard and fast rule. Consider the following query that you saw in the section "Group-by Clauses and the into Keyword":

```
var query = from method in typeof(System.Linq.Enumerable).GetMethods()
            where method.DeclaringType == typeof(Enumerable)
            orderby method.Name
            group method by method.Name into g
            select new { Name = g.Key, Overloads = g.Count() };
```

Here you see a call to `g.Count()` in the `select` clause. This query, however, is definitely deferred. You can confirm this by hovering the mouse cursor over the keyword `var`, or by trying to `foreach` over the computation it returns. Both tests come back positive for deferred execution.

Projections with SelectMany

When working with projections, LINQ developers occasionally need to wrestle with the distinction between the `Select` and `SelectMany` operators. `SelectMany` allows you to eliminate the hierarchical or graph-like structure of LINQ queries and instead returns the flat data that you would get from a SQL query.

This section will show you several queries against a single set of data. Listing 5.9, from the SimpleJoins program available on the book's web site (as described in the Appendix), shows the data that we will query over. This data is very similar to what you saw in the section "Joins," but this time a collection of `Instruments` is associated with each musician.

LISTING 5.9   This Code Defines the Data That Will Be Used by the Queries in This Section

```
public class Instrument
{
    public int InstrumentId { get; set; }
    public string Name { get; set; }

    public override string ToString()
    {
        return String.Format("{0}, {1}",
            InstrumentId, Name);
    }
}

public class Musician
{
    public int MusicianId { get; set; }
    public string Name { get; set; }
    public List<Instrument> instruments;
```

continues

LISTING 5.9   Continued

```
    public override string ToString()
    {
        return string.Format("{0}, {1}", MusicianId, Name);
    }
}

private static List<Musician> GetMusicians()
{
    List<Musician> musicians = new List<Musician>
        {
            new Musician { MusicianId = 1, Name = "Charlie Parker",
                instruments = new List<Instrument>
                {
                    new Instrument { InstrumentId = 1, Name =
                                    "Saxophone" }
                }
            },

            new Musician { MusicianId = 2, Name = "Sonny Rollins",
                instruments = new List<Instrument>
                {
                    new Instrument { InstrumentId = 1, Name =
                                    "Saxophone"},
                    new Instrument { InstrumentId = 2,
                        Name = "Soprano Saxophone"}
                }
            },

            new Musician { MusicianId = 3, Name = "Miles Davis",
                instruments = new List<Instrument>
                {
                    new Instrument { InstrumentId = 2, Name =
                                    "Trumpet" },
                    new Instrument { InstrumentId = 2, Name = "Organ" }
                }
            }
        };

    return musicians;
}

public void RunTest()
{
    List<Musician> musicians = GetMusicians();

    ... Our  queries will be inserted here.
}
```

Listing 5.9 initializes a collection of `Musicians`, each of which contains a collection of `Instruments`. Note that the method calls `RunTest`. It contains a call to `GetMusicians`. All the queries I'll show you in this section can be inserted immediately after this call to `GetMusicians`.

Consider the following query:

```
var query = from m in musicians
            where m.MusicianId == 2
            select m.instruments;

foreach (var item in query)
{
    Console.WriteLine(item);
}
```

This `foreach` loop prints the following unsatisfying result to the console:

```
System.Collections.Generic.List`1[ConsoleApplication1.Instrument]
```

The problem is that the query returns a collection of `Instruments`, and we can't see them unless we embed a second `foreach` loop inside our first `foreach` loop:

```
foreach (var item in query)
{
    foreach (var instrument in item)
    {
        Console.WriteLine(instrument);
    }
}
```

This awkward syntax produces the output we want:

```
1, Saxophone
2, Soprano Saxophone
```

Fortunately, LINQ provides us with an alternative to having to write nested `foreach` loops:

```
var query = from m in musicians
            from i in m.instruments
            where m.MusicianId == 2
            select i;
```

Here you can see that we make use of two `from` clauses. We can now use a simple `foreach` loop to yield the expected results:

```
foreach (var item in query)
{
    Console.WriteLine(item);
}
```

■ Order Does Not Matter

When using the `join` operator, I pointed out that the order of items around the `equals` keyword is important. In contrast to that situation, the order of the middle clauses in this query is not important. The following code yields the same results and is semantically identical to the previous query:

```
var query = from m in musicians
            where m.MusicianId == 2
            from i in m.instruments
            select i;
```

Let's pause to consider the implications of the code shown so far in this section. You have seen that a common LINQ scenario forces you to write nested `foreach` loops in order to discover the results of what should be a simple query. To fix this problem, the developers of C# provided you with a simple syntax that allows you to place two `from` clauses in your query. If you grasp this point, you understand the most important message in this section. Your understanding of LINQ will be increased considerably, however, if you can follow along with me for a few more paragraphs while I explore this subject in a bit more depth.

At this stage, you might have two questions:

* What does all this have to do with the `SelectMany` operator?
* Why is this explanation of two parallel `from` clauses included in a section on projections?

To help you understand the answers to these questions, I have to switch to query syntax. This is necessary because there is no way to directly call

`SelectMany` using the query expression syntax. In other words, there is no `selectmany` clause.

Our query with two `from` clauses can be translated into the following query method syntax:

```
var query = musicians
            .Where(p => p.MusicianId == 2)
            .SelectMany(musician => musician.instruments);
```

Because this code is semantically identical to the code shown previously, it should come as no surprise to learn that you can display the results of this query using a single `foreach` loop:

```
foreach (var item in query)
{
    Console.WriteLine(item);
}
```

However, if you changed the query to call `Select` rather than `Select-Many`, you would have to use the nested `foreach` loop syntax:

```
var query = people
            .Where(p => p.MusicianId == 2)
            .Select(musician => musician.instruments);
```

This query is semantically equivalent to the first query shown in this section:

```
var query = from m in musicians
            where m.MusicianId == 2
            select m.instruments;
```

If you look at the source code for LINQ, you will find that `SelectMany` is overloaded four times. Right now we are using the first of these four overloads:

```
public static IEnumerable<TResult>
    SelectMany<TSource, TResult>(this IEnumerable<TSource> source,
        Func<TSource, IEnumerable<TResult>> selector);
```

A relatively straightforward extension method takes a source parameter and a very simple delegate called `selector`:

```
Func<TSource, IEnumerable<TResult>> selector
```

This delegate takes the source object as its sole parameter and returns an `IEnumerable<TResult>`. In our particular case, the source is a `Musician` object, and the return value is a collection of `Instruments`. We can write a very simple lambda to implement this delegate:

```
.SelectMany(musician => musician.instruments);
```

As you can see, this simple lambda accomplishes our goal: It transforms `Musician` into a collection of the `Instruments`. We can iterate over these instruments with a single `foreach` loop. It would have taken nested `foreach` loops to iterate over the musicians and then extract their instruments.

You should now understand why I chose this section on projections to show you how to write a pair of `from` clauses. When you look beneath the surface, you see that a query containing two `from` clauses is translated into a call to `SelectMany`.

The SelectMany Overloads

I mentioned that `SelectMany` can help flatten out the results of a query. In Chapter 2, "Getting Started," I emphasized that one of the advantages of LINQ is that it allows you to work with hierarchies and graphs rather than the flat data arrayed in columns and rows that is returned from a SQL query. However, sometimes a flat SQL result set makes sense. In the preceding section, I hinted at how you can use `SelectMany` to get a SQL-like result set. In this section, I will show you how to use `SelectMany` or two `from` clauses to create a join between two classes that acts very much like a traditional SQL join.

Consider the data we worked with in the preceding section. Each `Musician` can be associated with multiple instruments. As you have seen, in a purely object-oriented world, we must have nested `foreach` loops to view that relationship properly. The first loop iterates over the musicians, and the nested `foreach` loop iterates over the instruments associated with that musician.

This code illustrates the "problem" we have with nested data:

```
var query = from p in musicians
            select new
            {
                Musician = p.Name,
                Instruments = from i in p.instruments
                                 select i.Name
            };

foreach (var item in query)
{
    Console.WriteLine(item.Musician);
    foreach (var instrument in item.Instruments)
    {
        Console.WriteLine("...{0}", instrument);
    }
}
```

This code, which does not use SelectMany, and which requires nested foreach loops, sends the following output to the console:

```
Charlie Parker
...Saxophone
Sonny Rollins
...Saxophone
...Soprano Saxophone
Miles Davis
...Trumpet
...Organ
```

If we want to escape from this nested world, we can simply write a query that has two from clauses:

```
var query = from p in musicians
            from i in p.instruments
            select new { Musician = p.Name, Instrument = i.Name };

foreach (var item in query)
{
    Console.WriteLine(item);
}
```

This foreach loop produces flat data like you would see returned from a SQL query that contains a join:

```
{ Musician = Charlie Parker, Instrument = Saxophone }
{ Musician = Sonny Rollins, Instrument = Saxophone }
{ Musician = Sonny Rollins, Instrument = Soprano Saxophone }
{ Musician = Miles Davis, Instrument = Trumpet }
{ Musician = Miles Davis, Instrument = Organ }
```

Hopefully you will rarely have to use it, but for the sake of completeness, I'll show you the equivalent query method syntax:

```
var query =
    musicians.SelectMany(person => person.instruments,
        (person, instruments) =>
            new { Musician = person.Name, instrument = instruments.Name });
```

This is an example of the third of the four overloads for `SelectMany`. That overload looks like this:

```
public static IEnumerable<TResult>
SelectMany<TSource, TCollection, TResult>(this IEnumerable<TSource>
            source,
    Func<TSource, IEnumerable<TCollection>> collectionSelector,
    Func<TSource, TCollection, TResult> resultSelector);
```

This version of `SelectMany` starts the same way as the previous version. It takes a lambda, which, in turn, takes a source object and returns a collection:

```
.SelectMany(person => person.instruments...
```

The second parameter of `SelectMany` is another lambda that receives the source for this extension method and the output from the first lambda:

```
Func<TSource, TCollection, TResult> resultSelector
```

In this case `TSource` is a `Musician` object, and `TCollection` is the collection of `Instruments` returned from the first lambda. This second lambda exists simply to give us a chance to massage the data in any way we find useful. In this case we create an anonymous type that returns the name of the musician and the instrument he plays:

```
(person, instruments) =>
    new { Musician = person.Name, instrument = instruments.Name });
```

Another means of accomplishing this same end can be seen if we take a look at the second overload of `SelectMany`:

```
public static IEnumerable<TResult>
    SelectMany<TSource, TResult>(this IEnumerable<TSource> source,
        Func<TSource, int, IEnumerable<TResult>> selector);
```

This overload is identical to the first overload, but it takes an integer parameter that tracks the index of the element within the source collection:

```
var query = musicians
            .SelectMany((person, index) => (person.instruments)
            .Select(p => new { person = musicians[index].Name,
                Instrument = p.Name }));
```

You don't have to initialize or compute the value of the parameter called index. The compiler takes care of that. Simply include the parameter in the lambda, and it will be available for you to use inside your lambda. In particular, you can use it to index into the original collection of musicians, yielding the same result as shown in the previous example:

```
{ Musician = Charlie Parker, instrument = Saxophone }
{ Musician = Sonny Rollins, instrument = Saxophone }
{ Musician = Sonny Rollins, instrument = Soprano Saxophone }
{ Musician = Miles Davis, instrument = Trumpet }
{ Musician = Miles Davis, instrument = Organ }
```

In the fourth overload, the SelectMany operator combines the features found in overloads two and three. You can see how to use it in the Simple-Joins program found with the source code available on the book's web site.

The SelectMany operator is very powerful, and it can help you write code quickly and easily. Nevertheless, it is usually easiest to use multiple from clauses in a query expression rather than making direct calls to SelectMany using query method syntax. In any case, you should take the time to experiment with this operator and see if you can find ways to master it.

Query Expressions and Other Flavors of LINQ

Over the course of the last two chapters, you have read about the features of the C# language that make LINQ possible, and you have read about the structure of LINQ query expressions. Throughout this discussion, we have been focused on LINQ to Objects.

As you know, LINQ comes in many different flavors. Two of them, LINQ to Objects and LINQ to XML, exactly follow the principles laid out in these chapters. In particular, they support a composable query syntax that both consumes and returns `IEnumerable<T>`. Here is the pattern they follow in a deferred query:

```
IEnumerable<T> result = from x in SomeIEnumerableOfT
                        select x;
```

However, other flavors of LINQ are not based on `IEnumerable<T>`. Most of these are LINQ to SQL, which is based not on `IEnumerable<T>`, but on `IQueryable<T>`. LINQ to SQL generally follows this pattern in deferred queries:

```
IQueryable<T> result = from x in SomeIQueryableOfT
                       select x;
```

This query operates on a variable type `IQueryable<T>` and returns a variable of type `IQueryable<T>`. It is, therefore, fully composable.

`IQueryable<T>` is a fairly complicated type. As a result, it does not serve as a good introduction to flavors of LINQ that are not based on `IEnumerable<T>`. Instead, I will create a very simple type and show you a very simple provider for it. After you understand the principles involved, I'll come back and say a few more words about `IQueryable<T>`.

LINQ to MyNumberServer

Query expressions are surprisingly obtuse about the data they query. They are merely syntactic sugar on top of LINQ query methods. They exist only because they provide developers with a simple, easy-to-use syntax for writing queries. The translation from a query expression to a query method is not complex. It is really just a pattern-matching exercise. The compiler looks at a query expression, applies a few simple rules, and translates it into query methods. If you create types that follow the few simple patterns that query expressions expect to see, you can use your types in a query expression, even if they are not based on `IEnumerable<T>`. In fact, there is nothing special about `IEnumerable<T>` other than the fact that it follows the simple patterns expected of any type used in a query expression.

Query expressions follow a pattern based on sequences of data. You learned in the preceding chapter that sequences of data are generated by iterators—in particular, by iterators that implement a method called `GetEnumerator`. Consider the simple class shown in Listing 5.10, which is found in the QueryProvider sample available on the book's web site.

LISTING 5.10   This Simple Class Serves up Multiple Copies of the Number You Pass to Its Constructor

```
public class MyNumberServer
{
    int numberToServer;
    int length;

    public MyNumberServer(int init, int length)
    {
        numberToServer = init;
        this.length = length;
    }

    public IEnumerator GetEnumerator()
    {
        for (int i = 0; i < length; i++)
        {
            yield return numberToServer;
        }
    }
}
```

This very simple class is designed to serve up a number *n* times. If you pass in the numbers 3 and 5 to its constructor, it serves up the number 3 five times. We want to be able to write queries against this type that ask it to show us the numbers it generates if we pass in any two arbitrary parameters. For instance, if we pass in the numbers 2 and 7, we want to see what values the class returns.

Although it does not mention `IEnumerable<T>` and does not even include generics, this simple class nevertheless follows two of the key patterns that a LINQ query expression expects to find:

- It works with sequences of data.
- It exposes the sequence in a method called `GetEnumerator` that returns the `IEnumerator` interface.

It looks like we are off to a good start. The next step is to try to use this type in a LINQ query:

```
var MyNumberServer = new MyNumberServer(323, 2);

var query2 = from a in MyNumberServer
             where a != 3
             select a;
```

Despite our efforts, the compiler bristles at this code and complains that it

```
could not find an implementation of the query pattern for source type
'MyNumberServer'. 'Where' not found.
```

The compiler wants us to implement the Where operator for MyNumberServer.

So far in this book, whenever we have wanted to write a query, we were working with a type that implemented IEnumerable<T>. As you have seen, the Enumerable type that ships with LINQ includes implementations of all the LINQ operators for IEnumerable<T>. This time, however, we are working with a new type called MyNumberServer. It is now up to us to implement the query operators we plan to use.

In the preceding chapter you learned how to write extension methods, and you even saw an implementation of the Where operator. Let's use that knowledge to create operators for MyNumberServer:

```
public static class NumberServicable
{
    public static IEnumerable Where(this MyNumberServer source,
        Func<int, bool> predicate)
    {
        foreach (int item in source)
        {
            if (predicate(item))
            {
                yield return item;
            }
        }
    }

    public static IEnumerable Select(this MyNumberServer source,
        Func<object, object> selector)
    {
        foreach (var item in source)
```

```
        {
            yield return selector(item);
        }
    }

    public static IEnumerable Cast(this MyNumberServer source)
    {
        foreach (var item in source)
        {
            yield return (int)(item);
        }
    }
}
```

Here you see implementations for the Where, Select, and Cast operators. It is clear why we need to implement Where and Select, because we
use them in our query expression. The Cast operator needs to be implemented only because our code is not using generics. Without generics to
help with type resolution, the compiler gets confused about the lambda that
we pass to the where clause:

```
from a in MyNumberServer
where a != 3
select a;
```

Our implementation of Cast shows LINQ exactly how to cast one of our
items to type int, which is what is needed in this case.

In the QueryProvider sample that accompanies this book, you will find
a second version of this sample that use generics and that does not implement the Cast operator. I elected not to show you that sample here simply
because I wanted to emphasize that not even generics are essential if you
want to create simple LINQ providers. My goal is to strip away everything
but the essentials so that you can see the core patterns used in LINQ query
expressions.

After implementing the Select, Where, and Cast operators, our code
compiles and runs as expected. If we pass in the numbers 323 and 2, our
query prints the number 323 twice. If we pass in the number 3, the query
does not return anything, because the number 3 does not pass the test in the
where clause.

This is obviously a very simple server and a very simple example of a
LINQ provider. Nevertheless, it shows that you can use types that do not

implement IEnumerable<T> in a LINQ query. All you need to do is create a type that implements GetEnumerator and then design a few simple extension methods that implement operators that work with our type.

You might have noticed that our type is not composable. In particular, our query takes a variable of type MyNumberServer and returns a variable of type IEnumerable:

```
IEnumerable result = from x in SomeNumberServer
select x;
```

We obviously won't be able to pass in the return type to a second query that expects to work with variables of type MyNumberServer. Chapter 17, "LINQ Everywhere," references third-party LINQ providers that ship with source. For now, however, you have seen enough to at least glimpse how we can use some other type besides IEnumerable<T> in a LINQ query. In fact, you have seen that IEnumerable<T> is important only because it very neatly, and very completely, fulfills the requirements for a LINQ provider.

All the principles you have seen so far in this book still apply when you query types other than IEnumerable<T>. You still have the same seven basic types of clauses, you still have operators that are implemented as extension methods, you still have deferred execution, you still need an iterator to generate a sequence, you still use *yield return* to create that iterator, you still use lambdas, you still have range variables, and you still have the into keyword. Everything you have learned about LINQ and query expressions applies equally well to other domains such as LINQ to SQL.

Thinking About IQueryable

IQueryable<T> is the type used in LINQ to SQL queries. IQueryable<T> differs from IEnumerable<T> in that it includes an expression tree. In particular, the type takes the following shape:

```
public interface IQueryable<T> : IEnumerable<T>, IQueryable, IEnumerable
{
}
```

The important interface in this declaration is `IQueryable`:

```
public interface IQueryable : IEnumerable
{
    Type ElementType { get; }
    Expression Expression { get; }
    IQueryProvider Provider { get; }
}
```

The key property here is the middle one, which is called `Expression`. You learned in the preceding chapter that `Expressions` convert code into data. LINQ then examines this data and uses the information it gleans to translate your query expression into a SQL query, which it then sends across the wire to a server. LINQ can't use `IEnumerable<T>` for LINQ to SQL because `IEnumerable<T>` does not include a variable of type `Expression`.

If you look closely at the declaration for `IQueryable<T>`, you will see that it implements `IEnumerable<T>`. Because of this shared heritage, and because all LINQ query expressions work much the same way, you will find that all the information I have given you in the last two chapters applies just as much to LINQ to SQL as it does to LINQ to Objects.

Summary

This chapter has been a general overview of query expressions. You have seen that only seven possible clauses can appear in a LINQ query expression:

- `from`
- `let`
- `where`
- `join`
- `orderby`
- `select`
- `group-by`

These clauses can be arranged as was shown in Table 5.1. Query expressions always start with a `from` clause and end with a `select` or `group-by` clause. In the middle you can find `from`, `where`, `orderby`, `join`, and `let` clauses.

A considerable portion of this chapter was dedicated to exploring `group-by` and `join` clauses and their relationship to the `into` operator. The section on joins covered inner joins, group joins, and left outer joins. Another section described how you can use dot notation to express joins that are encapsulated in the object model.

The next sections focused on projections. There you read explanations of how to examine the return type of a query expression to discover whether it is deferred. The text also discussed an alternative way to create a SQL-like join using multiple `from` clauses. That section also focused on `SelectMany` and its various overloads.

The final section drew back from our close study of `IEnumerable<T>` and showed you some of the simple patterns that make LINQ query expressions possible. There you learned that query expressions actually know very little about the types over which you want to query. Instead, they look for simple patterns. If you can create types that follow those patterns, you can use LINQ to run queries against them. This final section of the chapter also helped lay the foundation for Chapters 7 through 10 by explaining a few basic facts about `IQueryable<T>`. You heard that this type will be explored in more depth in Chapter 17, which references several LINQ providers.

Ultimately, there is no end to the study of query expressions. They lie very much at the heart of the functional extensions to C# that LINQ embodies. This chapter gave you enough information to help you get started using them in earnest.

The next chapter covers the LINQ operators. You have already had a look at some of them in this chapter, particularly in the sections on `Select-Many`. However, there is much more to learn about that subject. No study of query expressions is complete without an understanding of the power inherent in the LINQ operators.

■ 6 ■
Query Operators

THE PRECEDING CHAPTER covered the structure of query expressions. The next step is to begin embellishing queries with operators.

This book is not intended to be a reference; nevertheless, this chapter and the preceding one cover all the LINQ operators. You can supplement this material by referring to examples that are available for download on the book's Web site (as described in the Appendix), the online help, or the excellent SampleQueries program that ships with Visual Studio. Like the samples available for download, the SampleQueries program provides code showing how to use each of the operators. Written primarily by C# PM Alex Turner, SampleQueries contains more than 500 sample methods. Included in the sample program are more than 100 LINQ to SQL queries, 100 LINQ to Objects queries, 100 LINQ to XML queries, and LINQ to Dataset queries. See Appendix A for more information on how to locate and install SampleQueries.

Locating and Grouping the LINQ Operators

The C# team broke the LINQ operators into groups. I will use these categories to give the discussion structure. Some of these operators should already be familiar to you. For instance, five operators used to create query expressions were discussed in the preceding chapters—Where, Group-By, Join, Select, and SelectMany. Two of the operators, Concat and Reverse, stand on their own. I merged them into the Set and Ordering groups, respectively. All the other operators are sorted into the default groups established by the C# team.

You have, of course, been working with LINQ operators such as `where`, `orderby`, and `select` since Chapter 2, "Getting Started." You have seen that they are implemented as extension methods and are in a class called `Enumerable`. You know that you can extend LINQ by creating your own operators, and you can modify its behavior by overriding the existing operators. Nevertheless, it is the 49 LINQ operators that ship with the product that usually define what LINQ can and cannot do. Table 6.1 shows the complete set of those operators and three accompanying utilities (marked with a +). In this table and the others in this chapter, the operators that are not deferred are marked with a *.

TABLE 6.1 The LINQ Query Operators and Three Utilities Can Be Assigned to 12 Categories

Operator Type	Operator Name	Operator Type	Operator Name
Partitioning	Take	Conversion	AsEnumerable
	Skip		ToArray*
	TakeWhile		ToList*
	SkipWhile		ToDictionary*
Join	Join		ToLookup*
	GroupJoin		OfType
Ordering	OrderBy		Cast
	OrderByDescending	Element	First*
	ThenBy		FirstOrDefault*
	Reverse		Last*
Set	Distinct		LastOrDefault*
	Union		Single*
	Intersect		SingleOrDefault*

Operator Type	Operator Name	Operator Type	Operator Name
	Except		ElementAt*
	Concat		ElementAtOrDefault*
Projection	Select		DefaultIfEmpty
	SelectMany	Generation	Range$^+$
Aggregate	Count*		Repeat$^+$
	LongCount*		Empty$^+$
	Sum*		Any*, All*
	Min*		Contains*
	Max*	Grouping	GroupBy
	Average*	Equality	SequenceEqual*
	Aggregate*	Restriction	Where

These operators provide support for set operations, joins, ordering, grouping, and aggregation. Other operators, such as the Element and Partitioning types, allow you to easily access individual elements returned by a query.

Don't look at the list of operators shown in Table 6.1 as a democratic brotherhood of equals. As you learned in the previous chapter, you must master five core operators—Where, OrderBy, Group-By, Join, and Select— if you want to understand LINQ. The clauses based on these operators, plus those formed with let and from, are the body and limbs of a query expression. They are the structure on which a query expression is built.

When trying to decide which LINQ operator to use, there is no need to scan the list of all the operators to find the one that fits your current needs. Instead, you should first master the big five and then learn to pick and choose from the others as you find the need. Do you need to perform a calculation? If so, take a look at the Aggregate operators. Do you need to find the union or intersection of two sequences? Take a look at the Set operators. Do you want to convert an IEnumerable<T> to a List<T>? Take a look at the Conversion operators.

The LINQ operators form a rich and varied API. Studying them can help you reach a level of proficiency sufficient to support writing sophisticated LINQ queries. If you can create simple queries quickly and efficiently, you will find that the small gaps in your knowledge will be filled in automatically during the course of your daily work.

Code Reuse

Throughout this chapter I will need to repeat the foreach loop that displays the data returned from a LINQ to Objects query. Because the lines of code for this process rarely change, I have created the following simple method, which I will call instead of showing you the same foreach loop repeatedly:

```
public static void ShowList<T>(IEnumerable<T> list)
{
    foreach (var item in list)
    {
        Console.WriteLine(item);
    }
}
```

I will also frequently use this code to display a title to the console:

```
public static void ShowTitle(string p)
{
    Console.WriteLine("==================");
    Console.WriteLine(p);
    Console.WriteLine("==================");
}
```

Furthermore, I will use a list of famous Romans on several occasions:

```
public class Roman
{
    public int Id { get; set; }
    public string Name { get; set; }
    public char Gender { get; set; }

    public override string ToString()
    {
```

```
        return String.Format(
            "{{ Id = {0}; Gender = {1}; Name = {2} }}",
            Id.ToString().PadLeft(2, '0'), Gender, Name);
    }
}

public static List<Roman> romans = new List<Roman>()
{
    new Roman { Id=00, Gender='f', Name = "Aelia Paetina" },
    new Roman { Id=01, Gender='f', Name = "Agrippina the Younger" },
    new Roman { Id=02, Gender='m', Name = "Augustus" },
    new Roman { Id=03, Gender='f', Name = "Caesonia" },
    new Roman { Id=04, Gender='m', Name = "Caligula" },
    new Roman { Id=05, Gender='f', Name = "Claudia Octavia" },
    new Roman { Id=06, Gender='m', Name = "Claudius" },
    new Roman { Id=07, Gender='f', Name = "Clodia Pulchra" },
    new Roman { Id=08, Gender='f', Name = "Julia the Elder" },
    new Roman { Id=09, Gender='f', Name = "Junia Claudilla" },
    new Roman { Id=10, Gender='f', Name = "Livia Drusilla" },
    new Roman { Id=11, Gender='f', Name = "Livia Orestilla" },
    new Roman { Id=12, Gender='f', Name = "Lollia Paulina" },
    new Roman { Id=13, Gender='f', Name = "Messalina" },
    new Roman { Id=14, Gender='m', Name = "Nero" },
    new Roman { Id=15, Gender='f', Name = "Plautia Urgulanilla" },
    new Roman { Id=16, Gender='f', Name = "Poppaea Sabina" },
    new Roman { Id=17, Gender='f', Name = "Scribonia" },
    new Roman { Id=18, Gender='f', Name = "Statilia Messalina" },
    new Roman { Id=19, Gender='m', Name = "Tiberius" },
    new Roman { Id=20, Gender='f', Name = "Vipsania Agrippina" },
};
```

Locating the LINQ Operators

The LINQ to Objects operators are implemented in a class called System.Linq.Enumerable. You have already seen how to use LINQ to Objects to write a Reflection query that enumerates these methods. You can also find their declarations, but not their full source code, by using the tools built into the Visual Studio IDE. To find the declarations, first start a standard console application. In the main block, type in System.Linq.Enumerable, put the cursor on the word Enumerable, and press F12. Alternatively, you can right-click and select Go to Definition. You are taken to the metadata for the Enumerable class, as shown in Figure 6.1.

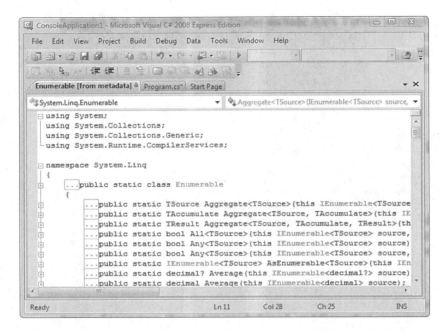

FIGURE 6.1   The IDE uses metadata to display the members of the `Enumerable` class.

You can learn a lot about these operators simply by looking at these declarations. After a time, you may even find that you can implement some of the simpler operators yourself just by looking at their declaration and having a little knowledge of how they behave.

When looking through these operators, you might notice that all but three of them are extension methods. The exceptions are a set of three utilities. Here are the declarations for `Empty`, `Range`, and `Repeat`, which clearly are not extension methods:

```
public static IEnumerable<TResult> Empty<TResult>();
public static IEnumerable<int> Range(int start, int count);
public static IEnumerable<TResult> Repeat<TResult>(TResult element,
                                                   int count);
```

If you're curious, the following query finds the three utility methods, returning the declaration for `Empty`, `Range`, and `Repeat`.

```
var query = from method in typeof(Enumerable).GetMethods()
            where method.DeclaringType == typeof(Enumerable)
            where method.GetCustomAttributes(true).Count() == 0
            select new { method };
```

This query is found in the sample program called LinqReflectionQuery that accompanies this book.

Generation Operators

The simple Generation operators shown in Table 6.2 allow you to create enumerations and test the contents of existing sequences that implement IEnumerable<T>. Some of these operators are designed to act as helper methods that you might use in test code, or for highly targeted scenarios in production code. The samples in this section are found in the GenerationOperators program that is available on the book's web site. None of the operators in the Generation group is deferred. Range, Repeat, and Empty are not implemented as extension methods.

TABLE 6.2   Generation Operators

Operator Name	Description
Range	Creates an enumeration with a range of values, such as the integers 1 to 10
Repeat	Creates an enumeration with a single repeated value
Empty	Creates an empty enumeration
Any*	Tests if a sequence is empty, or if any element in it meets a certain condition
All*	Tests if all elements in a sequence meet a certain condition
Contains*	Tests if a sequence contains a particular element

The Range, Repeat, and Empty methods are utilities that create lists. The Any, All, and Contains operators allow you to test the contents of a list against certain conditions.

Range

The Range operator allows you to quickly generate a sequence of integers. It is declared like this:

```
public static IEnumerable<int> Range(int start, int count);
```

Notice that it is not an extension method. For this reason, it is not really a traditional LINQ operator. But it is grouped with them and implemented in the Enumerable class because it is used frequently in LINQ programs as a utility. You can, however, use this utility any place in your code that you think appropriate. There is no reason to use it only with LINQ. Note that Range is deferred, which means that it is implemented with yield return, and hence does not execute until it is enumerated.

Here is how to call Range:

```
var list = Enumerable.Range(1, 3);
```

This call to Range returns a sequence containing the values 1, 2, and 3.

Because Range returns a sequence, you can use it as a data source in a query:

```
var query = from x in Enumerable.Range(1, 10)
            where (x % 2) == 0
            select x;
```

This produces a sequence containing the even numbers between 1 and 10.

Here the Range operator is used to calculate the area of a range of circles:

```
var query = from radius in Enumerable.Range(1, 9)
            let pi = 3.14159
            let area = (radius * radius) * pi
            select new { radius, pi, area };

ShowTitle("Radius | Area");

foreach (var item in query)
{
    Console.WriteLine("{0,6} |{1, 10}", item.radius, item.area );
}
```

This code produces the following results:

```
Radius | Area
==================
     1 |   3.14159
     2 |  12.56636
     3 |  28.27431
     4 |  50.26544
     5 |  78.53975
     6 | 113.09724
     7 | 153.93791
     8 | 201.06176
     9 | 254.46879
```

Here is a somewhat more complex query:

```
var query = from x in Enumerable.Range(1, 2)
            from y in Enumerable.Range(1, 3)
            select new { x, y };
```

This says, in effect, for each x, show me a range of numbers between 1 and 3. The result sequence looks like this if enumerated with our `ShowList` method:

```
{ x = 1, y = 1 }
{ x = 1, y = 2 }
{ x = 1, y = 3 }
{ x = 2, y = 1 }
{ x = 2, y = 2 }
{ x = 2, y = 3 }
```

The point here is that by using multiple `from` clauses you can start generating relatively complex sequences. Here we generate the sequence 1, 1, 1, 2, 2, 2. A simple modification to the code would allow you to extend this sequence for as long as you want. If this idea intrigues you, spend a little time playing with this code, passing in different parameters until you begin to get a feeling for what can be done.

Repeat

The `Repeat` utility is also not implemented as an extension method, so it is not a standard operator. It returns a sequence containing the same value repeated multiple times:

```
var list = Enumerable.Repeat(108, 12);
```

This call returns an enumeration containing 12 copies of the number 108. Consider the code shown in Listing 6.1. The ShowRepeat method stores 15 identical copies of an Item object with a Length of 5 and a Width of 6. Note also that I've implemented the ToString method so that a foreach loop can easily print the content of each instance of the Item class.

LISTING 6.1 The ShowRepeat Method Creates an Instance of the Item Class and Then Uses the Repeat Operator to Add the Instance to the Enumeration 15 Times

```csharp
class Item
{
    public int Width { get; set; }
    public int Length { get; set; }

    public override string ToString()
    {
        return string.Format("Width: {0}, Length: {1}", Width, Length);
    }
}

public void ShowRepeat()
{
    var item = new Item() { Length = 5, Width = 6 };
    var list = Enumerable.Repeat(item, 15);
    Console.WriteLine(
        Object.ReferenceEquals(list.ElementAt(1), list.ElementAt(2)));
    ShowList(list);
}
```

If you compare any two items from the list created in Listing 6.1, you will find that they have object identity: only one instance of the object is stored in the list 15 times. This is demonstrated by the call to Object. ReferenceEquals, which returns True.

Here is code that selects 12 random "Celsius temperatures" between 0 and 30 and converts them to Fahrenheit:

```csharp
Random random = new Random();

var query = from c in Enumerable.Repeat(0, 12)
                .Select(i => random.Next(0, 30))
            let f = (1.8 * c) + 32
            select new { c = c, f };
```

```
ShowTitle("Temp Convert");
foreach (var i in query)
{
    Console.WriteLine("{0, 3} c = {1, 4} f", i.c, i.f.ToString("F02"));
}
```

Note that `Repeat` never directly generates any numbers. Instead, the call to `Select` generates this list. It should not be hard to imagine how you could write this code in a more imperative fashion using a standard class constructor and a loop. This code accomplishes the same end with a more concise declarative syntax. The question you have to ask is whether the code is sufficiently readable to make the space savings worthwhile.

A Note on the Code and a Thank-You

In this text I've had to break the `from` clause into two lines because of line-width limitations. I should also add that I got the idea for using `Repeat` this way from a blog post written by Igor Ostrovsky, an engineer on Microsoft's parallel team.

The code produces the following output:

```
==================
Temp Convert
==================
 28 c = 82.40 f
  6 c = 42.80 f
 19 c = 66.20 f
 19 c = 66.20 f
 24 c = 75.20 f
 14 c = 57.20 f
 24 c = 75.20 f
 25 c = 77.00 f
  8 c = 46.40 f
  2 c = 35.60 f
  9 c = 48.20 f
 18 c = 64.40 f
```

To me this looks like a list of daily temperatures in a computer simulation of a world where the temperature is not very stable.

Empty

The Empty operator is the last of the three declarations in the Enumerable class that are not extension methods. It returns an IEnumerable<T> with no elements in the sequence. Consider this simple call to Empty, which creates a sequence of System.Double[0] that contains zero elements:

```
var list = Enumerable.Empty<double>();
Console.WriteLine(list);
```

I am unable to think of any good uses for this operator that you could not achieve just as easily using a standard constructor. I have a feeling the team included it for the sake of completeness, or to give you a declarative way to create a class of some arbitrary type.

Any

The Boolean Any operator can be used to tell whether a sequence is empty, or whether it meets the conditions of a particular predicate. The following code first checks to see if two lists are empty, and then it uses a simple predicate to detect whether a list contains the number 8:

```
public void ShowAny()
{
    var listA = Enumerable.Empty<double>();
    var listB = Enumerable.Range(1, 10);

    Console.WriteLine("Are there any items in ListA: {0}, ListB: {1}",
        listA.Any(), listB.Any());

    Console.WriteLine("Does listB contain the number {0}: {1}",
        8, listB.Any(i => i == 8));
}
```

The output for this method looks like this:

```
Are there any items in ListA: False, ListB: True
Does listB contain the number 8: True
```

The first version of Any called in this code takes no parameters, and you should be able to easily imagine the declaration for it:

```
public static bool Any<TSource>(this IEnumerable<TSource> source);
```

Note that it is a simple extension method for `IEnumerable<T>` that returns a `bool`.

The second version of `Any` is declared like this:

```
public static bool Any<TSource>(
    this IEnumerable<TSource> source,
    Func<TSource, bool> predicate);
```

Notice the simple delegate expected as the second parameter. As you recall, functions like this that return a Boolean value are called predicates by mathematicians—hence the name of this parameter to the `Any` operator. The lambda we pass in to fulfill the contract inherent in this parameter looks like this:

```
i => i == 8
```

This delegate returns a Boolean value specifying whether any item in the list is equal to 8.

The preceding example calls `Any` with a lambda, but the following code also compiles and runs correctly:

```
public bool Predicate(int value)
{
    return value == 8;
}

public void ShowAny()
{
    var listB = Enumerable.Range(1, 10);

    Console.WriteLine("Does listB contain the number {0}: {1}",
        8, listB.Any(Predicate));
}
```

Some developers might prefer to use lambdas in these situations because they can be guaranteed to be side-effect-free and hence thread-safe.

All

The `All` operator detects whether the elements of a list meet a certain condition specified in a predicate. In this example, the predicate asks whether all the items in a list are smaller than the number 11:

```
public void ShowAll()
{
    var list = Enumerable.Range(1, 10);

    if (list.All(i => i < 11))
    {
        Console.WriteLine("Condition met");
    }
    else
    {
        Console.WriteLine("Condition not met");
    }
}
```

Contains

The Contains operator can be used to test for the inclusion of a particular element in a sequence. This operator is overloaded several times. In its simplest case, you simply pass in an element of the same type as the list, and the method returns whether it is a member of the sequence. In this code, a sequence with the numbers 3 through 13 is generated, and the code checks to see which of the numbers between 0 and 15 are included in that list:

```
var list = Enumerable.Range(3, 10);

for (int i = 0; i < 15; i++)
{
    Console.WriteLine("List contains value {0}: {1}",
        i, list.Contains(i));
}
```

The second overload of the Contains operator uses the IEQualityComparer interface:

```
public static bool Contains<TSource>(this IEnumerable<TSource> source,
    TSource value, IEqualityComparer<TSource> comparer);
```

This gives you latitude to make more complex decisions about whether a particular value is in a list. Listing 6.2 shows an implementation of the IEqualityComparer interface.

LISTING 6.2   This `IEqualityComparer` Asks You to Implement the `Equals` and `GetHashCode` **Methods**

```
class EqualityCompare: IEqualityComparer<int>
{

    #region IEqualityComparer<int> Members

    public bool Equals(int x, int y)
    {
        if (x == y)
        {
            return y % 2 == 0;
        }
        else
        {
            return false;
        }
    }

    public int GetHashCode(int obj)
    {
        return obj.GetHashCode();
    }

    #endregion
}
```

Here is a method that uses this implementation of `IEqualityComparer`:

```
public void ShowContains()
{
  for (int i = 0; i < 15; i++)
  {
    Console.WriteLine("List contains value {0:D2}: {1}",
      i, list.Contains(i, new EqualityCompare()));
  }
}
```

The important method in Listing 6.2 is the implementation of `Equals`. It tests whether the values passed into it are equal and whether they are even. If both conditions are met, it returns true; otherwise, it returns false. I will show other implementations of `IEqualityComparer` later in this chapter. Note also that `Contains` has an overload that takes only a single parameter that uses a default implementation of `IEqualityComparer`:

```
list.Contains(i)
```

■ Contains Can Help You Write Succinct Code

One of the goals of LINQ is to help you write clear, succinct code that is easy to read. The Contains operator can help you achieve this goal. You might remember the IsState extension method from the preceding chapter:

```
public static bool IsState01(this string source)
{
    if (source == null) return false;
    source = source.ToUpper();
    foreach (var item in stateCodes)
    {
        if (source == item)
        {
            return true;
        }
    }
    return false;
}
```

This method contains 10 lines of code. Here is a rewrite of the IsState() extension method from the preceding chapter that contains one line of code, which I have wrapped here due to line-width considerations:

```
public static bool IsState02(this string source)
{
    return (source == null) ? false :
        stateCodes.Contains(source.ToUpper());
}
```

With LINQ, the goal is often to allow developers to create the simplest syntax possible that properly expresses their logic. This is an example of how that end can be achieved.

SequenceEqual

The SequenceEqual operator stands on its own and traditionally is not considered to be part of the Generation operators. I will include it in this section, however, because it bears some similarity to the Any, All, and Contains operators.

Consider the following code:

```
var listA = Enumerable.Range(1, 3);
var listB = Enumerable.Range(1, 5);

var query1 = from a in listB
             where a < 4
             select a;
```

The SequenceEqual operator tests to see if two sequences are equal. Given the first two lists we see here, the following query returns false:

```
listA.SequenceEqual(listB);
```

This returns false because listA does not contain the same sequence as listB. In particular, the sequence 1, 2, 3 is not equivalent to the sequence 1, 2, 3, 4, 5.

We find that query1 does have the same sequence as ListA. As a result, the following query returns true:

```
listA.SequenceEqual(query1)
```

This returns true because query1 returns the numbers from listB that are smaller than 4. These are the numbers 1, 2, and 3, which are the same numbers, found in the same order, as those found in listA.

You can also implement IEqualityComparer<T> and pass that in to SequenceEqual. Here is a simple implementation of that interface that works for our current example:

```
class EqualityCompare : IEqualityComparer<int>
{
    public bool Equals(int x, int y)
    {
        return (x == y);
    }

    public int GetHashCode(int obj)
    {
        return obj.GetHashCode();
    }
}
```

Given the existence of this class, you can write the following code, which returns true:

```
listA.SequenceEqual(query1, new EqualityCompare())
```

The EqualOperators sample that comes with this book contains the code shown in this section, and a few other samples that you might find interesting. For instance, it demonstrates that order matters when using this operator. For instance, the following code returns false:

```
var listC = new List<int> { 2, 1, 3 };
Console.WriteLine(listC.SequenceEqual(listA));
```

Partitioning Operators

The four Partitioning operators, shown in Table 6.3, allow you to divide a sequence into two sections where the partition between the sections is defined by a simple Boolean operation. All these operators are deferred.

TABLE 6.3   Partitioning Operators

Operator Name	Description
Take	Takes only the first n elements from a sequence
Skip	Skips the first n elements from a sequence
TakeWhile	Takes elements from a sequence while a condition is true
SkipWhile	Skips elements from a sequence while a condition is true

Throughout this section I'll run variations on a query run against the list of famous Romans shown near the beginning of this chapter. Here is an unadorned version of the query that does not use any Partitioning operators:

```
var query = from r in romans
            where r.Gender == 'm'
            select r.Name;
```

```
foreach (var e in query)
{
    Console.WriteLine(e);
}
```

The output from this query would look like this:

```
Augustus
Caligula
Claudius
Nero
Tiberius
```

This gives you a baseline to which you can compare this output with what is returned from the other queries in this section.

Take

The `Take` operator retrieves the first *n* elements from a list, where *n* is the number you pass as the operator's sole argument. Here is a query using the partitioning operator `Take`. This query returns the first two male emperors from the list of five shown in the preceding section:

```
var query1 = (from r in romans
              where r.Gender == 'm'
              select r.Name).Take(2);
```

If you write the results of the query with a `foreach` loop, you see the following output:

```
Augustus
Tiberius
```

Skip

The `Skip` operator takes the opposite tack. It skips *n* elements in a list and then shows the remainder:

```
query1 = (from r in romans
          where r.Gender == 'm'
          select r.Name).Skip(2);
```

This code skips Augustus and Tiberius and returns Caligula, Claudius, and Nero.

Here is how to take the third 25 items from a list of 100 items:

```
var list = Enumerable.Range(1, 100);
list.Skip(75).Take(25)
```

TakeWhile

The TakeWhile operator is perhaps most useful when you are working with an infinite list, or a very long list. Consider this somewhat contrived method:

```
public IEnumerable<long> GetInfiniteList()
{
    int bottom = 7000;
    long count = bottom;

    while (true)
    {
        yield return count;
        count += 7;
        if (count >= 20000) count = bottom;
    }
}
```

This code returns, in an infinite loop, the numbers between 7,000 and 20,000 that are divisible by 7. Here is one way to view the first five members of this list:

```
foreach (var item in GetInfiniteList().Take(5))
{
    Console.WriteLine(item);
}
```

The output from this list looks like this:

```
7000
7007
7014
7021
7028
```

The following code takes all the items from the list that are divisible by 11 and that are smaller than 10,000:

```
var query4 = (from r in GetInfiniteList()
              where r % 11 == 0
              select r).TakeWhile(r => r < 10000);
```

The result sequence contains many members, but here are the first few:

```
7007
7084
7161
```

Here is a variation on this same code, expressed in query method syntax:

```
var query = Enumerable
            .Range(1, 100)
            .Where(x => x % 3 == 0)
            .TakeWhile(x => x % 11 != 0);
```

Here we ask for the numbers between 1 and 100 that are evenly divisible by 3 and 11. Note that the Range operator generates all the numbers between 1 and 100, whereas our GetInfiniteList method generates only the numbers that are multiples of 7. Furthermore, our method generates only the exact number of items you request; it stops working when you stop asking for the next item in the sequence.

◾ An Interesting Case

Suppose we begin our series with a number that is not evenly divisible by 7, such as 8,000:

```
public IEnumerable<int> GetWeirdRepeatingList()
{
    int bottom = 8000;
    int top = 10000;
    int count = bottom;

    while (true)
    {
        count += 7;
        if (count >= 20000) count = bottom;
        yield return count;
    }
}
```

Now we ask for all the values in this list that are evenly divisible by 11, using the query just shown. The result is a list of numbers that

> begins like this: 8063, 8140, 8217, 8294, 8371. If you divide any of these
> numbers by 7, you end up with a repeating set of decimal values:
>
> ```
> 8063 / 7 = 1151.8571428571428571142857142
> 8140 / 7 = 1162.8571428571428571142857142
> 8217 / 7 = 1173.8571428571428571142857142
> ```
>
> As I say, it's an interesting case.

SkipWhile

The `SkipWhile` operator is very much like `TakeWhile`, except that it skips
the items from the beginning of a list that don't meet a particular condition.
We don't want to use this operator with an infinite list, because it would
never define a closing condition. We can, however, use it with a method
that could potentially generate a fairly long list:

```
public IEnumerable<long> GetLongList()
{
    int top = 1000;
    long count = -1001;

    while (count < top)
    {
        count += 7;
        yield return count;
    }
}
```

The sequence generated by this method runs in increments of 7 from –1001
to 1000, but it could easily be extended to range over all integers expressible
on a 64-bit system—that is, the numbers between `long.MinValue` and
`long.MaxValue`.

Here is a query run against `GetLongList`:

```
var query3 = (from r in GetLongList()
              where r % 11 == 0
              select r).SkipWhile(r => r < 0);
```

This code retrieves all the positive numbers from the list that are divisible by 11. The first viewed elements in the result sequence look like this:

```
0
77
154
231
308
385
```

Something about these operators tempts you to show how they can be used to manipulate numbers. Nevertheless, it would probably be wise to finish this section with a query against string data:

```
query1 = (from r in SimpleRomans
         where r.Gender == 'f'
         select r.Name)
        .SkipWhile(r => r.StartsWith("A"));
```

This query asks for all the female Romans from our list but asks that we skip those whose name begins with the letter A:

```
Caesonia
Claudia Octavia
Clodia Pulchra
Julia the Elder
Junia Claudilla
Livia Drusilla
Etc...
```

In reading this section you may have sensed three things:

- Although you have seen only a few LINQ operators so far, it should be clear that, taken together, these operators form a complete language for querying data. One senses the team's desire to be sure to include a way to express all the possible ways to query data.
- Some of these operators can be useful for writing mathematical formulas or expressing mathematical ideas.
- LINQ is quite at home working with infinite lists. You might, for instance, use LINQ to query an infinite stream of data coming in over the Internet, a stream of bytes from a network, a sequence of numbers such as primes, and so on.

Element Operators

As shown in Table 6.4, there are nine Element operators. Except for `DefaultIfEmpty`, which is deferred, their purpose is to force execution of a query and immediately return a single item from an enumeration. Examples of using all of these operators are found in the ElementOperators sample program available on the book's web site.

TABLE 6.4   Element Operators

Operator Name	Description
First*	Retrieves the first item from an enumeration
FirstOrDefault*	Gets the first element or a default value for the list type
Last*	Retrieves the last item from an enumeration
LastOrDefault*	Gets the last item or a default value for the list type
Single*	Returns the only element from a sequence that satisfies a condition
SingleOrDefault*	Returns a single element or a default value for the list type
ElementAt*	Retrieves an element at a specified offset in a list
ElementAtOrDefault*	Retrieves an element at a specified offset or a default value
DefaultIfEmpty	Retrieves a default value if the list is empty or null

The Element operators allow you to access individual items from a sequence. With the exception of `DefaultIfEmpty`, none of these operators are deferred.

First and FirstOrDefault

The following query uses the `First` operator to return the initial item from a query:

```
var query = (from r in romans
             where r.Gender == 'm'
             select r.Name).First();
```

When enumerated, this query returns Augustus.

Here is another common way to call the `First` operator:

```
Console.WriteLine("First item: {0}", romans.First());
```

Pass a predicate to `First` to specify a filter:

```
var firstLambda = (from r in romans
                   where r.Gender == 'm'
                   select r.Name).First(n => n.Length > 4);
```

If the sequence you are querying is empty, `First` throws an `InvalidOperationException`. If you think this probably will happen, call `FirstOrDefault`. This operator returns the default value for the type of element in your sequence. The default value for Reference types is null; for numeric Value types, it is 0. For instance, if you are working with a sequence of string, it returns null.

Because the filter in this query causes it to return a result sequence with zero elements, this call to the `Single` operator throws an exception when enumerated:

```
var query = (from r in romans
             where r.Gender == 'z'
             select r.Name).First();
```

This query, however, does not throw an exception and returns null:

```
var query = (from r in romans
             where r.Gender == 'z'
             select r.Name).FirstOrDefault();
```

`FirstOrDefault` is overloaded to allow you to pass in a lambda, just as you can when you use the `First` operator.

Last and LastOrDefault

You can use the `Last()` operator to retrieve the last item from a sequence. All the features of the `First` operator also work for `Last`. Here is a call to the `Last` operator that returns the name `Tiberius` from the list:

```
query = (from r in romans
        where r.Gender == 'm'
        select r.Name).Last();
```

You can pass in a predicate to filter a list:

```
var clawClawClaudius = (from r in romans
                        where r.Gender == 'm'
                        select r.Name).LastOrDefault(n =>
                                            n.StartsWith("C"));
```

This returns the value Claudius.

If you wrote a query that returned nothing, you would throw an exception, which you could capture in a `try/catch` block:

```
try
{
    var q = (from r in romans
            where r.Gender == 'z'
            select r).Last();
}
catch (System.InvalidOperationException)
{
    Console.WriteLine("You threw an InvalidOperationException");
}
```

You can call `LastOrDefault` to sidestep this problem:

```
var nullRoman = (from r in romans
                where r.Gender == 'z'
                select r).LastOrDefault();

WriteLine("{0}", (nullRoman == null) ? "Null" : nullRoman.Name);
```

Because this query returns zero elements, `LastOrDefault` returns the default value of `null` for a reference type such as `Roman`. In the `WriteLine` statement, the conditional operator is used to determine whether the query returned an instance of `Roman`.

Single

The `Single` operator returns one, and only one, element from a sequence. If your sequence contains only one element, you can use the operator with zero parameters, as shown here:

```
string name = (from r in romans
               where r.Name.Length == 4
               select r.Name).Single();

Console.WriteLine(name);
```

The point is that `Single` forces execution of the query. If we did not call `Single`, the return value would be an enumeration with one element. By calling `Single`, we get the result of the query without having to explicitly enumerate the list with `foreach`.

It is a runtime error to call `Single` on a sequence that contains more than one element:

```
try
{
    var n = (from r in romans
             select r.Name).Single();
}
catch (System.InvalidOperationException)
{
    Console.WriteLine("You threw an InvalidOperationException");
}
```

If you have multiple elements in your sequence, you may write a simple predicate that acts as a filter to return only the element you want. Your lambda must return only one element, or you receive an `InvalidOpera-tionException` at runtime.

```
string name = (from r in romans
               where r.Gender == 'm'
               select r.Name).Single(r => r.Length == 4);

Console.WriteLine("{0}", name);
```

ElementAt

Here is how to pull Claudius' name from the list:

```
query = (from r in romans
         where r.Gender == 'm'
         select r.Name).ElementAt(2);
```

Element Operators and Composition

I have been showing the Element operators in the context of a query expression, but you can use them directly on any type that supports `IEnumerable<T>`:

```
Console.WriteLine("{0,10}: {1}", "First", romans.First());
Console.WriteLine("{0,10}: {1}", "Last", romans.Last());
Console.WriteLine("{0,10}: {1}", "ElementAt", romans.ElementAt(2));
Console.WriteLine("{0,10}: {1}", "Single",
    romans.Single(q => q.Name.Length == 4));
```

These queries produce the following output:

```
    First: { Id = 00; Gender = f; Name = Aelia Paetina }
     Last: { Id = 20; Gender = f; Name = Vipsania Agrippina }
ElementAt: { Id = 02; Gender = m; Name = Augustus }
   Single: { Id = 14; Gender = m; Name = Nero }
```

Or you can use them on the results of a query:

```
var query = from r in romans
            where r.Gender == 'm'
            select r.Name;

ShowList(query.Take(2));
Console.WriteLine(query.First());
Console.WriteLine(query.Last());
Console.WriteLine(query.ElementAt(2));
```

The query expression found at the beginning of the method retrieves the list of Julio-Claudian emperors from our collection:

```
Augustus
Caligula
Claudius
Nero
Tiberius
```

It then uses

- The Take operator to pull the first two items: Augustus and Caligula.
- First to pull the name Augustus from the list.
- Last to pull the name Tiberius from the list.
- ElementAt(2) to pull our friend Claudius' name from the list.

This ability to reuse the results of a query is a form of composition, as described in Chapter 3, "The Essence of LINQ."

DefaultIfEmpty

Use the DefaultIfEmpty operator if you want to be sure that a result sequence has at least one element. Consider this query:

```
var query = from r in romans
            where r.Gender == 'z'
            select r;
```

It returns an empty list with zero elements.

This query, on the other hand, returns a list with one element that is set to null:

```
var query = (from r in romans
             where r.Gender == 'z'
             select r).DefaultIfEmpty();

Console.WriteLine("Count: {0}", query.Count());
foreach (var item in query)
{
    Console.WriteLine("{0}", (item == null) ? "null" : item.Name);
}
```

The output from these lines of code looks like this:

```
Count: 1
null
```

If a query returns a normal result sequence with one or more elements, a call to DefaultIfEmpty does nothing. It is as if you never called it. Here is an example:

```
var query = (from r in romans
             where r.Gender == 'm'
             select r).DefaultIfEmpty();
```

This query returns the names of our five male emperors.

You can specify a default value so that the single item in the list returned by `DefaultIfEmpty` contains a valid class rather than null:

```
var query = (from r in romans
             where r.Gender == 'z'
             select r)
             .DefaultIfEmpty(new Roman
                {
                    Id = -1,
                    Gender = 'N',
                    Name = "Empty Roman"
                });
```

This code uses our `ToString` implementation in the `Roman` class to return the following:

```
{ Id = -1; Gender = N; Name = Empty Roman }
```

Set Operators

Continuing our tour of the LINQ operators, we can now turn our attention to the Set operators, which are shown in Table 6.5. They allow you to perform set operations on various sequences. You can apply the Set operators to any two sequences that implement `IEnumerable<T>`. All the set operators are deferred. The `Concat` operator is also discussed in this section.

TABLE 6.5   Set Operators

Operator Name	Description
Distinct	Shows the distinct elements in a sequence
Union	Shows the unique items obtained by combining two sets
Intersect	Shows the elements that two sets have in common

Operator Name	Description
Except	Shows all the members of one set except those in a second set
Concat	Concatenates two sequences
SequenceEqual*	Tests if two sequences are equal

Union

The Union operator shows the unique items from two lists, as shown in Listing 6.3. Here we have two lists—one containing the numbers 1, 2, and 3, and the other 3, 4, 5, and 6. The union of these two lists is the numbers 1, 2, 3, 4, 5, and 6.

LISTING 6.3   The ShowUnion Method Displays the Numbers 1, 2, 3, 4, 5, and 6

```
public void ShowUnion()
{
    var listA = Enumerable.Range(1, 3);
    var listB = new List<int> { 3, 4, 5, 6 };

    var listC = listA.Union(listB);

    ShowList(listC);
}
```

After these two sequences are combined, only the unique members of each list are retained. The elements of listA appear before elements of listB in the merged sequence.

If you don't want the union of two lists, consider using the Concat operator:

```
var listA = Enumerable.Range(1, 3);
var listB = new List<int> { 3, 4, 5, 6 };

var listC = listA.Concat(listB);

ShowList(listC);
```

This operator returns a sequence containing all the items in both enumerations, including duplicates:

```
1
2
3
3
4
5
6
```

Intersect

The `Intersect` operator shows the items that two lists have in common. In this case we have one list containing the numbers 1, 2, 3, and 4 and a second list containing the numbers 3, 4, 5, and 6. The intersection of the two lists are the numbers 3 and 4, as shown in Figure 6.2. Listing 6.4 demonstrates how to use this operator.

FIGURE 6.2   The intersection of two lists.

LISTING 6.4   The ShowIntersect Method Prints the Numbers 3 and 4

```
public void ShowIntersect()
{
    var listA = Enumerable.Range(1, 4);
    var listB = new List<int> { 3, 4, 5, 6 };

    var listC = listA.Intersect(listB);

    ShowList(listC);
}
```

Here two collections are joined, and only the unique, shared members of each list are retained.

Consider what happens if we make the following change to the order in which the items are declared:

```
var listB = new List<int> { 4, 5, 3, 6 };
```

The result is still { 3, 4 } because `Intersect()` is applied on `listA`, whose order it kept.

Distinct

The `Distinct` operator finds all the unique items in a single list, as shown in Listing 6.5. This method works with a list containing the numbers 1, 2, 3, 3, 2, and 1. The unique, or distinct, numbers in this list are 1, 2, and 3, as illustrated in Figure 6.3.

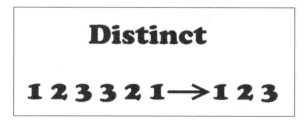

FIGURE 6.3   The unique, or distinct, items in the sequence 1, 2, 3, 3, 2, 1 are the numbers 1, 2, and 3.

LISTING 6.5   This Code Prints the Numbers 1, 2, and 3

```
public void ShowDistinct()
{
    var listA = new List<int> { 1, 2, 3, 3, 2, 1 };
    var listB = listA.Distinct();

    ShowList(listB);
}
```

Except

The `Except` operator shows all the items in one list minus the items in a second list, as shown in Listing 6.6. Here we have one list containing the numbers 1, 2, 3, 4, 5, and 6 and a second list containing the numbers 3 and 4. If we use the Except operator to remove the items in the second list from the first list, we end up with the numbers 1, 2, 5, and 6, as illustrated in Figure 6.4.

FIGURE 6.4 The items of one list minus, or except, the items in a second list. In this case we take 3 and 4 from the list 1, 2, 3, 4, 5, and 6 to yield the list 1, 2, 5, and 6.

LISTING 6.6 The ShowExcept Method Prints the Numbers 1, 2, 5, and 6

```
public void ShowExcept()
{
    var listA = Enumerable.Range(1, 6);
    var listB = new List<int> { 3, 4 };

    var listC = listA.Except(listB);

    ShowList(listC);
}
```

In the Context of LINQ

The type of code just shown is useful, but it might be helpful to see these same operators used in the context of LINQ query expressions. In that context, you can see how the Set operators can be used to analyze the results of queries to better understand the data that is returned.

You probably know that two similar collections are used to create lists. One is the generic List<T> collection, and the other is the old-style collection called ArrayList. We can use Set operators to help us better understand the difference between these two classes.

Here are two LINQ to Object providers that use Reflection-based queries to retrieve the methods from the List<int> class and the ArrayList class:

```
var queryList = from m in typeof(List<int>).GetMethods()
                where m.DeclaringType == typeof(List<int>)
                group m by m.Name into g
                select g.Key;
```

```
var queryArray = from m in typeof(ArrayList).GetMethods()
                 where m.DeclaringType == typeof(ArrayList)
                 group m by m.Name into g
                 select g.Key;
```

Here is code that shows the intersection of these two lists:

```
var listIntersect = queryList.Intersect(queryArray);
Console.WriteLine("Count: {0}", listIntersect.Count());

ShowList(listIntersect);
```

Alternatively, you could write the query like this:

```
var listIntersect = (from m in typeof(List<int>).GetMethods()
                     where m.DeclaringType == typeof(List<int>)
                     group m by m.Name into g
                     select g.Key).Intersect(
                         from m in typeof(ArrayList).GetMethods()
                         where m.DeclaringType == typeof(ArrayList)
                         group m by m.Name into g
                         select g.Key);
```

In either case, the following list would be displayed:

get_Capacity	GetRange
set_Capacity	IndexOf
get_Count	Insert
get_Item	InsertRange
set_Item	LastIndexOf
Add	Remove
AddRange	RemoveAt
BinarySearch	RemoveRange
Clear	Reverse
Contains	Sort
CopyTo	ToArray
GetEnumerator	

Here is how to see the items that the generic list supports that are not part of the old-style collection:

```
var listDifference = queryList.Except(listIntersect);
```

Here is the result of this query:

ConvertAll	FindLast
AsReadOnly	FindLastIndex
Exists	ForEach
Find	RemoveAll
FindAll	TrimExcess
FindIndex	TrueForAll

Aggregate Operators

The Aggregate operators allow you to perform simple mathematical operations over the elements in a sequence. Because they return the results of that operation, none of them is deferred. All the samples shown in this section are found in the AggregateOperators sample that accompanies this book. Table 6.6 lists the seven `Aggregate` operators.

TABLE 6.6   Aggregate Operators

Operator Name	Description
Count*	Counts the elements in a sequence
LongCount*	Counts the elements in a very, very long sequence
Sum*	Adds the elements in a sequence
Min*	Finds the smallest element in a sequence
Max*	Finds the largest element in a sequence
Average*	Finds the average value in a sequence
Aggregate*	Performs binary operations with the elements in a sequence

Except for the `Aggregate` operator, all these operators have a simple, obvious default use. Several of these operators, however, have overloads that need a few sentences of explanation. I will show you a simple example of using the operators' default behavior. Then we will look a bit deeper with a second example that shows how to use at least one of the overloads.

The Count and LongCount Operators

The Count and LongCount operators return the number of elements in a sequence. Classes such as List<T> that implement the ICollection<T> interface already track their count. This means that the Count operator can simply ask these objects for the count—an operation that executes very quickly.

The LongCount operator provides the same basic functionality but allows you to work with collections that contain more than the maximum value that an integer can handle. Calling Count on a List<long> returns quickly, because the list is tracking the total count, but calling Count on an IEnumerable<long> could become a very lengthy operation. In fact, working with any collection of that size is likely to be very cumbersome.

Listing 6.7 shows a simple example of using the Count operator. Long-Count works the same way.

LISTING 6.7   A Simple Example of Using the Count Operator

```
public void ShowCount()
{
    var list = Enumerable.Range(5, 12);
    Console.WriteLine(list.Count());
}
```

The overloads for Count and LongCount allow you to perform calculations to derive a count for a sequence. For instance, you can write code that counts the number of even numbers in a collection:

```
var list = Enumerable.Range(1, 25);

Console.WriteLine("Total Count: {0}, Count the even numbers: {1}",
    list.Count(),
    list.Count(n => n % 2 == 0));
```

Our list consists of the numbers between 1 and 25. We call Count once with the first version of the Count operator and get back the number 25.

The second overload of the Count operator takes a simple predicate that you can use for calculations of this type. The declaration looks like this:

```
public static int Count<TSource>(this IEnumerable<TSource> source,
    Func<TSource, bool> predicate);
```

The predicate takes an integer and returns a `bool` specifying whether a particular value from the list passes a test. In our case, we simply ask whether the number is even:

```
n % 2 == 0
```

This computation returns the values 2, 4, 6, and so on up to 24, for a total of 12 elements.

The Min and Max Operators

The `Min` and `Max` operators are equally simple, as you can see by glancing at Listings 6.8 and 6.9. The first shows the behavior of the first overload of `Min` and `Max`, and the second shows how to use one of the other overloads to pose more complex questions.

LISTING 6.8   A Simple Example of Using the `Min` and `Max` Operators to Determine the Highest and Lowest Values in a Sequence

```
public void ShowMinMax()
{
    var list = Enumerable.Range(6, 10);

    ShowList(list);

    Console.WriteLine("Min: {0}, Max: {1}", list.Min(), list.Max());
}
```

Our list consists of the numbers 6 through 15, so the code writes the values 6 and 15 to the console. If you pass in a null argument, you get an `ArgumentNullException`.

For the more complex examples, I need a few rows of simple data, which I provide in Listing 6.9.

LISTING 6.9   The Following `Item` Class and the `GetItems` Method Are Used by Most of the Examples in This Section

```
class Item
{
    public int Width { get; set; }
    public int Length { get; set; }
```

```
    public override string ToString()
    {
        return string.Format("Width: {0}, Length: {1}", Width, Length);
    }
}

private List<Item> GetItems()
{
    return new List<Item>
    {
        new Item { Length = 0, Width = 5 },
        new Item { Length = 1, Width = 6 },
        new Item { Length = 2, Width = 7 },
        new Item { Length = 3, Width = 8 },
        new Item { Length = 4, Width = 9 }
    };
}
```

The Item class has two simple properties called Length and Width. It also overrides the ToString method so that it can be displayed easily in a foreach loop.

It is easy to understand how to discover a default maximum value for a list of integers, but how can you find the maximum or minimum values for a list of Items? Do you choose the element with the greatest Length, the greatest Width, a combination of the two, or some other value? There is no set answer to this question. The user must make a custom decision based on the requirements of his or her application. You can define your solution by implementing a delegate used with an overload of the Min and Max operators:

```
public static int Max<TSource>(this IEnumerable<TSource> source,
    Func<TSource, int> selector);
```

This delegate is not a predicate. Instead, it asks you to return your custom Max value for an Item class. That is, it asks for the integer value that should be used to represent a given Item instance. The Min and Max overloads use this value to compute and return the minimum/maximum of a collection of Item instances. To see how this works, look at Listing 6.10.

LISTING 6.10　A Somewhat More Complex Use of `Min` and `Max`, Demonstrating How to Get Minimum and Maximum Values for Complex Types with Multiple Fields

```
List<Item> items = GetItems();

ShowList(items);

Console.WriteLine("MinItem: {0}, MaxItem: {1}",
    items.Min(x => x.Length + x.Width),
    items.Max(x => x.Length + x.Width));
```

The lambda passed to `Max` by our code looks like this: `x => x.Length + x.Width`. This delegate shows our definition of what we mean by max: the largest value returned by adding together the width and length of the `Item`.

■ Implementing `Max`

I mentioned earlier that many of these operators have very simple implementations. Without peeking at the real source code, it seems that `Max` might look like the code shown in Listing 6.11:

```
public static int
  Max<TSource>(this IEnumerable<TSource> source,
    Func<TSource, int> selector)
{
    int largest = int.MinValue;
    foreach (var item in source)
    {
        int nextItem = selector(item);
        if (nextItem > largest)
        {
            largest = nextItem;
        }
    }
    return largest;
}
```

The Average Operator

After you discover the pattern shown in our examination of the `Min` and `Max` operators, you find that it can be easily applied to most of the other Aggregate operators. Let's look at the `Average` operator, which returns the average value from an enumeration.

Obtaining the average for a range of numbers looks like this:

```
var list = Enumerable.Range(0, 5);
Console.WriteLine("Average: {0}", list.Average());
```

When run, this code tells us that the average of the numbers 0, 1, 2, 3, and 4 is the value 2.

When working with a collection of `Items`, we face the same problem we had with `Min` and `Max`: How do we discover the average value for a list of `Items` that define two properties called `Length` and `Width`? The answer, of course, is that we proceed just as we did with the `Min` and `Max` operators:

```
List<Item> items = GetItems();

double averageValue = items.Average(v => v.Length + v.Width);
Console.WriteLine("AverageValue: {0}", AverageValue);
```

The implementation of `Average` is probably similar to what is shown in the custom implementation for the `Max` operator found in the Note at the end of the preceding section. The code must iterate over the list, passing in each item to our lambda, which defines the value we want the `Average` operator to use in its calculations.

The Sum Operator

The `Sum` operator tallies the values in an enumeration. Consider the following simple example:

```
var list = Enumerable.Range(5, 3);
Console.WriteLine("List sum = {0}", list.Sum());
```

Our list consists of the numbers 5, 6, and 7. The `Sum` operator adds them together, producing the value 18.

When working with a list of `Items`, the `Sum` operator faces the same problem we saw with the `Min`, `Max`, and `Average` operators. It should come as no surprise that the solution is nearly identical:

```
var items = GetItems();
Console.WriteLine("Sum the lengths of the items: {0}",
  items.Sum(x => x.Length + x.Width));
```

This is the same pattern you saw with the `Average`, `Min`, and `Max` operators: We pass in a simple lambda to define what the `Sum` operator should use in its calculations. The result printed to the console is the value 10. If only the rest of our lives were this simple!

The Aggregate Operator

The `Aggregate` operator follows in the footsteps of the `Sum` operator but is more flexible. Rather than taking a simple delegate like the other operators in this series, it asks for one similar to the lambda we worked with in Chapter 3:

```
public static T Aggregate<T>(this IEnumerable<T> source,
    Func<T, T, T> func);
```

We know what do to with delegates that look like this. We could, for instance, revisit the lesson on lambdas in Chapter 3 and create a delegate that adds up a range of numbers:

```
var list = Enumerable.Range(5, 3);
Console.WriteLine("Aggregation: {0}", list.Aggregate((a, b) => (a + b)));
```

The `Aggregate` operator gets passed the numbers 5, 6, and 7. The first time the lambda is called, it gets passed 5 and 6 and adds them together to produce 11. The next time it is called, it is passed the accumulated result of the previous calculation plus the next number in the series: 11 + 7, which yields 18:

```
5+6 = 11
11 + 7 = 18
```

This overload of the `Aggregate` operator is more flexible than the `Sum` operator because it allows you to choose the operator. For instance, this code performs multiplication, yielding the value 210:

```
list.Aggregate((a, b) => (a * b))
```

The Aggregate Corner Cases

Everyone asks two questions about the Aggregate operator. I'll answer them here. If it is passed a list with one item, it returns that item. If it is passed a list with zero items, it throws an InvalidOperationException.

The second and perhaps most commonly used overload of the Aggregate operator allows you to seed the calculations it performs with an accumulator:

```
public static TAccumulate Aggregate<TSource, TAccumulate>(
    this IEnumerable<TSource> source, TAccumulate seed,
    Func<TAccumulate, TSource, TAccumulate> func);
```

This is essentially the same operator as shown in the previous example, but now you can decide the seed for the value that will be accumulated:

```
Console.WriteLine("Aggregation: {0}",
    list.Aggregate(0, (a, b) => (a + b)));
```

If we pass in a list with one item—say, the number 5—the first time the lambda is called, it is passed the seed plus the sole item in the list:

```
(0, 5) => (0 + 5)
```

The result, of course, is the number 5. Suppose we pass in an accumulator of 0 plus the numbers 5, 6, and 7:

```
var list = Enumerable.Range(5, 3);
Console.WriteLine("Aggregation: {0}", list.Aggregate(0, (a, b) =>
                                                        (a + b)));
```

In this case we would step through the following sequence:

```
0 + 5 = 5
5 + 6 = 11
11 + 7 = 18
```

Again, we are doing essentially what we did with the Sum operator.

If you pass in a different seed, you get a different result:

```
Console.WriteLine("Aggregation: {0}",
    list.Aggregate(3, (a, b) => (a + b)));
```

With a seed of 3, we get this:

```
 3 + 5 = 8
 8 + 6 = 14
14 + 7 = 21
```

If we use the multiplication operation, we should avoid passing in a seed of 0:

```
Console.WriteLine("Aggregation: {0}",
    list.Aggregate(1, (a, b) => (a * b)));
```

In this case the series looks like this:

```
 1 * 5 = 5
 5 * 6 = 30
30 * 7 = 210
```

If we passed in an accumulator of 0, we'd end up with the following series of operations:

```
0 * 5 = 0
0 * 6 = 0
0 * 7 = 0
```

In what I sometimes suspect might have been an excess of good spirits, the team added one final overload to the Aggregate operator:

```
public static TResult Aggregate<TSource, TAccumulate, TResult>(
    this IEnumerable<TSource> source, TAccumulate seed,
    Func<TAccumulate, TSource, TAccumulate> func,
    Func<TAccumulate, TResult> resultSelector);
```

This overload is identical to the previous one, but you are given one more delegate that you can use to transform the result of your aggregation. For instance, consider this use of the Aggregate operator:

```
Console.WriteLine("Aggregation: {0}",
    list.Aggregate(0, (a, b) => (a + b),
    (a) => (string.Format("{0:C}", a))));
```

Notice that the first two-thirds of this call mirror what we did earlier; only the third parameter is new.

Suppose we pass in a sequence with the values 5, 6, and 7. As we've already seen, the process begins by performing the following series of operations:

```
0 + 5 = 5
5 + 6 = 11
11 + 7 = 18
```

Now the `Aggregate` operator passes this result to our second lambda, which uses the string's `Format` method to transform it into a string in currency format:

```
$18.00
```

Like nearly everything in LINQ, this seems terribly complicated at first, only to end up being reasonably simple. These kinds of simple operations, however, provide us with the building blocks from which we can safely create complex programs. This is what we mean when we apply the word "elegant" to a technology.

Ordering Operators

You have already seen several examples of the `OrderBy` operator. I will, however, quickly show examples of `OrderByDescending` and `ThenBy`. In this section I also include the related `Reverse` operator. Table 6.7 lists the Ordering operators, all of which are deferred.

TABLE 6.7   Ordering Operators

Operator Name	Description
OrderBy	Sorts the elements in a selection
OrderByDescending	Sorts the elements in a selection in descending order
ThenBy	Orders by one criteria and then a second criteria
Reverse	Reverses the order of items in a sequence

In this section I'll run queries against one of the result sets from the section on joins in the preceding chapter. To keep things as simple as possible, I will embody the result of the query in a new class, as shown in Listing 6.11.

LISTING 6.11   This Code, and All the Sample Code from This Section, Is Found in the OrderingOperators Sample That Accompanies This Book

```
class Musician
{
    public int OrderId { get; set; }
    public string Name { get; set; }
    public string Instrument { get; set; }

    public override string ToString()
    {
        return string.Format("OrderId = {0}, Name = {1},
                            Instrument = {2}",
            OrderId, Name, Instrument);
    }

    public static List<Musician> GetList()
    {
        return new List<Musician>
        {
            new Musician { OrderId = 1, Name = "Sonny Rollings",
                Instrument = "Tenor Saxophone" },
            new Musician { OrderId = 2, Name = "Miles Davis",
                Instrument = "Trumpet" },
            new Musician { OrderId = 6, Name = "Miles Davis",
                Instrument = "Keyboard" },
            new Musician { OrderId = 4, Name = "John Coltrane",
                Instrument = "Tenor Saxophone" },
            new Musician { OrderId = 3, Name = "John Coltrane",
                Instrument = "Soprano Saxophone" },
            new Musician { OrderId = 5, Name = "Charlie Parker",
                Instrument = "Tenor Saxophone" }
        };
    }
}
```

OrderBy

Here is the simplest possible query we can run against the sequence of Musician objects shown in Listing 6.11:

```
var query = from m in list
            select m;
```

When passed to ShowList, the result of this query simply echoes our sequence to the console:

```
Name = Sonny Rollings, Instrument = Tenor Saxophone
Name = Miles Davis, Instrument = Trumpet
Name = Miles Davis, Instrument = Keyboard
Name = John Coltrane, Instrument = Tenor Saxophone
Name = John Coltrane, Instrument = Soprano Saxophone
Name = Charlie Parker, Instrument = Tenor Saxophone
```

We can order the sequence alphabetically by writing this code:

```
var query2 = from m in list
             orderby m.Name
             select m;
```

If run through the ShowList method, the output looks like this:

```
Name = Charlie Parker, Instrument = Tenor Saxophone
Name = John Coltrane, Instrument = Tenor Saxophone
Name = John Coltrane, Instrument = Soprano Saxophone
Name = Miles Davis, Instrument = Trumpet
Name = Miles Davis, Instrument = Keyboard
Name = Sonny Rollings, Instrument = Tenor Saxophone
```

OrderByDescending

If we use the descending keyword, the query and output are as shown in Listings 6.12 and 6.13.

LISTING 6.12   Using the Keyword descending in a Query

```
var query2 = from m in list
             orderby m.Name descending
             select m;
```

LISTING 6.13   The Output from the Query Shown in Listing 6.12

```
Name = Sonny Rollings, Instrument = Tenor Saxophone
Name = Miles Davis, Instrument = Trumpet
Name = Miles Davis, Instrument = Keyboard
Name = John Coltrane, Instrument = Tenor Saxophone
Name = John Coltrane, Instrument = Soprano Saxophone
Name = Charlie Parker, Instrument = Tenor Saxophone
```

When translated into query method syntax, the query shown in Listing 6.12 looks like this:

```
var query2 = list.OrderByDescending(m => m.Name);
```

The output from this query is identical to that shown in Listing 6.13.

ThenBy

In the queries shown in the previous two sections, we sorted on the Name field but ignored the Instrument field. You can, in fact, sort on multiple fields, or multiple keys, at the same time. Here is how it looks:

```
var query4 = from m in list
             orderby m.Name, m.Instrument
             select m;
```

The output shown after the query is enumerated with a foreach loop reveals that the artists are listed alphabetically, and the instruments played by Trane and Miles are also listed alphabetically:

```
Name = Charlie Parker, Instrument = Tenor Saxophone
Name = John Coltrane, Instrument = Soprano Saxophone
Name = John Coltrane, Instrument = Tenor Saxophone
Name = Miles Davis, Instrument = Keyboard
Name = Miles Davis, Instrument = Trumpet
Name = Sonny Rollins, Instrument = Tenor Saxophone
```

You may have noticed that this section of the text is titled ThenBy. The query I've shown, however, makes no mention of that word. The operator ThenBy becomes manifest only when you use method syntax rather than query expressions. When translated into method syntax, the query looks like this:

```
var query4a = list.OrderBy(m => m.Name).ThenBy(m => m.Instrument);
```

Now you can see the ThenBy operator! The output from this query is identical to that shown for the first query in this section.

The following syntax is also valid:

```
var query6 = from m in list
             orderby m.Instrument descending, m.Name descending
             select m;
```

You can also write code that looks like this, but it does not produce the same output as that derived from the previous query:

```
var query5 = from m in list
             orderby m.Instrument descending
             orderby m.Name descending
             select m;
```

I'll leave it up to you to open the OrderingOperators sample program that accompanies this book and experiment with these various combinations to see exactly how they work.

Reverse

Here is a simple example of how to use the Reverse operator:

```
List<int> list = new List<int> { 1, 2, 3 };

list.Reverse();

foreach (var item in list)
{
    Console.WriteLine(item);
}
```

This code prints out the values 3, 2, 1.

Conversion Operators

LINQ provides several Conversion operators that help you transform one list type into another. In this chapter I have shown that you can perform many powerful operations using the operators implemented on `IEnumerable<T>`. However, there will be times when you will want to transform the results of a query into a more familiar collection type, or when you will want to transform a type that does not support `IEnumerable<T>` into a type that you can use in a LINQ query. These operators are designed to help you achieve that goal. The Conversion operators are shown in Table 6.8.

TABLE 6.8 Conversion Operators

Operator Name	Description
AsEnumerable	Converts an IQueryable<T> to IEnumerable<T>
ToArray*	Converts an IEnumerable<T> into an Array
ToList*	Converts an IEnumerable<T> into a List<T>
ToDictionary*	Converts an IEnumerable<T> into a Dictionary
ToLookup*	Converts an IEnumerable<T> into an ILookup
OfType	Converts only those items in a list that are of a particular type
Cast	Provides LINQ with a way to cast from one type to another

The ToArray, ToList, ToDictionary, and ToLookup operators are not deferred. Like the element operators, they force immediate execution of a query.

ToList

By default, a typical LINQ query returns a computation on an IEnumerable<T>:

```
public IEnumerable<Roman> GetWives()
{
  var women = from r in romans
              where r.Gender == 'f'
              select r;

  return women;
}
```

You may have code that works with the common List<T> type, or you may want to call methods such as Add, which are unavailable on IEnumerable<T>. To convert the results of your query to a List<T>, just write this code:

```
public List<Roman> CreateList(char gender)
{
  return (from r in romans
```

```
            where r.Gender == gender
            select r).ToList();
}
```

The `List<T>` type is very commonly used by C# programmers, so there will obviously be many occasions when developers choose to work with that type rather than `IEnumerable<T>`. However, it also forces the execution of the query. In other words, calling `ToList` puts an end to deferred execution and all the other benefits that come with functional or declarative code. In saying this, I do not mean to discourage you from using the very useful `ToList` operator. I only ask that you be aware of the consequences of what you are doing.

Remember that you can always use Visual Studio's QuickInfo to retrieve the type that a query returns. For instance, in Figure 6.5 you can see that this call to `ToList` creates a `List<Roman>`.

FIGURE 6.5 Using QuickInfo to see the type returned by a call to the `ToList()` operator.

As mentioned earlier, `IEnumerable<T>`, sans its LINQ operators, is a very simple type:

```
public interface IEnumerable<T> : IEnumerable
{
    IEnumerator<T> GetEnumerator();
}
```

You cannot, for instance, `Add` an item to an item of type `IEnumerable<T>`:

```
IEnumerable<Int> list = from n in Enumerable.Range(1, 3)
                        where n < 3
                        select n;
list.Add(3); // Will not compile: member does not exist.
```

The following code, however, does compile, and it behaves as expected:

```
List<int> list = (from n in Enumerable.Range(1, 3)
                  where n < 3
                  select n).ToList();

list.Add(4);

ShowList(list);
```

ToArray

ToArray() can convert a sequence into an array, as shown in Listing 6.14. Thus, you can quickly convert the results of a LINQ query into an array of string or an array of Integer.

LISTING 6.14　You Can Use the ToArray() Method to Convert a Sequence—an IEnumerable<T>—into a More Traditional Array

```
List<int> list = new List<int> { 1, 2, 3 };

int[] data = (from num in list
              where num < 3
              select num).ToArray();

foreach (var item in data)
{
    Console.WriteLine(item);
}
```

Here we return not a computation, but an array of integers. Note that this forces execution of the query, so the query is no longer deferred.

OfType

Here is the OfType<T> operator, which converts only members of a collection that are of a specified type:

```
ArrayList list = new ArrayList { 1, "That", 2, "This" };

IEnumerable<string> elist = list.OfType<string>();

var query = from num in elist
            select num;
```

The output from this query looks like this:

```
That
This
```

Notice that the integers in the `ArrayList` are both ignored, and that only the strings are retrieved. This is because we asked explicitly for the members of the list that are "of type" string:

```
list.OfType<string>();
```

The point here is that an `ArrayList` is not type-safe, because it is not a generic collection. As a result, you can never completely trust that you know what type is in an `ArrayList`. This operator can help relieve your anxiety by ensuring that you will not end up with a runtime exception when you stumble across an unexpected type that was infesting an `ArrayList`.

ToDictionary

Here is an example of how to use the `ToDictionary` operator:

```
public void ToDictionary()
{
   var query = from r in romans
               select new { r.Name, r.Gender, r.Id };

   var romanDictionary = query.ToDictionary(r => r.Name);

   Console.WriteLine(romanDictionary["Augustus"]);
   Console.WriteLine(romanDictionary["Livia Drusilla"]);
}
```

This code produces the following output:

```
{ Name = Augustus, Gender = m, Id = 0 }
{ Name = Livia Drusilla, Gender = f, Id = 7 }
```

As you can see, the `ToDictionary()` operator converts the results of a LINQ query into a generic dictionary. `ToDictionary` takes as its sole argument a lambda expression that defines what field you want to use as the `Key` for the dictionary.

■ **Anonymous Types Usually have a Limited Scope**

The dictionary shown here uses the anonymous type returned from the original LINQ query shown in the first two lines of our method. This limits your options, because you can't declare a dictionary of type `Dictionary<MyAnonymousType>`, so you can't pass it outside the scope of this method. You could get around this problem by altering the code to return a `Dictionary<Roman>` or `Dictionary<SomeCustomType>` and then creating a `ToString` method for whichever type you used. An example of this is shown in the RomanOperators program that comes with this book.

Conversion Between IEnumerable and IQueryable

Although it is defined in the `Queryable` class, and not in `Enumerable`, this discussion would be incomplete without mentioning the `AsQueryable` operator and its companion, the `AsEnumerable` operator. `AsEnumerable` is defined with the other LINQ to Object operators in the `Enumerable` class. Here is a simple example, showing how it works:

```
var query = from r in romans
            where r.Gender == 'm'
            select r;

var queriable = query.AsQueryable();

Console.WriteLine(queriable.Expression.NodeType);

var query1 = queriable.AsEnumerable();

ShowList(query1);
```

The call to `AsQueryable` converts an `IEnumerable<T>` into an `IQueryable<T>`. As mentioned earlier, this is most often helpful when you want to create a LINQ provider. You can read about working examples of third-party providers that ship with source in Chapter 17, "LINQ Everywhere."

The sample code shown here demonstrates how to convert a variable of type `IQueryable<T>` into an `IEnumerable<T>`. Because `IQueryable<T>` implements the `IEnumerable<T>` interface, you probably won't often need to explicitly call this operator, but I mention it here for the sake of completeness.

Summary

In this chapter you have learned about the LINQ query operators. You have had a look at nearly all the operators, and you should now have a secure foothold in this landscape that will allow you to keep your balance in any situation.

This is the end of the introductory part of this book. If you understand the material that has been presented so far, you can consider yourself well established as an intermediate-level LINQ developer. The next chapter begins exploring LINQ to SQL, an important subject, and one that many developers will use every day in their work.

When thinking back on the material that has been covered, it is important to begin to understand how this style of programming differs from the traditional imperative style that has dominated programming for the last 20 or 30 years. The declarative style of programming offers interesting and exciting challenges for developers willing to explore this fascinating technology.

For additional information on the material covered in this chapter, see the page in the online help called "The .NET Standard Query Operators" at http://msdn.microsoft.com/en-us/library/bb394939.aspx. It is written by Anders Hejlsberg and Mads Torgersen.

▌7 ▪

A Quick Tour of LINQ to SQL

R ELATIONAL DATABASES contain important data that developers want to query and retrieve in their programs. LINQ to SQL lets developers access relational data as strongly typed objects by translating LINQ to SQL. It also provides a simple API to save to the database all the changes made to an object graph. Both query and changes are implemented by translating LINQ and API calls to SQL commands. Hence, users get the productivity of LINQ and the efficiency of the database query processor.

LINQ to SQL was created to bridge the differences between relational data and CLR objects. SQL is a rich query language, but it is not well integrated with programming languages such as C# and VB.NET. As a result, database developers have always struggled with the "impedance mismatch" between the relational data in their databases and the objects used in their programs running on the .NET framework.

An obvious manifestation of the mismatch is found when developers use string literals to embed SQL in their C# code. The resulting queries are opaque to the compiler. As a result, they are not type-checked and cannot benefit from IntelliSense.

Queries in strings are a serious problem, but it is only one manifestation of a deeper problem. The perennial difference between SQL and objects appears in many other forms:

* Relational tuples or records versus strongly typed objects
* Value-based identity versus reference-based identity
* Foreign key values versus object references
* Tabular results versus object graphs

Developers often have to think about the differences and write plumbing code to integrate relational data into their programs.

Before LINQ, several Object Relational Mapping (ORM) APIs helped transform the rows of data returned from a SQL query into objects and add them to graphs that could be consumed by C# developers. These tools managed identity when the user edited the data. They were smart enough to turn the objects back into rows when it was time to save the changes to the database. Despite their power, these tools continued to rely on string-based or API-based queries that were not fully integrated with the programming language. They also relied on awkward APIs that were poorly integrated with the programming language.

LINQ provides a much simpler way to integrate relational queries with the rest of the program. LINQ to SQL implements the LINQ standard query pattern and addresses the differences just mentioned. As a result, developers get a type-safe, IntelliSense-aware query language and a programming model for relational data that is fully integrated with their programming language.

LINQ to SQL is designed to be nonintrusive. Classes mapped to relational data can be defined just like normal classes. Developers need only decorate them with simple attributes to specify how properties correspond to columns. It is not even necessary to do this by hand. A design-time tool is provided to automate translating preexisting relational database schemas into object definitions. Together, the runtime infrastructure and design-time tools significantly reduce the workload for the database application developer.

Although this chapter uses C# to illustrate concepts and usage patterns, LINQ to SQL is language-agnostic. It can be used in any managed language that supports LINQ. In .NET Framework 3.5, similar code can be written in VB.NET. Other languages are also adding LINQ support and will be able to enable the use of LINQ to SQL.

Let's look at the key components of a program that uses LINQ to SQL to access relational data. We will begin by exploring a simple class that maps to a table.

Mapping Classes to Tables

LINQ to SQL needs to know how your class maps to a database table. Then you can use the LINQ to SQL API—primarily through a class called `Data-Context`—to query for objects of a mapped class and save the changes. We'll look at a mapped class and the `DataContext` class next.

Creating Entity Classes

The following code fragment shows a simple class, `Customer`, that is mapped to the Customers table in the Northwind sample database. The namespaces added with the `using` declarations contain the LINQ to SQL API used for data access and mapping, respectively.

```
using System.Data.Linq;
using System.Data.Linq.Mapping;

[Table(Name="Customers")]
public class Customer
{
    [Column(IsPrimaryKey=true)]
    public string CustomerID;

    [Column]
    public string City;
}
```

A class is mapped to a table by adding the `Table` attribute. The `Table` attribute has a `Name` property that specifies the name of the database table. If no `Name` property is supplied, the database table name is assumed to be the same name as the class. Instances of classes declared with the `Table` attribute are considered persistent and are known as *entities*; the classes themselves are called *entity classes*.

In addition to mapping classes to tables, each field or property must be mapped to a database column. This can be done by using the `Column` attribute. If you omit this attribute when declaring a field of your class, this class member is assumed to be unmapped or nonpersistent. This allows you to choose which members are persistent and augment the data from the database with additional, nonpersistent members. In the preceding class declaration, both of the fields of the `Customer` class are mapped to the corresponding columns in the Customers table.

The `Column` attribute has a variety of properties you can use to customize the exact mapping between fields and the database's columns. One property of note is the `IsPrimaryKey` property. It indicates that the database column is a member of the table's primary key.

As with the `Table` attribute, you need to supply information in the `Column` attribute only if it differs from what can be deduced from your field or property declaration. In this example, the `Id` property on the `Column` attribute conveys that the `CustomerID` field is part of the table's primary key. Note that you don't have to specify the exact name or type if the defaults work.

The DataContext

The `DataContext` is the main conduit by which you retrieve objects from the database and submit changes back to the database. It encapsulates an ADO.NET `Connection` property that is initialized with an instance of a connection object or a connection string that you supply in the constructor. You can use the `DataContext` to help retrieve customer objects by writing the following code:

```
// DataContext takes a connection string
DataContext db = new DataContext("c:\\northwind\\northwnd.mdf");

// Get a typed table to run queries
Table<Customer> Customers = db.GetTable<Customer>();

// Query for customers from London
IQueryable<Customer> CustomerQuery = from c in Customers
                                     where c.City == "London"
                                     select c;
```

```
foreach (var cust in CustomerQuery)
   Console.WriteLine("id = {0}, City = {1}", cust.CustomerID, cust.City);
```

This code creates an instance of the `DataContext` and then retrieves a set of `Customer` objects corresponding to rows where the `City` field is equal to `London`. The results bring back information for six customers:

```
id = AROUT, City = London
id = BSBEV, City = London
id = CONSH, City = London
id = EASTC, City = London
id = NORTS, City = London
id = SEVES, City = London
```

Looking more closely at this code, you can see that a database table is represented as a property of type `Table<T>`, accessible via the `GetTable()` method using its entity class `T` to identify it:

```
Table<Customer> Customers = db.GetTable<Customer>();
```

`Table<T>` is a LINQ to SQL class that implements the key LINQ interface—`IQueryable<T>`. That is how the LINQ query for customers from London is implemented by LINQ to SQL.

Rather than use this code in the midst of your query, it is recommended that you declare a strongly typed `DataContext` instead of relying on the basic `DataContext` class and the `GetTable()` method. A strongly typed `Data Context` declares all `Table` properties as members.

```
public partial class NorthwindDataContext : DataContext
{
    public Table<Customer> Customers;

    public NorthwindDataContext(string connection): base(connection) {}
}
```

The query for customers from London can then be expressed more simply:

```
NorthwindDataContext db = new
    NorthwindDataContext("c:\\northwind\\northwnd.mdf");

IQueryable<Customer> CustomerQuery = from c in db.Customers
                                     where c.City == "London"
                                     select c;
```

A derived class such as `NorthwindDataContext` provides a strongly typed view of your database. Henceforth, we will use the strongly typed `NorthwindDataContext` class instead of the base `DataContext` class. Also, we will use a more terse way to declare the query variable—var, where the return type is obvious from the query expression. See the section "Type Inference" in Chapter 4, "C# 3.0 Technical Overview," for more details.

Working with Relationships

Objects are not islands. They are connected to other objects through relationships. A customer may have orders, an order may have order details, an order detail may refer to a product that is being ordered, and so on. Relationships in relational databases typically are modeled as foreign key values referring to primary keys in other tables. To navigate between them, you must explicitly bring the two tables together using a relational join operation. Objects, on the other hand, refer to each other using property references or collections of references navigated using "dot" notation. Obviously, dotting is simpler than joining, because you don't need to recall the explicit join condition each time you navigate. Defining relationship properties allows you to navigate using the dot, so you don't have to use the explicit join operator available in LINQ for the common cases.

Defining Relationships

For data relationships that will remain constant, it becomes convenient to encode them as property references in your entity class. You can apply an `Association` attribute to a member used to represent such a relationship. An *association relationship* frequently consists of a foreign key and a primary key. Here is how to declare a class that captures the association between the Customers table and the Orders table:

```
[Table(Name="Customers")]
public class Customer
{
    [Column(IsPrimaryKey=true)]
    public string CustomerID;
    ...
    private EntitySet<Order> _Orders;
```

```
[Association(Storage="_Orders", OtherKey="CustomerID")]
public EntitySet<Order> Orders {
   get { return this._Orders; }
   set { this._Orders.Assign(value); }
}
}
```

The `Customer` class now has a property that declares the relationship between customers and their orders. The `Orders` property is of type `EntitySet` because the relationship is one-to-many—there may be many orders for a customer. We use the `OtherKey` property in the `Association` attribute to describe the property in the related class that needs to be matched to set up the association—in this case, the `CustomerID` member in the `Order` class. We have omitted the `ThisKey` property, which lists the key members on this side of the relationship. By default, it is inferred to be the primary key for the containing type—`Customer.CustomerID` in this case.

Notice how this is reversed in the definition for the `Order` class:

```
[Table(Name="Orders")]
public class Order
{
   [Column(IsPrimaryKey=true)]
   public int OrderID;
   [Column]
   public string CustomerID;
   private EntityRef<Customer> _Customer;
   [Association(Storage="_Customer", ThisKey="CustomerID")]
   public Customer Customer {
      get { return this._Customer.Entity; }
      set { this._Customer.Entity = value; }
   }
}
```

The `Order` class uses the `EntityRef` type to describe the relationship back to the customer. The `Association` attribute for the `Customer` property specifies the `ThisKey` property to relate `Order` to its `Customer`. In the class mapped to table with the foreign key, `ThisKey` needs to be specified.

The `Storage` property tells which private member is used to hold the property's value. This allows LINQ to SQL to bypass your public property accessors. This is useful if you want LINQ to SQL to avoid any custom business logic written into your accessors. If the storage property is not specified, the public accessors are used instead. You may use the `Storage` property with `Column` attributes as well.

As soon as you start introducing relationships into your entity classes, the amount of code you need to write grows as you introduce support for notifications and graph consistency. For instance, you might want to add event handlers that are fired when properties are accessed. This kind of work can become quite tedious if you have many fields in your tables. Fortunately, easy-to-use tools can be used to generate all the necessary definitions as partial classes, allowing you to use a mix of generated code and custom business logic. In the rest of this chapter, we assume that a tool has been used to generate a complete Northwind `DataContext` and all entity classes. Two commonly used tools called the Object Relational Designer and SqlMetal are described later in this chapter.

Querying Across Relationships

Now that an association has been defined between the `Customer` and `Order` classes, you can use it when you write queries. To do so, simply refer to the relationship properties defined in your class. In this case, `var` is not just a matter of terseness or convenience; the result is an anonymous type. Hence, no type name can be used in the declaration.

```
var CustomerQuery = from c in db.Customers
                    from o in c.Orders
                    where c.City == "London"
                    select new { c.CustomerID, o.OrderID };
```

This query uses the `Orders` property to form the cross-product between customers and their orders, producing a new sequence of `Customer` and `Order` pairs. The first two results are shown here:

```
CustomerID=AROUT        OrderID=10355
CustomerID=AROUT        OrderID=10383
...
```

It is also possible to do the reverse:

```
var CustomerQuery = from o in db.Orders
                    where o.Customer.City == "London"
                    select new { o.Customer.CustomerID, o  .OrderID };
```

In this example, the orders are queried, and the `Customer` relationship is used to access and filter on the properties of the associated `Customer` object. The results are the same as before.

Modifying and Saving Entities

Querying is only one use of relational data. Applications often need to create new relational data, modify existing data, and possibly delete some data too. LINQ to SQL is designed to offer maximum flexibility in manipulating and persisting changes made to your in-memory objects. As soon as entity objects are available, either by retrieving them through a query or constructing them anew, you may manipulate them as normal objects in your application, changing their values or adding them to and removing them from collections as you desire. `DataContext` tracks all your changes and is ready to transmit them back to the database as soon as you are done.

The following example uses the `Customer` and `Order` classes generated by a tool from the metadata of the entire Northwind sample database. To focus on the code for modifying entities, the class definitions are not shown. In the example, two customers are retrieved—one for update and one for deletion. A new order is created for insertion. All the operations are performed on the objects and collections in memory. The changes take effect in the database only when `SubmitChanges()` is called.

Before running the following code, make a copy of the sample Northwind database—in this case, the northwnd.mdf file. This will allow you to play with the code and make changes without altering the original sample database.

```
NorthwindDataContext db = new
NorthwindDataContext("c:\\northwind\\northwnd.mdf");

// Query for a specific customer
string id = "ALFKI";
var cust = db.Customers.Single(c => c.CustomerID == id);

// Change the name of the contact
cust.ContactName = "New Contact";
```

```
// Delete an existing Customer
string id2 = "FISSA";
var cust2 = db.Customers.Single(c => c.CustomerID == id2);
db.Customers.DeleteOnSubmit(cust2);

// Create and add a new Order to Orders collection
// LINQ to SQL discovers the new object and infers an insert
Order ord = new Order { OrderDate = DateTime.Now };
cust.Orders.Add(ord);

// Ask the DataContext to save all the changes
db.SubmitChanges();
```

When `SubmitChanges()` is called, LINQ to SQL automatically generates and executes SQL commands in order to transmit the changes back to the database. It is also possible to override this behavior with custom logic that can optionally call a stored procedure, as described in Chapter 10.

This completes the lifecycle of objects: creating, reading (querying), updating, and deleting. Collectively these operations are often known by the acronym CRUD. Through language integrated queries and simple API, LINQ to SQL provides CRUD operation support for relational data. This support uses the mapping between classes and tables to generate the necessary SQL to execute the operations in the database. We've looked at how this mapping can be added to code using attributes. The next section shows how the mapping can be created using a visual designer in Visual Studio.

Using the Graphical Designer for Mapping

Visual Studio 2008 includes a graphical designer, called the Object Relational Designer, that helps you map tables to classes. The following steps and associated figures outline how you can build a mapping that can be used with the queries in the previous sections:

1. **Preparation**: Using the View menu in Visual Studio, bring up Server Explorer, as shown in Figure 7.1, and Solution Explorer. In the Server Explorer pane, make sure that you can view the tables in your database. Appendix A contains tips for connecting to a database.

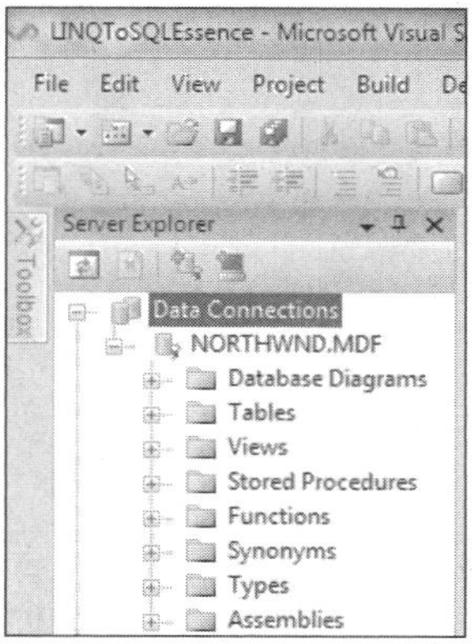

FIGURE 7.1   Server Explorer showing the Northwind database.

2. **Adding a designer file (dbml)**: Right-click the project in Solution
Explorer and select Add, New Item, as shown in Figure 7.2. In the
Add New Item window, select Data in the Categories pane. In the
Templates pane, select LINQ to SQL Classes. Type in the appropriate
name (Northwind.dbml, as shown in Figure 7.3) and click Add. A
blank design surface appears for creating classes. The design surface
corresponds to a dbml file in Solution Explorer. The file captures the
subset of databases you have dragged and dropped on the design
surface and your customizations of the classes and mapping.

3. **Mapping tables**: Drag and drop tables from Server Explorer onto
the design surface. As a table is dropped onto the surface, the
designer creates a class corresponding to it, and the class is visible
on the design surface. You can edit the name and type of the class
members using the property grid. If a newly dropped table is related
to one of the previously dropped tables, the designer automatically
creates a relationship, as shown in Figure 7.4. For example, when the
Customers and Orders tables from the Northwind database are
dragged and dropped, a relationship between the corresponding
generated `Customer` and `Order` classes is inferred.

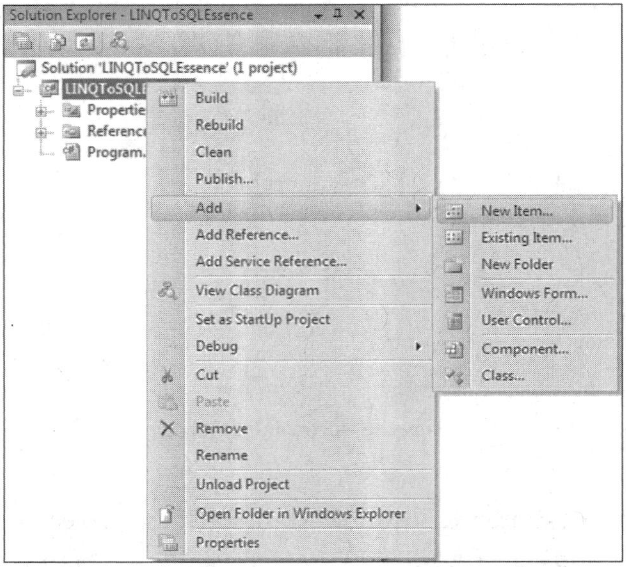

FIGURE 7.2   Adding a new item to the project.

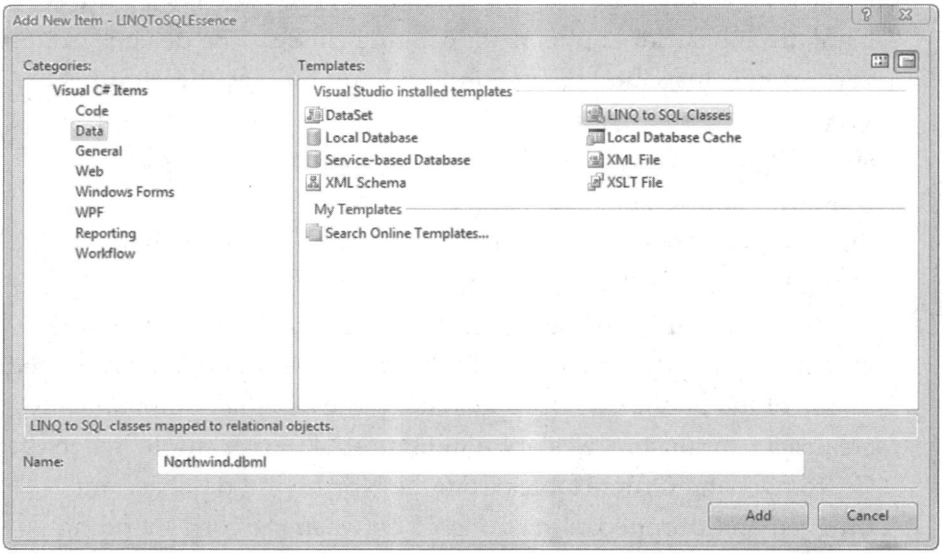

FIGURE 7.3   Adding a dbml file to create a mapping.

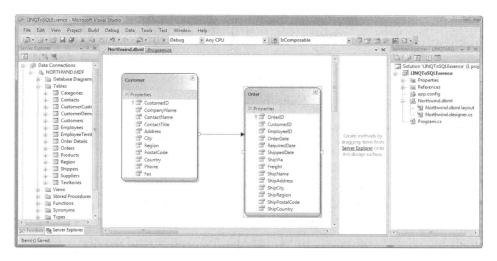

FIGURE 7.4 Classes generated from tables.

4. **Generating classes**: Save the file to trigger generation of C# (or VB.NET) code. The generated file appears in Solution Explorer with a designer.cs extension—Northwind.designer.cs in Figure 7.4. Now the classes are ready for use. We will cover the details of the generated code in the following chapters.

5. **Using the generated code**: The generated code can be used in lieu of the hand-crafted classes `NorthwindDataContext`, `Customer`, and `Order` to run the queries previously defined.

Using the Command-Line Tool for Mapping

The graphical designer provides an interactive way to customize mapping. However, sometimes it is more convenient to have a command-line tool for doing quick generation of classes and mapping. This allows additional options to be used for customization in an automated build process. It also provides a quicker way to generate an object model for an entire database.

The Windows SDK Version 6.0 includes a command-line tool, Sql-Metal.exe, that can be pointed at a database for quick generation of a set of

mapped classes. This tool can be found in the directory Program Files\
Microsoft SDKs\Windows\V6.0A\Bin\. The following line shows a sample usage for generating C# classes from the Northwind database using
SQL Server 2008 Express. The /? switch lists all the options that the tool
supports; we will not cover them in depth here.

```
SqlMetal /server:.\sqlexpress /database:northwind /code:northwind.cs
```

The SqlMetal tool can also be used in two stages—extracting the database schema to produce an intermediate dbml file, and generating code
from the dbml file. SqlMetal and the designer share a common code generator that consumes a dbml file and produces C# or VB.NET classes with
mapping. Hence, the code and mapping produced by the two tools are consistent. So, you can easily use a designer-generated dbml file to produce
code with SqlMetal.

SqlMetal also allows you to create an external XML mapping file instead
of mapping attributes. This capability currently is unavailable in the
designer. The following is an example of how you can create a dbml file for
further manipulation and then create an external mapping file for Northwind. In this case, the classes in the generated file northwind.cs do not contain mapping attributes; the mapping in northwind.xml can be
manipulated separately.

```
SqlMetal /server:.\sqlexpress /database:northwind /dbml:northwind.dbml
--- dbml file can be changed with another tool or XML editor as needed ---
SqlMetal /code:nothwind.cs /map:northwind.xml northwind.dbml
```

The details of an external mapping file and its usage are discussed
futher in Chapter 11.

Summary

This chapter has offered a quick tour of basic LINQ to SQL features. In a
nutshell, LINQ to SQL lets you query relational data as objects using the
LINQ query pattern. It provides a simple but expressive API to save the
changed objects. It works with entity classes mapped to tables and relationships between classes mapped to foreign keys in the database. You can

write your own classes and map them or use a convenient graphical designer or a command-line tool to generate mapped classes from an existing database. Next we'll cover the essential LINQ to SQL concepts and features in greater depth, starting with the reading of objects.

8

Reading Objects with LINQ to SQL

L ET'S EXPAND OUR quick tour to learn further details of querying and retrieving objects using LINQ to SQL. LINQ to SQL implements the standard query operators described in Chapter 5, "Writing Query Expressions," to retrieve objects from a relational database. It uses the mapping of classes to tables to translate LINQ queries to SQL commands and then materializes objects from the rows returned. The objects can be related to each other in a graph of objects that is managed by LINQ to SQL on your behalf.

Using LINQ and Databases

Relational databases contain a large amount of valuable data that applications want to use. An application written in a language such as C# can significantly benefit from querying and transforming this data using the power of LINQ. A straightforward but naive way of utilizing the LINQ capabilities would be to bring all the rows from one or more tables in memory as objects and then apply standard query operators to get exactly the objects you want. This would be very inefficient for two reasons: First, a large amount of data that is not a part of the query result may have to be brought from the database, wasting bandwidth, memory, and processing. Second, it would not utilize the power of the relational database query processor to optimize queries.

Relational databases such as Microsoft SQL Server provide very powerful query processors. The query processor includes a sophisticated optimizer that can find an efficient execution plan for complex queries and large amounts of data using indexes, statistics, and advanced algorithms. However, it is designed for processing SQL, which is all about tables and columns. If we want to get objects by querying this data using LINQ, we need to find a way to translate LINQ to SQL. As the name suggests, that is what LINQ to SQL is designed for. It provides the richness of LINQ while executing queries using the power of relational databases.

Translating LINQ to SQL

The magic of translating LINQ to SQL involves a beautiful dance between the C# compiler and the LINQ to SQL runtime that is a part of the .NET framework. The C# compiler translates LINQ queries to expression trees at compile time. Recall that this is how code is treated as data for easy composition and convenient collaboration among components. At runtime, LINQ to SQL translates the expression tree to SQL, executes the generated SQL, and converts the records obtained into objects. It uses the relational ADO.NET APIs to execute SQL and return results as records. Figure 8.1 shows this interaction between the components.

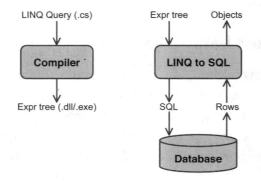

FIGURE 8.1   Compile-time and runtime handling of LINQ queries.

Consider the following simplified `Customer` and `NorthwindDataContext` classes to understand query translation:

```
using System.Data.Linq;

[Table(Name="Customers")]
public class Customer
{
    [Column(IsPrimaryKey=true)]
    public string CustomerID;
    [Column]
    public string City;
    [Column]
    public string Country;
}

public partial class NorthwindDataContext : DataContext
{
    public Table<Customer> Customers;

    public NorthwindDataContext(string connection): base(connection) {}
}
```

You can use a very convenient logging feature of the `DataContext` to monitor the generated SQL as follows. You need to use the appropriate connection string for the Northwind database on your machine.

```
NorthwindDataContext db = new NorthwindDataContext(connectionstring);
db.Log = Console.Out;
```

Using this logger, you can see the translation of the following LINQ query for a `Customer` class with `CustomerID`, `City`, and `Country` properties mapped to respective columns in the Northwind database:

```
var CustomerQuery = from c in db.Customers
                    where c.Country == "Spain"
                    select c;
```

The following SQL statement shows what is sent to the database for execution when the previous LINQ query is translated. The literal `Spain` is passed in as a parameter and is shown as a comment in the formatted SQL.

```
SELECT [t0].[CustomerID], [t0].[City],[t0].[Country]
FROM [dbo].[Customers] AS [t0]
WHERE [t0].[Country] = @p0
-- @p0: Input NVarChar (Size = 5; Prec = 0; Scale = 0) [Spain]
```

Interestingly, the C# compiler knows nothing about LINQ to SQL. It simply determines the right extension method corresponding to the `Table<Customer>` property in the `DataContext` and the query operators and produces an expression tree. LINQ to SQL takes the expression tree and looks up the mapping to translate from expression tree to SQL. The mapping also helps LINQ to SQL materialize objects from the retrieved records. Thus, LINQ to SQL is one of many possible consumers of expression trees that uses its own mapping information to bring relational data smoothly into the world of LINQ.

Understanding the Nuances of Translation

LINQ queries can contain all kinds of expressions, like the rest of the C# program. In the previous query, the expression involved comparing the member `Customer.City` with a constant. You also could have used another comparison operator or logical operators to form a more complex expression. Likewise, you could imagine using a method call as well. However, LINQ to SQL has to be able to translate the expression to its SQL counterpart. Hence, certain constraints on the expressions are supported. Three key categories of methods are supported:

- A rich subset of .NET framework methods and C# language operators
- Additional LINQ to SQL utility methods
- Mapped methods wrapping user-defined functions

The first category covers methods on the types defined in the base class library, such as `String` and `DateTime`. LINQ to SQL supports most commonly used methods that can be reasonably and efficiently translated into SQL. For example, the following query returns customers based on a text search for cities starting with the string `"M"`. It uses the method `String.StartsWith()` to do the text matching.

```
var CustomerQuery = from c in db.Customers
                    where c.City.StartsWith("M")
                    select c;
```

The `StartsWith()` method in this LINQ query is translated into the `Like` operator in SQL as follows:

```
SELECT [t0].[CustomerID], [t0].[City], [t0].[Country]
FROM [dbo].[Customers] AS [t0]
WHERE [t0].[City] LIKE @p0
-- @p0: Input NVarChar (Size = 2; Prec = 0; Scale = 0) [M%]
```

The second category covers a few nifty T-SQL functions that don't have direct counterparts in the .NET framework. LINQ to SQL adds a small number of static methods specific to SQL Server to the namespace `System.Data.Linq.SqlClient` in the `SqlMethods` class. The methods and their overloads cover the following:

- The `LIKE` operator in T-SQL
- The difference between `DateTime` types in different units
- The raw length of a byte array, its LINQ to SQL counterpart—binary and string

Here is an example of such a method. It requires an additional `using` statement.

```
using System.Data.Linq.SqlClient;
...
var CustQuery = from c in db.Customers
                where SqlMethods.Like(c.City, "%on%")
                select c;
```

The third category covers scalar user-defined functions (UDFs) from the database mapped to a C# method. The details of this subject are covered in Chapter 10. Think of a method mapped to a UDF as a method for which a call can be translated into the corresponding UDF call while generating SQL. LINQ to SQL takes care of binding the parameters appropriately.

LINQ to SQL cannot translate a method or operator that does not belong to any of these categories. There is no direct way to take arbitrary C# code and its execution environment and produce corresponding SQL. As mentioned in the preceding section, the C# compiler does not know about LINQ to SQL or its translation constraints. Hence, the compiler may successfully translate a LINQ query containing such a call to an expression tree.

However, LINQ to SQL throws an exception at runtime when it attempts to translate the method call from the expression tree to SQL. This is the upshot of the clean separation between expression tree generation at compile time and its translation at runtime. Although LINQ queries provide a significant amount of protection through compile-time checking compared to SQL, they do not insulate you from runtime exceptions.

■ **The Compiler Creates an Expression Tree; LINQ to SQL Creates SQL**

LINQ to SQL uses mapping to translate the class members to database column references or SQL functions. It also understands common framework methods and provides additional utility functions similar to SQL functions. The compiler catches your mistakes if you don't use the right member reference or have a type mismatch. LINQ to SQL throws an exception if you use an unmapped class, property, or method. In either case, the error you get is in terms of your object model, so your life is simpler while debugging.

Retrieving Objects: Entities and Projections

As you saw in the preceding chapter, the `Customer` class is mapped to the Customers table in the Northwind database so that LINQ to SQL can retrieve `Customer` instances from the rows retrieved from the Customers table. As in the case of the Customers table, a table often has a primary key or a unique key. When a class is mapped to such a table, it is called an *entity class* or *entity type*, and its instances are called *entities*. In the example in the preceding chapter, the Customer class is an entity class, and `Customer` objects are entities because the `CustomerID` member is mapped to the primary key column with the same name in the following mapping:

```
[Table(Name="Customers")]
public class Customer
{
    [Column(IsPrimaryKey=true)]
    public string CustomerID;
    [Column]
    public string City;
    [Column]
    public string Country;
}
```

This class is mapped to a table in Northwind that has a schema with a primary key `CustomerID`. Hence, each entity has a unique value for the `CustomerID` member. A query to retrieve entities simply selects the results of the entity type as follows:

```
var EntityQuery = from c in db.Customers
                  where c.Country == "Spain"
                  select c;

ObjectDumper.Write(EntityQuery,0);
```

ObjectDumper is a utility for printing object graphs to the console in a stylized fashion. It ships as a sample with Visual Studio 2008. You need to build it into a DLL so that it can be added as a reference in your project. You can think of `ObjectDumper.Write()` as an object-graph-enabled version of `Console.WriteLine()`. The optional second argument lets you control the level of navigation in the object graph. So the default value `0` doesn't go beyond top-level `Customer` entities, and value `1` lets you see `Customer.Orders` as well. Many results in this book, such as the following one, are output by ObjectDumper.

The execution of the preceding query produces the following results:

```
CustomerID=BOLID      City=Madrid      Country=Spain
CustomerID=FISSA      City=Madrid      Country=Spain
CustomerID=GALED      City=Barcelona   Country=Spain
CustomerID=GODOS      City=Sevilla     Country=Spain
CustomerID=ROMEY      City=Madrid      Country=Spain
```

In this result, each Customer entity represents a unique customer identified by a CustomerID. Hence, each entity has identity and can be updated. We will consider more implications of identity in the following sections, but first let's look at objects that don't have identity.

Sometimes we are interested in only a subset of the data. For example, to find out all the cities and countries where we have customers, the following class and query can be used. The query uses the `select` syntax available in LINQ to project only the interesting members:

```
public class CustomerCityInfo
{
   public string City;
   public string Country;
}
```

```
var ProjectionQuery = from c in db.Customers
                      where c.Country == "Spain"
                      select new CustomerCityInfo {
                                    City = c.City,
                                    Country = c.Country
                             };
```

This query is translated into the following SQL. Notice that exactly the projected information is retrieved. `CustomerID` is not projected, so it is omitted from the SQL `SELECT` clause.

```
SELECT [t0].[City], [t0].[Country]
FROM [dbo].[Customers] AS [t0]
WHERE [t0].[Country] = @p0
-- @p0: Input NVarChar (Size = 5; Prec = 0; Scale = 0) [Spain]
```

This code produces the following results:

```
City=Madrid       Country=Spain
City=Madrid       Country=Spain
City=Barcelona    Country=Spain
City=Sevilla      Country=Spain
City=Madrid       Country=Spain
```

The same query could also be performed using an anonymous type as follows:

```
var ProjectionQuery = from c in db.Customers
                      where c.Country == "Spain"
                      select new {
                                    City = c.City,
                                    Country = c.Country
                             };
```

In either case, we get a set of objects of type `CustomerCityInfo` or an anonymous type—both subsets of the entity type. The objects represent just a projection and don't have any identity by themselves. The translated SQL queries for these objects include appropriate filters and projections to retrieve a minimal amount of data from the server.

Thus, LINQ to SQL can be used to retrieve entities or projections efficiently. It lets you return entities or shape them to bring a subset as necessary. The next section further explores the difference between the two.

The Importance of Object Identity

When we retrieve a Customer entity, we may want to update it. If multiple copies of the entity exist—more than one instance with the same primary key values—confusion can occur about which instance is the authoritative one for the purpose of updates. Hence, it is important to ensure that no duplicates exist.

However, multiple queries can return overlapping results. For example, a query for customers with IDs that start with the letter B and customers from Spain overlap, as the previous query results show.

In this case, each of the two queries must return the appropriate results, and yet we must not have any duplicates for the customer with ID BOLID. LINQ to SQL implements *object identity* to ensure that the entity created for ID BOLID when the first query is executed is reused in the result for the second query. Object identity is scoped to a DataContext instance. Within a DataContext instance, no more than one object reference is associated with a primary key value of a given type. Conceptually you can think of each DataContext instance maintaining a hash table of object references indexed by the primary key values. For each row returned by the database, if the key value is not found in the hash table, a new entity instance with that key value is created and inserted into the hash table. Thereafter, if a row with the same key value is returned, the row is discarded, and the existing entity with the same key value is returned. In the previous example, conceptually, the first time a row with ID BOLID is returned, a Customer entity with that ID is created and inserted into the logical hash table. Thereafter, the same Customer instance is returned for a row with CustomerID BOLID; additional instances are not created for that ID by that DataContext instance.

Object reference is how identity is expressed in the .NET framework. Primary or unique key value is how identity is expressed in relational databases. LINQ to SQL bridges the two concepts of reference identity and value identity across the object-relational divide. The IsPrimaryKey property of the Column mapping attribute describes the value identity for the containing entity class. LINQ to SQL maintains the reference identity within the scope of a DataContext instance by not creating another entity instance (such as a different object reference) for a given identity value defined by the database columns.

A primary key may be composed of one or more columns. Each member mapped to a primary key column must have IsPrimaryKey set to true. If the primary key has multiple columns, such a key is often called a composite key. LINQ to SQL uniformly supports single-column and composite keys to ensure object identity.

Object identity is a property of an entity. It is not applicable to projections because projections don't have a well-defined identity. The query from the previous section for city information returns duplicate results containing multiple objects with the same City, Country value.

Object identity relies on immutability of members mapped to a unique key in the database. If these members that form the identity are changed, a loss of identity would occur. If the customer ID is changed from BOLID to something else, it is no longer the same customer. Hence, changes to members mapped to keys are *not* permitted. Any attempt to change key values results in undefined behavior. If you do need to update a primary key value, you can think of it as a pair of operations—deletion of the entity with the old key value and creation of a new entity with the new key value. However, for an entity, the identity must not change over the life of the entity.

This key concept of object identity allows updates and also enables relationships to be used effectively.

■ Consider Entity, Identity, and Updatability

An entity has identity defined by one or more key members. LINQ to SQL ensures that duplicate entity instances are not created for a given key value. Hence, entities typically are updatable. Arbitrary projections produce results of nonentity types and are not updatable.

Using Relationships

Entities are connected to each other through various relationships. An Order entity is associated with a Customer entity; an Employee entity is associated with other Employees through a manager-employee relationship. LINQ to SQL provides an easy way to represent such relationships and to effectively use them in queries and updates.

The relationship between objects is usually a property that references a related object, such as Order.Customer. In the case of a collection of related objects, the relationship is represented as a collection property containing references to related objects. For example, Customer.Orders usually is a collection of references to Order objects.

In relational databases, relationships usually are represented through keys. The relationships are often maintained using foreign key constraints. For example, in the Northwind database, the Orders table has a foreign key CustomerID referencing the CustomerID column in the Customers table.

LINQ to SQL bridges the database and object concepts of relationships using the Association attribute. A property referencing a related entity or entities is attributed as follows:

```
[Table(Name="Customers")]
public class Customer
{
    [Column(IsPrimaryKey=true)]
    public string CustomerID;
    [Column]
    public string Country;
    ...
    [Association(OtherKey="CustomerID")]
    public List<Order> Orders;
}

[Table(Name="Orders")]
public class Order
{
    [Column(IsPrimaryKey=true)]
    public int OrderID;
    [Column]
    public string CustomerID;
    ...
    [Association(ThisKey="CustomerID", IsForeignKey=true)]
    public Customer Customer;
}
```

The Association attribute provides information about the members in the containing class and the related class that map to the key values defining the relationship in the database. In the previous example, CustomerID names the class members mapped to the primary key of the Customers table and the foreign key in the Orders table. ThisKey refers to the key in the containing class, and OtherKey refers to the key member in the other, related class. The `IsForeignKey` attribute indicates that this relationship is enforced as a foreign key relationship in the database.

This relationship mapping can be used for querying as follows, with a few sample results shown:

```
var OrdersQuery = from o in db.Orders
                  where o.Customer.Country == "Spain"
                  select new { o.OrderID, o.Customer.CustomerID };


OrderID=10326    CustomerID=BOLID
OrderID=10801    CustomerID=BOLID
...
```

In this query, we can easily "dot through" the relationship in `where` and `select` expressions. `o.Customer.Country` refers to a property of the related entity Customer that can be referenced through the range variable o of type `Order`. Likewise, `o.Customer.CustomerID` accomplishes similar navigation. This is the real power of object relational mapping—an explicit join between the Customers and Orders tables is no longer needed. The association mapping combined with the power of LINQ makes it easy to write queries simply by using the "power of the dot" in the object model. Any joins that are required are handled by LINQ to SQL under the covers. The developer can just keep using dot notation to access the object and its properties. This is true whether they are mapped to a column in the same table, such as Order.OrderID, or whether they are mapped to a different table, such as Order.Customer.Country, which is mapped to the Customers table. Collection properties can be used similarly as follows, with the output shown at the end:

```
var CustomerQuery = from c in db.Customers
                    where c.Country == "Spain" && c.Orders.Any()
                    select c;


CustomerID=BOLID     Country=Spain    ...
CustomerID=GALED     Country=Spain    ...
CustomerID=GODOS     Country=Spain    ...
CustomerID=ROMEY     Country=Spain    ...
```

The only additional thing to keep in mind is that a collection valued property must be used with operators that work on collections. For example, the previous query uses the `Any()` operator to see if the collection has any orders. A collection property cannot be used like the property of an entity type. You cannot directly index an `Order` instance from the collection and navigate to its property. There is a difference between the members of `IEnumerable<Order>` versus `Order`. Fortunately, IntelliSense is very helpful in this case as well. The completion list shows the available set of members, as shown in Figure 8.2.

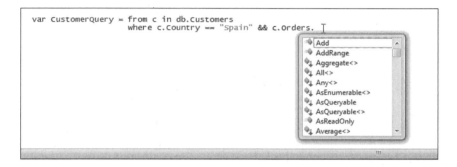

FIGURE 8.2 The completion list for a collection property.

Collection-valued properties may be used in the result of a query as well. SQL is designed for the relational domain; hence, the results in SQL are rectangular. If you want Customers and Orders, the result is tabular, with the customer information repeated for each order belonging to the customer. LINQ is designed for the object domain. Therefore, hierarchies of objects are naturally available in the result displayed using the ObjectDumper:

```
var CustomerQuery = from c in db.Customers
                    where c.Country == "Spain" && c.Orders.Any()
                    select new { c.CustomerID, c.Orders };

CustomerID=BOLID          Orders=...
    OrderID=10326   CustomerID=BOLID ...
    OrderID=10801   CustomerID=BOLID ...
    OrderID=10970   CustomerID=BOLID ...
CustomerID=GALED          Orders=...
    OrderID=10366   CustomerID=GALED ...
    ...
```

Joining Tables

Navigation based on mapped relationships is intended to cover most of the common scenarios for queries that relate two tables. The LINQ Join operator is available in addition to navigation. Consider querying for Customer and Suppliers in the same city in Northwind. Although there is no navigation property to go between Customers and Suppliers, LINQ to SQL allows the use of the Join standard query operator as follows:

```
var CustSuppQuery = from s in db.Suppliers
                    join c in db.Customers
                    on s.City equals c.City
                    select new
                    {
                        Supplier = s.CompanyName,
                        Customer = c.CompanyName,
                        City = c.City
                    };
```

This LINQ query is translated into SQL's inner join as follows:

```
SELECT [t0].[CompanyName] AS [Supplier], [t1].[CompanyName] AS
  [Customer], [t1].[City]
FROM [dbo].[Suppliers] AS [t0]
INNER JOIN [dbo].[Customers] AS [t1] ON [t0].[City] = [t1].[City]
```

This query eliminates suppliers that are not in the same city as some customers. But sometimes you don't want to eliminate one of the entities in an ad hoc relationship. The following query lists all suppliers, with groups of customers for each supplier. If a particular supplier does not have a customer in the same city, the result is an empty collection of customers corresponding to that supplier. Note that the results are not flat—each supplier has an associated collection. Effectively, this provides a group join. It joins two sequences and groups elements of the second sequence by the elements of the first sequence. Let's use an overload of the ObjectDumper.Write() call to drill down into the supplier and the corresponding group of customers:

```
var CustSuppQuery = from s in db.Suppliers
                    join c in db.Customers
                    on s.City equals c.City into scusts
                    select new { s, scusts };

ObjectDumper.Write(CustSuppQuery, 1);
```

Such a group join is translated into SQL's left outer join as shown in the following code. The long projection lists for each table are truncated to make the generated query easier to read. The SQL aggregate count helps LINQ to SQL build the collections of Customers for the join predicate—in this case, City.

```
SELECT [t0].[SupplierID], [t0].[CompanyName], ... ,
       [t1].[ContactName] AS [ContactName2], ... ,
       (
           SELECT COUNT(*)
           FROM [dbo].[Customers] AS [t2]
           WHERE [t0].[City] = [t2].[City]
       ) AS [value]
FROM [dbo].[Suppliers] AS [t0]
LEFT OUTER JOIN [dbo].[Customers] AS [t1] ON [t0].[City] = [t1].[City]
ORDER BY [t0].[SupplierID], [t1].[CustomerID]
```

Group joins can be extended to multiple collections as well. The following query extends the preceding query by listing employees who are in the same city as the supplier. Here, the result shows a supplier with (possibly empty) collections of customers and employees:

```
var EmpCustSuppQuery = from s in db.Suppliers
                       join c in db.Customers
                       on s.City equals c.City into scusts
                       join e in db.Employees
                       on s.City equals e.City into semps
                       select new { s, scusts, semps };
```

The results of a group join can also be flattened. The results of flattening the group join between suppliers and customers are multiple entries for suppliers with multiple customers in their city—one per customer. Empty collections are replaced with nulls. This is equivalent to a left outer equijoin in relational databases.

```
var CustSuppQuery = from s in db.Suppliers
                    join c in db.Customers
                    on s.City equals c.City into sc
                    from x in sc.DefaultIfEmpty()
                    select new
                    {
                        Supplier = s.CompanyName,
                        Customer = x.CompanyName,
                        City = x.City
                    };
```

The generated SQL query contains a simple left outer join, as expected.

```
SELECT [t0].[CompanyName] AS [Supplier],
       [t1].[CompanyName] AS [Customer],
       [t1].[City] AS [City]
FROM [dbo].[Suppliers] AS [t0]
LEFT OUTER JOIN [dbo].[Customers] AS [t1]
ON [t0].[City] = [t1].[City]
```

Thus, join is an additional tool for more complex relationships that are not mapped to navigational properties. It complements the more commonplace use of much simpler navigational properties. It can produce hierarchical or flattened results.

■■ Use the Power of the Dot

Where a mapped relationship is available, use the dot and navigate to related entities through relationship properties instead of explicitly using the join operator in the query. Unlike SQL, LINQ can produce hierarchies as results, so you can use collection valued properties in the results of a query, too. Pay special attention to the IntelliSense completion list shown after you type a period following a relationship property. This will help you avoid mistakenly using a collection like an entity.

Mapping Different Types of Relationships

The Customer-Orders example has a one-to-many relationship. There may be many orders for a given customer, but no more than one customer exists for a given Order. LINQ to SQL also supports the relatively less common one-to-one relationship, such as a Spouse for an Employee.

In a third kind of relationship called many-to-many, such as Order–Product, an order may cover multiple products, and a product is included in multiple orders. In relational databases, such a relationship typically is normalized through a "link table" or a table in the middle. The Order Details table in the Northwind database relates orders and products by including foreign keys from both the related tables. However, such relationships often have some important additional data in the link table. For example, Order Details specifies the quantity, price, and so on. Hence, in the interest of simplicity, LINQ to SQL supports the many-to-many relationship as a pair of one-to-many relationships—Order–Order_Detail and Product–Order_Detail. This allows the properties on the relationship entity to be naturally modeled, such as Order_Detail.Price. However, regardless of the presence of the additional properties, the class mapped to the link table is required in LINQ to SQL. Even if you do not intend to map Order_Detail.Price, Order_Detail class cannot be skipped with just Order.Products and Product.Orders collections.

As previously shown, the mapping for relationships can be written by hand. However, the designer makes relationships even simpler. When a pair of related tables are dragged and dropped onto the designer surface, the designer infers the relationship between them based on foreign keys in the database. It generates the necessary members and mapping automatically. The relationship between the Customer and Order classes is represented by an arrow between the classes, as shown in Figure 8.3.

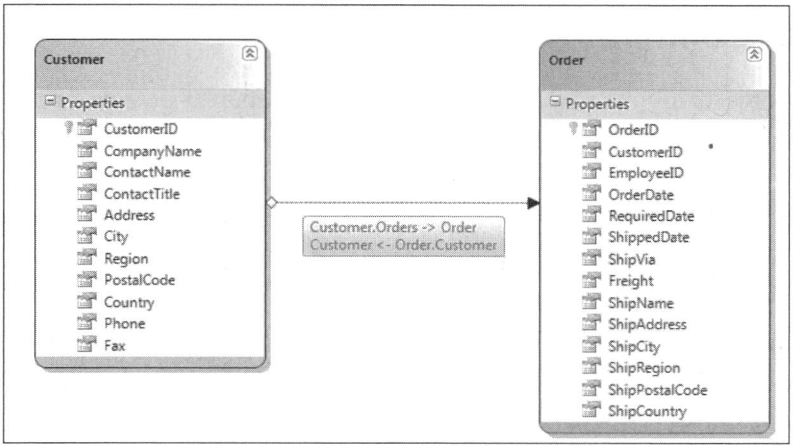

FIGURE 8.3   The relationship between entity classes.

The relationship represented by the arrow can be selected and edited through an association editor or the property grid. The Cardinality property in the grid indicates whether the relationship is one-to-many or one-to-one.

The direction of the arrow represents the parent-to-child direction. Following the Entity-Relationship model used for database modeling, the entity containing the foreign key is called the child, and the entity identified by the foreign key is called the parent. In the Customer–Order relationship shown in the figure, the arrow is from the parent, Customer, to the child, Order. By default, the designer creates a relationship property on each end of a relationship. The property in a child entity referencing the parent entity is required. The reverse property in the parent entity identifying the children or child is optional and can be removed.

Relationships allow you to think about your object model as a connected graph. LINQ to SQL operates on such a connected graph while generating SQL to operate on underlying tables joined using keys. Using the dot to refer to related entities in queries is one direct benefit of the object graph model. Another benefit is the ability to load the target of a relationship. Next we'll look at the options available for loading related entities.

Loading Options

Which objects are needed for processing often depends on some user action or business logic. Consider an example in which a set of orders is displayed to a user. The user, based on some criteria, may pick a particular Order entity to drill into. At that point, the Order_Detail entities related to that specific Order are needed. When the set of orders was initially retrieved, the specific Order entity of interest may not have been known. In such a case, it is interesting to be able to load the Order_Details in a deferred or lazy or on-demand fashion. The same applies even when there is business logic in place of a user that determines if further drill-down is needed for a subset of entities.

Deferred Loading

LINQ to SQL enables *deferred loading* through simple navigation. For a given Order, its Order_Details collection may be empty when the Order is first loaded. But when the collection is first iterated, LINQ to SQL fires off a query to load the collection. After it is loaded, the collection is then available for future use without requiring another query. A small delay involved in executing the query aside, the Order_Details collection property behaves as if it is available. If it is never iterated, the corresponding query is never executed, and unnecessary transfer of data is avoided. You can imagine the savings if a thousand orders, each with dozens of details, are present in the database, and the user picks just one or a few of the orders for further drill-down.

In the following example, using the `DataContext` log, you can see that a query is fired when the inner `foreach` loop is hit. Let's add a few extra `WriteLine()` statements to see when a query gets executed:

```
// Connect the log to console to see generated SQL
db.Log = Console.Out;

var OrdersQuery = from o in db.Orders
                  where o.ShipVia == 1
                  select o;

Console.WriteLine("Iterating over orders");
foreach(Order o in OrdersQuery)
{
    // Process Order here
    if (o.Freight > 400)
    {
        Console.WriteLine("Iterating over Order_Details for Order {0}\n",
                o.OrderID);
        // A query to load o.Order_Details is fired on first reference
        foreach (Order_Detail od in o.Order_Details)
        {
            // Process Order_Details
        }
    }
}
```

As explained before, `OrdersQuery` is executed at the beginning of the outer `foreach` loop due to deferred execution. The query for the deferred loaded collection `Order.Order_Details` is executed due to the inner `foreach` loop. *Deferred execution* of queries is a LINQ feature that is not specific to LINQ to SQL. *Deferred loading* is a LINQ to SQL feature. The following is the query generated for the deferred loading of the `Order_Details` property for the Order entity with ID 10430 when it is iterated the first time. It can be seen in the `DataContext` log.

```
Iterating over Order_Details for Order 10430

SELECT [t0].[OrderID], [t0].[ProductID], [t0].[UnitPrice],
        [t0].[Quantity], [t0].[Discount]
```

```
FROM [dbo].[Order Details] AS [t0]
WHERE [t0].[OrderID] = @p0
-- @p0: Input Int (Size = 0; Prec = 0; Scale = 0) [10430]
```

The deferred loading capability requires LINQ to SQL to intercept the access to a relationship property. The interception provides a way to check if the target is already loaded so that it can be populated on first access. Two special types, EntitySet<T> and EntityRef<T>, are used to provide the interception capability. EntitySet<T> is used where the target is a collection, and EntityRef<T> is used where the target is a singleton. For example, Order.Order_Details is of type EntitySet<Order_Detail>, and Order_Detail.Order is of type EntityRef<Order>. The designer and the command-line tool SqlMetal both use the correct types on each end of a relationship based on the cardinality of the relationship. As a result, the generated entities are automatically equipped to provide deferred loading for relationships.

Furthermore, deferred loading is also available for a nonrelationship property of a class. For example, if the Products table contains a large image of the product, you can choose to defer-load it by using a property of type Link<Binary>, where Binary is the type used for mapping to the image. In the designer, you can set the "Delay Loading" property to true for such a class member to change the type to Link <Binary> instead of Binary. The image would then be defer-loaded much like the Category entity referenced by the EntityRef<Category> property in the Product class. The difference between the two is that the image is not an entity—it is just a part of the Product entity. Category is a different entity with its own identity.

Eager Loading

Whereas deferred loading is handy when only an occasional relationship is navigated, in other cases all or most of the related entities are needed. Consider a variant of the previously shown logic in which the Order_Details for all Orders are needed, regardless of the freight. In such cases, deferred loading can be too chatty and inefficient due to the number of queries and resulting round-trips to the database.

Another option called *eager loading* (also called *immediate loading*) is available for just such a case. You can instruct the DataContext to automatically bring in Order_Details for all retrieved Orders, as shown in the following example. The `DataLoadOptions` on the `DataContext` can be used to specify a relationship that should be eager-loaded—`Order_Details` for `Order` entities in the example. The log shows that, unlike in the previous example, the inner `foreach` loop does not result in additional queries. All the related `Order_Details` are preloaded with the Order entities.

```
// Connect the log to console to see generated SQL
db.Log = Console.Out;

DataLoadOptions dlopt = new DataLoadOptions();
dlopt.LoadWith<Order>(o => o.Order_Details);
db.LoadOptions = dlopt;

var OrdersQuery = from o in db.Orders
                  where o.ShipVia == 1 && o.Freight > 400
                  select o;

foreach(Order o in OrdersQuery)
{
    // Order_Details are eager-loaded; additional queries are not needed
    foreach (Order_Detail od in o.Order_Details)
    {
        // Process Order_Details
    }
}
```

The following query for loading all the related `Order_Details` and the queried `Orders` is different from the queries used for multistep deferred loading. For simplicity, the SELECT clause with columns from the Orders and Order Details tables is trimmed and elided. LINQ to SQL takes the results of the left outer join and constructs the `Order–Order_Detail` hierarchy.

```
SELECT [t0].[OrderID], [t0].[CustomerID], [t0].[EmployeeID], ...
       (
          SELECT COUNT(*)
          FROM [dbo].[Order Details] AS [t2]
          WHERE [t2].[OrderID] = [t0].[OrderID]
       ) AS [value]
FROM [dbo].[Orders] AS [t0]
LEFT OUTER JOIN [dbo].[Order Details] AS [t1] ON [t1].[OrderID] =
  [t0].[OrderID]
WHERE ([t0].[ShipVia] = @p0) AND ([t0].[Freight] > @p1)
ORDER BY [t0].[OrderID], [t1].[ProductID]
-- @p0: Input Int (Size = 0; Prec = 0; Scale = 0) [1]
-- @p1: Input Decimal (Size = 0; Prec = 33; Scale = 4) [400]
```

Multiple relationships may be set up for eager loading using DataLoad-Options. The only restriction is that the options cannot form a cycle. For example, after Order.Order_Details is specified for eager loading, Order_Detail.Order cannot be specified, because it would form a cycle among the classes through the relationships—Order–Order_Detail–Order. This avoids the problem of unending traversal of cycles. One consequence is that certain relationships cannot be eager-loaded. For example, consider an Employee entity pointing to a collection of Employee entities in a manager-reports relationship. Because the target entity type in Employee.Reports is Employee, the relationship cannot be eager-loaded. However, deferred loading may be used in such cases because the relationship is loaded for a given instance without any danger of endless cycles.

```
// Error. Cyclic relationship cannot be eager-loaded
dlopt.LoadWith<Employee>(e => e.Reports);
```

The ability to load related objects is a crucial way to bridge the gap between object models and the underlying relational storage. Deferred and eager-loading options ensure that the bridging is done as efficiently as needed in the particular scenario. Yet an additional problem with relationships remains. Sometimes the sizes of related collections can be too large to be loaded in either eager or deferred fashion. Consider a database that stores orders over many years for customers. If the application is interested in showing only a small subset of the orders, perhaps for the last three months, it would be wasteful to load all the orders, whether eagerly or in a deferred fashion. Hence, LINQ to SQL provides an additional loading option to filter the collections in a consistent fashion.

```
dlopt.AssociateWith<Customer>(c => c.Orders.Where(
    o => o.OrderDate.Value.Year == 1998));
```

The load options for eager loading and filtering of relationships must be specified before any queries are performed. Specifying the options after the DataContext instance has been used for queries creates a risk of inconsistent results across queries. Hence, it results in an exception.

The AssociateWith option may be specified with or without the eager loading option. It is equally applicable to deferred loading as well. The following example shows how the option can be used with the eager loading option:

```
DataLoadOptions dlopt = new DataLoadOptions();
dlopt.LoadWith<Customer>(c => c.Orders);
dlopt.AssociateWith<Customer>(c => c.Orders.Where(
    o => o.OrderDate.Value.Year == 1998));
db.LoadOptions = dlopt;
```

> ### ■ Match the Loading Option to the Usage Pattern
>
> When you use the power of the dot by navigating relationships, think about the most common usage pattern. If a user action in a user interface or a programmatic choice based on data requires an occasional loading of a related object, use deferred loading. If all related data is needed, use eager loading. Even where you want to filter related data in a predetermined fashion, use eager loading and queries associated with the relationship.

Defining Inheritance

The relationship between entities is one key aspect of an object model. Inheritance is another. LINQ to SQL supports the mapping of an inheritance hierarchy to a single table or a view. Consider the example of three classes: base class `Customer` and two levels of derived classes, `PremierCustomer` and `EliteCustomer`, that map to the Customers table, as shown in Figure 8.4. Because the Northwind database does not have a table with such data, let's first create a suitable table for mapping such a hierarchy. The Data Definition Language (DDL) statements shown next create a table for instances of the Customer hierarchy.

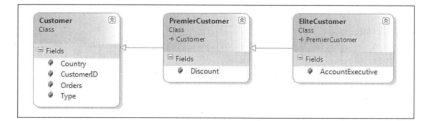

FIGURE 8.4   An inheritance class diagram.

Before running the following DDL statements, make sure that you are working with a copy of the Northwind database so that your original copy will remain unaffected. You can do so by copying the Northwnd.mdf database file to another directory and attaching it with SQL Server Express. Then you can run the following T-SQL commands in SQL Server Management Studio. (The Express version can be downloaded for free for SQL Express.) We will start by making copies of the Customers and Orders tables as the Customers2 and Orders2 tables and setting appropriate primary and foreign key constraints on them:

```sql
-- Copy Customers and Orders tables
select * into Customers2 from customers

select * into Orders2 from Orders

-- Set up primary keys and foreign key
alter table customers2 add constraint customers2_pk
primary key (customerid)

alter table orders2 add constraint orders2_pk
primary key(orderid)

alter table orders2 add constraint orders2_customers2_fk
foreign key(customerid) references customers2(customerid)

-- Add type discriminator and type-specific columns
alter table customers2 add Type smallint not null default 0

alter table customers2 add Discount decimal

alter table customers2 add AccountExecutive nvarchar(256)

-- Change some rows to premier and elite customer type
update customers2 set Type = 1, Discount = 5
where customerid in (
select customerid  from orders group by customerid
having count(customerid) between 10 and 15)

update customers2
set Type = 2, Discount = 10, AccountExecutive = 'Top Seller'
where customerid in (
select customerid  from orders group by customerid
having count(customerid) > 15)
```

Next, we need to make the schema and data suitable for an inheritance hierarchy. The rows for the three types of customers are differentiated using the inheritance discriminator column Type. The mapping uses the discriminator values to indicate how LINQ to SQL should materialize a given row from the Customers table. Here we will use the type values 0, 1, and 2 for Customer, PremierCustomer, and EliteCustomer, respectively. Additional, type-specific data is stored in nullable columns. PremierCustomer gets a non-null Discount, and EliteCustomer gets an AccountExecutive in addition to the inherited member Discount.

The following handcrafted mapping shows how the hierarchy can be mapped to the Customers2 and Orders2 tables. The mapped types in the class hierarchy need to be specified in the mapping of the base class using the InheritanceMapping attribute. This ensures that LINQ to SQL knows about all derived classes it might encounter while reading data from the table mapped to multiple types in the hierarchy. The Code property of the InheritanceMapping attribute indicates the discriminator values used for deciding the type of the object to be constructed from a given row in the table. It corresponds to the column that has IsDiscriminator set to true. In the preceding example, if the Type column contains the code 0, LINQ to SQL creates a Customer object. If it contains 1, a PremierCustomer is created, and so on. The default type is marked, setting the property IsDefault to true. It is used when LINQ to SQL encounters a value for the discriminator that is not specified in the InheritanceMapping attributes.

```
[Table(Name = "Customers2")]
[InheritanceMapping(Code = 0, Type = typeof(Customer), IsDefault = true)]
[InheritanceMapping(Code = 1, Type = typeof(PremierCustomer))]
[InheritanceMapping(Code = 2, Type = typeof(EliteCustomer))]
public class Customer
{
    [Column(IsPrimaryKey = true)]
    public string CustomerID;
    [Column(IsDiscriminator = true)]
    public short Type;

    [Column]
    public string Country;
```

```
        [Association(OtherKey = "CustomerID")]
        public List<Order> Orders;
    }

    public class PremierCustomer : Customer
    {
        [Column]
        public decimal Discount;
    }

    public class EliteCustomer : PremierCustomer
    {
        [Column]
        public string AccountExecutive;
    }

    [Table(Name="Orders2")]
    public class Order
    {
        [Column(IsPrimaryKey=true)]
        public int OrderID;
        [Column]
        public string CustomerID;

        [Association(ThisKey="CustomerID", IsForeignKey=true)]
        public Customer Customer;
    }

    class NorthwindDataContext : DataContext
    {
        public Table<Customer> Customers2;
        public Table<Order> Orders2;

        public NorthwindDataContext(string s) : base(s) { }
    }
```

The mapped classes can be used for queries that return results of mixed types or of a specific type, as shown in the next code segment. The first query returns rows for all the types and creates the instances of correct types based on the discriminator code. The second query returns results of types PremierCustomer and EliteCustomer due to the OfType extension method. The discriminator value is used to filter out results of other types, and the constructed type is determined by the discriminator code in the row. The third query returns only EliteCustomer instances.

```
// Get entities of each type including derived types
var AllCustQuery = db.Customers2;
var PremierCustQuery = db.Customers2.OfType<PremierCustomer>();
var EliteCustQuery = db.Customers2.OfType<EliteCustomer>();

// Use type-restricted sequence for further queries
var UKPremierQuery = from c in db.Customers2.OfType<PremierCustomer>()
                     where c.Country == "UK"
                     select c;
```

In each case, the OfType extension method is translated into an appro-priate WHERE clause in SQL on the discriminator column to reduce the amount of data fetched. The following SQL is generated for the Premier-CustQuery shown before. It uses the SQL WHERE clause to restrict the rows in the result to PremierCustomer and its derived types. Thus, LINQ to SQL ensures efficient execution and minimal data transfer for inheritance mapping.

```
SELECT [t0].[Type], [t0].[AccountExecutive], [t0].[Discount],
[t0].[CustomerID], [t0].[Country]
FROM [Customers2] AS [t0]
WHERE ([t0].[Type] = @p0) OR ([t0].[Type] = @p1)
-- @p0: Input SmallInt (Size = 0; Prec = 0; Scale = 0) [2]
-- @p1: Input SmallInt (Size = 0; Prec = 0; Scale = 0) [1]
```

The designer in Visual Studio also supports inheritance mapping. Fig-ure 8.5 shows the menu options used to define a derived class.

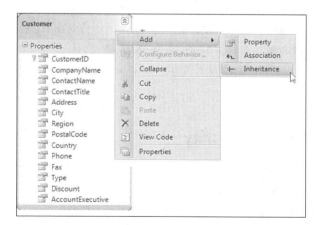

FIGURE 8.5   Defining inheritance in the designer.

After a derived class has been created using the New Inheritance dialog displayed by selecting the Inheritance menu option, the members from the base class need to be deleted from the derived class. This leaves only the members specific to the derived class. Then you can click the inheritance relationship, shown as an arrow from the derived class to the base class, to add information about the discriminant column and code values. Figure 8.6 shows the resulting class hierarchy for the Customers2 table.

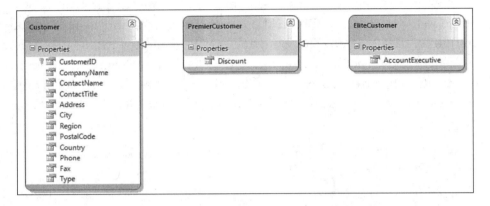

FIGURE 8.6   A class hierarchy on the designer surface.

An inheritance hierarchy may be a target of a relationship. `Order.Customer` may point to any of the classes in the hierarchy. Likewise, an `EntitySet` may also contain instances of any of the types in the hierarchy. For example, a salesperson managing multiple customers may have an `EntitySet<Customer>` that contains instances of derived classes as well. LINQ to SQL ensures that the materialization is done according to the inheritance mapping.

Performance and Security

LINQ to SQL supports a powerful set of abstractions defined in the C# language. In addition to enabling a rich set of query operators, it lets you navigate relationships and handles inheritance hierarchies. LINQ to SQL accomplishes this by automatically providing efficient translation to SQL. However, knowledge of a few more details is helpful for ensuring the best performance and secure usage. This section looks at some additional aspects of query translation to help you avoid common traps and pitfalls.

Query Versus Results

LINQ to SQL uses the deferred execution model defined for all LINQ components. There is no explicit "Execute" method that you need to call to get the results of a LINQ to SQL query. A query is executed only when you enumerate its results. As explained in Chapter 4, "C# 3.0 Technical Overview," this enables composition at almost no cost. The simplest example is the properties of type `Table<T>` in the `NorthwindDataContext` class. `Customers`, `Orders`, and so on are all queries corresponding to entire tables in the database; they are *not* local collections containing all the `Customer` or `Order` entities in your app domain. The same is true of query expressions composed on top of tables—say, customers from Spain. They represent queries that can be and need to be executed for results after all the desired composition. They let you avoid retrieving a large result set for local execution. You *don't* need all `Customer` entities in memory first to find customers from Spain. Such is the essential power of deferred execution. However, deferred execution also has two key implications for performance: latency for the first object in the result, and repeated execution if the results are not stored in a local collection.

First, the cost of query translation and execution is deferred until the results are enumerated. Hence, when you `foreach` over the results, the call to `IEnumerable.GetEnumerator()` is where you pay the price. Merely defining a query does not eliminate the latency for subsequent usage. Generally this is a beneficial feature, because you can define queries without worrying about their usage on various code paths. If you do not enumerate the results of a query, you do not pay the cost of translation and execution.

Second, re-enumerating the same query triggers another generation and execution of the corresponding SQL commands. No implicit caching of results occurs. Again, this is essential if you need to get the current results of the query when the second enumeration is done. However, this can result in significant cost if you treat a query like a list and try to enumerate it multiple times, as shown in the following code fragment:

```
var CustomerQuery = from c in db.Customers
                    where c.Country == "Spain"
                    select c;

// Some more work ...
// GetEnumerator() causes query translation, SQL query execution
// and object materialization.
foreach(Customer c in CustomerQuery) {...}
// The query is executed again
foreach(Customer c in CustomerQuery) {...}
```

Fortunately, here you can have your cake and eat it, too. If you want to prepay the price of query translation and execution, or if you want to enumerate the results multiple times, you can simply put the results in a list by calling `ToList()` or `ToArray()` on the query at the point of your choice, as shown in the following code line. Then you can use the list or array or whatever local collection you want to use as many times as you like without incurring any additional translation, execution, or object materialization costs.

```
List<Customer> CustomerList = CustomerQuery.ToList();
```

The list or array is a little "cache" of results that you can reuse. Of course, as in the case of any cache, you have to think about whether it is worth prepaying the cost, whether all objects in the cache are really needed, and whether stale data is a problem. But its creation and use are completely under your control. `ToList()` and `ToArray()` are convenience APIs for getting a list and an array of the result types, respectively. However, you could just as easily add the objects to a collection of your choice and use it like a cache.

Another example of the difference between a deferred query and a result is a query expression of a nondeferrable type. The following queries return results of type `int` and `Customer`, respectively. Hence, they do not require any enumeration and do not provide deferred execution. The results are produced when the assignment statement is executed.

```
int count = db.Customers.Count();
Customer cust = db.Customers.First();
```

Compiled Queries

Caching by enumerating the results is a fine way to reuse the results. But quite often you want to use the same query with different parameters. For example, if a form shows Orders for a customer, you want to be able to execute a query for orders for a given customer. Many applications provide results based on a set of parameters obtained from a UI form or another application. In such cases, cached results may not be useful, because the parameter values change from one execution to another, so caching the results for all parameter values may be impractical. Furthermore, if the data in the database keeps changing, the cached results of a query are likely to get stale.

Compiled queries provide an interesting capability to handle such cases. They allow you to compile or pretranslate a LINQ query with slots for specified parameters. Then, as soon as you know the values for the parameters, you can execute the "compiled" or pretranslated query by plugging in the values. If you use the query 10 times, the cost of translating the query is amortized over 10 executions. The greater the number of executions or the more complex the query, the more you are likely to save with compiled queries.

```
// Define a compiled query
var OrdByCustId = CompiledQuery.Compile(
        (NorthwindDataContext context, string custId) =>
        from o in context.Orders
        where o.CustomerID == custId
        select o);

// Execute the compiled query
string cust = 276AROUT";
var q = OrdByCustId(db, cust);
```

In fact, you can use this in a more stylized fashion by statically defining a set of compiled queries and then using them in response to a request. For each new request, you can simply execute the compiled query with the appropriate parameters. This pattern is particularly handy in case of web applications where you want to handle a large number of parameterized requests with minimum response time without holding a lot of state. Thus, compiled queries provide a mid-tier alternative to a T-SQL stored procedure or table-valued function and can be used as a complementary technology.

```
static class Queries
{
    public static Func<NorthwindDataContext, string, IQueryable<Order>>
        OrdByCustId = CompiledQuery.Compile(
            (NorthwindDataContext context, string custId) =>
            from o in context.Orders
            where o.CustomerID == custId
            select o);

    // More compiled queries for common query patterns
}
```

Compiled queries are in some ways analogous to the query and stored procedure cache maintained by a relational database such as SQL Server. However, the SQL Server cache can be used across multiple executions of applications. LINQ to SQL constructs, like compiled queries, live only as long as the containing CLR application domain lives. Hence, SQL Server uses implicit caching, whereas LINQ to SQL enables explicit caching and avoids implicit caching. This allows the application developer to decide which queries should be compiled and cached for use in a CLR application domain's lifetime.

The translation of compiled queries is independent of the data. Hence, the translation can be materially different in certain cases. The most important distinction is the use of a null value for a parameter. In the case of non-compiled queries, if the value of a parameter is known to be null at the time of translation, LINQ to SQL generates a special check for null required by SQL—IS NULL or IS NOT NULL, as appropriate. However, in the case of a compiled query, the translation is independent of data. Hence, null values should not be passed to a compiled query; they must be handled separately as constants in a query rather than as parameters.

Security

SQL users do have a certain degree of composability available to them. In principle, you can concatenate appropriate strings to programmatically build a SQL query based on various inputs. However, in practice, this is almost always very problematic because of the threat of SQL injection. Malicious user input can turn a benign-looking parameter into dangerous commands for doing something nefarious on the server.

LINQ to SQL addresses this issue in the generated SQL very effectively by always parameterizing inputs. A malicious user can try to provide input laced with commands, but the input will not get blindly concatenated into the SQL string. It will be left as a parameter, and the database will only treat it as a nonexecutable parameter.

Although most SQL users know about the threat of SQL injection and take steps to avoid string concatenation to build a command, LINQ to SQL does a more effective job of avoiding such concatenation. It provides a degree of additional security by ensuring that this basic principle is followed consistently.

Beyond thwarting SQL injection, restricting access to sensitive data or operations is another key security objective. If you use stored procedures or functions in your database, LINQ to SQL can use them to retrieve and save objects. We will discuss stored procedure support in depth in Chapter 10, "Using Stored Procedures and Database Functions with LINQ to SQL." For this discussion, remember that you can use fine-grained access control in the database with views, stored procedures, and functions just as effectively with LINQ to SQL as you do with plain SQL.

Finally, LINQ to SQL relies on the connection string for access to databases, just like the underlying ADO.NET relational APIs. If you use integrated security, the amount of sensitive data should be minimal. But if you do not use integrated security, it is important to protect the user ID and password used in the connection string. Typically such information is stored in a configuration file that is carefully secured. All precautions used for connection string information with `DataReader` or `DataSet` also apply to LINQ to SQL.

■ Get the Most from LINQ to SQL

Put the query results in a collection if you plan to enumerate them multiple times. Use compiled queries wherever possible for queries that are executed often. Although LINQ to SQL addresses SQL injection, you need to secure a connection string to protect any secrets, such as userid and password.

Summary

This chapter covered the details of reading objects with LINQ to SQL. LINQ queries are translated into SQL using mapping information for classes and relationships between classes. Mapped classes can be used to retrieve entities or projections. Relationships can be expressed as mapped properties that can be navigated using the dot or through joins. The target of a relationship can be loaded lazily or eagerly. Like relationships, inheritance is also supported by LINQ to SQL for a class hierarchy mapped to a table.

The distinction between a query with deferred execution and a cached result is a key to understanding the performance implications. Query performance can be significantly boosted by using compiled queries, which can be effectively cached in a web application. Finally, LINQ to SQL exclusively uses parameters to avoid SQL injection attacks. Thus, LINQ to SQL is a high-performance tool that provides a rich and relatively secure way to read objects from a database.

◾9◾

Modifying Objects with LINQ to SQL

Q UERYING IS THE FOCUS of all LINQ components, as the name Language Integrated Query suggests. However, applications that use relational data as objects need to go beyond querying by making changes to the retrieved objects and saving them back to the database. LINQ to SQL complements the LINQ query pattern with a simple API to modify and save objects.

Relational databases use SQL commands to insert, update, and delete rows. The LINQ pattern currently does not cover such commands because they are very specific to the relational domain. Furthermore, for most applications, it is more natural and efficient to work with objects and in-memory collections to modify objects until all the changes are done. Then they can be submitted to the database for insert, update, and delete operations. Hence, LINQ to SQL follows this approach by letting users modify their objects as they wish and then executing SQL commands for all the changes in one batch. This approach preserves the normal way of handling objects in the program and allows the developer to decide exactly when the changes are made persistent in the database.

This chapter starts with the foundational concept of creating new entity instances in the database and modifying or deleting existing instances from the database. We will then look at related concepts of concurrent changes, transactions, and support for moving entities between tiers to make changes. We will also look at how LINQ to SQL integrates with presentation technologies to display and modify data in Windows and web applications.

Entity Lifecycle

As mentioned in the preceding chapter, objects decorated with mapping information about the primary key are the only modifiable objects and are called entities. Typically, entities are retrieved through the use of one or more queries and then are manipulated until the application is ready to send back the changes to the server. This process may repeat a number of times until the application no longer needs the entities. At that point the entities are reclaimed by the runtime just like normal CLR objects. The data, however, remains in the database in persistent form. Even after the runtime representation is gone, the same data can still be retrieved. In this sense an entity's true lifetime exists beyond any single runtime manifestation.

The focus of this chapter is the *entity lifecycle*, in which a cycle refers to the time span of a single manifestation of an entity object within a particular runtime context. The cycle starts when the `DataContext` becomes aware of a new instance, and it ends when the object or `DataContext` is no longer needed. For both the runtime and persistent manifestations, let's start by looking at how entities are created for insertion and then are deleted.

Inserting and Deleting Entities

Consider the following code fragment that retrieves a `Customer` and adds a newly created order to its `Orders` collection. When the order is added to the collection, no change occurs in the database. In fact, the connection to the database is not even used at that point. Later, when `SubmitChanges()` is called, LINQ to SQL discovers the newly added order and generates the appropriate SQL `INSERT` command to create an Order in the database. Be sure to run the code in this chapter only against a copy of the Northwind database so that you keep the original copy intact. The following examples assume that the designer in Visual Studio or SqlMetal has been used to generate entity classes used against a copy of Northwind.

```
NorthwindDataContext db = new NorthwindDataContext(connectionString);
db.Log = Console.Out;

// Retrieve single customer with given ID - AROUT
Customer cust = (from c in db.Customers
                 where c.CustomerID == "AROUT"
                 select c).Single();

Order ord = new Order();
// Set properties for the new order
...
// Add order to the customer's Orders collection
cust.Orders.Add(ord);

db.SubmitChanges();

// Display the database generated id
Console.WriteLine(ord.OrderID);
```

A new Order could also be created using a slightly different approach, as shown in the next code fragment. The key differences in this code fragment are the lack of a query and a `DataContext.InsertOnSubmit()` call.

```
NorthwindDataContext db = new NorthwindDataContext(connectionString);

Order ord = new Order();
ord.CustomerID = "AROUT";
// Set other properties for the new order
...
// Add order to Table<Order> for eventual insertion
db.Orders.InsertOnSubmit(ord);

db.SubmitChanges();
```

In the first example, LINQ to SQL discovers a new order because it can be reached from the `Customer` object that was being tracked. The second example has no query, so there is no tracked object to start looking for new objects. The `InsertOnSubmit()`call introduces the new Order to the `DataContext` so that it can be inserted when `SubmitChanges()` is called. The first example shows the convenience of an inferred insert. The second example shows that when a new entity is not reachable from a known entity, it still can be introduced for insertion.

The example of inserting an Order is also interesting because it shows another requirement for inserting a new Order—retrieving a database-generated ID. The `Order.OrderID` column in the Northwind database is an autoincremented identity key. The mapping created using the designer or SqlMetal indicates that the value is database-generated by setting the IsDbGenerated property of the Column attribute to true. You can view this property in the property grid (called "Auto Generated Value") by right-clicking the class member on the designer surface and selecting Properties. Or you can look at the generated code under the dbml file node in the Solution Explorer in Visual Studio. In response to the IsDbGenerated setting, LINQ to SQL automatically retrieves the value after executing a successful INSERT command. As described in the preceding chapter, the text of the generated SQL commands sent to the database can be conveniently captured using DataContext's log, as shown in the following code snippet:

```
INSERT INTO [dbo].[Orders]([CustomerID], [EmployeeID], [OrderDate],
[RequiredDate], [ShippedDate], [ShipVia], [Freight], [ShipName],
[ShipAddress], [ShipCity], [ShipRegion], [ShipPostalCode],
[ShipCountry])
VALUES (@p0, @p1, @p2, @p3, @p4, @p5, @p6, @p7, @p8, @p9, @p10,
@p11, @p12)

SELECT CONVERT(Int,SCOPE_IDENTITY()) AS [value]
-- @p0: Input NChar (Size = 5; Prec = 0; Scale = 0) [AROUT]
...
```

An entity can be deleted by calling DeleteOnSubmit(), as shown in the next example. For simplicity, let's delete the order that was created in the previous example by setting the retrievedID variable to the OrderID value displayed by the last code fragment in place of the ellipsis (...) in the code.

```
// Set the value to newly inserted OrderID
int retrievedID = ...;

// Retrieve single order with given ID
Order ord = (from o in db.Orders
                where o.OrderID == retrievedID
                select o).Single();

// Mark the order for deletion
db.Orders.DeleteOnSubmit(ord);

db.SubmitChanges();
```

If the order was removed from the corresponding Customer's Orders collection by calling cust.Orders.Remove(), that would have been considered a case of "severing the association" between the Customer and the order entities; it would not be a case of deletion. The result would be an update to the Order setting the foreign key value to null to reflect the severance of association. Thus, unlike in the case of insertion, LINQ to SQL does *not* infer that a DELETE command should be generated for removal from a relationship collection. A DELETE command requires a DeleteOnSubmit()call to avoid accidental deletion. This is a safer choice.

Updating Entities

After entities are retrieved from the database, you are free to manipulate them as you like. They are your objects; use them as you will. As you do this, LINQ to SQL tracks changes so that it can persist them into the database when SubmitChanges() is called.

LINQ to SQL starts tracking your entities as soon as they are materialized, even before giving them to you as returned results of a query. Indeed, the identity management service discussed in Chapter 8, "Reading Objects with LINQ to SQL," has already kicked in as well. Change tracking costs very little in additional overhead until you actually start making changes. It allows LINQ to SQL to generate UPDATE statements when you call SubmitChanges(). Unlike in the case of deletion, which requires DeleteOnSubmit(), no additional API needs to be called before SubmitChanges(). The following code shows a simple example in which the ContactName property is changed for a Customer:

```
var cust = (from c in db.Customers
            where c.CustomerID == "AROUT"
            select c).Single();

// Change a property of retrieved customer
cust.ContactName = "Horatio Hornblower";

// Persist the change
db.SubmitChanges();
```

The automatic detection of a change is made possible by LINQ to SQL's ability to keep a copy of the original entity for comparison when `SubmitChanges()` is called. A new interface `INotifyPropertyChanging` was added to make this efficient by allowing a copy to be made just before an entity is changed through a property setter. The code generated by the designer or SqlMetal for entities implements this interface and notifies the LINQ to SQL runtime about an imminent change. The runtime makes a copy of the entity before the first property change. Entities that are queried but not modified do not need to have their original versions copied for comparison and update statement generation.

The original values also allow LINQ to SQL to generate a *minimal update statement*. Only the columns that are modified are set to new values. Unchanged column values are not set. The SQL generated for the previous C# code setting `Customer.ContactName` sets only the corresponding column with parameter `p10`, as follows:

```
UPDATE [dbo].[Customers]
SET [ContactName] = @p10
WHERE ([CustomerID] = @p0)
...
```

As in the case of insertions, some column values may be set in the database. A common example is a timestamp column. The value of the timestamp is set for an updated row in the database. Another example is a trigger-updated column. In such cases, using the `IsDbGenerated` and `Auto-Sync` properties of the `Column` mapping attribute, you can tell LINQ to SQL to skip updating the column and instead retrieve the value after successful update.

Automatically Maintained Relationships

Relationships pose an interesting challenge. They involve two entities. Hence, a change in the relationship affects two entities. In the database, this is simplified through normalized data models and foreign keys. In the case of the database relationship between `Customers` and `Orders`, the Orders table contains a foreign key recording the relationship, and the Customers table keeps no direct record of the relationship. In the corresponding object model, both the `Customer.Orders` collection and the `Order.Customer` references pointing back to `Customer` entities need to be in sync. If the `Customer.Orders` collection contains an `Order`, the corresponding `Order.Customer` better point back to the same Customer entity.

Maintaining such a bidirectional relationship would be quite a chore if you had to take care of it every time there was any change. Fortunately, LINQ to SQL automates this process through a combination of the generated code and the `EntitySet–EntityRef` classes. `Customer.Orders` is of type `EntitySet<Order>`, and `Order.Customer` is of type `EntityRef <Customer>`. Consider the following code, which moves an order from one `Customer` to another. Here, we use the terser but semantically identical lambda function syntax to retrieve single customers:

```
Customer cust1 = db.Customers.Single(c => c.CustomerID == id1);
Customer cust2 = db.Customers.Single(c => c.CustomerID == id2);

// Pick an order
Order o = cust1.Orders[0];

// Remove from first, add to the second
cust1.Orders.Remove(o);
cust2.Orders.Add(o);

// Prints 'true'
Console.WriteLine(o.Customer == cust2);
```

The same objective can be accomplished just as well through the following assignment instead of the `Remove()`, `Add()` sequence used in the preceding example:

```
o.Customer = cust2;
```

If you assign a null to a relationship reference, you are severing the relationship. This is distinct from deleting the target of the relationship. In the following code, the order is no longer associated with any `Customer` entity. The order's original target `Customer` is not deleted. Likewise, if you remove an order from the `Customer.Orders` collection, the effect is symmetric: the relationship is severed, but the order is not deleted. In each case, LINQ to SQL attempts to set the foreign key column `Order.CustomerId` to null in the database when `SubmitChanges()` is called. Such an operation may succeed if the foreign key column is nullable; otherwise, it will fail.

```
Customer cust1 = db.Customers.Single(c => c.CustomerID == id1);

// Pick an order
Order o = cust1.Orders[0];

// Set reference to null. db.DeleteOnSubmit() not called
o.Customer = null;

// Prints 'true'
Console.WriteLine(cust1.Orders.Contains(o));

// Updates Order
db.SubmitChanges();
```

Regardless of which direction you choose for severing a relationship—a `Customer.Orders.Remove()` call or assignment to `Order.Customer`—the net effect is an update to the entity containing a member mapped to the relationship's foreign key—in this case, `Order`. The key member for maintaining relationship is in the entity containing the foreign key, often called the child entity. Hence, LINQ to SQL requires the object reference from child to parent. The reference or collection of references in the other direction—from the parent entity to the child entity—is optional. In the `Customer–Orders` relationship, `Order.Customer` must be present and mapped, while the `Customer.Orders` member may be skipped.

References and collections of references are how object models handle relationships. But the underlying foreign key value (such as `Order.CustomerId`) is often valuable for showing the relationship in the presentation tier and for serializing the entities to another tier. Hence, it is available for use as a mapped member when you use the designer or SqlMetal. However, the foreign key value needs to remain consistent with the references. The generated LINQ to SQL code ensures that after it is initialized, an *in-memory* foreign key value is not accidentally directly changed. It is kept in sync with the in-memory references by the generated code.

Submitting Changes

The previous sections covered basic insert, delete, and update operations, as well as relationship management, as individual operations. However, a key advantage of accessing relational data as objects is that you can retrieve a bunch of objects, make changes to the object graph as needed, and then make all the changes persistent in one shot. LINQ to SQL uses this model by persisting all the pending changes in response to SubmitChanges(). This one-shot approach allows changes to be done or aborted atomically so that the database remains in a consistent state. It also provides a logical check-point for a set of changes and minimizes the overhead.

When you call SubmitChanges(), the set of tracked entities is examined. All entities with pending changes are ordered into a sequence based on dependencies between them. Objects whose changes depend on other objects are sequenced after their dependencies. Foreign key constraints and uniqueness constraints in the database play a big part in determining the correct ordering of changes. Then, just before any actual changes are trans-mitted, a transaction is started to encapsulate the series of individual com-mands unless one is already in scope. Finally, one by one the changes to the objects are translated into SQL commands and are sent to the server.

Any errors detected by the database cause the submission process to abort, and an exception is raised. All changes to the database are rolled back as if none of the submissions ever took place. The DataContext still has a full recording of all changes, so it is possible to attempt to rectify the prob-lem and resubmit the changes by calling SubmitChanges() again. The fol-lowing code shows the conceptual handling of exceptions. The following sections look at the processing of the specific exception that user code should check for and a richer set of transaction options.

```
NorthwindDataContext db = new NorthwindDataContext(connectionString);

// make changes to in-memory objects here

try {
    db.SubmitChanges();
}
catch (ChangeConflictException e) {
    // make some adjustments
    ...
    // retry
    db.SubmitChanges();
}
```

When the transaction around the submission completes successfully, the DataContext recognizes all the changes to the objects by simply forgetting the change-tracking information. However, failure of the transaction to complete successfully does not lead to a rollback of the local change tracking state. As just shown, you need to make the necessary changes to the entities based on the exception and then resubmit the changes. For example, if an update fails because a value is out of range, specified by a check constraint in the database, you need to change to value to fit within the range and then call SubmitChanges() again. Alternatively, if you decide not to retry the submission, you can discard the DataContext instance and restart with a new one. There is no rollback for the in-memory state held by a DataContext instance.

After successful completion of SubmitChanges(), you may use the DataContext for further queries and updates. Each successful SubmitChanges() call concludes a unit of work and effectively starts the next unit of work with no pending changes left. The following example shows a sequence of two units of work. Note that the Customer entity retrieved during the first unit of work remains available for the second unit of work and does not automatically get refreshed when a new unit of work begins.

```
// First unit of work
Customer cust =
        db.Customers.Where(c => c.CustomerID == "AROUT").Single();
// Defer load orders and modify some orders
...
db.SubmitChanges();
// Second unit of work begins
// Make more changes
...
db.SubmitChanges();
```

Simultaneous Changes

So far we have discussed changes as if only one instance of one application is manipulating data in a database. But a key purpose of a database is to allow sharing of data across multiple applications and users. Hence, we need to look at what happens when multiple applications modify data simultaneously and how we can ensure that the data remains consistent in such an environment. Ensuring consistency when simultaneous or *concurrent* changes are possible is called *concurrency control*. LINQ to SQL provides some key tools for implementing concurrency control.

Consider the example of a simplified Order entity with an `OrderId`, `ShippedDate`, and `ShipAddress` being modified by an interactive order management application and a fulfillment application. Further assume that the two applications retrieve the same order and modify their copies, as shown in Figure 9.1. The fulfillment application assumes that the `ShipAddress` it has read at instant t1 is valid. It proceeds with shipping the order and sets the `ShippedDate` at time t4. The order management application in turn reads the same Order at t2 and makes a change to `ShipAddress` in the database at time t3 based on the knowledge that the order has not yet been shipped.

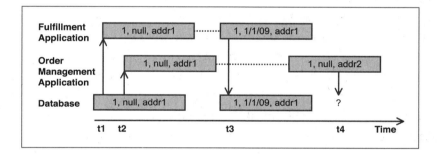

FIGURE 9.1   Concurrent changes to an entity.

Clearly, the data would be inconsistent if both the applications were allowed to make the changes and assume that their operations are successful. We would have an order that was shipped to an address that was different from the new address set by the user of the order management system. That is a conflict between two updates. So we need a way to either prevent such a conflict or detect it and take corrective actions.

A way to prevent such a conflict is to require the applications to acquire a lock on the order before making any changes. Then, only the application that can get a lock would have exclusive access to the order for making a change. This approach is an example of pessimistic concurrency control, because we are pessimistic about a conflict and always take preventive steps.

The pessimistic approach is problematic. A lock would always limit access to an order, regardless of whether other applications were looking to access the same order. In an interactive application where a user can go to lunch while keeping an order form open, such a lock could be held for a long time, and that could be unacceptable for other applications. Furthermore, it could potentially force the database server to manage a large number of locks for relatively uncommon conflicts. Hence, we need to look for a better alternative.

Optimistic Concurrency

An alternative is to take an optimistic approach: Proceed with changes as if there won't be any conflict, and then detect a conflict and take corrective actions so that consistency is ensured. In effect, instead of asking for permission to update in the form of a lock, we go ahead and update anyway and then apologize and make amends if a conflict is detected.

The optimistic concurrency approach is very suitable for data shared across applications in which the application can potentially spend a significant amount of time manipulating the data. Both applications involving user interaction and those involving significant processing without user input are good candidates for optimistic concurrency. Because such applications are the norm, LINQ to SQL relies on optimistic concurrency as the primary approach for concurrency control. Optimistic concurrency has two aspects: detection of conflicts and resolution of conflicts. LINQ to SQL provides support for both aspects.

Conflict Detection

Let's revisit the example shown in Figure 9.1. The order management application assumed that the ShippedDate was null when it was not. To avoid the conflict, it needed to detect that the value of ShippedDate had changed since it was read. In short, it could have used the original value of null and compared it against the value in the database before applying the current value for ShipAddress. In fact, you can imagine doing the comparison with the original values automatically in the data access layer. This is how the original values are used by LINQ to SQL on behalf of the application. Figure 9.2 shows how the order example can be changed to make use of the original values.

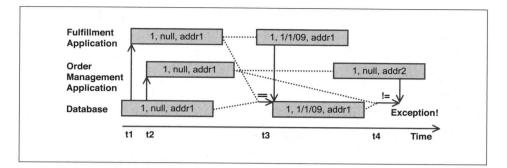

FIGURE 9.2   The original value check for conflict detection.

The following code fragments show the C# code performing the update and the corresponding generated SQL. In the absence of a conflict, the WHERE clause in the generated SQL simply confirms that there has been no change to the original values, and the update succeeds. In the case of the conflict described before, the check for the original value of ShippedDate fails and, as a result, the update fails.

```
ord.ShipAddress = "123 Main St., Paradise";
db.SubmitChanges();

UPDATE [dbo].[Orders]
SET [ShipAddress] = @p2
WHERE ([OrderID] = @p0)
AND ([ShippedDate] IS NULL)
AND ([ShipAddress] = @p1)
```

The optimistic concurrency check in the previous SQL statement covered all the mapped properties of the Order entity. Common variations include a subset of the properties that acts as a proxy for the entire entity. For example, you may exclude large values such as images or notes in certain cases, because they do not affect the business logic like ShippedDate did in the previous case. One interesting special case is where a special timestamp column (or similar DateTime column) is updated for every update to the row. Where available in the database schema, such a column provides a great conflict-detection proxy for the entire row.

LINQ to SQL designer and SqlMetal automatically detect timestamp columns and use them for the optimistic concurrency check. In the absence of such a column, all mapped columns are used for the optimistic concurrency check. This provides a safe default. However, you can override these defaults by changing the UpdateCheck property of the Column attribute for the properties you want to exclude from the check.

In the previous example, we looked at a single entity update. In many applications, multiple entities are modified, and the changes are submitted together with one SubmitChanges() call. In such a case, it is more efficient to gather information about all the conflicts that can be detected in one shot instead of dealing with one conflict at a time and discovering successive ones with additional calls to SubmitChanges(). The following code illustrates how to collect all conflicts for a set of changes submitted together. The outer loop in the catch block iterates over entities in conflict, and the inner loop iterates over the entity members in conflict.

```csharp
using System.Reflection;

// Modify Customer entities
try
{
    db.SubmitChanges(ConflictMode.ContinueOnConflict);
}
catch (ChangeConflictException e)
{
    // Take corrective actions for all detected conflicts
    foreach (ObjectChangeConflict occ in db.ChangeConflicts)
    {
        Customer customerInConflict = (Customer)occ.Object;

        foreach (MemberChangeConflict mcc in occ.MemberConflicts)
        {
            object currVal = mcc.CurrentValue;
            object origVal = mcc.OriginalValue;
            object databaseVal = mcc.DatabaseValue;
            MemberInfo mi = mcc.Member;
            // Change customerInConflict's members as appropriate
        }
    }
}

// Retry
db.SubmitChanges(ConflictMode.FailOnFirstConflict);
```

This code example also illustrates the two different failure-handling options: ContinueOnConflict and FailOnFirstConflict. The first attempt collects all the conflicts and reports them in a single exception. The second attempt is failed on the first conflict that is encountered while executing a sequence of insert, update, and delete commands. In the absence of an explicit request to continue, the default behavior of SubmitChanges() is to fail on first conflict.

Conflict Resolution

When a conflict is detected, the SubmitChanges() operation fails, and LINQ to SQL throws a ChangeConflictException. The following code shows *one way* to deal with such an exception. It generalizes the previously shown approach of using retries. In most cases, a very small number of retries are sufficient or appropriate before a user has to intervene or the processing has to start over again by retrieving the data again.

```
while (retries < maxRetries)
{
   try
   {
      db.SubmitChanges(ConflictMode.ContinueOnConflict);
      break;
   }
   catch (ChangeConflictException e)
   {
      // Adjust properties of objects with conflicts
      retries++;
   }
}
```

LINQ to SQL provides tools for reporting errors and adjusting objects with conflicting changes. In some applications, user input may be the best choice for deciding what adjustments, if any, should be made. In others, policy-based resolution may be programmatically applied for automatic handling of conflicts.

Three steps are involved in handling conflicts: catching ChangeConflictException, resolving each reported conflict using the built-in resolution mechanism or through additional programmatic work, and calling SubmitChanges() again. Three resolution policy options often are referred to by simplified names: client wins, database wins, and merge. Alternatively and more informally, the first two also are called stomp on the database and stomp on my updates. The RefreshMode enumeration has three corresponding values. To illustrate the difference, let's consider a slightly modified version of the entity class that contains three nonkey values— ShippedDate, ShipAddress, and ShipVia. Figure 9.3 shows the effect of each of the options for an Order object that was concurrently updated, causing a conflict between the original and database values.

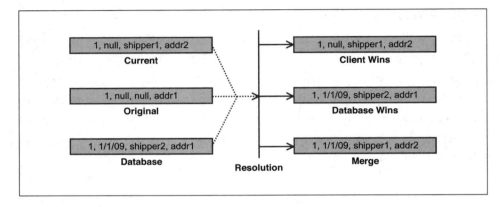

FIGURE 9.3 Conflict resolution options.

- Client wins, or the KeepCurrentValues option: The original values are reset to the database values so that when SubmitChanges() is called again, the "new" original values are the same as those that caused the conflict. Hence, no conflict occurs during the second SubmitChanges() call, and the current, in-memory values overwrite the concurrent update. Hence, this option circumvents optimistic concurrency by pushing through the updates anyway, despite the optimistic concurrency check specified in the mapping. So this is most appropriate after some check about the values or a user override. This is the default value used by the Resolve() method when the option is not explicitly specified.

- Database wins, or the OverwriteCurrentValues option: The current values in the DataContext are overwritten and effectively lost. This allows changes to other entities that were *not* in conflict to succeed with the next SubmitChanges() call. The conflicting update is simply omitted.

• Merge, or the `KeepChanges` option: The concurrent changes are merged such that the values of properties updated in the current version in the `DataContext` are retained. As a result, if conflicting changes are made to a property, the client values win over the database values. Note that in the particular example in Figure 9.3, this option does not make much sense based on the semantics of the three properties.

The `Resolve()` method also supports an additional Boolean parameter to ignore conflicts in case of delete operations.

Conflict resolution requires two key decisions: selecting the resolution option, and deciding on the number of retries before abandoning the current set of changes and starting over. Each resolution option involves overwriting someone's change or potentially merging inconsistent changes. Hence, it is worth seeking human input from a user if the application has a user interface. Otherwise, automatic conflict resolution based on predetermined choices may be the only option. The number of retries typically is decided in advance and is defined in the program. Optimistic concurrency is intended for cases in which conflicting concurrent changes are rare. Hence, a small number of retries, often just one, is appropriate and sufficient. In practice, repeated conflicts in succession may indicate that optimistic concurrency is an unsuitable option. Perhaps a more pessimistic approach using transactions is appropriate.

Refreshing Entities

Simultaneous changes also can affect entities that have been retrieved but not modified. Modified entities can be refreshed when a conflict is detected by using the `Resolve()` method. For unmodified entities, an explicit `Refresh()` call is required to retrieve the latest values. Refresh capability is particularly handy when a unit of work runs for a long time. An example is when the results are bound to a user interface and the user comes back after a lunch break. Another example is when certain entities need to be selectively refreshed for a second unit of work. The following code is a modified version of a previous code sample with a `Refresh()` call added. Note that `Refresh()` changes only the scalar values and does not affect relationship properties such as `Order.Order_Details`.

```
// First unit of work
Customer cust =
        db.Customers.Where(c => c.CustomerID == "AROUT").Single();
// Defer load orders and modify some orders
...
db.SubmitChanges();

// Second unit of work begins
// Select a specific order with a LINQ to Objects query
// Refresh the order before making changes
Order ord = cust.Orders.Where(...).Single();
db.Refresh(RefreshMode.OverwriteCurrentValues, ord);
// Change the order
...
db.SubmitChanges();
```

LINQ to SQL computes the set of changes before generating SQL commands to make the changes persistent. You can ask for the set of changes using the GetChangeSet() method. This gives you a way to inspect the changes and possibly do some validations before deciding to call SubmitChanges(). It also provides a handy tool for debugging your applications without affecting the rows in the database. The changes are returned as three read-only collections containing entities to be inserted, updated, and deleted, respectively. ChangeSet also has a convenient ToString() implementation that lists the number of inserts, updates, and deletes. Alternatively, you can use the ObjectDumper class from the Visual Studio sample project mentioned in the preceding chapter to see the results. The following listing shows a usage pattern:

```
Customer cust = new Customer();
cust.CustomerID = "AAAA";
// Set other properties

Order ord = db.Orders.Where(o => o.OrderID == 10355).Single();
Order_Detail od = ord.Order_Details[0];

// New customer (insert), changed order, deleted detail
ord.Customer = cust;
db.Order_Details.DeleteOnSubmit(od);

// Get change set without submitting anything to database
ChangeSet cs = db.GetChangeSet();

// The following prints "{Inserts: 1, Deletes: 1, Updates: 1}"
Console.WriteLine(cs);
```

```
// See contents of Inserts, Deletes, Updates collections
// ObjectDumper sample must be built into a DLL and added
ObjectDumper.Write(cs,1);

// Submit to database after additional processing
db.SubmitChanges();
```

In summary, LINQ to SQL provides a rich set of tools to handle simultaneous changes. You can specify what properties should be used to detect conflicts, choose to end on first conflict, or get information about all conflicts and resolve conflicts with simple built-in options. You can also refresh the state for unmodified objects. These tools cover concurrent changes between the time that objects are read and the time that the changes are submitted. But an equally important issue is to ensure that all the changes are done atomically as one unit of work or are not done at all. This is accomplished using transactions, which are covered next.

Transactions and Connection Management

LINQ to SQL lets you retrieve a graph of objects for modification. All changes to the graph can then be submitted as a single unit of work with a `SubmitChanges()` call. A unit of work may include multiple updates, inserts, and deletes. Each operation on an entity is handled as a single database command. So the set of changes requires a set of commands. This raises some obvious questions:

- What happens when one of the commands fails—say, due to a change conflict or some other failure?
- What happens if someone else makes changes between two commands in a set of changes?

LINQ to SQL addresses these issues by executing the set of SQL commands as a single transaction. Here is the conceptual multistep process for a `SubmitChanges()` call:

1. Compute the change set for the entities in the `DataContext`. The result is a list of entities to be updated, a list of entities to be inserted, and a list of entities to be deleted.

2. Order the changes based on foreign key dependencies. For example, an Order must be inserted before an OrderDetail can be inserted, because the latter requires the key value of the former.

3. Open a connection to the database, and start a transaction or use the ambient transaction.

4. Execute INSERT, UPDATE, and DELETE SQL commands, with appropriate checks for conflict detection.

5. Run queries for database-generated values.

6. If all commands execute successfully, commit the transaction to make the changes persistent in the database. Otherwise, roll back the transaction and throw exception to inform the caller that SubmitChanges() failed.

The transaction around all the SQL commands addresses these questions. It ensures that either all the changes are persisted or all of them are ignored, leaving the database in the same state as before the beginning of the transaction. Second, depending on the transaction's isolation level, the database server prevents conflicting changes between the commands.

LINQ to SQL starts a transaction by default to minimize the chance of an error. You do not have to remember to start a transaction for every SubmitChanges() call. However, you still have control over the transaction boundary if you so desire. You have two additional options at your disposal for more advanced scenarios. In most common cases, you do not need the following options; you can just rely on the implicit transaction started by a SubmitChanges() call.

Use a TransactionScope to perform additional operations in the context of the transaction. LINQ to SQL detects an ambient transaction and uses it for SubmitChanges(). The transaction is committed or aborted based on the usual TransactionScope model. Failures other than SubmitChanges() also get to veto the transaction's completion.

Create a DbTransaction yourself, and use it to execute other commands as necessary. Then tell LINQ to SQL to use it by setting the DataContext.Transaction property. You still get to start and commit or roll back the transaction as you want.

Use of `TransactionScope` is convenient when you want to perform additional operations. A common scenario for such a broader scope is to include queries and `SubmitChanges()` in one transaction, as shown in the following code. This provides a pessimistic concurrency control option, where you want to avoid conflicts rather than detecting and resolving them. Another usage scenario is to enable access to multiple transactional sources using a promotable or distributed transaction.

```
using System.Transactions; // Add reference to System.Transactions.dll

using (TransactionScope ts = new TransactionScope())
{
   NorthwindDataContext db = new NorthwindDataContext();
   List<Order> orders =
      db.Orders.Where(o => o.Customer.CustomerID == "ALFKI").ToList();
   // Modify order entities here
   db.SubmitChanges();
   ts.Complete();
}
```

Use of `DbTransaction` allows interoperability with code using ADO. NET relational APIs, as shown in the following code. It lets you mix direct SQL commands and LINQ to SQL operations, and it also allows you to change the isolation level on the transaction if you want.

```
using System.Data.SqlClient;

DbTransaction myTxn = db.Connection.BeginTransaction();
// Execute some SqlCommands with the transaction
db.Transaction = myTxn;
try
{
    db.SubmitChanges();
}
catch(ChangeConflictException e)
{
    // handle conflicts and roll back transaction
}
// Do additional work with the transaction
myTxn.Commit();
```

Optimistic concurrency checks and transactions provide complementary support. The former allows disconnected operation. No resources are held on the database server while working with entities retrieved in memory, and yet conflicting changes are detected. The latter ensures that either all changes are persisted successfully, or nothing is persisted in case of a failure.

The two mechanisms also illustrate how connections are managed by LINQ to SQL. When a user issues a query, LINQ to SQL issues a command and creates a `DataReader`. As soon as the results are consumed, the connection goes back to the connection pool for use by other users of the connection (unless you explicitly change the connection pooling setting on the connection). This pattern repeats for all LINQ to SQL queries. Meanwhile, the retrieved objects can be used for potentially long-running computations involving user input (including coffee breaks) or for complex processing. When all the changes are done and `SubmitChanges()` is called, LINQ to SQL again opens a connection to the database and uses it to execute `INSERT`, `UPDATE`, and `DELETE` SQL commands in a transaction. LINQ to SQL then returns the connection to the connection pool. This minimizes connection usage while providing flexibility of operating in disconnected mode and yet making changes to the retrieved objects. Thus, precious database resources such as connections are managed carefully to provide a more scalable solution.

Attaching Multitier Entities

In two-tier applications, a single `DataContext` instance handles queries and updates to results of queries. However, for applications that have additional tiers, it is often necessary to use separate `DataContext` instances for query and update. For example, in the case of an ASP.NET application, query and update are executed as separate requests to the web server where most of the code is supposed to operate in a stateless fashion. The requests may even go to different machines in a server farm. Hence, it is not possible to use the same `DataContext` instance across multiple requests. In such cases, a `DataContext` instance needs to be able to update objects that it has not retrieved. The `Attach()` method allows the `DataContext` to deal with entities coming from another tier. An `Attach()` call tells the `DataContext` to start tracking the entity as if it were retrieved with a query but without actually requiring a database query. Just like the `InsertOnSubmit()`

method, this capability is exposed by `Table<T>` for each given entity type `T`. The following example shows a typical usage:

```
NorthwindDataContext db1 = new NorthwindDataContext();
Customer c1 = db1.Customers.Single(c => c.CustomerID == "AROUT");

// Customer entity changed on another tier - e.g. through a browser
// Back on the mid-tier, a new context needs to be used
NorthwindDataContext db2 = new NorthwindDataContext();
// Create a new entity for applying changes
Customer c2 = new Customer();
c2.CustomerID = originalID;

// Set other properties needed for optimistic concurrency check
c2.CompanyName = originalCompanyName;
...
// Tell DataContext to track this object for an update
db2.Customers.Attach(c2);
// Now apply the changes
c2.ContactName = "Horatio Hornblower";
// DataContext has original/current values to update the customer
db2.SubmitChanges();
```

In the absence of `Attach()`, during `SubmitChanges()` processing, an entity that was not retrieved in a query is considered to be a new entity for insertion into the database. `Attach()` tells the `DataContext` that the entity is not new but merely serialized from another tier.

`Attach()` needs to preserve the optimistic concurrency capability by ensuring that current and original values are available. As a result, three different overloads deal with the current and original values:

- Original values used for conflict detection: `Attach(originalCustomer)` should be used to attach the original values. The instance can then be modified by playing back the changes serialized from another tier before calling `SubmitChanges()`.

- Original and current copies available: `Attach(currentCustomer, originalCustomer)` does it in one shot. This requires two instances with original and current values, respectively.

- Timestamp or no optimistic concurrency members: `Attach(currentProduct, true)` lets you attach the current value without requiring the original values. No playback is needed before `SubmitChanges()`

is called. The current version of `Product` is attached with updated members but the original timestamp. The original timestamp takes care of the optimistic concurrency check. If the mapping is set up to skip the optimistic concurrency check, the current version is all that is needed for an update when `SubmitChanges()` is called.

In many multitier applications, the entire entity often is not sent across tiers for simplicity, interoperability, or privacy. For example, a supplier may define a data contract for a web service that differs from the Order entity used on the middle tier. Likewise, a web page may show only a subset of the members of an Employee entity. Hence, the multitier support also accommodates such cases. Only the members belonging to one or more of the following categories need to be transported between tiers and set before calling `Attach()`:

- Members that are part of the entity's identity
- Members that have been changed
- Members that participate in the optimistic concurrency check

LINQ to SQL uses minimal updates. It checks which columns are changed from the original to the current version and creates a SQL `UPDATE` command to set just the corresponding columns. So when you create an entity instance on the mid-tier for attaching, anything that is not changed and not required for the optimistic concurrency check can be skipped. The remaining members can have default values in both the original and current versions. For example, if an `Order` uses a timestamp and only the `ShipAddress` has been changed, you need to set only three properties when you new up an Order entity—`OrderID`, `ShipAddress`, and the timestamp property.

When attaching objects in original state, the entity graph is recursively explored for each attached entity until a known entity is reached. By default, no further action is taken for attached entities. For example, if you attach an `Order` in original state, all related `Order_Detail` entities are also attached. You are free to make changes to `Order_Details` to effect an update, or you can even take action to have them inserted or deleted.

However, entities for insertion and deletion *do not* require the `Attach()` method. The methods used for two-tier applications—`Table.InsertOn-Submit()` and `Table.DeleteOnSubmit()`—need to be used for inserting and deleting multitier entities. As in the case of two-tier usage, a user is responsible for handling the foreign key constraints in the multitier case as well. A customer with orders cannot just be deleted without handling its orders if a foreign key constraint in the database is preventing the deletion of a customer with orders.

`Attach()` is designed for multitier entities obtained through deserialization from another tier or a web service. It is not intended for moving objects from one live `DataContext` instance to another. When an entity is already in the scope of a live `DataContext`, it may be "tethered" to the `DataContext` instance to enable deferred loading. If you try to `Attach()` such an entity to another `DataContext` instance, you get an exception. In short, you should call `Attach()` only if you have an entity that is detached. There is no specific API to detach an entity from a `DataContext`. When you serialize the entity, it is effectively detached when it is re-created through deserialization.

Thus, `Attach()` provides a core operation that brings a deserialized entity into the world of entities retrieved from the database. After it is attached, the entity then can be used for update, delete, or refresh operations exactly like the entities retrieved from the database. With the foundation of these operations, let's now look at how to build a presentation tier for entities retrieved using LINQ to SQL.

Data Binding

Many applications have a presentation tier that uses the data retrieved by a Data Access Layer (DAL) technology such as LINQ to SQL. In the presentation tier, the data is bound to user interface (UI) controls—either with one-way data binding for a read-only display of data or two-way data binding for updatable data. Two-way data binding ensures that the control and the object bound to it remain in sync as the values in either of them are changed. You can use the objects retrieved and saved by LINQ to SQL for two-way data binding either with smart client technologies such as

Windows Forms and Windows Presentation Foundation (WPF) or with web technology such as ASP.NET Web Forms.

Smart Client Data Binding

The entities retrieved using LINQ to SQL are normal CLR objects that can be used for data binding just like any other CLR object. The role of LINQ to SQL in supporting data binding comes into focus for the results of a query. In general, the results of a LINQ to SQL query are of type `IEnumerable<T>`. Hence, they can be displayed easily, like any other `IEnumerable<T>`. For two-way data binding, LINQ to SQL implicitly implements the necessary interface so that you can bind the results of a typical query to a `DataGrid`. The following sequence of steps gets a simple form that binds to `Orders` and `Order_Details`:

1. Create a new Windows Forms Application called NorthwindForms, and add a new item for LINQ to SQL classes named Northwind.dbml. Use the design surface to build an object model by dragging and dropping two tables from the Northwind database—Orders and Order Details. After you have the model, the first step for data binding is to create a new data source using the Data menu in Visual Studio, as shown in Figure 9.4.

FIGURE 9.4   The Add New Data Source menu option.

2. The Add New Data Source menu option brings up the Data Source Configuration Wizard, as shown in Figure 9.5. Because LINQ to SQL returns normal CLR objects, choose Object as the Data Source Type.

3. Click Next to bring up a list of available objects, including `Order` and `Order_Detail`, as shown in Figure 9.6.

FIGURE 9.5   Choosing a data source type.

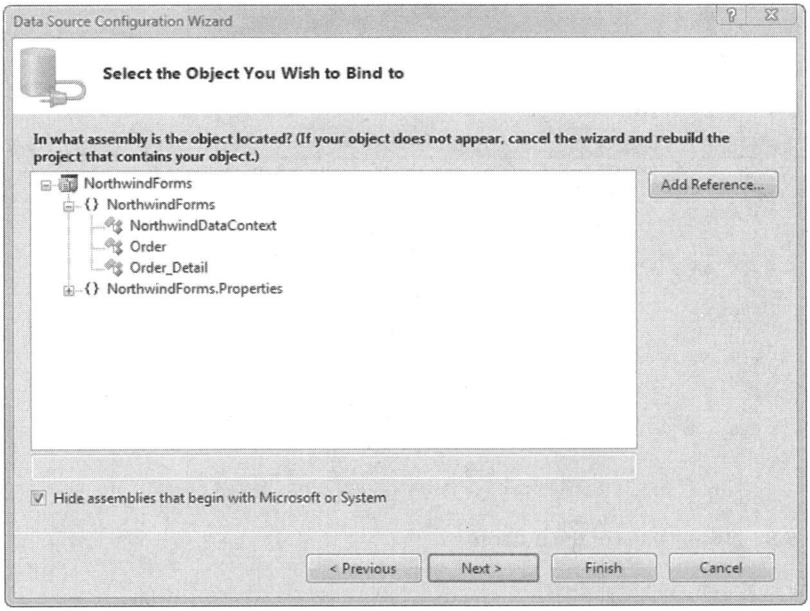

FIGURE 9.6   Choosing the object you want to bind to.

4. Select Order and click Finish to put Order in the Data Sources window, as shown in Figure 9.7. You can get to the Data Sources window by selecting Data, Show Data Source in Visual Studio.

FIGURE 9.7   The Data Sources window populated by the wizard.

5. Drag and drop Order from the Data Sources window onto the form to get the grid shown in Figure 9.8.

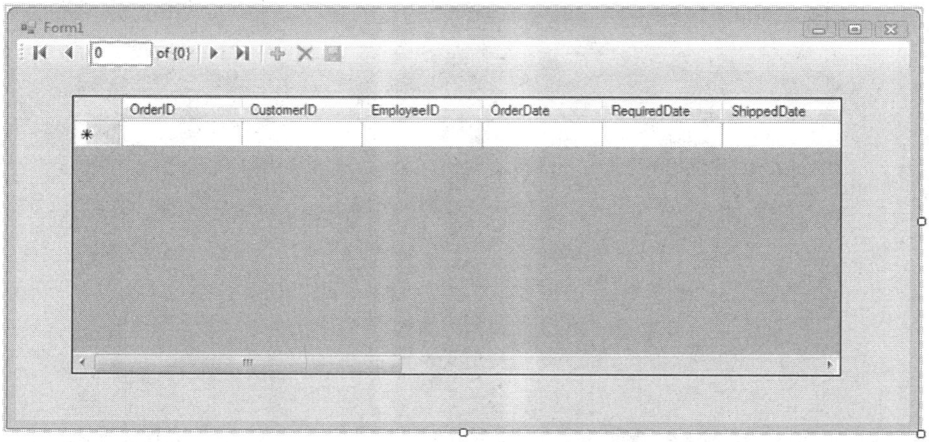

FIGURE 9.8   Design view of the order form.

6. Notice that Order_Details is available as a data source under Order. This is possible because LINQ to SQL recognizes the foreign

key-based relationship and automatically creates a collection of `Order_Details` that is available as a data source. To see a master-details view showing `Orders` and their `Order_Details`, drag `Order_Details` from the Data Sources window onto the form. The result is shown in Figure 9.9.

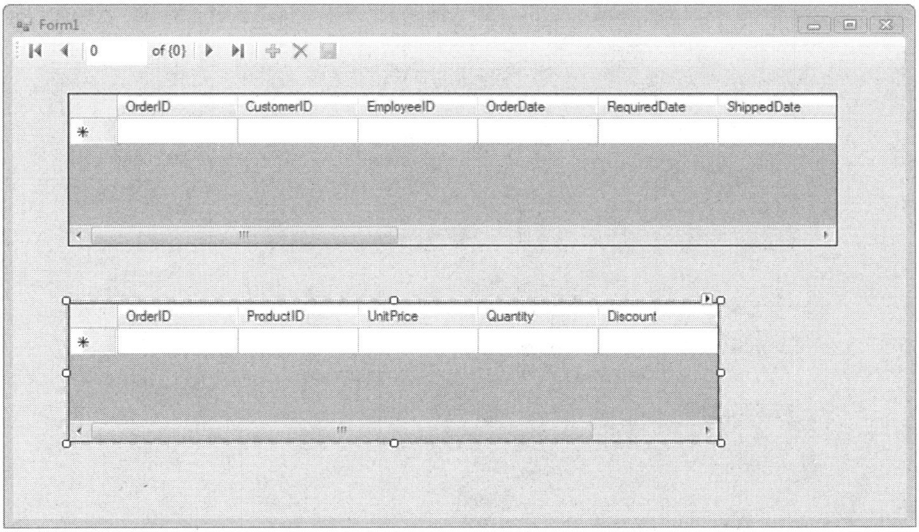

FIGURE 9.9   Design view of the master-details form.

Now it is time to instantiate a `DataContext` instance and specify the query whose results we want to bind. In general, it is not a good idea to bind the entire contents of a database table to a form, because the amount of data may be too large for a user of the form to consume. Here, we will get the orders for one customer with ID `"AROUT"`. The following listing shows the result of adding code to instantiate a `DataContext` and specifying the query for orders:

```
public partial class Form1 : Form
{
    private NorthwindDataContext db = new NorthwindDataContext();
    public Form1()
    {
        InitializeComponent();
        orderBindingSource.DataSource = from o in db.Orders
                                        where o.CustomerID == "AROUT"
```

```
                                        select o;
        }
    }
```

A sample application displaying orders is now ready to run. Figure 9.10 shows the data retrieved when the application is run.

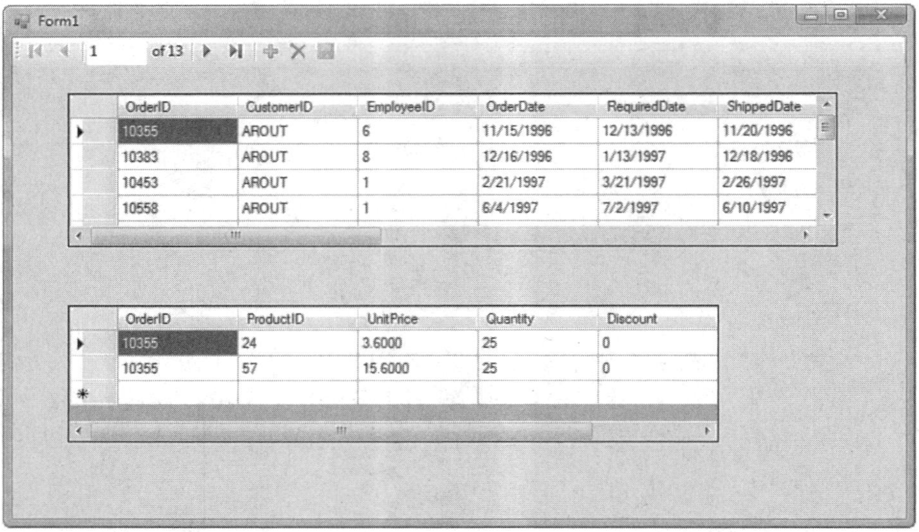

Figure 9.10   Results in the master-details form.

ASP.NET Data Binding

The experience for basic data binding of query results is very similar in ASP.NET. Create a new ASP.NET web application and add the existing model previously created in the Windows Forms applications sample. Use the Toolbox in Visual Studio to drag and drop a GridView control and add the title "Order Details" to Default.aspx as follows:

```
<h3>Order Details</h3>
<asp:GridView ID="GridView1" runat="server">
</asp:GridView>
```

Save Default.aspx and add the following code to the Page_Load() method in Default.aspx.cs:

```
protected void Page_Load(object sender, EventArgs e)
{
    NorthwindDataContext db = new NorthwindDataContext();

    GridView1.DataSource = from od in db.Order_Details
                           where od.OrderID == 10356
                           select od;
    GridView1.DataBind();
}
```

With just three lines of code, we have a simple sample application that is ready to run. Running it produces the output shown in Figure 9.11.

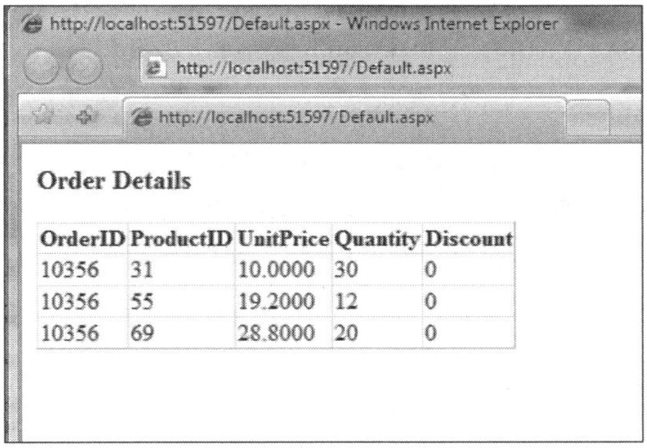

FIGURE 9.11   Order details in a web page.

This sample shows how to display results easily. However, more functionality is needed to edit the results. In the ASP.NET stateless server model, when a change is posted back, the original `DataContext` instance that retrieved the data bound results is no longer around. As discussed in the section "Attaching Multitier Entities," a new `DataContext` instance serves the second request to make a change. You could programmatically do the work for update, insert, or delete using the APIs discussed in earlier sections. But `LinqDataSource` simplifies everything with a declarative way to handle changes on postback. `LinqDataSource` implements the `Data-SourceControl` pattern defined in ASP.NET 2.0. It knows how to take a mini-string language for filtering, sorting, and paging and turn it into LINQ queries. It also knows how to round-trip the original values and `Attach()` to a new `DataContext` instance to make updates. Let's look at a quick way to enhance the previous sample to use LinqDataSource. First, remove the C# code added in the previous sample. Instead, we will use a wizard to set up a LinqDataSource, as shown in Figure 9.12.

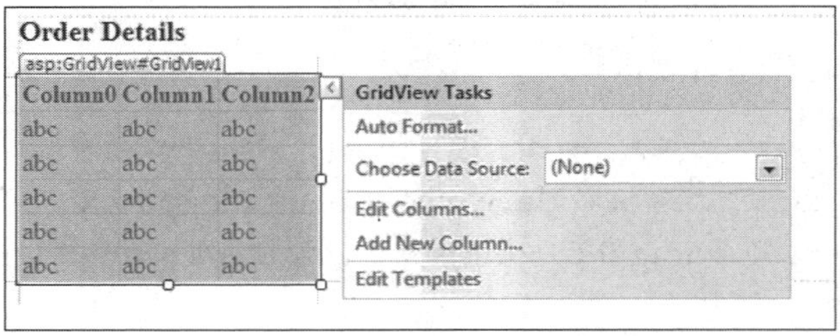

FIGURE 9.12 Launching the Data Source Configuration Wizard.

1. Select the <New data source...> option for the Choose Data Source property. The selection starts the Data Source Configuration Wizard. Select LINQ as the source, and provide a name for the LinqData-Source—Order_Details, as shown in Figure 9.13.

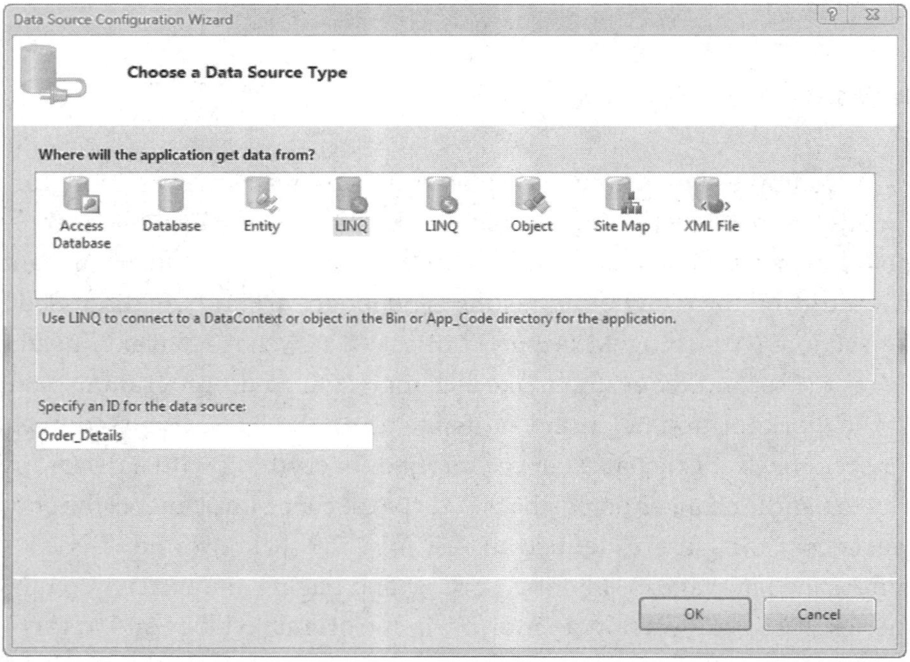

FIGURE 9.13 Launching the LinqDataSource Configuration Wizard.

2. Click OK to see the LINQ to SQL `DataContext` types available in the project and the `Table<T>` instances in them, as shown in Figure 9.14.

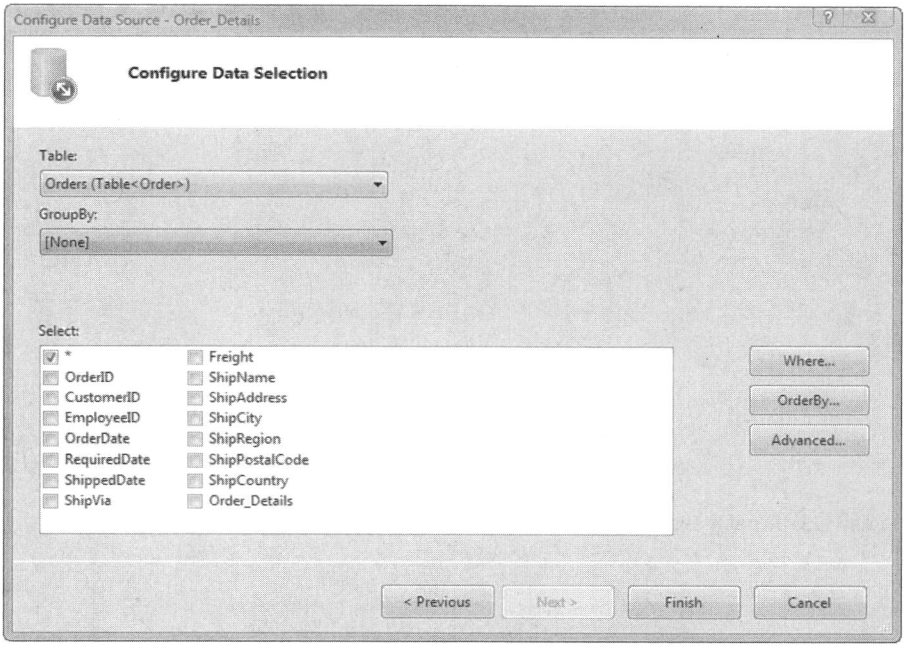

FIGURE 9.14   Selecting data in the `LinqDataSource` Configuration Wizard.

3. Click the Where button to specify a filter for the LINQ query, as shown in Figure 9.15. This dialog is suitable for relatively simple predicates in the LINQ `where` clause. For more complex cases, you could simply edit the `LinqDataSource` element in the aspx file.

4. Click OK to go back to the Configure Data Selection dialog (see Figure 9.14). You can similarly set up sorting by clicking the OrderBy button. Clicking the Advanced button brings up the key dialog shown in Figure 9.16. It is essential for ensuring that the query results are set up for modification.

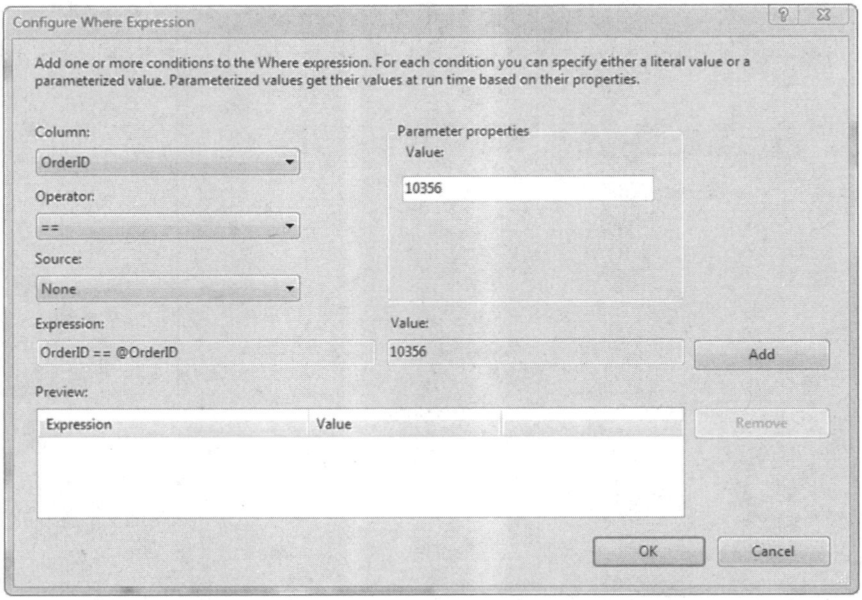

FIGURE 9.15   Specifying a filter for the LINQ query.

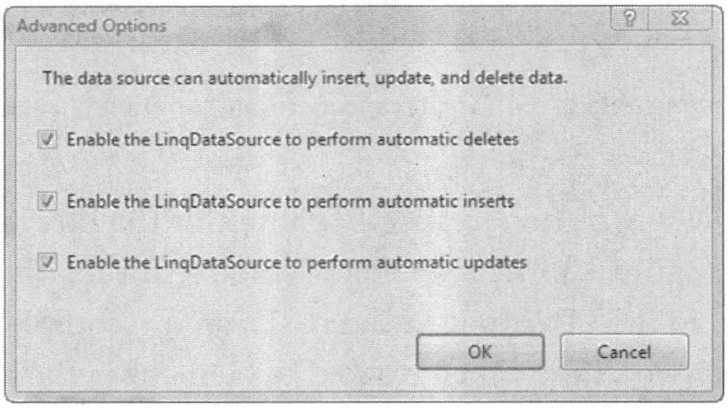

FIGURE 9.16   Setting up LinqDataSource for insert, update, and delete operations.

5. The final design view step is to configure the GridView to provide links for editing and deleting, as shown in Figure 9.17.

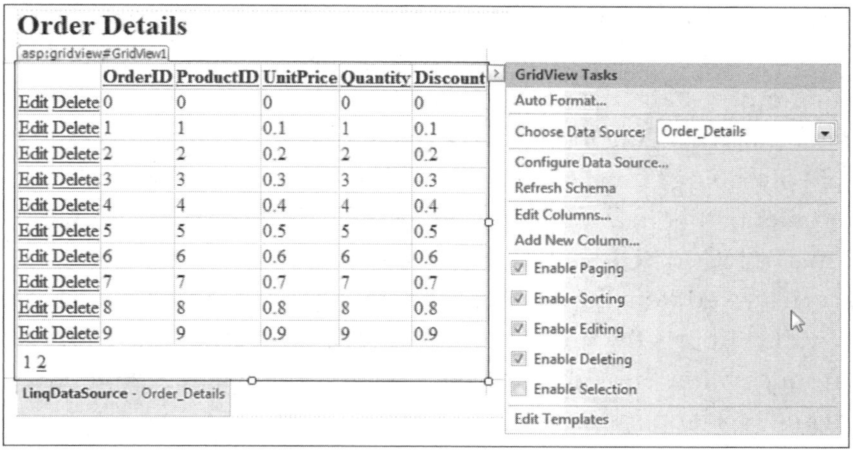

FIGURE 9.17   Setting up `GridView` for additional operations.

This completes the basic `LinqDataSource` sample. Run the application to get results, as shown in Figure 9.18. Now the entities can be edited or deleted as well.

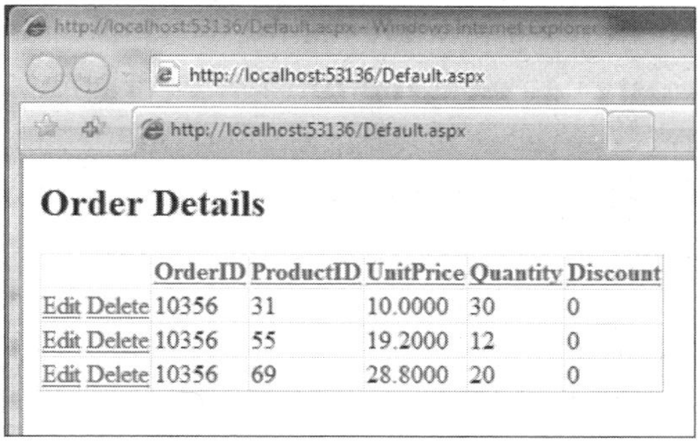

FIGURE 9.18   Results displayed by the `LinqDataSource` sample application.

Overall, `LinqDataSource` takes care of a number of complex tasks and provides a simple design-time data-binding capability. At runtime, it takes care of creating a `DataContext`, forming LINQ queries from string properties, and returning the results for consumption by a control such as `GridView`. After the user has made a change, it also handles the postback by creating a new `DataContext` instance, calling `Attach()` for entities to be updated, and handling inserts and deletes as well. By taking care of a number of "plumbing" details, it provides simple building blocks for creating a presentation tier in a web application.

Thus, LINQ to SQL provides a broad array of options for bridging the objects retrieved from the database and your desired presentation tier technology. It supports the presentation tier actions affecting the entity lifecycle, from creation through retrieval, update, and deletion, for both smart client and web applications.

Creating a Database

LINQ to SQL is designed to allow you to think in terms of your objects. That is true whether you are retrieving data from the database or binding the results to a presentation tier control. In fact, the same principle even extends to creating a database. Because entity classes have attributes describing the structure of the relational database tables and columns, you can use this information to create new instances of your database.

You can call the `CreateDatabase()` method on the `DataContext` to construct a new database instance with a structure defined by your classes. This allows you to build an application that automatically installs itself on a customer system. It also allows you to build a client application that needs a local database to save its offline state. For these scenarios, `CreateDatabase()` is ideal.

However, the data attributes may not encode everything about an existing database's structure. The contents of additional indexes, user-defined functions, stored procedures, triggers, and check constraints are not represented by the attributes. The `CreateDatabase()` function creates a replica of the database using only the information it knows. It is not designed to be a substitute for full-fledged schema design or DDL creation for a complex production database with tuning needs. Yet, for a variety of databases, this is sufficient and very expedient from a productivity standpoint.

Here is an example of how you can create a new database named MyDVDs.mdf:

```
[Table(Name="DVDTable")]
public class DVD
{
   [Column(IsPrimaryKey = true)]
   public string Title;
   [Column]
   public string Rating;
}

public class MyDVDs : DataContext
{
   public Table<DVD> DVDs;
   public MyDVDs(string connection) : base(connection) {}
}
```

The object model can be used to create a database using the SQL Server Express 2005 database as follows:

```
MyDVDs db = new MyDVDs("c:\\mydvds.mdf");
db.CreateDatabase();
```

A complementary API allows you to check an existing database and drop it before creating a new one. Here is a modified version of the database creation code that first checks for an existing version of the database using `DatabaseExists()` and then drops it using `DeleteDatabase()`:

```
MyDVDs db = new MyDVDs("c:\\mydvds.mdf");

if (db.DatabaseExists()) {
   Console.WriteLine("Deleting old database...");
   db.DeleteDatabase();
}

db.CreateDatabase();
```

After the call to `CreateDatabase()`, the new database exists and can accept queries and commands such as `SubmitChanges()` to add objects to the MDF file.

It is also possible to use `CreateDatabase()` with normal SQL Server, using either an MDF file or just a catalog name. You need to use the appropriate connection string, which you can find from the connection properties in Server Explorer in Visual Studio. The information in the connection string is used to define the database that will exist, not necessarily one that already exists. LINQ to SQL finds the relevant bits of information and uses them to determine what database to create and on what server. Of course, you need the appropriate rights granted to you on the database server to do so.

Summary

LINQ to SQL implements the LINQ query pattern to retrieve entities from the database. Applications require additional support for the retrieved entities beyond the LINQ query pattern. LINQ to SQL supports modification of entities through create, update, and delete operations. It also provides rich capabilities for handling concurrent changes through optimistic concurrency checks, conflict resolution, and transactions. In addition to the database operation, entities from other tiers can be processed using attach functionality.

LINQ to SQL also provides rich features for building a presentation tier quickly. Retrieved entities are ready for data binding in both the Windows smart client and ASP.NET web forms presentation tiers.

In addition to data access and presentation, LINQ to SQL covers simple deployment through a runtime capability for creating a database from the object model. Together these features make it easier to write database applications in an object model-centric fashion.

▛ 10 ▟

Using Stored Procedures and Database Functions with LINQ to SQL

L INQ TO SQL GENERATES dynamic SQL for queries and inserts, updates, and deletes. However, in some cases data access must be made through stored procedures, also called *sprocs*. Stored procedures may encapsulate business logic, ensure security restrictions, or provide an optimized and restricted way to query or modify data. Occasionally a database may be accessible exclusively through stored procedures. Hence, LINQ to SQL fully supports stored procedures for CRUD operations. This chapter looks at how to specify the stored procedures and database functions for mapping and how to use them to perform CRUD operations.

Stored Procedures and Functions for Querying

Let's begin by exploring techniques for querying data using stored procedures, user defined functions, and table value functions. Later in the chapter, we will see how to use stored procedures to perform create, update, and delete operations.

Mapping and Using a Stored Procedure

The sample Northwind database contains a stored procedure titled SalesByCategory. To use it in LINQ to SQL, open the project used for the code in previous chapters and follow these simple steps:

1. Open the Northwind.dbml file in the project.

2. In the Server Explorer pane, expand the Stored Procedures node under the Northwind database, and select the SalesByCategory stored procedure.

3. Drag and drop the selected stored procedure on the designer surface to generate a method with the same name. The left pane shows classes generated from tables, and the right pane shows methods generated from stored procedures and database functions. As a result of the drag-and-drop operation, the LINQ to SQL designer displays a method with the same name—SalesByCategory.

4. Right-click the method and choose Properties to see additional details, as shown in Figure 10.1.

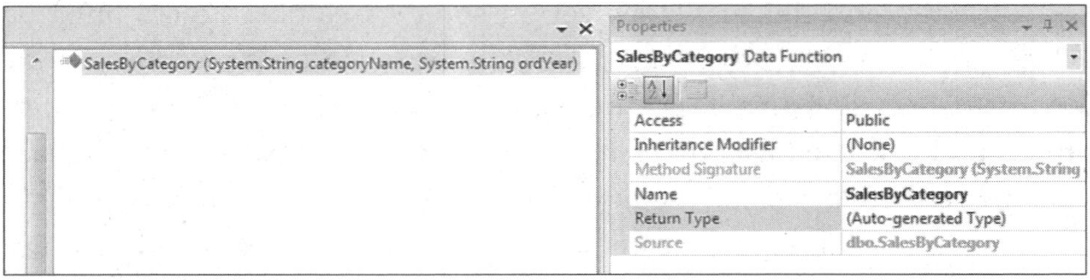

FIGURE 10.1   A stored procedure mapped to a method.

5. Save the dbml file to regenerate code and mapping to include the displayed method.

6. In Solution Explorer, double-click Northwind.designer.cs to view the generated method NorthwindDataContext.SalesByCategory().

You could also use SqlMetal with the /sprocs option to automatically map stored procedures. However, unlike in the case of the designer, you cannot selectively map stored procedures or change their return types easily without editing the intermediate dbml file.

As shown in Figure 10.1, LINQ to SQL autogenerates a type to match the shape of the result returned by the stored procedure. The method signature in step 6 shows that the return type is `ISingleResult<SalesByCategory Result>`. `ISingleResult` is a generic return type that LINQ to SQL uses for methods used to call stored procedures returning a single result set. LINQ to SQL generates the `SalesByCategoryResult` type for the `SalesByCategory` stored procedure.

The generated method is ready for use, as shown next. The period after the `DataContext` variable `db` shows the `SalesByCategory` method in IntelliSense.

```
using System.Data.Linq;

NorthwindDataContext db = new NorthwindDataContext();
db.Log = Console.Out;

ISingleResult<SalesByCategoryResult> SalesResult =
    db.SalesByCategory("Produce", "1997");

Console.ReadLine();
ObjectDumper.Write(SalesResult);
```

The execution produces translated SQL with stored procedure invocation; the results are as follows. Notice that unlike the case of a normal `IQueryable<T>` query expression, the execution of the method `Sales ByCategory` is not deferred. Even before you press Enter for the `Console. ReadLine()` call, the stored procedure has been executed.

```
EXEC @RETURN_VALUE = [dbo].[SalesByCategory] @CategoryName = @p0,
    @OrdYear = @p1
-- @p0: Input NVarChar (Size = 7; Prec = 0; Scale = 0) [Produce]
-- @p1: Input NVarChar (Size = 4; Prec = 0; Scale = 0) [1997]
-- @RETURN_VALUE: Output Int (Size = 0; Prec = 0; Scale = 0) [Null]
-- Context: SqlProvider(Sql2005) Model: AttributedMetaModel Build:
3.5.30729.1


ProductName=Longlife Tofu       TotalPurchase=1001.00
ProductName=Manjimup Dried Apples       TotalPurchase=24571.00
ProductName=Rossle Sauerkraut   TotalPurchase=13949.00
ProductName=Tofu        TotalPurchase=6234.00
ProductName=Uncle Bob's Organic Dried Pears     TotalPurchase=9186.00
```

Thus, using the designer, you can execute a stored procedure by simply invoking the corresponding generated methods with suitable parameters. LINQ to SQL does all the plumbing associated with creating parameters, executing the stored procedure, and materializing objects from the rows in the stored procedure result.

The preceding example shows how to get results of the shape specified by the stored procedure. The type SalesByCategoryResult is not a class with a key; it is not an entity class that can be used for insert, update, and delete operations. It is limited to read-only use. But the designer also lets you specify an existing entity type if you want to retrieve entities using a stored procedure. Let's look at a stored procedure that returns rows with key values that can be used to create entities. Because the sample Northwind database available for download on the web does not contain a suitable entity-shape returning stored procedure, we will add the following stored procedure to Northwind for use in this example:

```
CREATE PROCEDURE OrdersByCustomer   @CustomerID nchar(5)
AS
SELECT *
FROM Orders
WHERE CustomerID = @CustomerID
```

You can add the OrdersByCustomer stored procedure to a copy of the Northwind database by running the preceding SQL in Visual Studio 2008 or SQL Server Management Studio or a similar tool. In Visual Studio, right-click the database in Server Explorer, select New Query, and run the SQL just shown. As soon as the stored procedure is created in the database, it is available for use in the Server Explorer. Using the steps outlined a moment ago, you will map this newly created stored procedure. The resulting method with the same name, OrdersByCustomer, returns a result type that the designer autogenerates by default. To use an existing entity type obtained by dragging and dropping a table, change the return type, and pick Order instead of the autogenerated type, as shown in Figure 10.2.

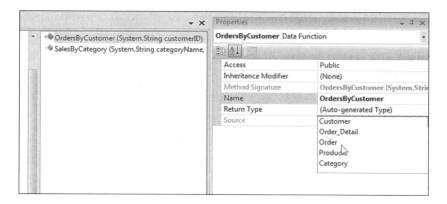

FIGURE 10.2 A stored procedure returning an entity type.

The replacement of the autogenerated type brings up the confirmation dialog shown in Figure 10.3. Click the Yes button, and save the dbml file to regenerate the code, including the OrdersByCustomer method.

FIGURE 10.3 Stored procedure returning an entity type.

The OrdersByCustomer method returns ISingleResult<Order>. It can be used as follows:

```
NorthwindDataContext db = new NorthwindDataContext();
db.Log = Console.Out;

ISingleResult<Order> OrdersQuery = db.OrdersByCustomer("BOLID");

ObjectDumper.Write(OrdersQuery);
```

The result of executing this code is the execution of the corresponding stored procedure and the materialization of a set of Order entities for the customer with ID BOLID. The returned entities can be modified just like entities retrieved using dynamic SQL. The following listing shows the generated SQL for stored procedure execution and the first order in the results:

```
EXEC @RETURN_VALUE = [dbo].[OrdersByCustomer] @CustomerID = @p0
-- @p0: Input NChar (Size = 5; Prec = 0; Scale = 0) [BOLID]
-- @RETURN_VALUE: Output Int (Size = 0; Prec = 0; Scale = 0) [Null]
-- Context: SqlProvider(Sql2005) Model: AttributedMetaModel Build:
3.5.30729.1

OrderID=10326    CustomerID=BOLID        EmployeeID=4
OrderDate=10/10/1996    RequiredDate=11/7/1996
ShippedDate=10/14/1996  ShipVia=2       Freight=77.9200
ShipName=Bolido Comidas preparadas      ShipAddress=C/ Araquil, 67
ShipCity=Madrid         ShipRegion=null         ShipPostalCode=28023
ShipCountry=Spain       Order_Details=...
Customer={ }
...
```

Using Stored Procedures That Return Multiple Results

So far we have looked at stored procedures that return single results. However, stored procedures can also return multiple results. Currently, the graphical designer doesn't support mapping of such stored procedures. However, you can use the command-line tool SqlMetal.exe or map them manually, as shown next.

You will go through three steps to learn how to use a stored procedure that returns multiple results. First you will create a stored procedure, and then you will map it to a method. Finally, you will execute the method to obtain multiple results.

The sample Northwind database does not have a suitable stored procedure returning multiple entities. So first, add a suitable stored procedure to the sample Northwind database. The following stored procedure returns suppliers and customers from a given city as two distinct results. As before, right-click the Northwind database in Server Explorer, select New Query, and run the following SQL:

```
CREATE PROCEDURE SuppliersAndCustomers @City nvarchar(15)
AS

SELECT *
FROM Suppliers
WHERE City = @City

SELECT *
FROM Customers
WHERE City = @City
```

Next, add a partial class for the generated `NorthwindDataContext` class. Right-click the designer surface and select View Code. The designer creates a separate file for you to write code, with a stub declaration for the corresponding partial class. Add the following code for mapping the newly created stored procedure. The mapping specifies the stored procedure name and the result types. The method parameter indicates the corresponding stored procedure parameter. The method body is similar to the one generated by the designer for executing any stored procedure based on the mapping attributes. The return type `IMultipleResults` exposes multiple results that you will use next.

```csharp
public partial class NorthwindDataContext
{
   [Function(Name = "dbo.SuppliersAndCustomers")]
   [ResultType(typeof(Supplier))]
   [ResultType(typeof(Customer))]
   public IMultipleResults SuppliersAndCustomers(
      [Parameter(Name = "City", DbType = "NVarChar(15)")] string city)
   {
      IExecuteResult result = this.ExecuteMethodCall(this,
      ((MethodInfo)(MethodInfo.GetCurrentMethod())), city);
      return ((IMultipleResults)(result.ReturnValue));
   }
}
```

Now the method is available for getting suppliers and customers. Add the following code to Program.cs to use the multiple results returned by the stored procedure:

```csharp
using(IMultipleResults results = db.SuppliersAndCustomers("London"))
{
   List<Supplier> suppliers = results.GetResult<Supplier>().ToList();
   List<Customer> customers = results.GetResult<Customer>().ToList();
```

```
ObjectDumper.Write(suppliers);
ObjectDumper.Write(customers);
}
```

Executing this code brings back suppliers and customers from London as two separate results. Here, only the first customer is shown; the others are elided:

```
EXEC @RETURN_VALUE = [dbo].[SuppliersAndCustomers] @City = @p0
-- @p0: Input NVarChar (Size = 6; Prec = 0; Scale = 0) [London]
-- @RETURN_VALUE: Output Int (Size = 0; Prec = 0; Scale = 0) [Null]
-- Context: SqlProvider(Sql2005) Model: AttributedMetaModel Build:
3.5.30729.1

SupplierID=1    CompanyName=Exotic Liquids    ContactName=Charlotte
Cooper    ContactTitle=Purchasing Manager
Address=49 Gilbert St.  City=London    Region=null  PostalCode=EC1 4SD
Country=UK      Phone=(171) 555-2222
Fax=null        HomePage=null    Products=...

CustomerID=AROUT        CompanyName=Around the Horn
    ContactName=Thomas Hardy        ContactTitle=Sales Representative
        Address=120 Hanover Sq.        City=London      Region=null
PostalCode=WA1 1DP      Country=UK      Phone=(171) 555-7788
    Fax=(171) 555-6750        Orders=...
...
```

Using Table-Valued Functions

Stored procedures return results but do not allow further query composition on the server. You cannot use a stored procedure in place of a table to write a SQL query. You can use LINQ to Objects to further query the results of a stored procedure. However, such a query is executed entirely on the mid-tier or client machine and cannot benefit from the indexes in the database or the capabilities of the SQL query optimizer.

A table-valued function (TVF) can be used in place of a table in an SQL query. LINQ to SQL lets you exploit this capability by allowing a method mapped to a TVF in a LINQ query in a composable fashion. Such a query expression is translated to SQL, and it is executed entirely by the database server.

Let's add the following TVF to the copy of the sample Northwind database. You can use the same steps described earlier to run the following SQL

for a TVF in Visual Studio using the Server Explorer. The TVF returns the orders shipped by a particular shipper identified by the TVF parameter.

```
CREATE FUNCTION OrdersByShipper(@shipper integer)
RETURNS TABLE
AS
RETURN (SELECT *
        FROM Orders ord
        WHERE ord.ShipVia = @shipper)
```

The LINQ to SQL designer lets you map a TVF just like a stored procedure. Expand the Functions node in Server Explorer to view the newly created TVF. Drag it to the designer surface. In the property grid, change the return type from autogenerated to Order. Next, save the dbml file to generate the corresponding method. In Northwind.designer.cs, a new method appears as follows:

```
[Function(Name="dbo.OrdersByShipper", IsComposable=true)]
public IQueryable<Order> OrdersByShipper([Parameter(DbType="Int")]
   System.Nullable<int> shipper)
{
   return this.CreateMethodCallQuery<Order>(this,
      ((MethodInfo)(MethodInfo.GetCurrentMethod())), shipper);
}
```

Unlike the case of a stored procedure, the resulting method is marked as composable using the IsComposable property of the Function mapping attribute. This tells the LINQ to SQL runtime that the method may be used in place of a table. The following code in Program.cs does just that:

```
IQueryable<Order> orders = from o in db.OrdersByShipper(1)
                           where o.Customer.City == "London"
                           select o;

Console.ReadLine();

ObjectDumper.Write(orders);
```

The first statement shows how the mapped method OrdersByShipper() can be used with the appropriate parameter in place of the Orders table. The second statement, Console.ReadLine(), lets us see the execution semantics. As in the case of LINQ to SQL queries shown in previous chapters, and unlike the stored procedure executions shown in this chapter so far, the TVF-mapped method can be composed inside an expression tree that is translated into SQL only when the results are consumed. Pressing the Enter key provides the following results. As in the previous results, Customer entities beyond the first one are elided in the following listing:

```
SELECT [t0].[OrderID], [t0].[CustomerID], [t0].[EmployeeID],
[t0].[OrderDate], [t0].[RequiredDate], [t0].[ShippedDate],
[t0].[ShipVia], [t0].[Freight], [t0].[ShipName], [t0].[ShipAddress],
[t0].[ShipCity], [t0].[ShipRegion], [t0].[ShipPostalCode],
[t0].[ShipCountry]
FROM [dbo].[OrdersByShipper](@p0) AS [t0]
LEFT OUTER JOIN [dbo].[Customers] AS [t1] ON [t1].[CustomerID] =
    [t0].[CustomerID]
WHERE [t1].[City] = @p1
-- @p0: Input Int (Size = 0; Prec = 0; Scale = 0) [1]
-- @p1: Input NVarChar (Size = 6; Prec = 0; Scale = 0) [London]
-- Context: SqlProvider(Sql2005) Model: AttributedMetaModel Build:
3.5.30729.1

OrderID=10355    CustomerID=AROUT    EmployeeID=6    OrderDate=11/15/1996
        RequiredDate=12/13/1996
ShippedDate=11/20/1996  ShipVia=1       Freight=41.9500
ShipName=Around the Horn  ShipAddress=Brook Farm Stratford St. Mary
ShipCity=Colchester       ShipRegion=Essex  ShipPostalCode=CO7 6JX
ShipCountry=UK  Order_Details=...
Customer={ }
...
```

Using Scalar-Valued Functions

Scalar-valued functions return a single value, such as an integer, string, or DateTime. Like their table-valued counterparts, scalar-valued functions are also free from side effects; hence, they can be composed into a SQL query. Hence, LINQ to SQL also supports scalar-valued functions in LINQ queries.

Let's add the following scalar-valued function to a copy of the sample Northwind database using the steps described in the previous sections. The function AverageProductUnitPriceByCategory returns the average price for the given product category.

```
CREATE FUNCTION AverageProductUnitPriceByCategory
(@categoryID int)
RETURNS Money
```

```
AS
BEGIN
   DECLARE @ResultVar Money

   SELECT @ResultVar = (SELECT Avg(UnitPrice)
                        FROM Products
                        WHERE CategoryID = @categoryID)

   RETURN @ResultVar
END
```

In the LINQ to SQL designer, drag and drop the newly created function onto the designer surface. The designer lists a method with the same name as the database function. The property grid shows that the method returns System.Decimal—the default mapping for the database type Money. Save the dbml file, and use the generated method in a query as follows:

```
var categoryQuery =
    from c in db.Categories
    where db.AverageProductUnitPriceByCategory(c.CategoryID) < 22
    select c;

ObjectDumper.Write(categoryQuery);
```

This LINQ to SQL query uses the method mapped to the scalar-valued function inside a regular LINQ query. It produces the following SQL query and results. The scalar-valued function is composed inside the generated SQL query.

```
SELECT [t0].[CategoryID], [t0].[CategoryName],
       [t0].[Description], [t0].[Picture]
FROM [dbo].[Categories] AS [t0]
WHERE [dbo].[AverageProductUnitPriceByCategory]([t0].[CategoryID]) <
@p0
-- @p0: Input Decimal (Size = 0; Prec = 33; Scale = 4) [22]
-- Context: SqlProvider(Sql2005) Model: AttributedMetaModel Build:
3.5.30729.1

CategoryID=5      CategoryName=Grains/Cereals
Description=Breads, crackers, pasta, and cereal    Picture={ }
Products=...
CategoryID=8      CategoryName=Seafood      Description=Seaweed and fish
Picture={ }       Products=...
```

Stored Procedures for Inserts, Updates, and Deletes

Stored procedures are often used in databases for create (insert), update, and delete (CUD) operations. They may ensure access restrictions or include business logic related to the operations. Hence, in certain cases, a developer may have no option but to use the stored procedures provided by a database administrator (DBA) for persisting changes to the database. LINQ to SQL supports such stored procedures through a combination of designer and runtime support.

Stored procedures can be used via a more general-purpose mechanism in LINQ to SQL for overriding CUD operations. The mechanism works as follows: if the DataContext class contains a method with a canonical name and signature of a CUD operation, that method is considered to *override* the generation of normal dynamic SQL commands for CUD operations. The CUD override methods use convention rather than configuration as follows. For the Order entity, the three methods are

```
void InsertOrder(Order instance) {...}
void UpdateOrder(Order instance) {...}
void DeleteOrder(Order instance) {...}
```

The method bodies can contain arbitrary logic, including a call to a stored procedure for carrying out the corresponding operation. During SubmitChanges() processing, for each CUD operation, the LINQ to SQL runtime checks if there is a corresponding CUD override method for that entity and invokes the method if one is found.

The code generator used in the designer and SqlMetal provides additional help by pregenerating the method signatures as partial method declarations in the DataContext class as follows:

```
partial void InsertOrder(Order instance);
partial void UpdateOrder(Order instance);
partial void DeleteOrder(Order instance);
```

The LINQ to SQL designer further simplifies the use of stored procedures in the bodies of such override methods with a dialog for specifying the operation and the stored procedure parameters. Let's add the following stored procedure for updating an Order row to the copy of the sample Northwind database using the steps mentioned in previous sections.

```
CREATE PROCEDURE UpdateOrder
  @OrderID int,
  @CustomerID nchar(5),
  @EmployeeID int,
  @OrderDate datetime,
  @RequiredDate datetime,
  @ShippedDate datetime,
  @ShipVia int,
  @Freight money,
  @ShipName nvarchar(40),
  @ShipAddress nvarchar(60),
  @ShipCity nvarchar(15),
  @ShipRegion nvarchar(15),
  @ShipPostalCode nvarchar(10),
  @ShipCountry nvarchar(15)
AS
UPDATE Orders
SET
      CustomerID = @CustomerID,
      EmployeeID = @EmployeeID,
      OrderDate = @OrderDate,
      RequiredDate = @RequiredDate,
      ShippedDate = @ShippedDate,
      ShipVia = @ShipVia,
      Freight = @Freight,
      ShipName = @ShipName,
      ShipAddress = ShipAddress,
      ShipCity = @ShipCity,
      ShipRegion = @ShipRegion,
      ShipPostalCode = @ShipPostalCode,
      ShipCountry = @ShipCountry
WHERE
      OrderID = @OrderID
RETURN @@ROWCOUNT
```

Next, drag and drop the stored procedure onto the designer surface to obtain the UpdateOrder() method, as shown in Figure 10.4.

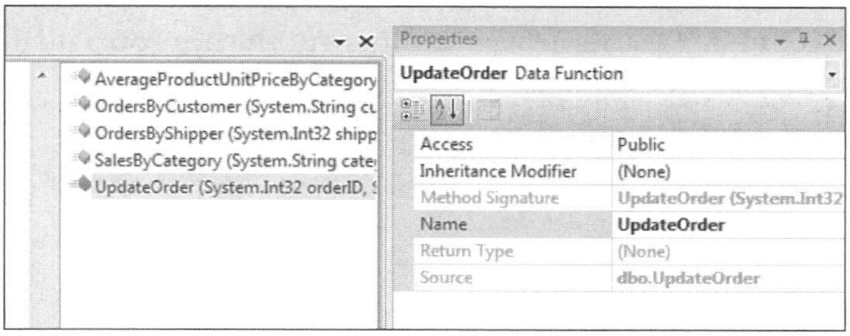

FIGURE 10.4   An update stored procedure mapped to a method.

In the left pane, which contains entity classes, right-click the Order class, and select Configure Behavior, as shown in Figure 10.5.

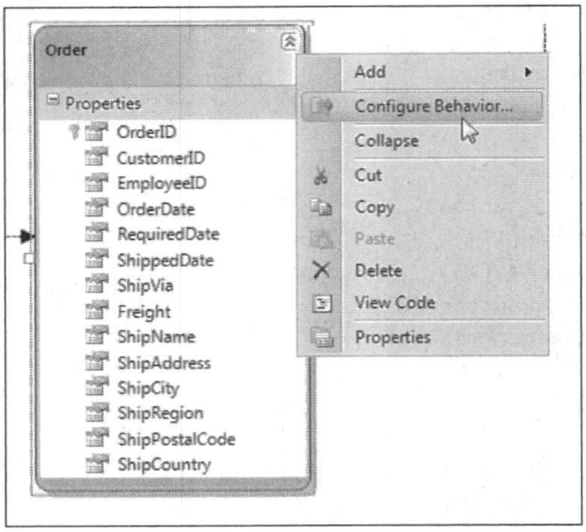

FIGURE 10.5   Configuring CUD operation on an entity.

The Configure Behavior dialog lets you specify a stored procedure for CUD operations and map its parameters, as shown in Figure 10.6.

Select Order from the Class drop-down, Update from the Behavior drop-down, and UpdateOrder from the Customize drop-down. The stored procedure parameters and entity properties are matched by name and presented. In this case, you don't need to change any parameter mappings, so click OK to complete the generation of an update override method. Now all Order update operations will be routed through the override method and, in turn, through the UpdateOrder stored procedure listed earlier. Insert and delete operations can be configured in a similar fashion. Note that the override methods are not meant to be called in your code; they are defined so that the LINQ to SQL runtime can call them at the appropriate point when your code calls SubmitChanges().

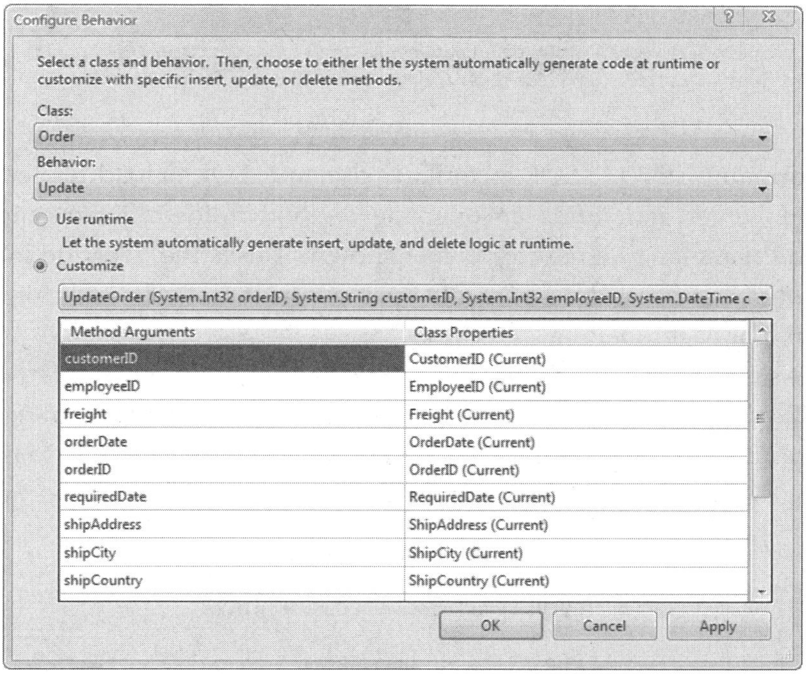

FIGURE 10.6   Specifying a stored procedure for CUD operations on an entity.

Stored Procedures for Loading Relationships

Query and CUD operations are the foundation of any object-relational mapping solution. All these operations can be easily done using stored procedures. However, as discussed in Chapter 8, "Reading Objects with LINQ to SQL," the real attraction of an object-relational mapping solution is the "power of the dot." You can navigate from a Customer to its Orders by simply referencing the Customer.Orders property. There is no need to do explicit queries or joins. Hence, LINQ to SQL also lets you load related entities using stored procedures. It uses a similar override pattern to load related objects. For example, the following signatures define override methods to load Customer.Orders and Order.Customer, respectively:

```
partial class NorthwindDataContext
{
    private IEnumerable<Order> LoadOrders(Customer customer) { ... }
    private Customer LoadCustomer(Order order) { ... }
}
```

Normally, LINQ to SQL formulates dynamic SQL to load related entities. However, if it finds an override method following the canonical
method name and signature, as just shown, it uses the override method
instead of executing dynamic SQL. Such overrides may be used for either
deferred or eager loading.

Let's use the previously defined stored procedure OrdersByCustomer to
load Customer.Orders. As in the case of stored procedures returning multiple results, this requires the addition of code to a partial class. Add the following code to the partial class created in the previous section:

```
private IEnumerable<Order> LoadOrders(Customer customer)
{
    return this.OrdersByCustomer(customer.CustomerID);
}
```

LINQ to SQL uses this override method to load the corresponding collection, as in the following code:

```
var cust = db.Customers.Where(c => c.CustomerID == "BOLID").Single();
ObjectDumper.Write(cust.Orders);
```

The query and results for this code show that the OrdersByCustomer
stored procedure is called for loading cust.Orders as follows. The query
for loading the customer with ID BOLID is done using dynamic SQL, but the
deferred loading of cust.Orders does not use dynamic SQL; it uses the
mapped stored procedure instead.

```
SELECT [t0].[CustomerID], [t0].[CompanyName], [t0].[ContactName],
[t0].[ContactTitle], [t0].[Address], [t0].[City], [t0].[Region],
[t0].[PostalCode], [t0].[Country], [t0].[Phone], [t0].[Fax]
FROM [dbo].[Customers] AS [t0]
WHERE [t0].[CustomerID] = @p0
-- @p0: Input NVarChar (Size = 5; Prec = 0; Scale = 0) [BOLID]
-- Context: SqlProvider(Sql2005) Model: AttributedMetaModel Build:
3.5.30729.1
```

```
EXEC @RETURN_VALUE = [dbo].[OrdersByCustomer] @CustomerID = @p0
-- @p0: Input NChar (Size = 5; Prec = 0; Scale = 0) [BOLID]
-- @RETURN_VALUE: Output Int (Size = 0; Prec = 0; Scale = 0) [Null]
-- Context: SqlProvider(Sql2005) Model: AttributedMetaModel Build:
 3.5.30729.1


OrderID=10326    CustomerID=BOLID      EmployeeID=4     OrderDate=10/10/1996
    RequiredDate=11/7/1996  ShippedDate=10/1
4/1996  ShipVia=2         Freight=77.9200          ShipName=Bolido Comidas
 preparadas       ShipAddress=C/ Araquil, 67
ShipCity=Madrid          ShipRegion=null          ShipPostalCode=28023
    ShipCountry=Spain      Order_Details=...
Customer={ }
...
```

Summary

Stored procedures are not only a key mechanism for data access. In some cases, they may be the only available mechanism. LINQ to SQL supports queries using stored procedures returning single or multiple results. It also supports composable queries using table-valued functions (TVF) or scalar-valued functions. Stored procedures can also be used in overrides for insert, update, and delete operations. Finally, the set of operations is significantly expanded by the ability to use stored procedures or table-valued functions for relationship loading. These capabilities can be used together or in combination with dynamic SQL to get the best combination of flexibility, security, and performance.

11

Customizing Entity Persistence and Adding Business Logic

T HE LINQ TO SQL DESIGNER, which is also known as the Object Relational Designer, and SqlMetal help you by generating classes and mapping from a database. The generated code targets the most common and standard way to persist objects and is not meant to be modified. However, it includes mechanisms for customizing how the objects are retrieved, modified, and persisted. It also provides easy extensibility for the addition of business logic. Finally, the generated code is only one way to use the LINQ to SQL runtime libraries. You can also write your own classes and specify mapping external to the classes if you want to. In this chapter we will look at the common ways to customize generated classes and write your own classes to use LINQ to SQL in the most effective fashion for your applications.

Customizing Generated Code

Let's revisit the code generated by the LINQ to SQL designer when the Customers and Orders tables from the Northwind database are dropped on the designer surface in a new project. Recall that the command-line tool SqlMetal uses the same code generator. So a few project configuration items aside, you will get substantially the same code from SqlMetal as well.

The generated code in Northwind.designer.cs has two main sets of classes—a `DataContext` class, `NorthwindDataContext`, and a set of entity classes—`Customer` and `Order` in this case. Both sets of classes allow a rich set of customizations without any need to modify the generated source code. This is done through the use of partial classes, partial methods, and virtual methods. Partial classes and virtual methods have been available in C# and VB.NET prior to the LINQ-enabled release. Partial *methods* were added along with LINQ support and are covered in detail in Chapter 4, "C# 3.0 Technical Overview."

The LINQ to SQL designer provides an easy way to create a partial class stub to add your code. For the `DataContext` class, right-click the designer surface, and select the View Code option. A corresponding file, North-wind.cs, is created with a partial class declaration for `NorthwindDataContext`. This is where you can write your own code without worrying about the designer overwriting it when you make changes in the designer and regenerate code. Likewise, right-clicking an entity class gives you a partial class stub in Northwind.cs for the corresponding entity class. The generated stubs along with manually added code are shown in a following listing.

Customizing the DataContext Class

The generated `NorthwindDataContext` class contains the following partial methods tucked away in a code region:

```
#region Extensibility Method Definitions
partial void OnCreated();
partial void InsertCustomer(Customer instance);
partial void UpdateCustomer(Customer instance);
partial void DeleteCustomer(Customer instance);
partial void InsertOrder(Order instance);
partial void UpdateOrder(Order instance);
partial void DeleteOrder(Order instance);
#endregion
```

As explained in Chapter 4, the partial methods provide placeholders for you to write code if you want to. In this case, the implementations of the partial methods are called either in the generated code, as in the case of `OnCreated()`, or by the LINQ to SQL runtime, as in the case of insert, update, and delete methods for an entity type. If you choose not to customize the specific behavior, the compiler simply omits the method calls in the generated code and optimizes away the method metadata. The method declaration just acts as a stub. The LINQ to SQL runtime provides its default insert, update, and delete behavior when it cannot find an overriding implementation of the method.

The `OnCreated()` method is called in the `NorthwindDataContext` constructors and provides you a way to write the code you want in the constructor. For example, it lets you initialize any additional properties you choose to create in your partial class.

We briefly covered the partial methods for insert, update, and delete customization in Chapter 10, "Using Stored Procedures and Database Functions with LINQ to SQL," for using stored procedures. That is by far the most common use of these methods. However, the implementation of the methods can do any other operation as well. In fact, it can even add pre- and post-operation logic and simply use the LINQ to SQL capabilities to perform the actual operation, as shown in the following code fragment. It shows how insert, update, and delete operations can be customized for Customer entities while using LINQ to SQL methods such as `DataContext.ExecuteInsert()` that generate dynamic SQL on your behalf. In each case, you can add the logging code before and/or after the actual operation. You do not need to take over the entire operation, which involves generating a command, opening a connection, executing the command, and flowing back the database-generated values.

The code fragment also shows how to obtain the original values for an entity in case you want to use them for your pre- or post-processing. It also illustrates that you can change a delete operation into an update—a common practice in which database records are marked as deleted or are moved to a "tombstone" table instead of being deleted. Finally, the code fragment shows how relationship loading can be customized—in this case by using a stored procedure as described in the preceding chapter. Together the methods let you customize the CRUD operations per entity type—in this case shown for the `Customer` type.

```
partial class NorthwindDataContext
{
    partial void OnCreated()
    {
        // Set up the log for logging operations
    }
```

```
        partial void InsertCustomer(Customer instance)
        {
            // pre-insert processing; e.g. log attempted operation
            this.ExecuteDynamicInsert(instance);
            // post-insert processing; e.g. log completed operation
        }

        partial void UpdateCustomer(Customer instance)
        {
            // Get the original version for logging
            Customer original =
                this.Customers.GetOriginalEntityState(instance);
            // Add code for pre-update processing
            // e.g. log the original and current state

            // Use LINQ to SQL method for the update operation
            this.ExecuteDynamicUpdate(instance);
        }

        partial void DeleteCustomer(Customer instance)
        {
            // pre-"delete" processing
            // set some status field to deleted and issue an update instead
            this.ExecuteDynamicUpdate(instance);
            // post-"delete" processing
        }

        private IEnumerable<Order> LoadOrders(Customer customer)
        {
            // Call a stored procedure for loading
            return this.OrdersByCustomer(customer.CustomerID);
        }
    }
```

Overriding SubmitChanges

In addition to the per-entity-type customization just described, you can customize the overall SubmitChanges() operation by overriding the method in your partial class. As in the case of InsertCustomer() and other methods in the previous example, the heavy lifting can be done by the SubmitChanges() method in the base class implemented in LINQ to SQL code. You can just add the functionality specific to your application—in this case logging of the set of changed entities.

```
public override void SubmitChanges(ConflictMode failureMode)
{
   ChangeSet cs = this.GetChangeSet();
   // Add code to log the entire change set

   // Use base class operation for bulk of the work
   base.SubmitChanges(failureMode);
}
```

Customizing the Entity Classes

A common need for entity class customization is the ability to specify your own base class with common functionality. LINQ to SQL does not require a specific base class. In other words, it does not "hijack" your base class. Hence, you are free to use your base class. The command-line tool SqlMetal lets you specify a base class with the /entitybase option. The designer currently does not expose this capability, but you can work around that limitation by using SqlMetal to generate code with the /entitybase option from the designer-generated dbml file.

Another common need is to use the entity classes as return values from a web method. To serialize entities using the Windows Communication Foundation (WCF), DataContract and DataMember attributes are needed on entity and entity properties, respectively. LINQ to SQL designer and SqlMetal provide an easy way to add the DataContract serialization attributes. In the designer, right-click the designer surface, and select Properties. Figure 11.1 shows the serialization options. Select Unidirectional to get the DataContract attributes. Because the serializer in .NET Framework Version 3.5 did not permit cycles,[1] the Unidirectional option ensures that the DataMember attribute is placed in only one direction of a bidirectional relationship. Customer.Orders gets the DataMember attribute, but Order. Customer does not.

---

[1] The WCF DataContract serializer enabled the handling of circular object references in 3.5 SP1 using the IsReference property on DataMember after LINQ to SQL shipped in Version 3.5 (pre-SP1). Earlier releases required serializer configuration (not the default setting).

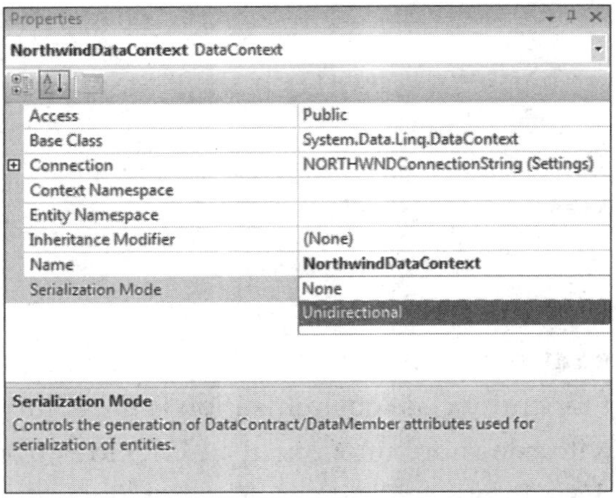

FIGURE 11.1   Generating DataContract attributes in the designer.

When the dbml file is saved, the generated code includes serialization attributes as follows:

```
[Table(Name="dbo.Customers")]
[DataContract()]
public partial class Customer : INotifyPropertyChanging, INotifyPropertyChanged
{
   ...
   [Column(Storage="_CustomerID", DbType="NChar(5) NOT NULL",
    CanBeNull=false, IsPrimaryKey=true)]
   [DataMember(Order=1)]
   public string CustomerID
   {
    ...
```

This entity class can now be used as a return type in a WCF web service. The following is a simple implementation to illustrate how the class can be used with an appropriate service contract. You need to add a reference to System.ServiceModel.dll in your project through the Visual Studio Solution Explorer.

```
[ServiceContract]
public interface ICustomerService
{
   [OperationContract]
   Customer GetCustomer(string id);
```

```
   }

public class CustomerService : ICustomerService
{
   public Customer GetCustomer(string id)
   {
      NorthwindDataContext db = new NorthwindDataContext();
      return (db.Customers.Where(c => c.CustomerID == id).Single());
   }
}
```

Beyond the use of designer and SqlMetal options, you can extend entity classes by adding your own partial class, as in the case of the `DataContext` class. In the designer, if you right-click an entity class and select the View Code option, a partial class stub for the corresponding entity is generated. The stub is generated in the same file mentioned before. For Northwind. designer.cs, the stub class is created in Northwind.cs. The newly created partial class provides a place to add methods containing business logic or additional nonpersistent properties. For example, you could add a method for discount computation to an Order entity in the partial class, or you could add a `Discount` property that does not map to any database column. The two members are shown in the following code snippet:

```
partial class Order
{
   public decimal ComputeDiscount(string CouponCode)
   {
      // call a web service and obtain the discount percentage
   }

   public decimal Discount { get; set; }
}
```

Any field or property you add in your partial class typically is not be mapped to a column in the database. Hence, it cannot be used in the LINQ to SQL query. LINQ to SQL cannot find it in the mapping. Hence, you get a runtime exception when LINQ to SQL attempts to translate the unmapped property to a column for use in the generated SQL.

Using Entity Lifecycle Events

When a LINQ query is executed against a database, LINQ to SQL constructs entities and sets the values of its properties. Likewise, when

SubmitChanges() is called, LINQ to SQL computes the set of changed entities and submits the changes as database commands. When you are relying
on generated code for entities, it is useful to be able to add custom behav-
iors at these persistence-related points in an entity's lifecycle. LINQ to SQL
provides ways to add code during the lifecycle using partial methods.

Generated entity classes contain partial method declarations and calls
for customization similar to those in the DataContext class. The following
methods are declared for the Order class. Three partial methods are related
to the entity's lifecycle, and then one pair of methods per property, such as
OnRequiredDateChanging() and OnRequiredDateChanged(). The method
pairs for one property are shown; the others are omitted.

```
#region Extensibility Method Definitions
partial void OnLoaded();
partial void OnValidate(System.Data.Linq.ChangeAction action);
partial void OnCreated();
...
partial void OnRequiredDateChanging(string value);
partial void OnRequiredDateChanged();
...
#endregion
```

The OnCreated() method is called in the entity class constructor as a
part of the Initialize() method. You can see the call to OnCreated() in the
generated code. The OnLoaded() method is called after the entity's properties are set using the values retrieved during the execution of a LINQ query.
It is invoked by the LINQ to SQL runtime if an implementation is provided.
The OnValidate() method is called on an instance that is a part of the
change during SubmitChanges() processing. It is invoked before the SQL
commands for insert, update, and delete operations are executed. Hence,
it provides a way to validate an entity that is about to be changed in the
database, as shown in the following code example.

The per-property method pair allows you to hook in your code before
and after the value is set. The following example shows how a change in
Order.RequiredDate can be checked before setting the value and how the
new value can be used to kick off additional processing:

```
partial void OnCreated()
{
    // Provide 5% discount by default
```

```
        this.Discount = (decimal)0.05;
    }

    partial void OnLoaded()
    {
        // Increase the discount if this order is late
        if (this.ShippedDate == null && this.RequiredDate.Value <
            DateTime.Now)
            this.Discount = (decimal)0.10;
    }

    partial void OnValidate(ChangeAction action)
    {
        // Check discount rules and throw in case of violation
    }

    partial void OnRequiredDateChanging(DateTime? value)
    {
        if (this.ShippedDate != null) throw new ArgumentOutOfRangeException();
    }

    partial void OnRequiredDateChanged()
    {
        // Change freight and shipper accordingly
    }
```

Writing Your Own Persistent Classes

The customization entry points are designed to take care of the most common cases with small, incremental work. However, if you have your own separate code generator, or you need to heavily customize your entity classes, you are free to do so while using the LINQ to SQL runtime. Data-Context and entity classes generated by the designer or SqlMetal are meant to simplify your tasks—they are not essential for using LINQ to SQL runtime capabilities. In fact, Chapters 7 through 9 gave examples of handwritten (not designer-generated) classes with mappings in attributes. Let's revisit the handwritten classes from Chapter 8, "Reading Objects with LINQ to SQL," but this time with the mapping moved from .NET attributes to an external XML file.

Authors of handwritten classes often prefer to keep the classes free of attributes and use a different artifact such as an XML file to specify the mapping. In part, this is a matter of personal preference. However, in certain cases, it may be useful to modify the mapping file without changing the files containing the C# or VB.NET classes that are mapped in the mapping file. This may be true for trivial database schema changes such as renaming a column. In practice, many mapping changes due to database schema changes may require some changes in the mapped classes.

```csharp
public class Customer
{
    public string CustomerID;
    public string Country;
    ...
    public List<Order> Orders;
}

public class Order
{
    public int OrderID;
    public string CustomerID;
    ...
    public Customer Customer;
}
```

The external XML mapping provides the same information as the mapping in attributes. The .NET attributes appear as XML elements, and properties of .NET attributes appear as XML attributes. The contextual information about the class or property that the .NET attribute is placed on is added to the mapping element because it is external to the entity classes. The following is a fragment of the mapping you can generate using Sql-Metal. Specifically, most columns in the Customers table are omitted. So you need to use the longer mapping file generated using SqlMetal to run the C# code that appears after the mapping listing.

```xml
<?xml version="1.0" encoding="utf-8" ?>
<Database Name="northwind"
 xmlns="http://schemas.microsoft.com/linqtosql/mapping/2007">
  <Table Name="dbo.Customers" Member="Customers">
    <Type Name="Customers">
      <Column Name="CustomerID" Member="CustomerID"
       Storage="_CustomerID" DbType="NChar(5) NOT NULL"
       CanBeNull="false" IsPrimaryKey="true" />
      ...
      <Association Name="FK_Orders_Customers" Member="Orders"
       Storage="_Orders" ThisKey="CustomerID" OtherKey="CustomerID"
       DeleteRule="NO ACTION" />
    </Type>
```

```
    </Table>
    <Table Name="dbo.Orders" Member="Orders">
      <Type Name="Orders">
        <Column Name="OrderID" Member="OrderID" Storage="_OrderID"
          DbType="Int NOT NULL IDENTITY" IsPrimaryKey="true"
          IsDbGenerated="true" AutoSync="OnInsert" />
        <Column Name="CustomerID" Member="CustomerID"
          Storage="_CustomerID" DbType="NChar(5)" />
        ...
        <Association Name="FK_Orders_Customers" Member="Customer"
          Storage="_Customer" ThisKey="CustomerID"
          OtherKey="CustomerID" IsForeignKey="true" />
      </Type>
    </Table>
  </Database>
```

The mapping file can be specified using a `DataContext` constructor over-load as follows. The code assumes that the mapping is stored in North-windMapping.xml and that a variable named `connectionString` contains the connection string for the Northwind database.

```
MappingSource ms = XmlMappingSource.FromXml("NorthwindMapping.xml");

NorthwindDataContext db =
    new NorthwindDataContext(connectionString, ms);
```

Just as the entity classes are free from LINQ to SQL concepts, you can also choose to wrap the `DataContext` so that all the objects used are your objects and LINQ to SQL just provides persistence service. This enables *persistence ignorance*, because your class is not tied to LINQ to SQL classes and generated code patterns. It can be used as is against different stores, including mocks created for testing.

There are some key differences between the preceding classes and the corresponding designer or SqlMetal-generated classes. Each difference has its own set of implications:

- There are no mapping attributes on classes and members; hence, external mapping needs to be supplied.
- It is up to you to decide which interfaces to implement and whether to use a base class. If you want to data-bind to a UI control, you need to implement `INotifyPropertyChanged`. If you want more efficient change tracking by ensuring that the original values are copied only

in case of a modification, you need to implement `INotifyProperty-Changing`.

- Relationship members use `List<T>` and normal object reference instead of LINQ to SQL classes `EntitySet` and `EntityRef` that enable deferred loading. Hence, deferred loading is unavailable. Eager loading may still be specified.
- The generated code to keep the two ends of the relationships and the foreign key in sync is unavailable. The author of the class now has to provide this capability.
- Entity customization methods discussed in this chapter are not needed, because you are free to add whatever code you want in the constructors and in the property setters.

There is a trade-off between the convenience and the productivity of generated code versus the full flexibility of writing your own classes to suit your needs. However, it is important to remember that you can use your own entity classes if you want to.

Summary

LINQ to SQL provides a range of customization options for customizing entity classes and the `DataContext`. It also provides opportunities for you to add business logic. For the most common customization patterns, the generated code contains a set of partial classes, a set of partial methods, and calls to those partial methods. Partial classes allow you to add your own business logic in the form of nonpersistent properties and methods. You can provide partial method implementations for a `DataContext` class to control how entities are persisted or even loaded. Partial methods in entity classes can be implemented to add logic during key persistence-related points in the entity lifecycle.

LINQ to SQL also supports persistence ignorance if you want to author your own entity classes and control the persistence mechanism. The runtime effectively utilizes the patterns in the generated code but works well without them.

■ 12 ■

LINQ to Entities Overview

T HE ENTITY FRAMEWORK (EF) is another object-relational data access technology from Microsoft that includes a LINQ implementation. Commonly called LINQ to Entities, EF shipped in Service Pack 1 of the .NET Framework 3.5 release. It is expected to evolve significantly in the coming releases. The first release includes runtime libraries and designer support in Visual Studio for generating classes and metadata files. It supports database and model-driven styles of development.

EF emphasizes model-driven development. It has its own set of concepts and vocabulary that go beyond the CLR classes and database objects. EF can be used with LINQ or Entity SQL. Entity SQL is a query language based on SQL but designed for Entity Framework. However, in this book we are focusing on LINQ, and hence, we will cover the subset of EF pertinent to the use of LINQ. The next section looks at the core concepts and then walks through an example using the EF tools and the runtime.

Understanding Entity Framework Concepts and Components

EF is based on the Entity Data Model (EDM). EDM is an entity relationship (ER) model, as shown in Figure 12.1. EDM uses its own vocabulary, concepts, and artifacts to define data in a format independent of programming languages and relational databases. EDM schemas are used to specify the details of entities and relationships and to implement them in terms of programming languages and database constructs.

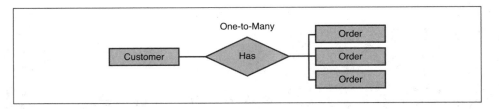

FIGURE 12.1   The EDM entity-relationship model.

EF separates the conceptual model from the storage model, as shown in Figure 12.2. The conceptual model covers types, inheritance, complex members, and relationships. It is described by a conceptual schema normally realized as a .csdl section in an .edmx file. To see the XML, right-click the .edmx file and choose Open With, XML editor. The storage model describes how the data is stored. For relational databases, it covers tables, columns, stored procedures, and so on. It is described by a storage schema typically realized as an .ssdl section in the .edmx file. The conceptual and storage models are bridged with a mapping that relates the concepts from the two models. It is typically captured in an .msl section in the .edmx file. The three spaces—conceptual, storage, and mapping—together bridge the artifacts commonly used by a developer—entity classes in a .cs or .vb file, and the database that stores the data.

The Entity Data Model
An entity is an abstract carrier of data in the application domain. Examples include Customer, Order, and Product. It can be described using a specification language based on XML. It is typically realized in the programming language domain as a C# or VB.NET class that derives from the framework base class `EntityObject` in the `System.Data.Objects.DataClasses` namespace. Its metadata is represented by the `EntityType` class in the `System.Data.Metadata.Edm` namespace.

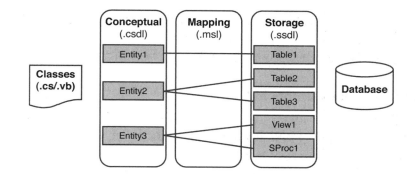

FIGURE 12.2   The logical EDM model spaces described by the XML found in an .edmx file.

A relationship may be between two or more entities. A binary relationship is between two entities such as Customer and Order. They are called ends of the relationship. A unary relationship (sometimes called a self-referencing relationship) involves a single entity typically in two roles, such as Employee and Manager. A ternary relationship involves more than two entities, such as an enrollment relationship that involves Student, Professor, and Course entities. Association is the basic type of relationship, in which each end of the relationship can exist independent of the other and the entities are considered peers. Composition is a more specialized relationship in which one entity is composed in another. Currently, EDM supports unary and binary associations. An association also has a multiplicity attribute that specifies the number of instances of each end. EDM supports the commonly used one-to-many, one-to-one, and many-to-many associations. An association is bidirectional in EDM. You can logically navigate from Customer to Order and from Order to Customer—at least in the model.

The main noteworthy point is that an association is a first-class concept in EDM. It is not merely the navigation properties or the foreign key values. It is realized as navigation properties in the conceptual space and foreign keys in the storage space. Collection-valued navigation properties (such as Customer.Orders) typically use EntityCollection<T>, whereas singleton navigation properties (such as Order.Customer) use the type of the other end. We will look at concrete examples when we review the code generated by the EF designer. The metadata for an association is represented by the `AssociationType` in the `System.Data.Metadata.Edm` namespace.

Entity Framework Components

EF is implemented in two separate layers, as shown in Figure 12.3. The EntityClient Data Provider layer is the lower layer that translates from EDM concepts into native SQL concepts. The Object Services layer provides additional services such as entity classes, a LINQ implementation, and an `ObjectContext` for change tracking.

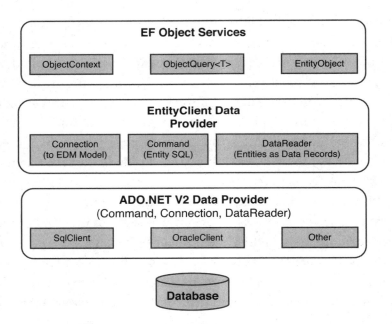

FIGURE 12.3   Entity framework layers and components.

LINQ extension methods are implemented for `ObjectQuery<T>`. LINQ queries against `ObjectQuery<T>` are translated into Entity SQL and, in turn, into native flavors of SQL supported by an ADO.NET V2 Data Provider. The concepts in the EntityClient layer closely resemble the ADO.NET V2 concepts of Connection, Command, and DataReader. However, they are enhanced by EDM constructs. For example, the connection in the Entity-Client layer contains not only the database connection information but also information about the EDM model files.

The EF Object Services layer is very similar to a typical Object Relational Mapping layer. It knows how to translate queries, materialize objects, ensure identity, and track changes. It also manages optimistic concurrency and transactions.

Using the Entity Framework

This section walks you through the steps for using the Entity Framework in Visual Studio 2008 SP1. We will use the graphical designer to generate a model from the Northwind sample database. Then we will use the generated classes for a simple set of operations on objects created from Northwind data.

As described in Chapter 7, "A Quick Tour of LINQ to SQL," be sure that you have set up a connection to the database. In Visual Studio, select View, Server Explorer, *Solution Explorer*. In the Server Explorer pane, shown in Figure 12.4, be sure that you can view the tables in your database. Appendix A contains tips for connecting to a database. Next we will outline the steps to generate an entity data model so that it can be used for CRUD operations.

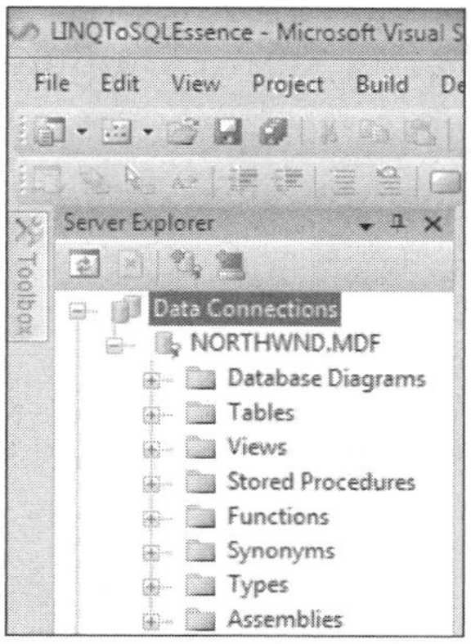

FIGURE 12.4   Server Explorer showing the Northwind database.

Entity Model Generation

Create a new project in Visual Studio. Here we will use a C# console application named NorthwindEF. In Solution Explorer, right-click the NorthwindEF project and choose Add, as shown in Figure 12.5.

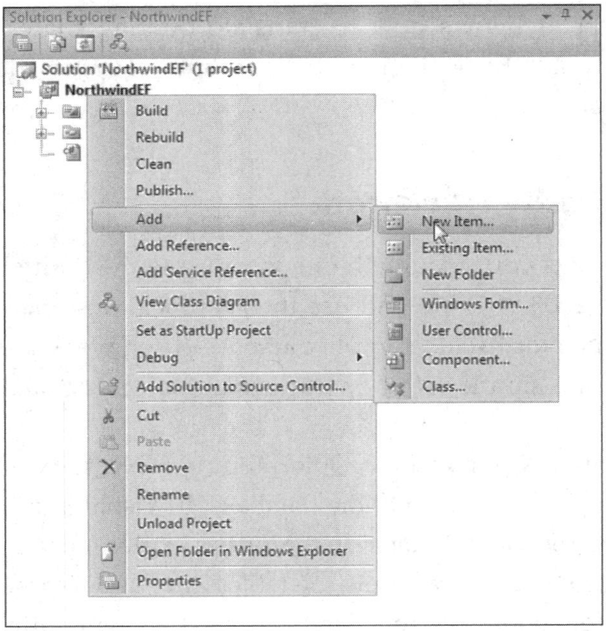

FIGURE 12.5   Add New Item for using EF.

In the Add New Item dialog, shown in Figure 12.6, select *Data* in the left pane and ADO.NET *Entity Data Model* in the right pane, and click Add. Select ADO.NET Entity Data Model, and choose a suitable name, such as Northwind.edmx.

Click Add to bring up the Entity Data Model Wizard, as shown in Figure 12.7. This wizard helps you set up the connection and create a model from a database. Choose Generate from Database and click Next.

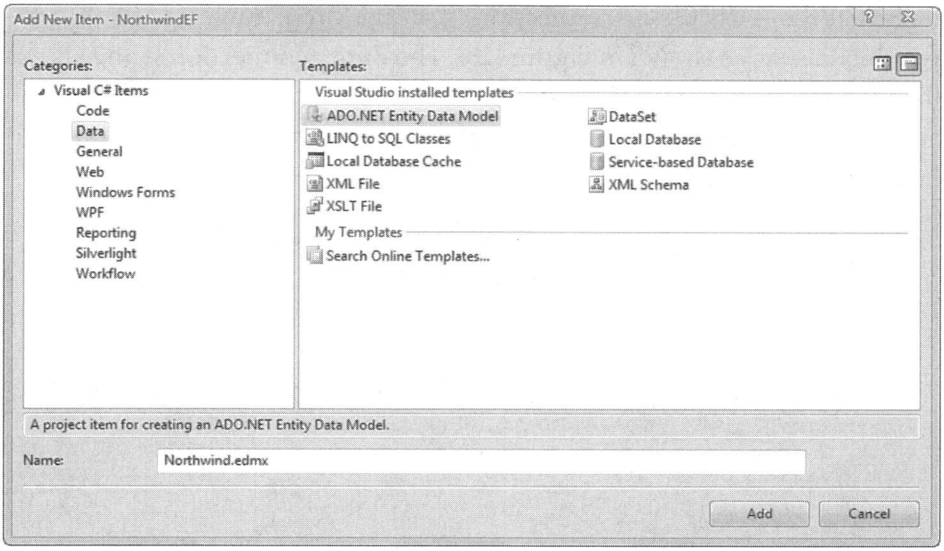

FIGURE 12.6   The Add Entity data model.

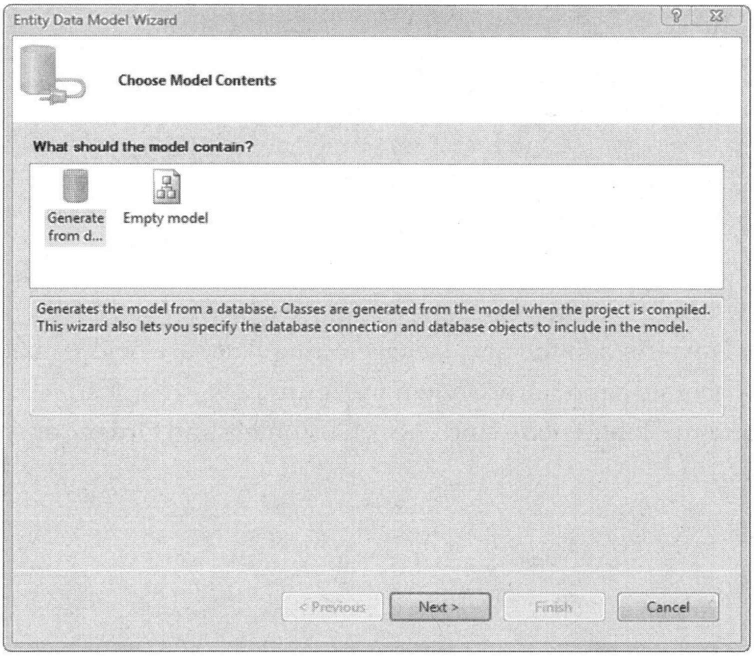

FIGURE 12.7   Entity Data Model Wizard step 1: Generate from the database.

Select the .mdf file or connection from the drop-down for the North-wind database, as shown in Figure 12.8. The Entity connection string shows the information used by the EntityClient Data Provider. It has information about the three model files and the connection string for use by the next layer—the relational data provider.

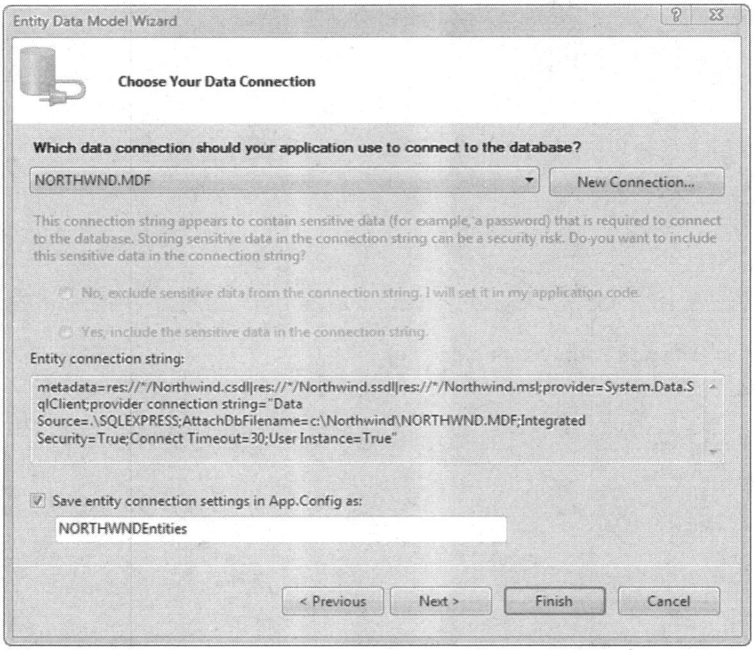

FIGURE 12.8 Entity Data Model Wizard step 2: Select a connection.

Click Next to go to the next step: selecting database objects that will be used to generate a model, as shown in Figure 12.9.

Expand the Tables node, and check Customers and Orders, as shown in Figure 12.10.

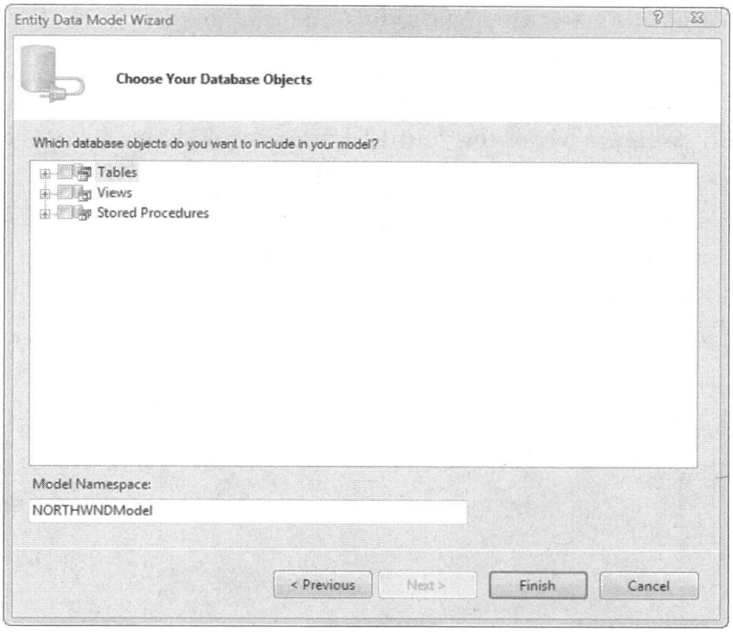

FIGURE 12.9   Entity Data Model Wizard step 3: Expand database objects for the model.

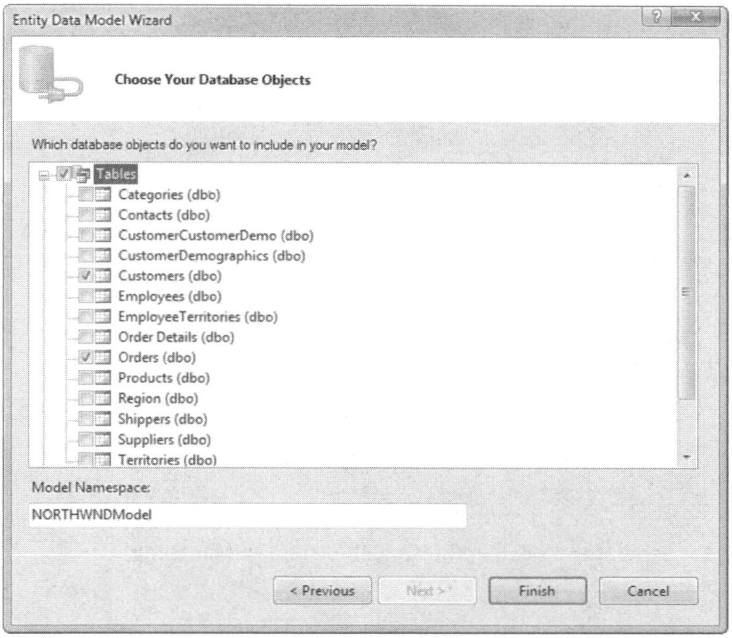

FIGURE 12.10   Entity Data Model Wizard step 4: Select database objects for the model.

Click Finish to generate the model. The wizard generates the North-wind.edmx file, which shows the two entities and the relationship between them (see Figure 12.11). Each entity also shows the navigation properties that let you navigate to another entity. For example, the Customers entity has a property named Orders for navigating to Orders entities. The lower pane shows the mapping information for the entity selected on the designer surface. Note that unlike LINQ to SQL designer, because EF designer does not perform smart plural-singular changes, you may want to use the renaming feature in Visual Studio to create more palatable entity names, such as Customer and Order.

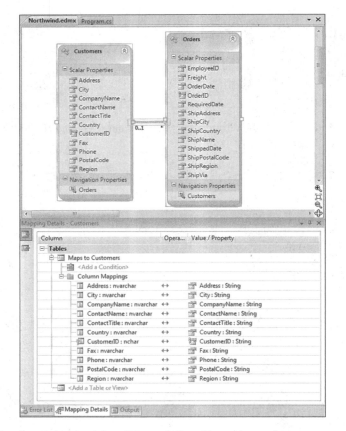

FIGURE 12.11   Generated model: entities, relationship, and mapping.

In addition to the designer, EF provides a command-line tool, edmgen.exe, for generating classes and model files from a database. We will not cover the details of the tool here because most users typically prefer to use the designer. Refer to the MSDN documentation if you intend to use the command-line tool instead of the graphical designer. (For additional information, see the topic called EDM Generator [EdmGen.exe] found at http://msdn.microsoft.com/en-us/library/bb387165.aspx.)

Understanding the Generated Code

From Solution Explorer, open Northwind.designer.cs under Northwind.edmx. It shows three classes generated by the wizard. The following code segment shows the key parts of the generated classes and attributes without the extensive details that you can see in the file. The main class is NORTH-WNDEntities, which is an ObjectContext. It contains an ObjectQuery<T> for each of the mapped tables. It supports only queries. AddToCustomers() and AddToOrders() have separate methods to add new entities for eventual insertion. Delete operations are handled through the base class method DeleteObject().

```
public partial class NORTHWNDEntities :
   global::System.Data.Objects.ObjectContext
{
   public global::System.Data.Objects.ObjectQuery<Customers> Customers
   {...}
   public global::System.Data.Objects.ObjectQuery<Orders> Orders
   {...}
   public void AddToCustomers(Customers customers)
   {...}
   public void AddToOrders(Orders orders)
   {...}
}
```

The two entity classes—Customers and Orders—inherit from the Entity Framework base class EntityObject. Hence, you cannot use your own base class. They contain attributes that point to model information in the conceptual space, which, in turn, is mapped to the appropriate counterpart in the storage space via mapping. The storage space connects to the database table. Thus, the model is at the center of programming in the Entity Framework.

The entity classes contain members with EDM attributes. The interesting members are the factory method, the key properties, and the navigation properties. The static factory method `CreateCustomers()` takes the company name and ID as parameters and stores them through nonnullable properties and returns a new valid Customers entity instance. The key property `Customers.CustomerID` is used to ensure object identity. The navigation property `Customers.Orders` is of the framework type `EntityCollection<T>`, which encapsulates framework functionality for EDM association. On the singleton side, such as `Orders.Customers`, no special framework type is needed. Unlike in LINQ to SQL, the loading of relationships is explicit using the `Load()` method. There is no implicit deferred loading. Notice that the foreign key member `Orders.CustomerID` is also absent. That information is abstracted in the EDM association.

```csharp
[global::System.Data.Objects.DataClasses.EdmEntityTypeAttribute
(NamespaceName="NORTHWNDModel", Name="Customers")]
public partial class Customers :
    global::System.Data.Objects.DataClasses.EntityObject
{
    ...
    public static Customers CreateCustomers
        (string companyName, string customerID)
    {...}

    [global::System.Data.Objects.DataClasses.EdmScalarPropertyAttribute
    (EntityKeyProperty=true, IsNullable=false)]
    public string CustomerID
    {...}

    [global::System.Data.Objects.DataClasses.
    EdmRelationshipNavigationPropertyAttribute
    ("NORTHWNDModel", "FK_Orders_Customers", "Orders")]
    public global::System.Data.Objects.DataClasses.EntityCollection<Orders>
        Orders
    {...}
}

public partial class Orders :
    global::System.Data.Objects.DataClasses.EntityObject
{
    public static Orders CreateOrders(int orderID)
    {...}

    [global::System.Data.Objects.DataClasses.EdmScalarPropertyAttribute
    (EntityKeyProperty=true, IsNullable=false)]
```

```
    public int OrderID
    {...}

    [global::System.Data.Objects.DataClasses.
    EdmRelationshipNavigationPropertyAttribute
    ("NORTHWNDModel", "FK_Orders_Customers", "Customers")]
    public Customers Customers
    {...}
}
```

Performing CRUD Operations

In Program.cs, add the following code to perform a simple query. Recall from Chapter 8, "Reading Objects with LINQ to SQL," that ObjectDumper is a handy utility for printing object graphs that ship with Visual Studio 2008 in source form. We will use it to display query results.

```
static void Main(string[] args)
{
    NORTHWNDEntities db = new NORTHWNDEntities();

    var CustInfoQuery = from c in db.Customers
                        where c.Country == "Spain"
                        select new
                        {
                            Id = c.CustomerID,
                            Contact = c.ContactName,
                            City = c.City
                        };

    ObjectDumper.Write(CustInfoQuery);
}
```

Building and running the project provides the following results for customers from Spain:

```
Id=BOLID        Contact=Martin Sommer        City=Madrid
Id=FISSA        Contact=Diego Roel           City=Madrid
Id=GALED        Contact=Eduardo Saavedra     City=Barcelona
Id=GODOS        Contact=Jose Pedro Freyre     City=Sevilla
Id=ROMEY        Contact=Alejandra Camino     City=Madrid
```

We'll look at insert, update, and delete operations next. We will run code very similar to that in Chapter 7. It has small differences:

- LINQ to Entities does not support the LINQ extension method `Single()`. Hence, `First()` must be used.
- The method for deletion is on the context, not on `ObjectQuery<T>`.

As mentioned in Chapter 7, remember to work with a copy of the Northwnd.mdf file (or the database) so that insert/update/delete operations do not affect the main copy of Northwind.

Here is code that you can enter into Program.cs to get some experience with deleting an existing customer and creating a new order:

```
NORTHWNDEntities db = new NORTHWNDEntities();

// Query for a specific customer
string id = "ALFKI";
var cust = db.Customers.First(c => c.CustomerID == id);

// Change the name of the contact
cust.ContactName = "New Contact";

// Delete an existing Customer: one without any Orders
string id2 = "FISSA";
var cust2 = db.Customers.First(c => c.CustomerID == id2);
db.DeleteObject(cust2);

// Create a new Order and set its Customers property
// EF discovers the new object and infers an insert
Orders ord = new Orders { OrderDate = DateTime.Now };
ord.Customers = cust;

// Save all the changes in one shot
db.SaveChanges();
```

Using Stored Procedures

EF supports stored procedures for CRUD operations. We will use two stored procedures—`OrdersByCustomer`, which returns entities, and `UpdateOrder`, which updates an entity. These stored procedures are not a part of the Northwind sample database, but the code and instructions for creating them are provided in Chapter 10, "Using Stored Procedures and Database Functions with LINQ to SQL."

Unlike in LINQ to SQL designer, EF designer uses the wizard instead of drag-and-drop from Server Explorer. To access the wizard, switch to the

Northwind.edmx file handled by the designer. Right-click the designer surface to bring up the menu shown in Figure 12.12.

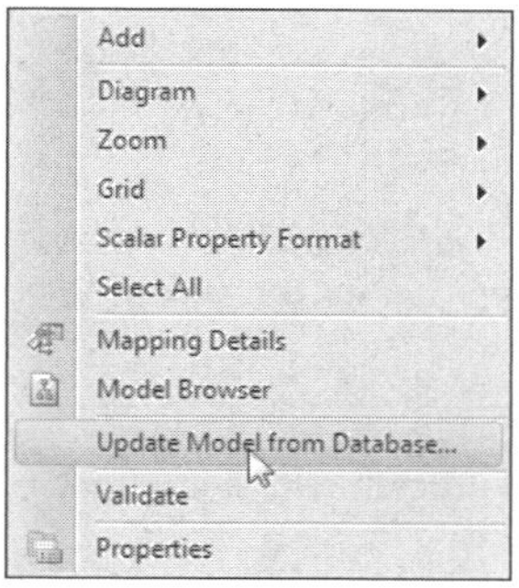

FIGURE 12.12   Adding to an existing entity data model.

Select Update Model from Database to bring up the Update Wizard. Using the wizard as described in earlier sections, add the two stored procedures to the model. Then right-click the designer surface to bring up the menu shown in Figure 12.12. Select Model Browser, open the Stored Procedures folder, right-click `OrdersByCustomer`, and select Create Function Import, as shown in Figure 12.13.

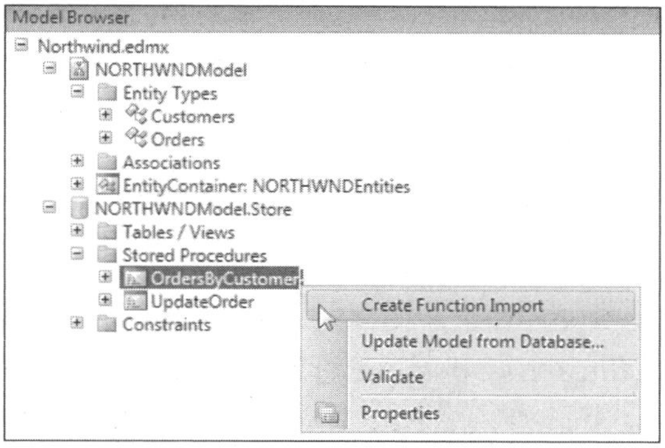

FIGURE 12.13   Adding a F procedure.

The Add Function Import dialog appears, as shown in Figure 12.14. Select a Return Type of Entities, and pick Orders from the drop-down.

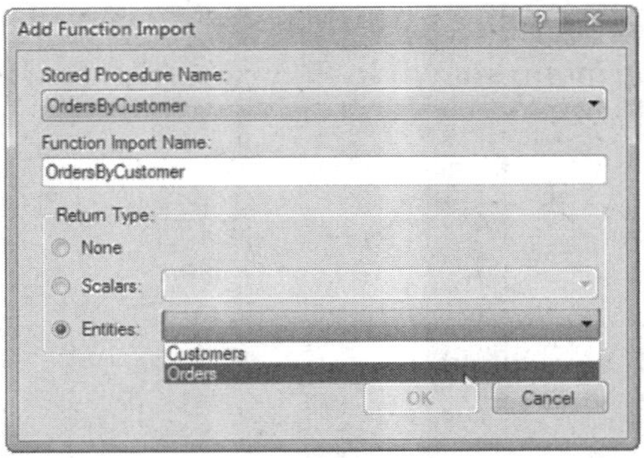

FIGURE 12.14   Mapping a stored procedure to a method.

Click OK to add a function with the same name. Save Northwind.edmx, and browse the regenerated Northwind.designer.cs file. It shows a new method, OrdersByCustomer, in the NORTHWNDEntities class. You can use it by adding the following code to Program.cs:

```
NORTHWNDEntities db = new NORTHWNDEntities();
var ords = db.OrdersByCustomer("BOLID");
ObjectDumper.Write(ords);
```

As expected, it brings back the orders for the specified customer. Additional members of Orders entities are omitted in the following result:

```
EmployeeID=4    Freight=77.9200    OrderDate=10/10/1996    OrderID=10326
...
EmployeeID=4    Freight=97.0900    OrderDate=12/29/1997    OrderID=10801
...
EmployeeID=9    Freight=16.1600    OrderDate=3/24/1998     OrderID=10970
...
```

For the update procedure, we need to switch back to the designer—the Northwind.edmx file. In the designer, click the Orders entity, and then click the second icon on the left side (the ToolTip says Map Entity to Functions). Click Select Update Function and choose UpdateOrder from the drop-down, as shown in Figure 12.15.

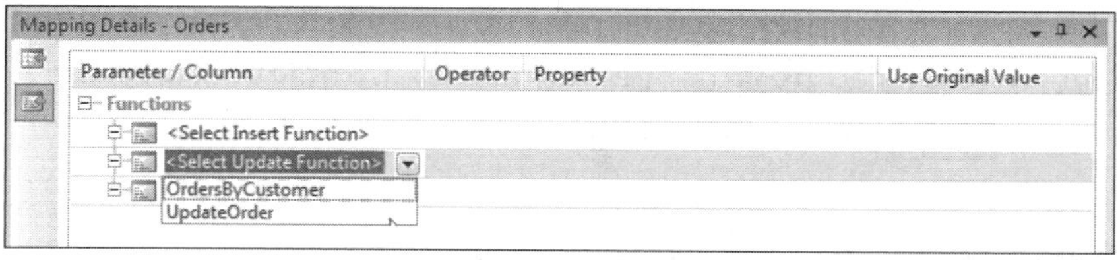

FIGURE 12.15   Mapping insert, update, and delete operations to stored procedures.

The Mapping Details window shows the mapped stored procedure. You can change the parameter to entity member mapping or pick the original value instead of the current value for some of the parameters. However, UpdateOrder does not use original values. Hence, we will use the defaults shown in Figure 12.16 based on name matching. One parameter that the designer cannot map is CustomerID. Map it manually to Customers. CustomerID by clicking the corresponding cell in the Property column and selecting the navigation property displayed.

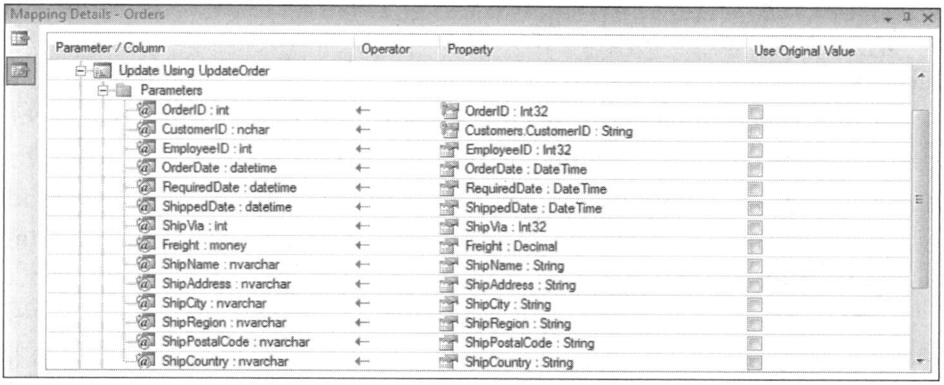

FIGURE 12.16   Mapping stored procedure parameters.

Unfortunately, due to a restriction in the first release of the schema, you cannot map just an update function; you need to map the insert and delete functions as well. So create stored procedures for inserting and deleting orders, and map them using the steps outlined before. For this discussion, simple stored procedures that just raise errors are enough to show how an update stored procedure is mapped. After they are mapped, the stored procedures are automatically used in lieu of dynamic SQL.

Making Sense of LINQ to Relational Choices

LINQ has proven to be a popular technology. Soon after the release of the first set of LINQ-enabled components in .NET Framework 3.5, a number of implementations came out. In this book we look at two implementation in the .NET Framework—LINQ to SQL and LINQ to Entities. Additional implementations exist, such as that in LLBLGen. At the time of this writing, there is also a rudimentary nhibernate LINQ project. Given the very strong positive response to LINQ, the number and quality of implementations are likely to go up. This is a very positive sign for the developer community, because they will have a good range of choices, and competition will ensure continuing improvements.

Given the choice, a common question is which LINQ to Relational technology is the most appropriate for current and future needs. A number of blogs and online papers provide guidance on this matter. Although you could get some information from these, it is best to experiment with the candidate technologies and decide which one suits your needs best. The design approach, complexity, scope, limitations, performance, cost, and community support levels are quite different across various implementations of LINQ.

In the .NET Framework, as of the first release, LINQ to SQL is very lightweight and intentionally keeps the mapping simple. It lets you write your own classes and map them directly if you want to. It also lets you use a graphical or command-line tool to generate classes and mapping from a database. On the other hand, EF has a much richer and more complex concept of a model between classes and tables. It follows a more prescriptive pattern, with a required base class and an emphasis on separation of the classes, the model, and the database. LINQ to SQL is designed to help you build robust applications quickly while helping you keep a simple, easy-to-maintain architecture. Use it if you can, and move on to LINQ to Entities if you see that your application has a clear need for model-driven development, complex mappings, or supported providers.

Developers interested in strong testability, a wide selection of providers, and a strong community may find nhibernate attractive as it improves its LINQ support.

Summary

The Entity Framework (EF) provides an implementation of LINQ for relational databases. It is based on the Entity Data Model (EDM) and emphasizes model-driven development. Entities and associations are first-class concepts in EDM and are at the heart of the design and runtime experience. EF is implemented as two layers—object services for a typical C#/VB.NET, and LINQ user and EntityClient for the implementation of the services in terms of EDM-aware connections, commands, and DataReaders.

EF designer provides a wizard for generating classes and model files from the database. The generated classes inherit from `EntityObject` and follow a strong prescribed pattern. The EF designer also enables the use of stored procedures.

EF is one of several LINQ to Relational solutions. It is likely to receive additional investments for more providers and a broader set of scenarios. However, other choices are available for the LINQ user with different characteristics.

■ 13 ■
LINQ to XML: Creation

INQ TO XML PROVIDES support for querying, creating, and transforming XML documents. XML namespaces are included in the API, as well as support for XML schemas. LINQ to XML stands on its own as a compelling alternative to technologies such as XPath, XQuery, XSLT, and the XML DOM.

Although LINQ to XML is not a small subject, the learning curve is nonetheless gentle. You learned earlier in this book that LINQ has a unified querying model. The skills you learned reading about LINQ to objects and LINQ to SQL also apply to LINQ to XML. This can seem like a minor point at first. It is not. The unified model that allows you to apply a single set of rules to a wide variety of data sources is one of the most valuable benefits of the LINQ programming model.

A series of practical examples explored in this chapter exemplify the key themes underlying LINQ to XML development. The focus is on learning the basics and then slowly introducing more complex subjects over the course of three chapters:

- This chapter focuses on creating XML.
- Chapter 14, "Querying and Editing XML," shows you how to query XML.

- The final chapter (Chapter 15, "XML Namespaces, Transformations, and Schema Validation") in the series shows more advanced topics:
  - XML namespaces
  - XML transforms
  - XML schemas

I like XML because it provides a simple, humble solution for use with a range of advanced technologies. For instance, XML can help you

- Transfer data across the Web.
- Create and call web services (SOAP).
- Create RSS documents that form a simple subscription model for information of all types.
- Define the object model for WPF (XAML).
- Define a host of other services too numerous to mention.

I've tried to make this chapter fit the subject matter by keeping the text easy to read. Hopefully you will be able to relax while reading, finding that each subject unfolds in a logical manner. When you are done, you will have learned about a relatively simple technology that is in wide use throughout many areas of both desktop and Internet-based computing.

XML Fundamentals

This chapter discusses several important features of XML with which you may already be conversant. Let's take a moment, however, to make sure that you understand the fundamentals. I think I can safely assume that you probably know the basics of XML, but I want to pin down some nomen-clature.

Consider the simple XML document shown in Listing 13.1.

LISTING 13.1   A Simple XML Document Containing Two Planets and One Moon

```xml
<?xml version="1.0" encoding="utf-8" standalone="yes"?>
<!--The planets Venus and Earth-->
<Planets>
  <Planet>
```

```
        <Name>Venus</Name>
      </Planet>
      <Planet Id="3">
        <Name>Earth</Name>
        <Moons>
          <Moon>Moon</Moon>
        </Moons>
      </Planet>
    </Planets>
```

The data captured in this document enumerates the second and third planets in our solar system. The code easily captures the fact that the Earth has a satellite that we call the moon. An `Id` field, set to the number 3, is also associated with the planet Earth.

This document contains four distinct pieces of XML syntax called a *declaration*, *comment*, *element*, and *attribute*. The top element, called `Planets`, is called a *root node*. These bits of syntax are illustrated in Figure 13.1.

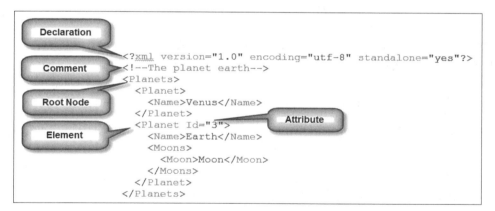

FIGURE 13.1   This simple XML file includes a declaration, a comment, multiple elements, an attribute, and a root node.

At the top you see an XML declaration, containing information about the version, the encoding, and whether the file depends on any other files. In this case, it does not; it can stand on its own. After the declaration you see an XML comment.

The root node, called `Planets`, is the beginning of an XML tree. This tree has various nodes, most of which are elements. These elements include the nodes called `Planets`, `Planet`, `Name`, `Moons`, and `Moon`.

The `Planets` element is the *parent* of the `Planet` element. The `Planet` element is a *child* of the `Planets` element. The `Planet`, `Name`, `Moons`, and `Moon` elements are all *descendants* of the `Planets` element. The `Planet` element is an *ancestor* of the `Name`, `Moons`, and `Moon` elements.

Figure 13.2 shows a simple XML element consisting of some text and an opening and closing tag. The text field is also frequently called *content*. We call this an XML element because it has an opening tag delineated by brackets and a closing tag delineated by brackets and a slash. The actual text inside the brackets is arbitrary.

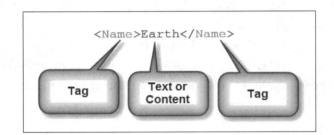

FIGURE 13.2   Elements typically consist of tags and content. In LINQ to XML, the text or content field is called `Value`.

Some of the XML elements in the sample document are nested:

```
<Moons>
    <Moon>Moon</Moon>
</Moons>
```

In this case both the `Moons` and `Moon` nodes are elements and can be treated as single entities. In other words, LINQ to XML allows you to address `Moons` as a single element, even though it contains a nested element.

The document shown in Listing 13.1 has a root node called `Planets`. The root node, or root element, is the outermost node in the portion of an XML file that contains its data. The declaration and some comments are located outside the root nodes, but they do not contain the data, which is the primary payload for an XML document. Locating the root can help you get your bearings in even the largest and most complex XML file.

The Planet element has an XML attribute, as shown in Figure 13.3. Attributes are nested inside an element tag, and they have a name, an equals sign, and a value in quotation marks.

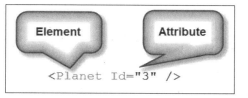

FIGURE 13.3 This entire XML node is an element. It contains an attribute called Id with a value of 3.

■ Elements Versus Attributes

XML has no clearly defined rules about when data should be placed in an attribute and when it should reside in an element. I tend to follow the common practice of placing data that I want to display to a user in elements, and placing housekeeping data such as an Id in attributes. In general, I find elements easier to read than attributes, so I tend to favor them. However, these are simply my prejudices; opinions on this subject differ. Where necessary, I will happily suffer minor inconsistencies in my style.

XML declarations are optional in XML 1.0 and mandatory in XML 1.1. Therefore, any document without a declaration is assumed to be an XML 1.0 document. XML documents support the Unicode standard, and UTF-8 is a common way to implement that standard. A document is stand-alone if it does not rely on an external DTD file or other entities.

Only the version is required in an XML declaration. Most parsers can automatically determine if a document is UTF-8 or UTF-16, so specifying the encoding usually is unnecessary unless you are using some other format. By default, XML documents are not considered to be stand-alone, but it is not an error to omit external references from such a document.

My goal in this introductory section has been to provide the minimum information you need to follow the discussion in the rest of the chapter. As mentioned earlier, Chapter 14 describes XML namespaces and schemas. But this is all I'll say about the basics. If you want more information, feel free to read any of the excellent books on XML that currently crowd bookstore shelves.

Understanding the LINQ to XML API

This section introduces the LINQ to XML API, which supplements the standard LINQ query operators with a set of XML-specific methods. Our exploration of LINQ to XML begins with samples of how to create, save, and read XML documents using the LINQ to XML API.

These opening sections focus on the objects shown in Figure 13.4. The XDocument, XElement, and XAttribute classes play central roles in this chapter. Other classes, such as XComment and XDeclaration, will be included in the discussion, but they have secondary importance. Most of your work with LINQ to XML will involve just a handful of classes, each of which has only a small number of important methods that you will use repeatedly. Many of the most important of those methods will be introduced during the discussion of querying XML data.

Figure 13.4 does not show the complete LINQ to XML hierarchy of objects, because I have omitted classes that are not particularly important. So as not to leave gaps in the hierarchy, I've included in Figure 13.4 supporting classes such as XObject, XNode, and XText. You will rarely encounter these classes in your day-to-day programming work, but knowing of their existence can help inform your decision-making process.

■ The Role of Nodes

The hierarchy shown in Figure 13.4 correctly suggests that the term node is a general way of talking about virtually any entity found in an XML document. Comments and elements are both nodes. Even the content, or text, inside an element, such as the one shown in Figure 13.2, is considered to be a node in an XML document. As the hierarchy shown in Figure 13.4 suggests, LINQ does not regard attributes as nodes, although some developers may disagree.

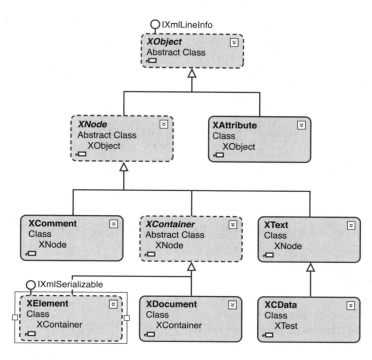

FIGURE 13.4   This hierarchy contains most of the important classes found in the LINQ to XML API.

Creating XML Elements

A "Hello World" program for the LINQ to XML API might look something like this:

```
using System.Xml.Linq;

var x = new XElement("Planet", "Earth");
Console.WriteLine(x);
```

These few lines of code create the following simple XML element:

```
<Planet>Earth</Planet>
```

Note the presence of the System.Xml.Linq using directive. Unlike System.Linq, this directive is not automatically added to your new source files when you are working in Visual Studio. You must add it yourself.

> ### ■ Inserting using Directives
>
> When working in Visual Studio, the simplest way to add a using directive to your program is to type in a member of a namespace not included in your using directives. In this case you might type XElement. Notice the red Smart Tag under the last letter of the word. This lets you know that Visual Studio thinks it knows a way to help you. Hold down the Ctrl key and press the period key. A window appears that allows you to automatically insert the appropriate using directive at the top of your current file.

You can access the name of an XML element through the Name property and access its content through the Value property. Consider the following code:

```
XElement element = new XElement("Planet", "Earth");
Console.WriteLine(element.Name);
Console.WriteLine(element.Value);
```

This code writes the words Planet and Earth.

The constructor for the XElement class shown here allows you to pass in the name and content for a single XML element. Here is the complete list of overloads for the XElement constructor:

```
public XElement(XElement other);
public XElement(XName name);
public XElement(XStreamingElement other);
public XElement(XName name, object content);
public XElement(XName name, params object[] content);
```

We are currently using the fourth overload. This is probably the most commonly used overload. The fifth overload is also very important, but I will delay showing it to you until we reach the section "Creating an XML Declaration."

Here are examples of using the first and second overloads:

```
var y = new XElement("Planets");
var z = new XElement(y);
Console.WriteLine(y);
Console.WriteLine(z);
```

The output from this code looks like this:

```
<Planets />
<Planets />
```

This syntax specifies that these elements do not have any value; they are empty.

Creating XML Attributes

LINQ to XML uses the XAttribute class to encapsulate the idea of an XML attribute. Here is how to create an XAttribute:

```
var xml = new XElement("Planet", new XAttribute("Id", 3));
```

If written to the console, this XElement produces the following code:

```
<Planet Id="3" />
```

XAttribute has only two constructors:

```
public XAttribute(XAttribute other);
public XAttribute(XName name, object value);
```

The second of these constructors is used in the previous example and in the majority of cases.

If you want to add two or more XAttributes to an XML element, you can write the following lines of code:

```
var xml = new XElement("Planet",
    new XAttribute("Id", 3),
    new XAttribute("ModelColor", "blue"));
```

When this code is written to the console, the output from this simple statement looks like this:

```
<Planet Id="3" ModelColor="blue" />
```

Most of the important properties and methods of XElement and XAttribute are used primarily in the context of querying data, so I will show you how to use them in that section of this chapter. For now, it is important only that you understand how to use their constructors to create XML nodes.

Creating an XML Document

The XElement class is remarkably flexible, and it will fit your needs in many cases. However, a second class called XDocument is similar to XElement. There is no reason to create an XDocument unless you have a use for one. Typically, those uses would include a desire to explicitly access the Root element in your XML tree, or wanting to include an XML declaration in a document you are creating.

Here is code that creates a simple XML document:

```
var xml = new XDocument(new XElement("Planets",
            new XElement("Planet", "Earth")));
```

You can print the output from this document to the console with the following line of code:

```
Console.WriteLine(xml);
```

The output looks like this:

```
<Planets>
  <Planet>Earth</Planet>
</Planets>
```

Creating an XML Declaration

An XML declaration is found on the first line of this simple XML document:

```
<?xml version="1.0" encoding="utf-8" standalone="yes"?>
<Planets>
  <Planet>Earth</Planet>
</Planets>
```

To add this node to your XML file, you must use an XDocument. XElement cannot handle declarations. As shown in Listing 13.2, LINQ to XML makes it easy for you to create and configure the various sections of an XML declaration. The code shown in Listing 13.2 includes an XML declaration, an XML comment, and an XML attribute. Listing 13.3 shows the simple XML file produced by this code.

LISTING 13.2   Using a Single Statement to Create an XML Document That Includes a Declaration, Comment, Elements, and Attributes

```
var xml = new XDocument(new XDeclaration("1.0", "utf-8", "yes"),
    new XComment("The planets Venus and Earth"),
    new XElement("Planets",
        new XElement("Planet",
            new XElement("Name", "Venus")),
        new XElement("Planet", new XAttribute("Id", 3),
            new XElement("Name", "Earth"),
            new XElement("Moons",
                new XElement("Moon", "Moon")))));

Console.WriteLine(xml.Declaration);
Console.WriteLine(xml);
```

LISTING 13.3   The Output from Listing 13.2

```
<?xml version="1.0" encoding="utf-8" standalone="yes"?>
<!-- The planets Venus and Earth -->
<Planets>
  <Planet>
    <Name>Venus</Name>
  </Planet>
  <Planet Id="3">
    <Name>Earth</Name>
    <Moons>
      <Moon>Moon</Moon>
    </Moons>
  </Planet>
</Planets>
```

A single nested statement, written in the declarative style, is used to create this XML document. If you indent your code properly, this kind of statement is easy to use, because it mirrors the structure of the document you want to create. Later in this chapter, I will show you how to create a similar document from a series of discrete statements. However, the declarative style shown in this example is preferred and is generally held up as one of the attractions of the LINQ to XML API.

Note that you need to use two `WriteLine` statements to display the output from the code in Listing 13.2 in its entirety. The first statement writes out the declaration, and the second writes out the body of the XML, including the comment:

```
Console.WriteLine(xml.Declaration);
Console.WriteLine(xml);
```

Five LINQ to XML classes are used in this example. You have already seen three of these classes: XDocument, XAttribute, and XElement. Two more classes are introduced in Listing 13.2:

- An XDeclaration is used to adorn our XML with some metadata that includes the version, the file encoding, and whether the document is stand-alone.
- XComment creates an XML comment.

I can't think of anything useful to say about the constructors for these simple classes other than they are easy to use and have obvious utilitarian value. Simply lift the code directly from Listing 13.2, and insert it into your own programs.

This excerpt from Listing 13.2 includes examples of how to use the fifth overload of the XElement constructor:

```
new XElement("Planet", new XAttribute("Id", 3),
     new XElement("Name", "Earth"),
     new XElement("Moons",
     new XElement("Moon", "Moon")))
```

Recall that this fifth overload of the XElement constructor looks like this:

```
public XElement(XName name, params object[] content);
```

This is a deceptively powerful line of code. The unusual type called params object[] allows you to pass an array of from 0 to *n* classes that derive from type object. This means, in effect, that you can pass an array of any type of object in this parameter. In particular, you can pass in a lengthy sequence of XAttribute and XElement constructors like those shown in this example. This is a form of compiler magic that enables LINQ to support the declarative style of programming.

Included with the programs that accompany this book is a sample called `CreatePlanets`. It shows you how to write a single declarative statement that generates a document listing all the planets and all the moons in our solar system. That sample includes the following constructor for the planet Jupiter, the body of which is nested inside a much larger declaration for all the planets and their moons:

```
public const string planet = "Planet";
public const string moon = "Moon";
public const string moons = "Moons";

... Code omitted here ...

new XElement(planet,
   new XElement(name, "Jupiter"),
   new XElement(moons,
      new XElement(moon, "Io"),
      new XElement(moon, "Europa"),
      new XElement(moon, "Ganymede"),
      new XElement(moon, "Callisto"),
      new XElement(moon, "Leda"),
      new XElement(moon, "Himalia"),
      new XElement(moon, "Lysithea"),
      new XElement(moon, "Elara"),
      new XElement(moon, "Ananke"),
      new XElement(moon, "Carme"),
      new XElement(moon, "Pasiphae"),
      new XElement(moon, "Sinope"),
      new XElement(moon, "Metis"),
      new XElement(moon, "Adrastea"),
      new XElement(moon, "Amalthea"),
      new XElement(moon, "Thebe"))),
```

The fifth overload of the `XElement` constructor accepts this code with nary a blink.

Designing and implementing code like this clearly requires an advanced degree in compiler magic. Nevertheless, the code itself is easy to use. This is declarative code at its best, allowing us to write a constructor that closely mirrors the shape of the complex XML documents that many developers frequently create.

Creating a Document from Raw Text

Here is an alternative means of creating an XML document:

```
string str = @"<?xml version=""1.0"" encoding=""utf-8""
  standalone=""yes""?>
    <!--The first three planets-->
  <Planets>
    <Planet>Mercury</Planet>
    <Planet>Venus</Planet>
    <Planet Moon=""Moon"">Earth</Planet>
  </Planets>";

XDocument doc = XDocument.Parse(str);
```

As you can see, the Parse method of the XDocument class allows you to pass in raw XML directly as a string literal. Sometimes this is the fastest and easiest way to create an XML document in your code.

Building a Document One Node at a Time

Although it is usually simplest to create an XML document with a single statement in the declarative style, it is possible to take other approaches. Listing 13.4 shows how to build a document one node at a time with a series of Add statements. See the program that accompanies this book called GettingStartedWithLinqToXml.

LISTING 13.4   Creating an XML Document One Node at a Time Using Add Statements

```
public void BuildDocument()
{
    var xml = new XDocument();

    xml.Add(new XComment("Some of the Solar System"));
    xml.Add(new XElement("Sun"));
    XElement temp = new XElement("Planet");
    temp.Add(new XAttribute("Name", "Earth"));
    xml.Root.Add(temp);
    temp = new XElement("Planet");
    temp.Add(new XAttribute("Name", "Mars"));
    temp.Add(new XElement("Moon", "Phobos"));
    temp.Add(new XElement("Moon", "Deimos"));
    xml.Root.Add(temp);

    Console.WriteLine(xml);
}
```

The Add method shown here is found in both the XDocument and XElement classes. I recommend using this technique primarily when you need to edit an existing document. An XML document is a single, heavily nested hierarchy of nodes, but the code shown in Listing 13.4 gives the impression that the document consists of separable, discreet pieces. As a result, many developers prefer to use the declarative style shown in Listing 13.2. Note also that the code shown in Listing 13.4 gives you no sense of the shape of the document you are creating. The failure of this imperative code to give you a sense of the shape of the document highlights one of the virtues of declarative code.

■ Declarative Versus Imperative Revisited

It is my belief that declarative code is better than imperative code when it is used at the right time and place. Both methods of programming have advantages, and it is important to learn how to get the best from both styles. It just happens that the declarative style lends itself well to the act of creating XML documents, just as it suits the act of querying data. This doesn't mean that it is the best tool to use in all cases, however.

Reading and Writing XML

Listing 13.5 shows how to create an XML document and then save it to disk.

LISTING 13.5   Saving a File to Disk

```
var xml = new XDocument(new XDeclaration("1.0", "utf-8", "yes"),
    new XComment("The planet earth"),
    new XElement("Planets",
        new XElement("Planet",
            new XElement("Name", "Venus")),
        new XElement("Planet", new XAttribute("Id", 3),
            new XElement("Name", "Earth"),
            new XElement("Moons",
                new XElement("Moon", "Moon")))));

xml.Save("Planets.xml");
```

Figure 13.5 shows the document created by Listing 13.4. It appears as it would if you typed it from the command prompt. Note the small set of unreadable characters at the start of the second line. This is the UTF-8 header. The header becomes visible at the command prompt, but it usually is not shown in most editors.

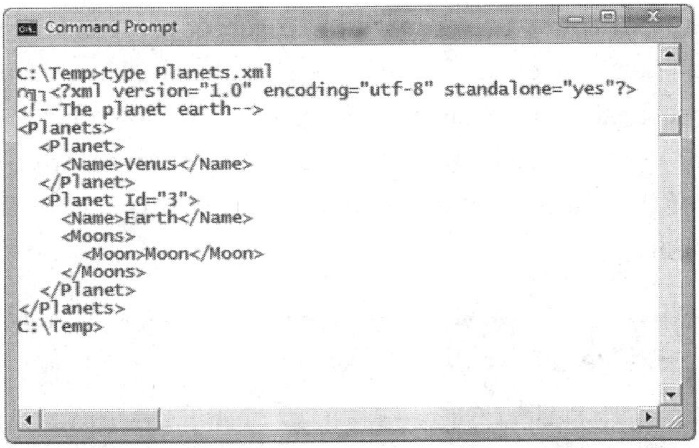

FIGURE 13.5　The UTF-8 document created by the code shown in Listing 13.4.

This is not a reference book, so I won't discuss each part in depth, but here are the overloads for the XElement and XDocument Save method:

```
public void Save(string fileName);
public void Save(TextWriter textWriter);
public void Save(XmlWriter writer);
public void Save(string fileName, SaveOptions options);
public void Save(TextWriter textWriter, SaveOptions options);
```

XDocument.Save saves declarations and similar information that appear before the root node, but XElement does not. The SaveOptions enumeration allows you to decide how to treat white space.

Both XDocument and XElement provide a Load method:

```
var xml = XDocument.Load(fileName);
var xml = XElement.Load(fileName);
```

XElement does not load information such as a declaration that appears before the root node. XDocument reads in that kind of information.

As mentioned, if you load the document this way and then try to write it to the console, you will discover that the default ToString() method for the XDocument class does not write out the XML declaration. If you want to see the entire XML document, you need to write two lines of code:

```
Console.WriteLine(xml.Declaration);
Console.WriteLine(xml);
```

Alternatively, you can use the File object to read the text back in so that you can see how it appears on disk:

```
string data = File.ReadAllText(tempxml);
Console.WriteLine(data);
```

The Load method has six overloads. LoadOptions allows you to preserve white space and capture line number information:

```
public static XDocument Load(string uri);
public static XDocument Load(TextReader textReader);
public static XDocument Load(XmlReader reader);
public static XDocument Load(string uri, LoadOptions options);
public static XDocument Load(TextReader textReader, LoadOptions options);
public static XDocument Load(XmlReader reader, LoadOptions options);
```

For example, here is how to load an RSS feed from the Internet into an XDocument:

```
XDocument xml = XDocument.Load(@"http://blogs.msdn.com/charlie/rss.xml");
Console.WriteLine(xml.Declaration);
Console.WriteLine(xml.FirstNode);
Console.WriteLine(xml);
```

If this were a call to XElement instead of XDocument, the attempt to write out the Declaration would be a compile-time error, and the call to write out the FirstNode would dump the entire document, minus the declaration and other header information. As it is, the first two WriteLine statements print the following:

```
<?xml version="1.0" encoding="UTF-8"?>
<?xml-stylesheet type="text/xsl"
   href=http://blogs.msdn.com/utility/FeedStylesheets/rss.xsl
   media="screen"?>
```

You must use `XDocument` if you want the declaration, the doctype, and related information. If you have no need for that information, call `XElement.Load`.

Summary

This chapter began with a brief overview of key features of the XML standard. With the preliminaries out the way, the text moved on to explain how LINQ to XML provides the tools you need to create, read, and write XML documents.

All the code shown in this chapter is also found on the book's web site. If you haven't done so already, download these programs and run them. There is nothing like working with live code to increase your understanding of a subject.

In the next chapter, you will learn how to query an XML document and how to edit an existing XML document. The final chapter on LINQ to XML covers XML namespaces, transformations, and schemas.

■ 14 ■
Querying and Editing XML

T HE PREVIOUS CHAPTER covered creating, reading, and saving XML documents. The next steps are to learn how to query and edit them.

This chapter deals with XML documents similar to the ones shown in the previous chapter. You will learn how to navigate through these documents to find individual nodes or series of nodes. You can start your query at any point in a document. You can begin at the top node and drill down into the hierarchy, or you can start on a leaf node and climb back up toward the root node. Wherever you are in a document, you can start your search there and either look at the sibling nodes nearest you, or navigate up to a root node or down to a leaf node. Detailing the range of options open to you is one of the primary goals of this chapter.

You will also learn how to edit, append, and delete XML nodes. These skills usually depend on your ability to search through a document, so I cover them only after completing a survey of common techniques of querying and navigating a document. After all, you usually need to find a particular node before you can edit it, delete it, or insert data next to it.

More on XDocument, XElement, and XAttribute

Before we begin, I want to step back for a moment and discuss the structure of the hierarchy of classes in which the XDocument, XElement, and XAttribute classes reside. This may seem an academic exercise, but you will see that there is a practical reason for understanding the shape of these objects.

Figure 14.1 shows the hierarchy for both the XDocument and XElement classes. Notice in particular that both classes descend from a class called XContainer, which in turn descends from a class called XNode. Other descendents of the XNode class include XComment and XCData.

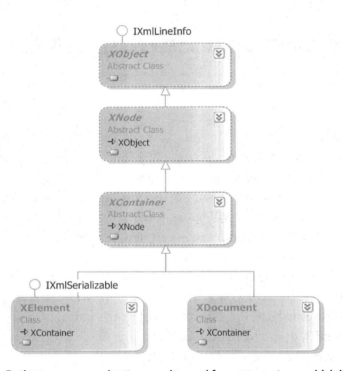

FIGURE 14.1 Both XDocument and XElement descend from XContainer, which in turn descends from XNode.

Figures 14.2 and 14.3 reveal that the abstract classes XNode and XContainer contain the declarations for many of the most important methods accessed by consumers of the XElement and XDocument classes. Having at least a passing familiarity with what these classes offer will stand you in good stead when you are working with LINQ to XML.

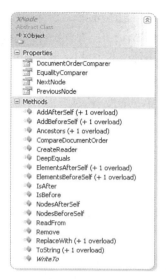

FIGURE 14.2 Besides XElement and XDocument, other important classes that descend from XNode include XComment, XText, and XCData.

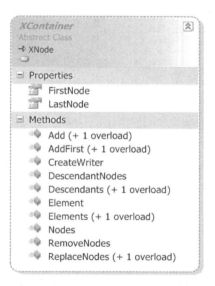

FIGURE 14.3 The XContainer class defines some of the most important methods shared by XDocument and XElement.

As shown in Figure 14.4, although XDocument is clearly smaller than XElement, both classes inherit quite a bit of power from XContainer and XNode. Therefore, they are more equal in capability than a simple glance at their declarations might suggest.

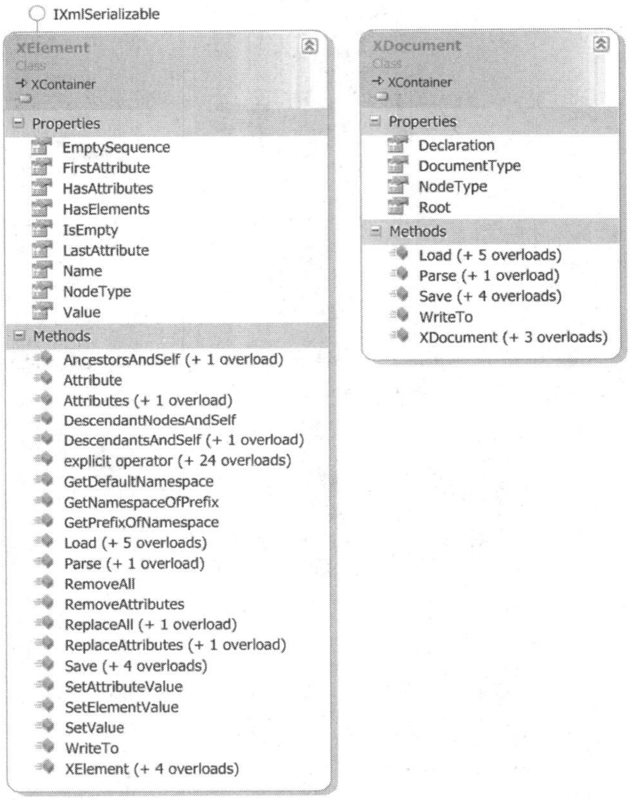

○ IXmlSerializable

XElement
Class
↗ XContainer

Properties
- EmptySequence
- FirstAttribute
- HasAttributes
- HasElements
- IsEmpty
- LastAttribute
- Name
- NodeType
- Value

Methods
- AncestorsAndSelf (+ 1 overload)
- Attribute
- Attributes (+ 1 overload)
- DescendantNodesAndSelf
- DescendantsAndSelf (+ 1 overload)
- explicit operator (+ 24 overloads)
- GetDefaultNamespace
- GetNamespaceOfPrefix
- GetPrefixOfNamespace
- Load (+ 5 overloads)
- Parse (+ 1 overload)
- RemoveAll
- RemoveAttributes
- ReplaceAll (+ 1 overload)
- ReplaceAttributes (+ 1 overload)
- Save (+ 4 overloads)
- SetAttributeValue
- SetElementValue
- SetValue
- WriteTo
- XElement (+ 4 overloads)

XDocument
Class
↗ XContainer

Properties
- Declaration
- DocumentType
- NodeType
- Root

Methods
- Load (+ 5 overloads)
- Parse (+ 1 overload)
- Save (+ 4 overloads)
- WriteTo
- XDocument (+ 3 overloads)

FIGURE 14.4　XDocument **compared to** XElement.

Figures 14.2, 14.3, and 14.4 show the methods and properties found in XNode, XContainer, XElement, and XDocument. I'm showing you these classes not because I want you to memorize which methods are in which classes, or because you need to overly concern yourself with the actual class in which a method is declared. Instead, I want to be sure you understand that XDocument and XElement derive much of their power from XNode and XContainer.

Here are the methods in XContainer that you will use most often when querying data:

```
public IEnumerable<XNode> DescendantNodes();
public IEnumerable<XElement> Descendants();
public IEnumerable<XElement> Descendants(XName name);
public XElement Element(XName name);
public IEnumerable<XElement> Elements();
public IEnumerable<XElement> Elements(XName name);
public IEnumerable<XNode> Nodes();
```

Notice that all of them, except Element, return an IEnumerable<T>. As a result, they are all fully LINQ-enabled.

The XNode class has a similar set of methods:

```
public IEnumerable<XElement> Ancestors();
public IEnumerable<XElement> Ancestors(XName name);
public IEnumerable<XElement> ElementsAfterSelf();
public IEnumerable<XElement> ElementsAfterSelf(XName name);
public IEnumerable<XElement> ElementsBeforeSelf();
public IEnumerable<XElement> ElementsBeforeSelf(XName name);
public bool IsAfter(XNode node);
public bool IsBefore(XNode node);
public IEnumerable<XNode> NodesAfterSelf();
public IEnumerable<XNode> NodesBeforeSelf();
```

When you query data, the only member declared in XDocument that you will use frequently is Root. The XElement class is a bit richer, because it contains the Attribute and Attributes properties, as well as Descendant NodesAndSelf, DescendantsAndSelf, and AncestorsAndSelf:

```
public IEnumerable<XElement> AncestorsAndSelf();
public IEnumerable<XElement> AncestorsAndSelf(XName name);
public XAttribute Attribute(XName name);
public IEnumerable<XAttribute> Attributes();
public IEnumerable<XAttribute> Attributes(XName name);
public IEnumerable<XNode> DescendantNodesAndSelf();
public IEnumerable<XElement> DescendantsAndSelf();
public IEnumerable<XElement> DescendantsAndSelf(XName name);
```

Finally, a class called Extensions is declared in the System.Xml.Linq namespace. A set of extensions methods are declared in that class, all but one of which return IEnumerable<T>:

```
IEnumerable<XElement> Ancestors<T>(...);
IEnumerable<XElement> AncestorsAndSelf(...);
IEnumerable<XAttribute> Attributes(...);
IEnumerable<XNode> DescendantNodes<T>(...);
IEnumerable<XNode> DescendantNodesAndSelf(...);
IEnumerable<XElement> Descendants<T>(...);
IEnumerable<XElement> DescendantsAndSelf(...);
IEnumerable<XElement> Elements<T>(...);
IEnumerable<T> InDocumentOrder<T>(...);
IEnumerable<XNode> Nodes<T>(...)
public static void Remove(this IEnumerable<XAttribute> source);
```

I should perhaps add that XObject, the base class for these other classes, contains two methods that LINQ to XML developers will find frequent reason to use:

```
public XElement Parent { get; }
public abstract XmlNodeType NodeType { get; }
```

Also included in the XObject class is the ability to annotate a node. I discuss this relatively minor feature near the end of the next chapter.

Now that you understand a little of how XElement and XDocument get their power, it is time to begin writing LINQ to XML queries. I'll begin that process in the next subsection and continue until near the end of the chapter. At that point I'll switch gears and talk about editing XML files with LINQ to XML.

Querying with Element and Elements

The Element and Elements properties are two of the workhorses of LINQ to XML. They are the simplest means of gaining access to the nodes of an XML tree.

To write LINQ to XML queries, you need an XML document that is complex enough to offer a moderate challenge. To get us started, I've created a document called FirstFourPlanets.xml, which is shown in Listing 14.1 and which you can find on disk. Take a moment to familiarize yourself with this document. This file and files similar to it are referenced often throughout this chapter and the next. You might even want to consider using a bookmark to help you return to this listing while you are reading.

LISTING 14.1   FirstFourPlanets.xml

```xml
<Planets>
  <Planet>
    <Name>Mercury</Name>
  </Planet>
  <Planet>
    <Name>Venus</Name>
  </Planet>
  <Planet>
    <Name>Earth</Name>
    <Moons>
      <Moon>
        <Name>Moon</Name>
        <OrbitalPeriod UnitsOfMeasure="days">27.321582</OrbitalPeriod>
      </Moon>
    </Moons>
  </Planet>
  <Planet>
    <Name>Mars</Name>
    <Moons>
      <Moon>
        <Name>Phobos</Name>
        <OrbitalPeriod UnitsOfMeasure="days">0.318</OrbitalPeriod>
      </Moon>
      <Moon>
        <Name>Deimos</Name>
        <OrbitalPeriod UnitsOfMeasure="days">1.26244</OrbitalPeriod>
      </Moon>
    </Moons>
  </Planet>
</Planets>
```

The root element of this listing is called Planets. It contains four elements called Planet. In turn, these elements have two nested elements called Name and OrbitalPeriod and an optional element called Moons, which has nested elements called Moon. Each Moon has two nested elements called Name and OrbitalPeriod. Each OrbitalPeriod has an attribute called UnitsOfMeasure. This document is just complex enough to provide an interesting challenge for those who want to query it.

Listing 14.2 (from the sample program called CreatePlanets) shows you how to write a simple two-line query that retrieves the names of the planets, creating the output shown in Listing 14.3.

> ### ▪ Ensuring That Your Program Can Find an XML File
>
> In this section of the book, you will frequently need to access XML files from your project. Visual Studio makes this easy. Simply copy the XML file to the directory where your project file is located. Add the XML file to your project. In the Properties window, set the property Copy to Output Directory to the value Copy if Newer. This ensures that the XML file is in the same directory as the project executable and, hence, can be loaded directly into the project without your having to consider the path to the file. For a more in-depth explanation of how this works, see the section in Appendix A titled "Including Data Files in Your Project."

LISTING 14.2   Code That Writes out the Names of the Planets Found in FirstFourPlanets.xml

```
var xml = XDocument.Load("FirstFourPlanets.xml");

var query = from p in xml.Root.Elements("Planet")
            select p.Element("Name").Value;

foreach (var x in query)
{
    Console.WriteLine(x);
}
```

LISTING 14.3   The Output When You Run the Code Shown in Listing 14.2 Against the XML Shown in Listing 14.1

```
Mercury
Venus
Earth
Mars
```

The first line of code in Listing 14.2 loads the XML we want to query. We then start a simple LINQ query that begins like this:

```
from p in xml.Root.Elements("Planet")
```

The reference to the Root node allows us to address the top-level element in the XML file. Because the rest of the file is nested inside the Planets element, the Root node addresses the entire file minus the declaration. The following code is semantically identical:

```
from p in xml.Element("Planets").Elements("Planet")
```

Now add a select statement:

```
from p in xml.Root.Elements("Planet")
select p;
```

This code returns the entire XML file except the outer Planets node. You need to foreach over the results to see them:

```
foreach (var x in query)
{
    Console.WriteLine(x);
}
```

This displays the following output:

```
<Planet>
  <Name>Mercury</Name>
  <Moons />
</Planet>
<Planet>
  <Name>Venus</Name>
  <Moons />
</Planet>
<Planet>
  <Name>Earth</Name>
  <Moons>
    <Moon>
      <Name>Moon</Name>
      <OrbitalPeriod UnitsOfMeasure="days">27.321582</OrbitalPeriod>
    </Moon>
  </Moons>
</Planet>
<Planet>
  <Name>Mars</Name>
  <Moons>
    <Moon>
      <Name>Phobos</Name>
      <OrbitalPeriod UnitsOfMeasure="days">0.318</OrbitalPeriod>
    </Moon>
    <Moon>
```

```
        <Name>Deimos</Name>
        <OrbitalPeriod UnitsOfMeasure="days">1.26244</OrbitalPeriod>
      </Moon>
    </Moons>
  </Planet>
```

It is important to understand that this code does not simply dump one large chunk of XML to the screen. Instead, our query returns four elements, one for each `Planet` element in the document. This differs from the `xml.Element("Planets")` query, which returns only one very large item, because the file has only one `Planets` node.

To see exactly how this works, let's modify that `foreach` loop just slightly by asking it to "take" the first two results from the query:

```
foreach (var x in query.Take(2))
{
    Console.WriteLine(x);
}
```

This produces the following output:

```
<Planet>
  <Name>Mercury</Name>
  <Moons />
</Planet>
<Planet>
  <Name>Venus</Name>
  <Moons />
</Planet>
```

This is one way of demonstrating that we are returning four elements, and not just one big element.

Now take a look at the `select` clause in Listing 14.2. It projects a return set that contains the `Value` of the `Name` element:

```
select p.Element("Name").Value;
```

Our `from` clause returns a set of four planets. Each planet in our file contains two elements called `Name` and `Moons`. Our new projection simply asks for the `Value` of the `Name` node. In the case of the second planet, that value would be the string `"Venus"`.

Consider what would happen if we wrote the following code:

```
var query = from p in xml.Root.Elements("Planet")
            select p.Element("Name");
```

Our output would look like this:

```
<Name>Mercury</Name>
<Name>Venus</Name>
<Name>Earth</Name>
<Name>Mars</Name>
```

The point is that the code returns the entire element.

> ### ▪ Casting an Element
>
> If you cast an element as a string using an explicit conversion operator, you get its value:
>
> ```
> var query = from p in xml.Root.Elements("Planet")
>             select (string)p.Element("Name");
> ```
>
> This query projects the element's `Value`, producing output like that shown in Listing 14.3. We'll return to this subject in the section "Working with Missing Nodes."

XML Descendants

If you have to dig more than two levels deep into your XML file, using `Elements` to compose a query can become cumbersome. For instance, this code is perhaps a bit too verbose:

```
xml.Element("Planets").Elements("Planet").Elements("Moons").Elements("Moon")
```

Fortunately, there are many cases when you will not need to use this kind of syntax. LINQ to XML provides a shortcut that allows you to dig down directly to the node you want:

```
var query = from x in xml.Descendants("Moon")
            select x.Element("Name");
```

Let's step back for a moment and see if we can understand how Descendants works. One version of the Descendants method takes no parameters. I found it useful to take a moment to study this overload. Consider the following code:

```
var query = from c in xml.Descendants()
            select c;

Console.WriteLine("Descendant Count: " + query.Count());

int count = 1;
foreach (var item in query)
{
    Console.WriteLine("{0} Descendant {1} {2}", ">>",
        count++.ToString(), "<<");
    Console.WriteLine(item);
}
```

In the sample program that accompanies this book called Descendants, I ran this query against the following short XML file:

```
<?xml version="1.0" encoding="utf-8" ?>
<Planet>
  <Name>Mars</Name>
  <Moons>
    <Moon>Phobos</Moon>
    <Moon>Deimos</Moon>
  </Moons>
</Planet>
```

The program produces the output shown in Listing 14.4. Note that the code "annotates" the results with some simple descriptive statements designating the descendant count.

LISTING 14.4   An Annotated Look at the Results of a Simple Query That Uses a Call to Descendants

```
Descendant Count: 5

Descendant 1:
<Planet>
  <Name>Mars</Name>
  <Moons>
    <Moon>Phobos</Moon>
    <Moon>Deimos</Moon>
  </Moons>
</Planet>
```

```
Descendant 2:
<Name>Mars</Name>

Descendant 3:
<Moons>
  <Moon>Phobos</Moon>
  <Moon>Deimos</Moon>
</Moons>

Descendant 4:
<Moon>Phobos</Moon>

Descendant 5:
<Moon>Deimos</Moon>
```

As you can see, the first descendant is the entire document. The next one is the `Name` element with the value `Mars`, and then the element `Moons`, and finally each individual `Moon`. This is a very logical descent through the nodes of the document. Whenever you become confused about how LINQ to XML views the structure of your document, it may be worth writing code like this to see exactly how LINQ thinks about the descendants in your document.

If you pass in a parameter to `Descendants`, you can single out one of the nodes shown in Listing 14.4. Consider this code:

```
var query = from c in xml.Descendants("Name")
            select c;
```

It retrieves the following data:

```
Descendant Count: 1

>> Descendent 1 <<
<Name>Mars</Name>
```

As you can see, this code skips directly to the `Name` node and ignores the `Planet` node that precedes it.

You will find LINQ to XML much more fun to use if you if you take the time now to fully understand the difference between calling `Descendants()` and calling `Descendants("Name")`. The first call retrieves all the elements that descend from the caller. The second node picks out the descendant elements that have the specified name.

Consider what would happen if you ran the following code against the same document:

```
var query = from c in xml.Descendants("Moon")
            select c;
```

It would produce the following output:

```
Descendant Count: 2

>> Descendant 1 <<
<Moon>Phobos</Moon>

>> Descendant 2 <<
<Moon>Deimos</Moon>
```

As you can see, the output from this query consists of the two nodes named Moon. The call to Descendants simply skips all the previous nodes and focuses only on the name we passed in as a parameter. If you pass in a parameter to Descendants, it does not drill down into the hierarchy as the parameterless version does. Instead, it grabs only the siblings of the node you specify.

Composition and XML Queries

It probably has occurred to you that calls to Descendants might not work as hoped in documents that contain nodes that have the same name but at different levels. For instance, consider what happens when we run the following query against the FirstFourPlanets.xml file:

```
var nameQuery = from x in xml.Descendants("Name")
                select x;

foreach (var x in nameQuery)
{
    Console.WriteLine(x);
}
```

This code grabs Name nodes from multiple levels. In other words, it finds both the names of planets and the names of moons.

```
<Name>Mercury</Name>
<Name>Venus</Name>
<Name>Earth</Name>
<Name>Moon</Name>
<Name>Mars</Name>
<Name>Phobos</Name>
<Name>Deimos</Name>
```

This is fine if you want to find all the `Name` nodes in the document. But if you are looking for only the names of moons, it would be the wrong answer. As you will see in the next chapter, you can solve this problem by using XML namespaces. Alternatively, you could revert to the type of code you saw earlier in this chapter, which is slightly more verbose than a call to `Descendants()`, but also more precise:

```
var moonName = from x in xml.Descendants("Moon")
               select x.Element("Name");
```

This query locates the unique node that is nearest to the `Name` element you seek and then uses it as a point of reference.

Solutions like this work fine with relatively simple documents, but with complex documents it could become painful to try to isolate a particular node. If you are working with a complex document, you might want to use LINQ composability to help simplify your query. As you recall, composability allows you to break queries into composable parts, thereby limiting the complexity of any one query. Because LINQ queries are deferred, this does not result in a significant performance penalty.

The code shown in Listing 14.5 is run against the FirstFourPlanets.xml file. It separates the `Mars` node from the rest of the XML in our file.

LISTING 14.5   A Short Query Showing How to Access a Single Node in an XML Tree

```
var query = from x in xml.Descendants("Planet")
            where x.Element("Name").Value == "Mars"
            select x;

foreach (var x in query)
{
  Console.WriteLine(x);
}
```

The output from this query expression looks like this:

```
<Planet Name="Mars">
  <Name>Mars</Name>
  <Moons>
    <Moon>
      <Name>Phobos</Name>
      <OrbitalPeriod UnitsOfMeasure="days">0.318</OrbitalPeriod>
    </Moon>
    <Moon>
      <Name>Deimos</Name>
      <OrbitalPeriod UnitsOfMeasure="days">1.26244</OrbitalPeriod>
    </Moon>
  </Moons>
</Planet>
```

We can now write a second query based on the results of the query shown in Listing 14.5:

```
var query1 = from x in query.Descendants("Moon")
             select x;
```

The output from this query is as follows:

```
<Moon>
  <Name>Phobos</Name>
  <OrbitalPeriod UnitsOfMeasure="days">0.318</OrbitalPeriod>
</Moon>
<Moon>
  <Name>Deimos</Name>
  <OrbitalPeriod UnitsOfMeasure="days">1.26244</OrbitalPeriod>
</Moon>
```

This particular example is perhaps a bit contrived. Nevertheless, many developers may find it easier to break a query into two parts like this rather than writing one long query. Feel free to use this kind of composition whenever possible if you think it will help you write code that is simpler to write, simpler to test, and simpler to understand. The compositional aspect of LINQ is one of its great features. Use it when you think it will be helpful.

DescendantNodes, XText, and CData

The `DescendantNodes` method returns a collection of not just the elements, but of all the nodes descending from the source collection. Contrast it with the `Descendants` method, which retrieves only the `Elements`.

Here is an example from the `CreatePlanets` sample program of embedding a query in a `foreach` statement:

```
foreach (var x in query.Descendants("Moon").DescendantNodes())
{
  Console.WriteLine(x);
}
```

This query uses both the `Descendants` methods and the `DescendantNodes` method to produce the output shown in Listing 14.6.

LISTING 14.6   The Output from a Call to `DescendantNodes` Includes Not Only Elements, but Also Text Nodes

```
<Name>Moon</Name>
Moon
<OrbitalPeriod UnitsOfMeasure="days">27.321582</OrbitalPeriod>
27.321582
<Name>Phobos</Name>
Phobos
<OrbitalPeriod UnitsOfMeasure="days">0.318</OrbitalPeriod>
0.318
<Name>Deimos</Name>
Deimos
<OrbitalPeriod UnitsOfMeasure="days">1.26244</OrbitalPeriod>
1.26244
```

If this query asked only for the `Descendants("Moon")`, it would return three nested nodes, one for each of the moons in the FirstFourPlanets.xml file:

```
<Moon>
  <Name>Moon</Name>
  <OrbitalPeriod UnitsOfMeasure="days">27.321582</OrbitalPeriod>
</Moon>
<Moon>
  <Name>Phobos</Name>
  <OrbitalPeriod UnitsOfMeasure="days">0.318</OrbitalPeriod>
</Moon>
<Moon>
  <Name>Deimos</Name>
  <OrbitalPeriod UnitsOfMeasure="days">1.26244</OrbitalPeriod>
</Moon>
```

`DescendantNodes` breaks the descendants of the top-level nodes in this query into their constituent parts. Look, for instance, at this descendant:

```
<Moon>
  <Name>Moon</Name>
  <OrbitalPeriod UnitsOfMeasure="days">27.321582</OrbitalPeriod>
</Moon>
```

It is broken down by `DescendantNodes` into these three constituent parts:

```
<Name>Moon</Name>
Moon
<OrbitalPeriod UnitsOfMeasure="days">27.321582</OrbitalPeriod>
27.321582
```

As mentioned earlier, attributes such as `UnitsOfMeasure` are not regarded as nodes.

DescendantNodesAndSelf

If you called `DescendantNodesAndSelf`, as shown in Listing 14.7, you would find one extra node in the results of your query. Compare the code in Listing 14.8 with that in Listing 14.6. Notice that `DescendantNodesAndSelf` returns not only the descendants of the Moon node, but also the Moon node itself. In Listing 14.8, I have put in bold the code that is retrieved by `DescendantNodesAndSelf` but not by `DescendantNodes`.

LISTING 14.7   A Call to `DescendantNodesAndSelf`

```
var dsnodes = from x in
                planets.Descendants("Moon").DescendantNodesAndSelf()
                select x;

foreach (var x in dsnodes)
{
    Console.WriteLine(x);
}
```

LISTING 14.8   The Results of the Simple Query Shown in Listing 14.7

```
<Moon>
  <Name>Moon</Name>
  <OrbitalPeriod UnitsOfMeasure="days">27.321582</OrbitalPeriod>
</Moon>
<Name>Moon</Name>
Moon
<OrbitalPeriod UnitsOfMeasure="days">27.321582</OrbitalPeriod>
27.321582
<Moon>
```

```
  <Name>Phobos</Name>
  <OrbitalPeriod UnitsOfMeasure="days">0.318</OrbitalPeriod>
</Moon>
<Name>Phobos</Name>
Phobos
<OrbitalPeriod UnitsOfMeasure="days">0.318</OrbitalPeriod>
0.318
<Moon>
  <Name>Deimos</Name>
  <OrbitalPeriod UnitsOfMeasure="days">1.26244</OrbitalPeriod>
</Moon>
<Name>Deimos</Name>
Deimos
<OrbitalPeriod UnitsOfMeasure="days">1.26244</OrbitalPeriod>
1.26244
```

Searching for Text Nodes

One quick way to find a unique Value in an XML tree is to combine Descen-
dantNodes with a call to the standard LINQ operator OfType:

```
var phobos = from XText x in xml.DescendantNodes().OfType<XText>()
             where x.Value == "Phobos"
             select x;
Console.WriteLine(phobos.First());
```

This simple query writes the word Phobos. The call to OfType ensures that
the query retrieves only nodes of type XText—that is, content nodes that
contain a simple text value. Consider this element:

```
<Name>Venus</Name>
```

The content for this XML element is the text node Venus. LINQ to XML
regards text like the word Venus as being of type XText.

Write code like this to ensure that your query retrieves a single value:

```
var phobos = (from XText x in planets.DescendantNodes().OfType<XText>()
              where x.Value == "Phobos"
              select x).Single().Value;
```

As you learned in Chapter 6, "Query Operators," the LINQ query operator Single raises an exception if your query returns more than one result.
Thus, a developer is alerted if the document contains two instances of a
string that he assumed appeared only once.

CData

We have been working with very "well-behaved" text nodes. However, sometimes you need to work with text fields that do not conform so nicely to the expected syntax for an XML file. Consider, for instance, what would happen if you inserted a text node that itself contained markup as text in an XML element:

```
<Alt>Use "<PlanetName>Earth</PlanetName>"?</Alt>
```

Code like this would upset any XML parser and cause it to return unexpected results. To fix the problem, you could write something like this:

```
<Alt>Use &quot;&lt;PlanetName&gt;Earth&lt;/PlanetName&gt;&quot;?</Alt>
```

Here standard XML *character entity references* such as < and > are used in place of characters such as < and >. Few people would consider this an optimal solution.

The CData section, where CData stands for "character data," is designed to help alleviate the pain. Consider the code shown in Listings 14.9 and 14.10. (See the CDataQuery sample program that accompanies this book for the complete Listing 14.9.)

LISTING 14.9　An Example of How to Parse XML That Contains CData

```
XDocument xml = XDocument.Load("WithCData.xml");

var query = from p in xml.Descendants("Alt")
            select p;

foreach (var item in query)
{
    Console.WriteLine("The entire node");
    Console.WriteLine(item);
}

var alt = from p in xml.Descendants("Alt")
          select p.Value;

foreach (var item in alt)
{
    ShowTitle("Just the title");
    Console.WriteLine(item);
}
```

LISTING 14.10   A Simple XML File Containing CData

```
<?xml version="1.0" encoding="utf-8" ?>
<Planets>
  <Planet>
    <Name>Earth</Name>
    <Alt><![CDATA[Use "<PlanetName>Earth</PlanetName>"?]]></Alt>
  </Planet>
</Planets>
```

The Alt element shown in Listing 14.10 uses a CData section to embed text that contains XML markup. Although admittedly it's a bit awkward to read, this is nonetheless much simpler than directly inserting character entity references into XML.

Consider the query shown in Listing 14.9. This code loads the XML file from Listing 14.10 and produces the following output:

```
==================
The entire node
==================
<Alt><![CDATA[Use "<PlanetName>Earth</PlanetName>"?]]></Alt>
==================
Just the value
==================
Use "<PlanetName>Earth</PlanetName>"?
```

As you can see, LINQ to XML interprets the Value of the Alt node as if it were the plain text without the machinery of the CDATA syntax.

Here is one way to search for a node that contains CData:

```
var query1 = from p in xml.DescendantNodes().OfType<XCData>()
             where p.ToString().Contains("Earth")
             select p;
```

This query would retrieve our CData node from the document in Listing 14.10. As always in LINQ, there are many different ways to achieve the same end, but this is a reasonable approach.

Parents and Ancestors

After you have found a node, you can navigate backward from it to a Parent node. In this code fragment, the program navigates to a text node and then finds the parent of its parent:

```
var parent = from XText x in planets.DescendantNodes().OfType<XText>()
             where x.Value == "Phobos"
             select x.Parent.Parent;

Console.WriteLine(parent.First());
```

This code writes the following:

```
<Moon>
  <Name>Phobos</Name>
  <OrbitalPeriod UnitsOfMeasure="days">0.318</OrbitalPeriod>
</Moon>
```

Even though we specified a node of type XText in our search, this query returns an XElement because the projection returns the Parent of Parent, and Parents return XElements:

```
public XElement Parent { get; }
```

The Ancestors method is the mirror image of the Descendants method. Instead of walking down the graph of the XML file, it walks backward through it toward the root:

```
var ancestors = from XText x in planets.DescendantNodes().OfType<XText>()
                where x.Value == "Phobos"
                select x.Ancestors();

count = 1;
foreach (var item in ancestors)
{
    foreach (var i in item)
    {
        Console.WriteLine("<< Ancestor: {0} >>", count++);
        Console.WriteLine(i);
    }
}
```

This code walks backward through the FirstFourPlanets.xml document:

```
<< Ancestor: 0 >>
<Name>Phobos</Name>

<< Ancestor: 1 >>
<Moon>
  <Name>Phobos</Name>
  <OrbitalPeriod UnitsOfMeasure="days">0.318</OrbitalPeriod>
</Moon>
```

```
<< Ancestor: 2 >>
<Moons>
  <Moon>
    <Name>Phobos</Name>
    <OrbitalPeriod UnitsOfMeasure="days">0.318</OrbitalPeriod>
  </Moon>
  <Moon>
    <Name>Deimos</Name>
    <OrbitalPeriod UnitsOfMeasure="days">1.26244</OrbitalPeriod>
  </Moon>
</Moons>
Etc, up to the root...
```

To save space, I cut off this listing about halfway through. The next node in the series would be `Planet`. The final element in the series would be the entire document, starting at the `Root` node. Like the `Descendants` method, you can pass in a string with an element name as a parameter to the `Ancestors` method. You then are taken directly to the particular set of elements associated with that name.

It's hard to overemphasize the importance of understanding how `Descendants` and `Ancestors` work. The more readily you can visualize what nodes would be returned by a call to these methods, the more quickly you will become comfortable with navigating through a document with LINQ to XML.

Elements After or Before Self

It can be confusing to call `ElementsBeforeSelf` or `ElementsAfterSelf` right after calling `Ancestors` or `Descendants`. You can tend to think that these methods drill up or down into the XML hierarchy like `Descendants` and `Ancestors`, when in fact they reference the next item after the caller at the current level in the XML graph. They return sibling nodes, not parent or child nodes.

Consider the following XML node:

```
<Planet>
    <Name>Earth</Name>
    <Moons>
      <Moon>
        <Name>Moon</Name>
        <OrbitalPeriod>27.321582d</OrbitalPeriod>
```

```
        </Moon>
      </Moons>
    </Planet>
```

The Ancestor of the Moons node is Planet, and its Descendants are Moon, Name, and OrbitalPeriod. The ElementsBeforeSelf in this file is Name. There are no ElementsAfterSelf.

To illustrate how these methods work, open the ReadXml sample that accompanies this book. Here is the ElementsBeforeSelf method from that program:

```
var query = from p in xml.Descendants("Moons")
            select new
            {
                eas = p.ElementsAfterSelf(),
                ebs = p.ElementsBeforeSelf()
            };

foreach (var item in query)
{
    // After self
    foreach (var i in item.eas)
    {
        Console.WriteLine("Before...{0}...{1}", i.Name, i.Value);
    }
    // Before self
    foreach (var i in item.ebs)
    {
        Console.WriteLine("Before...{0}...{1}", i.Name, i.Value);
    }
}
```

When run against the FirstFourPlanets.xml file, this code yields these results:

```
Before...Name...Earth
Before...Name...Mars
```

As you can see, the code finds the Name node that appears before itself on the same level in the XML hierarchy, but it finds nothing after itself. In either case, it is searching for sibling nodes, not parents or children.

Here are similar lines of code run against the same file:

```
var query = from p in xml.Descendants("Planet")
            select new { val = p.Element("Name").Value,
                         eas = p.Element("Name").ElementsAfterSelf() };

foreach (var item in query)
{
    Console.WriteLine(item.val);
    foreach (var i in item.eas)
    {
        Console.WriteLine("...{0}", i.Name);
    }
}
```

It produces this code:

```
Mercury
Venus
Earth
...Moons
Mars
...Moons
```

This code searches for and finds the two planets in the file that have moons and then gets the elements after the Name element. Each planet has only one such element, and it is called Moons. In other words, this sample does the opposite of what we saw in the previous sample.

Working with Missing Nodes

LINQ to XML developers frequently encounter the "problem of the missing node." Consider this simple XML document from the MissingElements sample that accompanies this book:

```
<?xml version="1.0" encoding="utf-8" ?>
<Planets>
  <Planet Id="1">
    <Name>Mercury</Name>
  </Planet>
  <Planet Id="2">
    <Name>Venus</Name>
  </Planet>
```

```
<Planet>
  <Name>Earth</Name>
</Planet>
<Planet Id="4">
  <Name>Mars</Name>
</Planet>
</Planets>
```

All but one of the `Planet` elements in this document has an `Attribute` called `Id`. Following the lead of its dominant species, the planet Earth is the one that breaks with precedent.

If you run the following code against this document and then try to `foreach` over the results, you get a `NullReferenceException`:

```
var venusMoons = from x in xml.Descendants("Planet")
                 where x.Attribute("Id").Value == "2"
                 select x;
```

The problem, of course, is that there is no `Attribute` called `Id` for the planet Earth, and when LINQ tries to find the `Value` of the `Id` attribute for Earth, a null reference exception is thrown.

To avoid this problem, you can write the following code, or some variation of it:

```
var venusMoons = from x in planets.Descendants("Planet")
                 let id = x.Attribute("Id") ?? new XAttribute("Id", "-1")
                 where id.Value == "2"
                 select x;
```

Here the `??` (null coalescing) operator is used to test if an `Attribute` called `Id` exists:

```
let id = x.Attribute("Id") ?? new XAttribute("Id", "-1")
```

If it does not, a new `Attribute` called `Id` with a value of `-1` is created. This new attribute ensures that we don't get a `NullReferenceException`. I've passed in `-1` as the `Value` of this attribute to ensure that this node does not accidentally pass our filter.

In some cases the null coalescing operator won't meet a developer's needs. In those situations, you may use a regular ternary operator (`if` statement):

```
var venusMoons = from x in planets.Descendants("Planet")
                 let id = (x.Attribute("Id") == null) ?
                    "-1" : x.Attribute("Id").Value
                 where id == "2"
                 select x;
```

This is less elegant, but it works in certain circumstances where the null coalescing operator will not work.

Another very useful technique is to use explicit conversion operators to access the value of an attribute:

```
var venusMoons = from x in planets.Descendants("Planet")
                 let id = (string)x.Attribute("Id")
                 where id == "2"
                 select x;
```

Code like this is quite terse and very easy to read. It relies on the existence of a series of more than 20 very esoteric conversion operators that happen to exist in the XAttribute and XElement classes. If you cast the XAttribute class to a string, it returns the Value of the attribute if it is available; otherwise, it returns the empty string. This means you don't get a null reference exception.

▪ Explicit Conversion

This is absolutely not the right place to explore explicit and implicit conversion operators. However, you might want to open one of your LINQ to XML source files and hover the cursor over a valid instance of the word XElement. Press F12 to go to the metadata definition of the XElement class. You will see the declarations for the explicit conversion operators at the top of the listing. Here are two of them:

```
public static explicit operator int?(XAttribute attribute);
public static explicit operator int(XAttribute attribute);
```

For more information, search the online C# help for the topic "Using Conversion Operators."

If none of these solutions fits your tastes, you can simply use an external method to resolve any potential null reference exceptions in your code:

```
private static void UseExternalMethod()
{
    XDocument planets = XDocument.Load("FirstFourModified.xml");

    var venusMoons = from x in planets.Descendants("Planet")
                     let id = ExternalResolution(x)
                     where id == "2"
                     select x;

    foreach (var item in venusMoons)
    {
        Console.WriteLine(item);
    }
}

private static string ExternalResolution(XElement x)
{
    if (x.Attribute("Id") == null)
    {
        return "IdEarth";
    }
    else
    {
        return (string)x.Attribute("Id");
    }
}
```

Here we create a method that checks if the node we want to examine is null. If it is, the code returns `IdEarth`; otherwise, it returns the `Id` of the attribute. This is not particularly terse, and perhaps not really in the spirit of LINQ, but it is easy to read.

The examples I've shown you here are fairly easy to understand. In the next chapter, I will revisit the subject of missing nodes and show how you can solve more complex problems with this same technology.

Working with Line Numbers

Sometimes it is helpful to know the line number of a node in a file. Reporting the line number of a node you have found can be a very useful feature, particularly if you want to report an error. It can also be convenient to search for a node by line number. However, that can, of course, be a very risky endeavor, because documents can be modified accidentally, and their line numbers changed without notice.

If you look at either the first or last figure in this chapter, you will see that a class called XObject sits at the top of the LINQ to XML class hierarchy. This class supports an interface called IXmlLineInfo:

```
public interface IXmlLineInfo
{
  int LineNumber { get; }
  int LinePosition { get; }
  bool HasLineInfo();
}
```

An instance of this interface is used to store the line number information when you call XDocument.Load with LoadOptions.SetLineInfo:

```
XDocument xml = XDocument.Load(fileName, LoadOptions.SetLineInfo);
```

If you load an XML file into memory using this technique, line numbers are associated with the nodes in your document.

Here is code that uses the IXmlLineInfo interface to report the line number of a node you have found through a standard LINQ to XML search:

```
XText phobos = (from x in xml.DescendantNodes().OfType<XText>()
                where x.Value == "Phobos"
                select x).Single();

var lineInfo = (IXmlLineInfo)phobos;
Console.WriteLine("{0} appears on line {1}",
    phobos, lineInfo.LineNumber);
```

This code is taken from the XmlLineNumber program that accompanies this book.

The query shown here searches through our document for the word "Phobos." It uses the query operator Single to ensure that the query returns only a single node, which in this case is of type XText. The program then casts the result as IXmlLineInfo and reports the line number to the user:

```
Phobos appears on line 21
```

Let's now turn things around and see how to search through an XML and look for a node by line number. If you look at the FirstFourPlanets.xml file, you will see that line 18 looks like this:

```
<Name>Mars</Name>
```

Here is code from the XmlLineNumber sample showing how to search for that node by line number:

```
XDocument xml = XDocument.Load(fileName, LoadOptions.SetLineInfo);

var line = from x in xml.Descendants()
           let lineInfo = (IXmlLineInfo)x
           where lineInfo.LineNumber == 21
           select x;

foreach (var item in line)
{
    Console.WriteLine(item);
}
```

Note that the first line uses `LoadOptions.SetLineInfo` to ensure that line information is recorded when the document is loaded into memory.

The LINQ query shown here uses `Descendants` to iterate over the elements in the FirstFourPlanets.xml file. The `where` filter in the query checks to see if any of those elements has its line number set to 21. It happens that the 15th element returned by the call to `Descendants` fits that search criteria, so that node, and that node alone, is found when we `foreach` over the results.

Notice the cast to convert the `XElement` nodes returned by the call to `Descendants`:

```
let lineInfo = (IXmlLineInfo)x
```

This cast is necessary because the actual fields of the `IXmlLineInfo` interface are not exposed as `Public` by `XElement`. As soon as we know the line number of an element, we can use a `where` clause to filter the result set, returning only the node that appears on line 21.

Again, I want to stress that reporting the line number of a node seems like a reasonable thing to do, but searching for an element by line number usually is not a good idea. In any case, you now know enough to begin working with line numbers in a LINQ to XML program.

Modifying XML

To modify the nodes of an XML tree, you need to work with only a small set of easy-to-use calls. The program called ModifyNodes that accompanies this book illustrates how to proceed.

The ModifyNodes program uses the document called FirstFour-Planets.xml, which lists the first four planets and their moons, as shown in Listing 14.11. Alternatively, you can use the file called NewPlanets.xml, which lists 8 planets and their 66 moons, plus the dwarf planet Pluto and its moons Charon, Nix, and Hydra.

In this section of the chapter, I will modify the same document multiple times. The results of each query are cumulative. For instance, in the section on removing nodes, the code lops off all the moons in the document. The next section, on editing, assumes that the moons have been removed from the document, and it shows the results of editing the modified document.

Removing Nodes

The code shown in Listing 14.11 strips all the planetary moons by calling Remove. The Element and Elements methods navigate to the relevant nodes. As soon as we have arrived at our destination, a call to Remove excises the moons. We then navigate to the next set of satellites and again excise them with a call to Remove. You can see the results of this operation in Listing 14.12.

LISTING 14.11   Using Remove to Delete Nodes from an XML Document

```
XDocument xml = XDocument.Load("FirstFourPlanets.xml");
planets.Element("Planets")
       .Elements("Planet")
       .Elements("Moons")
       .Remove();
```

LISTING 14.12   The Results of the Method Shown in Listing 14.11

```
<Planets>
  <Planet>
    <Name>Mercury</Name>
  </Planet>
  <Planet>
    <Name>Venus</Name>
  </Planet>
  <Planet>
    <Name>Earth</Name>
  </Planet>
  <Planet>
    <Name>Mars</Name>
  </Planet>
</Planets>
```

The code shown in Listing 14.11 uses LINQ method syntax. Alternatively, you could write this code:

```
XDocument planets = XDocument.Load("FirstFourPlanets.xml");
var nodes = from m in planets
              .Element("Planets")
              .Elements("Planet")
              .Elements("Moons")
          select m;

nodes.Remove();
```

Here the effect is exactly the same, but the code uses a traditional LINQ query expression, and the program calls Remove on the results returned from the query. Remember that query expressions are converted into method syntax at compile time, so the runtime performance of both techniques is close to identical. In most cases, you should use the syntax that you find easiest to read.

Editing Nodes

Here is how to edit the value of the first planet node:

```
planets.Element("Planets")
       .Element("Planet")
       .Element("Name")
       .Value = "Mercury is near the sun";
```

Note that this code picks out the first planet in the document by using `Element("Name")` rather than `Elements("Name")`. The latter technique would return a list of all the names of the planets, which is not what we want in this case. If we make this edit after removing the moons, the document looks like this:

```
<Planets>
  <Planet>
    <Name>Mercury is near the sun</Name>
  </Planet>
  <Planet>
    <Name>Venus</Name>
  </Planet>
  <Planet>
    <Name>Earth</Name>
  </Planet>
  <Planet>
    <Name>Mars</Name>
  </Planet>
</Planets>
```

This code uses a `where` clause to pick out one node by name and edit it:

```
Console.WriteLine("Modify Planet by Name");

var q = (from p in planets.Element("Planets").Elements("Planet")
         where p.Element("Name").Value == "Venus"
         select p).Single();

q.Element("Name").SetValue("Venus is love!");
Console.WriteLine(planets);
```

The code uses `Single()` to specify that we want to get the only item from the XML file that meets our criteria. If more than one element is returned, the call to `Single` ensures that an `InvalidOperation` exception is raised. The exception would state that the "Sequence contains more than one element."

After this action, the document would look like this:

```
<Planets>
  <Planet>
    <Name>Mercury is near the sun</Name>
  </Planet>
```

```
<Planet>
  <Name>Venus is love</Name>
</Planet>
<Planet>
  <Name>Earth</Name>
</Planet>
<Planet>
  <Name>Mars</Name>
</Planet>
</Planets>
```

Inserting Nodes

There are simple methods for inserting nodes in or adding nodes to an existing XML file. You read about these methods in the section "Building a Document One Node at a Time" in the preceding chapter, but they take on a different flavor in this context.

In the samples shown in this section, the code first searches for a location in the document where you want to add the node. When it is safely at its destination, the code proceeds to insert the new node.

Adding Attributes

Here is how you add an attribute to a node:

```
XElement sun = planets.Element("Planets");
sun.Add(new XAttribute("MassOfSun", "332,946 Earths"));
```

After this edit, the XML for the `Planets` element looks like this:

```
<Planets MassOfSun="332,946 Earths">
```

Here is how you add an attribute to the `Mars` node:

```
var query = (from x in planets.Elements("Planets").Elements("Planet")
             where x.Element("Name").Value == "Mars"
             select x).Single();

query.Add(new XAttribute("Mass", "0.107 Earths"));
```

After you execute this code, the `Mars` node looks like this:

```
<Planet Mass="0.107 Earths">
  <Name>Mars</Name>
</Planet>
```

Here is how you edit that attribute:

```
var attr = (from x in planets.Elements("Planets").Elements("Planet")
            where x.Element("Name").Value == "Mars"
            select x.Attribute("Mass")).Single();

attr.Value = "6.4185?1023 kg";
```

After you execute this code, the Mars node looks like this:

```
<Planet Mass="6.4185x1023 kg">
  <Name>Mars</Name>
</Planet>
```

Adding Elements

Here is a how to add an element to our existing list of planets:

```
planets.Root.Add(new XElement("DwarfPlanet",
    new XElement("Name", "Eris")));
```

Note that we are adding a nested set of XElement nodes, one called Dwarf-Planet and the other called Name. Here is what the XML looks like when we are done:

```
<Planets MassOfSun="332,946 Earths">
  <Planet>
    <Name>Mercury is near the sun</Name>
  </Planet>
  <Planet>
    <Name>Venus is love</Name>
  </Planet>
  <Planet>
    <Name>Earth</Name>
  </Planet>
  <Planet Mass="6.4185x1023 kg">
    <Name>Mars</Name>
  </Planet>
  <DwarfPlanet>
    <Name>Eris</Name>
  </DwarfPlanet>
</Planets>
```

In this section, you have learned about the three basic operations you can perform when modifying a document: delete, modify, and insert. You have seen that the code for performing these actions is usually very simple.

Using these methods, however, does require that you first know how to search for the node upon which you want to operate.

Summary

In this chapter, you have learned how to query an XML document. The text focused on several key methods and properties, including `Element`, `Elements`, `Descendants`, `Parents`, and `Ancestors`. You also read about removing, editing, and inserting nodes in an XML document.

Figure 14.5 shows the complete hierarchy of the classes that make up the core of LINQ to XML. A few other classes in this namespace are not part of this hierarchy, such as `XNamespace` and `XDeclaration`. But most of the key LINQ to XML classes are shown in this diagram. Take a moment to study it as a means of reviewing the subjects covered in this and the previous chapter, and also to see some of the topics to be covered in the next chapter.

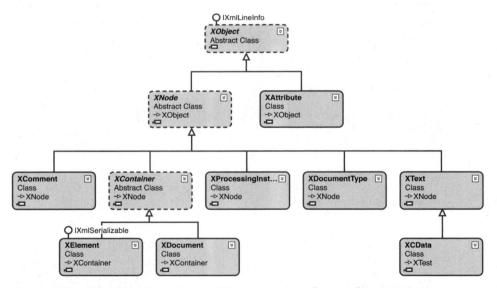

FIGURE 14.5   This object hierarchy provides an overview of many of the key classes explored in this chapter and the preceding one.

By this stage you know many of the most important features of LINQ to XML. The next chapter covers slightly more advanced material on XML namespaces, transforms, and schemas. You will see examples of how to move XML data into and out of a relational database.

▪ 15▪

XML Namespaces, Transformations, and Schema Validation

I N THIS CHAPTER, you will learn about XML namespaces, transformations (also called transforms), and schemas. LINQ to XML has modern techniques for working with each of these technologies. Understanding how these technologies work is an important step toward mastering both XML and LINQ.

In this chapter, you will learn the following:

- Namespaces provide a scoping mechanism for XML data. LINQ to XML can both create namespaces and navigate through them.

- There are several types of XML transformations. For instance, you will see how to transform relational data into XML and vice versa. You will also see how to transform an XML document from one format to another. For instance, you will see how to transform a standard XML document into an XHTML document.

- XML schemas can ensure not only that a document is well formed, but also that it follows a set of rules that govern the types and locations of nodes in a document.

XML and Namespaces

XML namespaces are much like namespaces in C#. Their primary purpose is to scope the range of a tag in an XML file. The FirstFourPlanets.xml file introduced in Listing 13.1 in the preceding chapter has two elements called Name. One is the name of a planet, and the other is the name of a moon. XML namespaces allow you to put one element in namespace A and the second in namespace B. These namespaces can then be used to distinguish the name of a moon from the name of a planet. This is analogous to placing two classes with the same name in two different namespaces and thus distinguishing between them.

You can also use namespaces to distinguish data in two different files. For instance, suppose we had one XML file with planets listed in it and a second XML file with moons listed in it. If both documents had a Name tag similar to the one in our FirstFourPlanets.xml file, we could distinguish the Name tag from the planet file from the Name tag in the moon file by the namespace that encapsulated it.

URIs are used as unique identifiers for XML namespaces. In Windows programming we frequently use GUIDs for the same purpose. The goal is to find an identifier that is unlikely to be duplicated so that each namespace can be uniquely identified. The URIs are used simply as identifiers. Typically they are not used to connect to a server over HTTP. Don't think of them as web sites; think of them simply as unique names, just as a GUID is a unique identifier.

Consider these two simple XML documents:

```
<Moons xmlns="http://www.elvenware.com/moons">
  <Moon>
    <Name>Phobos</Name>
  </Moon>
</Moons>

<Planets xmlns="http://www.elvenware.com/planets">
  <Planet>
    <Name>Mars</Name>
  </Planet>
</Planets>
```

Each of these documents has its own namespace designated by the attribute `xmlns`, which stands for "XML namespace." The first document is uniquely identified by a URL ending with the word `moons`, and the second by a URL ending with the word `planets`.

If each document were in a separate file, we could ignore the individual filenames and distinguish the two documents by their namespaces. Furthermore, we could use the namespace to distinguish between the `Name` node in the moons file and the `Name` node in the planets file.

You could, at least in theory, use this type of namespace to gain more fine-grained control by placing one namespace in each node of your file:

```
<Planets xmlns="http://www.elvenware.com/planets">
  <Planet xmlns="http://www.elvenware.com/planets">
    <Name xmlns="http://www.elvenware.com/planets">Mars</Name>
    <Moons xmlns="http://www.elvenware.com/moons">
      <Moon xmlns="http://www.elvenware.com/moons">
        <Name xmlns="http://www.elvenware.com/moons">Phobos</Name>
      </Moon>
    </Moons>
  </Planet>
</Planets>
```

We can distinguish between the two different `Name` nodes in this file by looking at the default namespaces in which they reside. Furthermore, we can tell that the `Moons` and `Moon` nodes belong to one namespace, and the `Planets` and `Planet` nodes to another. This system works, but it is very verbose.

To help write more concise code that is easier to read, the developers of XML created a second kind of namespace that uses prefixes to designate whether a particular node belongs to a particular namespace. The kind of namespace I have shown you so far is called a default namespace. Here is a document that uses prefixes rather than default namespaces:

```
<planets:Planets
  xmlns:planets="http://www.elvenware.com/planets"
  xmlns:moons="http://www.elvenware.com/moons">
  <planets:Planet>
    <planets:Name>Mars</planets:Name>
    <planets:Moons>
      <moons:Moon>
```

```
        <moons:Name>Phobos</moons:Name>
      </moons:Moon>
    </planets:Moons>
  </planets:Planet>
</planets:Planets>
```

Notice that we declare two different namespaces in the root node of this document. The URLs for these namespaces are designated with a slightly different syntax than that used in a default namespace. The markup `xmlns` is followed by a colon, and then the name of the namespace:

```
xmlns:planets="http://www.elvenware.com/planets"
```

We can now use this new namespace as a prefix to distinguish the other nodes in our document. For instance, we can see at a glance which `Name` node belongs to the `planets` namespace, and which to the `moons` namespace:

```
<planets:Name>Mars</planets:Name>
<moons:Name>Phobos</moons:Name>
```

Now that you understand the basics of XML namespaces, I'll show you how to work with these namespaces in a LINQ to XML program.

Default Namespaces

This code contains a default namespace called `http://www.charliecalvert.com/planets` that wraps the `Planets` node and all its subnodes:

```
<?xml version="1.0" encoding="utf-8" ?>
<Planets xmlns="http://www.charliecalvert.com/planets">
  <Planet>
    <Name>Mercury</Name>
    <OrbitalPeriod>Unknown</OrbitalPeriod>
    <Moons />
  </Planet>
  <Planet>
    <Name>Venus</Name>
    <OrbitalPeriod>Unknown</OrbitalPeriod>
    <Moons />
  </Planet>
  <Planet>
    <Name>Earth</Name>
    <OrbitalPeriod>1.0000175y</OrbitalPeriod>
    <Moons>
```

```
      <Moon>
        <Name>Moon</Name>
        <OrbitalPeriod>27.321582d</OrbitalPeriod>
      </Moon>
    </Moons>
  </Planet>
</Planets>
```

This document uses a default namespace, so all the tags enveloped by the node called `Planets` belong to that namespace. For instance, the nodes `Planet`, `Name`, `OrbitalPeriod`, and `Moons` are all considered to be inside the `Planets` namespace. In fact, all the nodes in this document are part of that namespace.

If you ran the following query against this document, it would fail to retrieve any data, but it would have succeeded had there been no namespace:

```
var query = from x in xml.Descendants("Name")
            select x;

foreach (var item in query)
{
    Console.WriteLine(item.Value);
}
```

This query fails because there is no `Element` in the document called `Name`. Instead, there is an `Element` that looks like this:

```
<Name xmlns=http://www.charliecalvert.com/planets>
```

Alternatively, you could designate the same thing with this syntax:

```
<{http://www.charliecalvert.com/planets}Name>
```

You can take a node's namespace into account by using a LINQ to XML class called `XNamespace`. After incorporating that class, your code would look like this:

```
XNamespace planets = "http://www.charliecalvert.com/planets";

var query = from x in xml.Descendants(planets + "Name")
            select x;
```

```
foreach (var item in query)
{
    Console.WriteLine(item.Value);
}
```

The points of interest here are the declaration for the namespace, and also the use of that namespace in the call to Descendants:

```
XNamespace planets = "http://www.charliecalvert.com/planets";
xml.Descendants(planets + "Name")
```

With these two items in place, the call succeeds.

Here is another, very different XML document called XmlPresComplex.xml:

```
<?xml version="1.0" encoding="utf-8" ?>
<pres xmlns:pres="http://www.charliecalvert.com/pres">
  <vp xmlns:vp="http://www.charliecalvert.com/vp">
    <Presidents>
      <President sequence="1">
        <pres:Name>George Washington</pres:Name>
        <termStart>1789</termStart>
        <termEnd>1797</termEnd>
        <party>none</party>
        <born>1732</born>
        <died>1799</died>
        <VicePresidents>
          <VicePresident>
            <vp:Name>John Adams</vp:Name>
            <termStart>1789</termStart>
            <termEnd>1797</termEnd>
            <born>1735</born>
            <died>1826</died>
            <party></party>
          </VicePresident>
        </VicePresidents>
      </President>
    </Presidents>
  </vp>
</pres>
```

This document has two XML elements called Name. One designates the name of a president, and the other the name of a vice president. To distinguish between them, the code includes two prefix namespaces—one for the president, and one for the vice president. Notice that the namespaces are used only to single out the two `Name` fields. They are not used to address the other fields in the document.

When looking at the XML document, notice that we explicitly use the namespace followed by a colon for the nodes we want to call out:

```
<pres:Name>George Washington</pres:Name>
    <vp:Name>John Adams</vp:Name>
```

In this excerpt from the XmlNamespaces sample available for download from the book's web site, you can see how to query the president and vice president document:

```
XDocument presDoc = XDocument.Load("XmlPresComplex.xml");

XNamespace president = "http://www.charliecalvert.com/pres";
XNamespace vp = "http://www.charliecalvert.com/vp";

var query2 = from c in presDoc.Descendants(president + "Name")
             select c;
```

This code returns the name of the president. The following code, however, which uses the `vp` namespace, returns the name of the vice president:

```
var query3 = from c in presDoc.Descendants(vp + "Name")
             select c;
```

Notice how both calls use the `XNamespace` class to set up a namespace that can be used as a prefix in the calls to `Descendants`.

To get one of the elements from the file that is not explicitly designated as belonging to either namespace, just query without the namespace:

```
var query4 = from c in presDoc.Descendants("termStart")
             select c;
```

That's all I want to say about querying XML documents that contain namespaces. In the next section, on XML transformations, you will see how to create XML documents that contain namespaces.

XML Transformations

Transformations are an important part of all the flavors of LINQ, but they play a particularly large role when you're working with XML. Rather than run through all the possible permutations, I'll focus on three important ways to transform XML data:

- Transform XML from one format to another
- Transform relational data into XML
- Transform XML into relational data

The focus will stay primarily on these tasks. Additional examples of working with text and XML are found in the sample programs that accompany this book.

Transforming XML from One Format to Another

Transforming XML from one format to another is one area where LINQ to XML is particularly strong. Complex documents can make the task more challenging, but the basic skills involved are not difficult to master. I should perhaps add that many of the queries you looked at in the preceding chapter are really transformations: They queried one document and transformed it into a second document.

Let's begin by transforming the FirstFourPlanets XML file from the preceding chapter into the following XML:

```
<Planets>
  <Planet>Mercury</Planet>
  <Planet>Venus</Planet>
  <Planet>Earth</Planet>
  <Planet>Mars</Planet>
</Planets>
```

The following code from the TransformPlanets program that accompanies this book performs this task:

```
var xml = new XElement("Planets",
    from x in doc.Root.Elements("Planet")
    select new XElement("Planet", x.Element("Name").Value));

Console.WriteLine(xml);
```

This code first creates a Root node for the new document:

```
var xml = new XElement("Planets",
```

A simple LINQ query then retrieves the data to insert into the other elements of the new document:

```
from x in doc.Root.Elements("Planet")
select new XElement("Planet", x.Element("Name").Value);
```

The projection in the `select` statement begins with a call to the `XElement` constructor, which creates an XML node called `Planet`. The content, or `Value` field for this element, is filled in by a call to `x.Element("Name")`. `Value`. This code returns the name of the planet. If you then write the output from this query to the console or to disk, you will have completed the transformation.

In this example a few bits of information from the original XML file were added to our new file, and much data was stripped away. In the end, however, the data from one document was transformed into data for another document.

Creating XHTML Through a Transformation

XHTML is a specification for writing HTML documents that conform to the XML standard. Both types of documents conform to the XML standard, but an XHTML document is a form of HTML and, hence, can be easily displayed in a browser. XML parsers, such as LINQ to XML, can be used to query an XHTML document. This means that you can, at least in some cases, reliably automate the processing of XHTML documents.

XHTML documents contain familiar HTML tags such `<p>`, `<pre>`, and `<h1>`. Each tag must be used in conformance with the XML standard. For instance, every `<p>` tag must have a matching `</p>` tag, and every `<li>` tag must have a matching `</li>` tag. We even have to close a break tag using `<br />`.

Converting an XML document into XHTML is a common task. It is also a transformation in that we are transforming an XML document from one format into another.

XHTML is not a complicated format, but enough subtleties are involved that you need a way to confirm that a document is valid. Later in this chapter, I will show you how to use the LINQ APIs to confirm that a document is valid XML. Here we need to go beyond that and confirm that the document conforms to the XHTML standard. For that task we can use a service found at this URL:

```
http://validator.w3.org
```

On that web page, you can submit your XHTML as raw text and have its syntax validated, as shown in Figure 15.1.

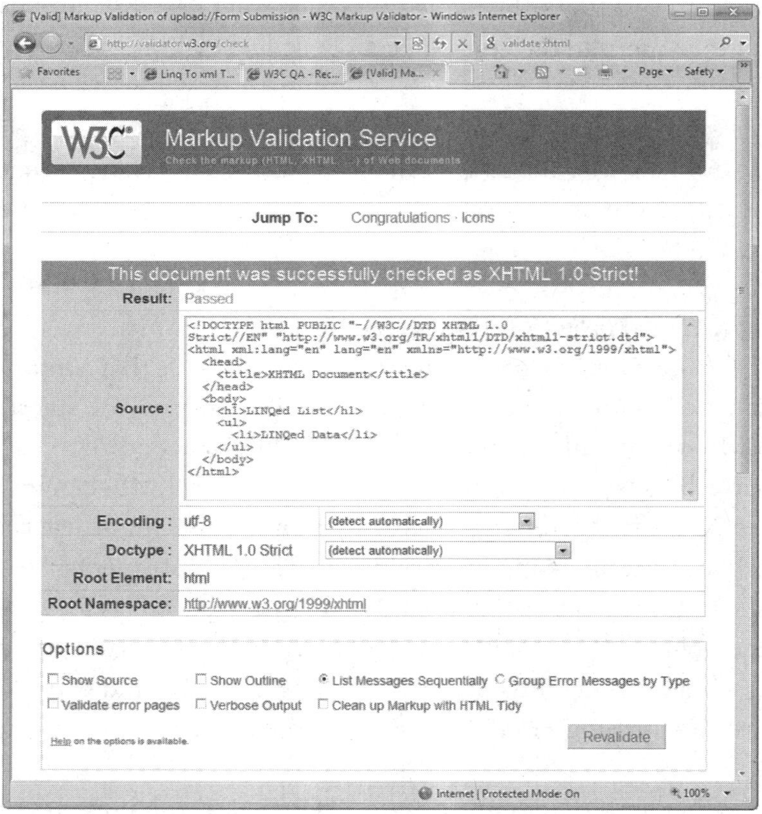

FIGURE 15.1 The w3.org Web site provides a validation service that can confirm that XHTML conforms to the official standards.

The code shown in Listing 15.1 illustrates how to create a simple XHTML document. It is an excerpt from the TransformPlanets sample project that accompanies this book. The output from the code shown in Listing 15.1 is displayed in Listing 15.2.

LISTING 15.1   The LINQ to XML Code for Creating a Simple XHTML Document

```
using System.Collections.Generic;
using System.Xml.Linq;

namespace TransformPlanets
{
    class TransformToXhtml: Utilities
    {
        string publicId = @"-//W3C//DTD XHTML 1.0 Strict//EN";
        string sysId =
        @"http://www.w3.org/TR/xhtml1/DTD/xhtml1-strict.dtd";
        XNamespace xhtml = @"http://www.w3.org/1999/xhtml";


        public XDocument ProcessList()
        {
            XDeclaration declaration =
                new XDeclaration("1.0", "utf-8", "no");
            XDocumentType docType =
                new XDocumentType("html", publicId, sysId, null);

            // Create main body of HTML
            XDocument doc = new XDocument(declaration, docType,
            new XElement(xhtml + "html",
                new XAttribute(XNamespace.Xml + "lang", "en"),
                new XAttribute("lang", "en"),
                new XElement(xhtml + "head",
                    new XElement(xhtml + "title", "XHTML Document")),
                new XElement(xhtml + "body",
                    new XElement(xhtml + "h1", "LINQed List"),
                    new XElement(xhtml + "ul",
                        new XElement(xhtml + "li", "LINQed Data")))));

            return doc;
        }
    }
}
```

Listing 15.2   The XHTML Produced by the Code Shown in Listing 15.1

```
<?xml version="1.0" encoding="utf-8" standalone="no"?>
<!DOCTYPE html PUBLIC "-//W3C//DTD XHTML 1.0 Strict//EN"
    "http://www.w3.org/TR/xhtml1/DTD/xhtml1-strict.dtd">
<html xml:lang="en" lang="en" xmlns="http://www.w3.org/1999/xhtml">
  <head>
    <title>XHTML Document</title>
  </head>
```

continues

Listing 15.2   Continued

```
  <body>
    <h1>LINQed List</h1>
    <ul>
      <li>LINQed Data</li>
    </ul>
  </body>
</html>
```

The code in the `ProcessList` method begins with a standard `XDeclaration` and includes an `XDocumentType`. This latter class creates the `DOCTYPE` declaration found in Listing 15.2.

A document type, or `DOCTYPE`, should be included in all XHTML documents. It appears after the XML declaration and before the root node. The `DOCTYPE` declaration can help ensure that a browser renders your document correctly.

Don't Focus on the Content of a DOCTYPE

If you search on the Web, you can easily find places that show you how to declare a valid `DOCTYPE`. You should simply duplicate these declarations verbatim without trying to parse or tweak their content. Most browsers simply check the `DOCTYPE` and render a document accordingly. Much of the syntax inside the `DOCTYPE` is ignored. For instance, near the end of the `DOCTYPE`, you can see the URL for a Document Type Definition (DTD) file called xhtml1-strict.dtd. This DTD contains rules that can, at least in theory, be used to confirm that this XML file conforms to the XHTML standard. In practice, however, a browser rarely uses this DTD to validate a document. You will read more about DTDs and schemas near the end of this chapter.

After creating the document type declaration, the code sets up the namespace for the `<html>` element at the root of the document. This default namespace is like the ones described earlier in this chapter, but it was created by a standards body.

The `<html>` element where this namespace is declared should look like this:

```
<html xml:lang="en" lang="en" xmlns="http://www.w3.org/1999/xhtml">
```

Here you see the official XHTML namespace, circa 1999, and attributes declaring that the document is written in English.

Here is how to create this <html> element:

```
XNamespace xhtml = @"http://www.w3.org/1999/xhtml";
new XElement(xhtml + "html",
        new XAttribute(XNamespace.Xml + "lang", "en"),
        new XAttribute("lang", "en"),
```

The first line declares the XHTML namespace. The second line includes the namespace in the root node of our document:

```
new XElement(xhtml + "html"
```

The next two lines of code add in the attributes that specify the natural language we are using.

```
new XAttribute(XNamespace.Xml + "lang", "en"),
  new XAttribute("lang", "en"),
```

Taken together, this is a valid way to introduce an XHTML 1.0 document, with all the proper headings, namespaces, and related information in place. You need only ensure that the rest of the XHTML you generate is valid. As explained earlier, it should contain the familiar set of HTML tags, such as <p>, <pre>, and <h1>.

You can see that most of the code for generating the beginnings of an XHTML document is just boilerplate. As a result, I have created a simple file that you can add into your program and use whenever you need to create an XHTML document. It is shown in the ProcessList method from Listing 15.3. The PlanetsXhtml method from the same listing shows how to use it.

LISTING 15.3   This Code from the TransformPlanets Sample Combines Code from the Planets XML File with Code from the Boilerplate for Opening an XHTML Document

```
using System.Linq;
using System.Xml.Linq;

namespace TransformPlanets
{
    class TransformToXhtml: Utilities
    {
        // Code omitted here for brevity. See Listing 15.2.
```

continues

LISTING 15.3   Continued

```
public XDocument PlanetsXhtml()
{
    XDocument doc = XDocument.Load("FirstFourPlanets.xml");

    XDocument xdoc = ProcessList();

    var xml = new XElement(xhtml + "ul",
        from x in doc.Root.Elements("Planet")
        select new XElement(xhtml + "li",
                            x.Element("Name").Value));


    xdoc.Descendants(xhtml + "body").Single().Add(xml);


    return xdoc;
}

}
}
```

The Price of Accidentally Omitting a Namespace

You can learn a lot about namespaces by failing to include some of the tags for this document. Suppose the xhtml namespace were not included in our ul element, as shown in the first line of this code:

```
var xml = new XElement("ul",
    from x in doc.Root.Elements("Planet")
    select new XElement(xhtml + "li",
    x.Element("Name").Value));
```

With this omission, the line items (<li>) will have huge namespace declarations in them:

```
<html xml:lang="en" lang="en"
    xmlns="http://www.w3.org/1999/xhtml">
  <head>
   <title>XHTML Document</title>
  </head>
  <body>
   <ul xmlns="">
     <li xmlns="http://www.w3.org/1999/xhtml">Mercury</li>
     <li xmlns="http://www.w3.org/1999/xhtml">Venus</li>
```

```
        <li xmlns="http://www.w3.org/1999/xhtml">Earth</li>
        <li xmlns="http://www.w3.org/1999/xhtml">Mars</li>
      </ul>
    </body>
  </html>
```

Clearly it is best to include the namespace in the nodes you declare.

Transforming Relational Data into XML

Converting the results of an SQL query into XML is another common task in the lives of many programmers. Code for performing this task can be seen in the sample program that accompanies this book called Transform-Customers.

To build the program from scratch, first create a console application, and then add an Object Relational designer to your project. (Choose Project, Add New Item from Visual Studio, and then select LINQ to SQL Classes.) Locate a copy of the Northwind database, as explained in Appendix A. Select the Northwind database and drag the `Customers`, `Orders`, `Order_ Details`, `Products`, and `Employees` tables from Server Explorer to the designer. Now open the program's main file, and add the code shown in Listing 15.4 into the `Main` method. Listings 15.5 and 15.6 show the output.

Server Explorer = Database Explorer

In the Express products, Server Explorer is called Database Explorer.

LISTING 15.4   Two Different Ways to Transform Relational Data into XML

```
DataClasses1DataContext db = new DataClasses1DataContext();

var xml = new XElement("Customers",
          from c in db.Customers
          where c.City == "Paris"
          select new XElement("Company",
            new XElement("Name", c.CompanyName),
            new XElement("Address", c.Address),
```

continues

LISTING 15.4   Continued

```csharp
                new XElement("City", c.City),
                new XElement("PostalCode", c.PostalCode),
                new XElement("County", c.Country),
                new XElement("Phone", c.Phone)));


    Console.WriteLine(xml);


    xml = new XElement("Customers",
            from c in db.Customers
            where c.City == "London"
            select new XElement("Company",
                new XElement("Name", c.CompanyName),
                new XElement("Orders",
                from o in c.Orders
                where o.ShipVia == 2
                select new XElement("Order",
                    new XElement("EmployeeName", o.Employee.LastName),
                    new XElement("Id", o.OrderID),
                    new XElement("Date", o.OrderDate)))));


    Console.WriteLine(xml);
```

LISTING 15.5   The Output from the First Query Shown in Listing 15.4

```xml
<><Customers>
  <Company>
    <Name>Paris specialites</Name>
    <Address>265, boulevard Charonne</Address>
    <City>Paris</City>
    <PostalCode>75012</PostalCode>
    <County>France</County>
    <Phone>(1) 42.34.22.66</Phone>
  </Company>
  <Company>
    <Name>Specialites du monde</Name>
    <Address>25, rue Lauriston</Address>
    <City>Paris</City>
    <PostalCode>75016</PostalCode>
    <County>France</County>
    <Phone>(1) 47.55.60.10</Phone>
  </Company>
</Customers>
```

LISTING 15.6   A Heavily Elided Version of the Output from the Second Query Shown
in Listing 15.4

```
<?xml version="1.0" encoding="utf-8" ?>
<Customers>
  <Company>
    <Name>Consolidated Holdings</Name>
    <Orders>
      <Order>
        <EmployeeName>Callahan</EmployeeName>
        <Id>10435</Id>
        <Date>1997-02-04T00:00:00</Date>
      </Order>
      <Order>
        <EmployeeName>King</EmployeeName>
        <Id>10848</Id>
        <Date>1998-01-23T00:00:00</Date>
      </Order>
    </Orders>
  </Company>
  <Company>
    <Name>Eastern Connection</Name>
    <Orders>
      <Order>
        <EmployeeName>Callahan</EmployeeName>
        <Id>11056</Id>
        <Date>1998-04-28T00:00:00</Date>
      </Order>
    </Orders>
  </Company>
  <Company>
    <Name>North/South</Name>
    <Orders />
  </Company>
</Customers>
```

Listing 15.4 shows two different queries. The first converts two company records from the Customers table into XML. The second joins data from three tables and converts it into XML.

Both queries begin by creating a root element:

```
var xml = new XElement("Customers",
```

The next step is to begin the query that retrieves the data from the database:

```
from c in db.Customers
where c.City == "Paris"
```

Nested XElements are used to put the company name into the XML file:

```
select new XElement("Company",
  new XElement("Name", c.CompanyName),
```

The XML written so far produces this output:

```
<Customers>
  <Company>
    <Name>Paris specialites</Name>
```

Up to this point, both queries follow almost exactly the same pattern. It is here, however, that their paths diverge. The first query simply adds XElements to fill out the remaining fields of the Customer table:

```
new XElement("Name", c.CompanyName),
new XElement("Address", c.Address),
new XElement("City", c.City),
new XElement("PostalCode", c.PostalCode),
new XElement("County", c.Country),
new XElement("Phone", c.Phone)));
```

The second query, however, follows a very different course. It begins a second query, diving into the Orders table, which is bound to the Customers table in a one-to-many relationship:

```
select new XElement("Company",
  new XElement("Name", c.CompanyName),
  new XElement("Orders",
    from o in c.Orders
    where o.ShipVia == 2
    select new XElement("Order",
      new XElement("EmployeeName", o.Employee.LastName),
    // Code omitted here for brevity
```

You have seen this kind of code before in this book, so I won't explain it again. In this case, however, it is being used to transform relational data into XML elements and not just into text.

Digging Deeper

The code you see in the second example from Listing 15.4 typifies the virtues and complexities of the declarative style of programming. The whole operation is a bit like a set of Russian nesting dolls, with one pattern nested inside another of the same type. As soon as you get the rhythm, it is a relatively simple matter to extend the whole process one layer deeper, thereby retrieving information from the `Products` table:

```
xml = new XElement("Customers",
      from c in db.Customers
      where c.City == "London"
      select new XElement("Company",
          new XElement("Name", c.CompanyName),
          new XElement("Orders",
          from o in c.Orders
          where o.ShipVia == 2
              select new XElement("Order",
              new XElement("Id", o.OrderID),
              new XElement("EmployeeName", o.Employee.LastName),
              new XElement("Date", o.OrderDate),
              from d in o.Order_Details
              select new XElement("Product",
                  new XElement("Name", d.Product.ProductName),
                  new XElement("Quantity",
                              d.Product.QuantityPerUnit))))));
```

Here you see yet another `from` clause, thereby nesting our Russian nesting dolls one layer deeper. Here is an excerpt from the XML produced by this query, complete with new information about the products associated with each order:

```
<Customers>
  <Company>
    <Name>Eastern Connection</Name>
    <Orders>
      <Order>
        <Id>11056</Id>
        <EmployeeName>Callahan</EmployeeName>
        <Date>1998-04-28T00:00:00</Date>
        <Product>
          <Name>Uncle Bob's Organic Dried Pears</Name>
          <Quantity>12 - 1 lb pkgs.</Quantity>
        </Product>
```

```
        <Product>
          <Name>Pate chinois</Name>
          <Quantity>24 boxes x 2 pies</Quantity>
        </Product>
        <Product>
          <Name>Camembert Pierrot</Name>
          <Quantity>15 - 300 g rounds</Quantity>
        </Product>
      </Order>
    </Orders>
  </Company>
  <Company>
    <Name>North/South</Name>
    <Orders />
  </Company>
</Customers>
```

In this section you have moved from a relatively simple example, to a moderately complex example, to a final example that is more heavily nested than the first two. This gives you a chance to assess the virtues of the declarative style of programming. With imperative code, it is relatively easy for experienced programmers to break each problem into discrete sections. In the imperative mode, bugs come singly, with large sections of the program running correctly, and isolated problem areas. With declarative programming, you often wrestle with a nested statement that will be completely out of whack one second and then quite suddenly snap into place after you make that last tweak.

With imperative code I often use logic to solve problems; with declarative code, I simply apply rules. In this last example, for instance, there are three occasions when I apply a single rule for creating joins with from statements. The result is nested code, like three Russian dolls nested one within the other.

Programmatically Creating the Database

In this section, the direction of flow is the opposite of what you encountered in the previous section. In the previous section, you moved data from a database into an XML file. Now the process is reversed, and data flows from an XML file into a database.

When using LINQ to XML, moving data from an XML file to a database is a three-step process:

1. Find the data in your XML file.
2. Create objects shaped like the data you found in the XML file.
3. Write LINQ to SQL code that automatically creates tables based on the objects in your program.

Chapter 9, "Modifying Objects with LINQ to SQL," introduced the techniques for creating a database with LINQ to SQL. In this chapter you will dig a bit more deeply into that same technology.

Database Generation

To create a database and its tables with LINQ to SQL, first you need to manually create a set of classes that define the structure of your data. You can then give a simple command to create tables based on those classes. In effect, this reverses the task performed by the Object Relational Mapper. That tool creates classes based on the tables in a database. The part of LINQ I'm about to show you creates tables based on the classes in your program. In either case, the same syntax is used to define the classes that mirror the objects in a database.

Before creating a class, you need to study the data in your XML file to discern its shape. Take a moment to study this excerpt from our FirstFour-Planets XML file:

```
<Planets>
  <Planet>
    <Name>Mars</Name>
    <Moons>
      <Moon>
        <Name>Phobos</Name>
        <OrbitalPeriod uom="days">0.318</OrbitalPeriod>
      </Moon>
      <Moon>
        <Name>Deimos</Name>
        <OrbitalPeriod uom="days">1.26244</OrbitalPeriod>
      </Moon>
    </Moons>
  </Planet>
</Planets>
```

You can see that this XML can be encapsulated in two classes called Planet and Moon:

```
public class Planet
{
    public int Id { get; set; }
    public string PlanetName { get; set; }
    public string OrbitalPeriod { get; set; }
    public List<Moon> Moons;
}

public class Moon
{
    public int Id { get; set; }
    public int PlanetId { get; set; }
    public string MoonName { get; set; }
    public string OrbitalPeriod { get; set; }
}
```

Each class has an Id field, a Name field, and an OrbitalPeriod. The Name and OrbitalPeriod are taken directly from the XML file. The Id field is added to form the basis of a primary key in the database. Also included is a list of Moons associated with a particular Planet, as well as a PlanetId. This latter field forms the basis of a one-to-many relationship between a Planet and a Moon.

Listing 15.7 shows the simplest possible take on how to decorate these classes with the mapping attributes needed to create tables in a database. As explained in Chapters 7 through 10, the two key pieces of syntax here are the Table attribute, used to map the class to a table in the database, and the Column attribute, used to map a field in a class to a column in a database.

LISTING 15.7   Classes That Can Be Used to Create the Tables in a Database

```
[Table(Name = "dbo.Planet")]
public class Planet
{
    [Column(IsPrimaryKey = true)]
    public int PlanetId { get; set; }
    [Column]
    public string PlanetName { get; set; }
    [Column]
    public string OrbitalPeriod { get; set; }
    [Association(Name = "Planet_Moon", OtherKey = "PlanetId")]
    public List<Moon> Moons;

    public override string ToString()
```

```
    {
        return string.Format("{0} {1} {2}",
            PlanetId, PlanetName, OrbitalPeriod);
    }
}

[Table(Name = "dbo.Moon")]
public class Moon
{
    public Moon()
    {
        planet = null;
    }

    [Column(IsPrimaryKey = true)]
    public int MoonId { get; set; }
    [Column(CanBeNull = true)]
    public int PlanetId { get; set; }
    [Column]
    public string MoonName { get; set; }
    [Column]
    public string OrbitalPeriod { get; set; }
    [Association(Name = "Planet_Moon", ThisKey = "PlanetId",
        IsForeignKey = true)]
    Planet planet;
}

public class PlanetsDataContext : DataContext
{
    public Table<Planet> planets;
    public Table<Moon> moons;

    public Planets(string connection)
        : base(connection)
    {
    }
}
```

When looking at this code, you might be particularly interested in the `Association` attribute. It is used to create a foreign key linking the `Planet` and `Moon` tables on the `PlanetId` field.

The third class in this series is perhaps the most important. Derived from the `DataContext` class, it contains two collections called `planets` and `moons`. The `Table` class, you may recall, is part of LINQ to SQL, and it is designed to hold a collection of classes mapped to tables in a database.

The next step is to actually create the database and insert some data into it. You can do that with this code:

```
public const string connectionString = @"c:\data\planets.mdf";

public void CreateDatabase()
{
    using (Planets db = new PlanetsDataContext(connectionString))
    {
        db.CreateDatabase();

        Planet p = new Planet { PlanetName = "Alpha", OrbitalPeriod =
                                    "1" };

        db.planets.InsertOnSubmit(p);
        db.SubmitChanges();
        db.Connection.Close();
    }
}
```

After declaring the connection string, the next step is to initialize an instance of the DataContext. After instantiating the class, you can use it to create the database:

```
db.CreateDatabase();
```

This simple call

- Creates the database in the C:\Data directory.
- Creates the Moon and Planet tables.
- Adds the columns with the names and types we specified in our class declaration.
- Sets up our primary and foreign keys.

In short, our Moon and Planet classes are converted into tables. The attributes and types we use in our classes are the basis of the types and relationships created in the database.

The next step is to initialize a row of data and insert it into the database. You can do that with this code:

```
Planet p = new Planet { PlanetName = "Alpha", Rating = "Beta" };
```

After an instance of our `Planet` class is instantiated, an object initializer assigns data to its two properties. Now we have a fully initialized object with data we would like to insert into the database. To actually insert the data, call `InsertOnSubmit` and `SubmitChanges`:

```
db.planets.InsertOnSubmit(p);
db.SubmitChanges();
```

While still focused on the basics, take a moment to consider this code, which demonstrates how to delete a database:

```
public void DeleteDatabase()
{
    using (Planets db = new Planets(connectionString))
    {
        if (db.DatabaseExists())
        {
            Console.WriteLine("Deleting old database...");
            db.DeleteDatabase();
        }
    }
}
```

This method first creates an instance of the `DataContext` and then uses it to test if the database exists. If it does, the method deletes it.

There is no built-in command for dropping a table, but you can use the `DataContext`'s `ExecuteCommand` method to construct one. This command allows us to execute a T-SQL query directly. In this case, we pass in the simple T-SQL command "drop table `Planet`." The result is that the table `Planet` is deleted from the database:

```
public void DeleteTable()
{
    using (Planets db = new Planets(connectionString))
    {
        db.ExecuteCommand("drop table Planet");
    }
}
```

Transferring Data from an XML File to a Database

Now you know how to create a simple database using LINQ to SQL. The final step is to transfer all the data in the planet's XML file into the C#

classes called `Planet` and `Moon`, and then insert the data stored in those classes into the database. Here is code that performs that very task:

```
var query =
    from a in doc.Elements("Planets").Elements("Planet")
    select new Planet
    {
        PlanetName = (string)a.Element("Name"),
        OrbitalPeriod = (string)a.Element("OrbitalPeriod"),
        Moons =
            (from b in a.Elements("Moons").Elements("Moon")
             select new Moon
             {
                 MoonName = (string)b.Element("Name"),
                 OrbitalPeriod = (string)b.Element("OrbitalPeriod")
             }).ToList()
    };
```

This query iterates over the planets in the XML file and returns the data it finds in them. The first `select` clause initializes the fields of the `Planet` class with the data retrieved from the XML file:

```
PlanetName = (string)a.Element("Name"),
OrbitalPeriod = (string)a.Element("OrbitalPeriod"),
```

The code then instantiates instances of the `Moon` class and uses the second `select` statement and explicit conversion operators to initialize its fields:

```
MoonName = (string)b.Element("Name"),
OrbitalPeriod = (string)b.Element("OrbitalPeriod")
```

The final step is to use the LINQ operator called `ToList()` to insert each newly created `Moon` object into the `Moons` collection of the `Planet` class. The effect of the entire query is to query the data from the XML file and insert it into instances of the `Planet` and `Moon` classes.

We can now take the computation returned from this query and use it to insert our data into the database:

```
int planetCount = 0;
int moonCount = 0;
foreach (var item in query)
{
    item.PlanetId = planetCount++;
    db.planets.InsertOnSubmit(item);
    foreach (var moon in item.Moons)
```

```
    {
        moon.PlanetId = moonCount++;
        moon.PlanetId = planetCount - 1;
        db.moons.InsertOnSubmit(moon);
    }
}

db.SubmitChanges();
```

This code is complicated slightly by the fact that a list of moons is associated with each planet. In other words, we have a list of lists. By this point in the book, however, that arrangement should be as comfortable as a warm bath in the evening. Hopefully you will have little trouble following how the nested `foreach` loops use calls to `InsertOnSubmit` to move our data into the database.

■ Learning How to Create Database Entities

It should be clear that you can learn the details of how to create a particular kind of table, or other database entity, by first creating one in your database and then using the Object Relational Designer to create a class based on it. You can then study the class you created and mimic its syntax in your own classes. Alternatively, you can use code like what I've shown here to create an approximation of the data structure you want in your tables. Then use the SQL tools to refine your data model, and use the Object Relational Designer to convert your tables back into C# classes. These may not be the most elegant of solutions, but they have a certain practical efficacy.

Viewing the Data Schemas

When creating a database programmatically, it is sometimes convenient to find a way to check if the tables conform to our plans. SQL server provides the information we need in the form of the INFORMATION_SCHEMA tables. We need only find an easy way to access this information.

One simple approach would be to create a view in the database. As shown in Figure 15.2, you can do this by opening Database (or Server) Explorer, expanding the nodes for your database, right-clicking the Views nodes, and selecting Add New View.

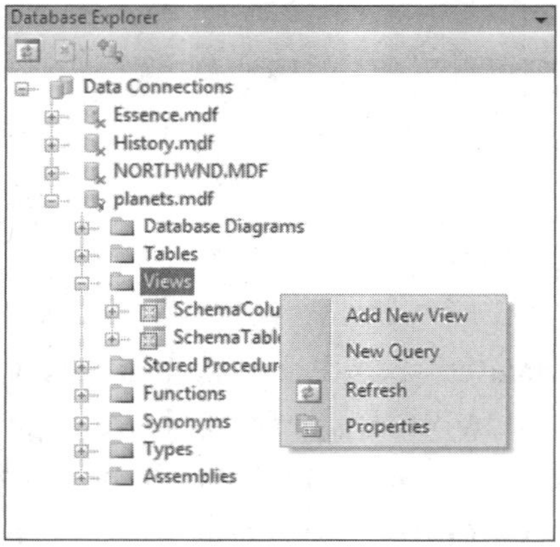

FIGURE 15.2   Creating a new view in Database Explorer.

Dismiss the Add Table dialog that pops up, and insert an SQL statement like this in the query designer:

```
select * from information_schema.tables;
```

Click the red Execute Query button, or press Ctrl-R to confirm that you have written the correct SQL. If you are satisfied, save the view by choosing File, Save All. Drag the newly created view from the Explorer onto the Object Relational Designer. Now you can access these classes using LINQ to SQL just as you would any other database entity.

Alternatively, you can simply create your own declarations for these classes and place them in a file or assembly that you can include in any project you create. Because the tables have the same definition in all databases, you need to declare them only once and then reuse them as often as you want. Declarations for these tables are shown in Listing 15.8, and examples of how to use them are provided in the CreateDatabase sample program that accompanies this book.

Listing 15.8   A Complete Declaration for information_schema.tables and a Partial Declaration for information_schema.columns

```
[Table(Name = "INFORMATION_SCHEMA.tables")]
public class TableSchema1
{
    [Column(Name = "TABLE_CATALOG", DbType = "NVarChar(128)")]
    public string TableCatalog { get; set; }
```

```
    [Column(Name = "TABLE_SCHEMA", DbType = "NVarChar(128)")]
    public string TableSchema { get; set; }
    [Column(Name = "TABLE_NAME", DbType =
        "NVarChar(128) NOT NULL", CanBeNull = false)]
    public string TableName { get; set; }
    [Column(Name = "TABLE_TYPE", DbType = "VarChar(10)")]
    public string TableType { get; set; }
}

[Table(Name = "INFORMATION_SCHEMA.columns")]
public class ColumnSchema
{
    [Column(Name = "TABLE_CATALOG", DbType = "NVarChar(128)")]
    public string TableCatalog { get; set; }
    [Column(Name = "TABLE_SCHEMA", DbType = "NVarChar(128)")]
    public string TableSchema { get; set; }
    [Column(Name = "TABLE_NAME", DbType =
        "NVarChar(128) NOT NULL", CanBeNull = false)]
    public string TableName { get; set; }
    [Column(Name = "COLUMN_NAME", DbType = "NVarChar(128)")]
    public string ColumnName { get; set; }
}
```

XML Schema Validation

LINQ to XML makes it easy for you to validate an XML document by test-ing it against a schema. I'll walk you through the process, taking a few moments to explain the basics of XSD and schema validation.

When used properly, XML can be easy to read and easy to understand. This clarity derives in part from the sparseness of the XML specification. Although people manage to create hard-to-read XML documents, the syn-tax nevertheless can be simple if developers want it to be.

The sparseness of XML comes at a price. Unlike C#, XML has no built-in type checking. The absence of this feature helps keep XML simple and easy to understand but leaves it exposed to misinterpretation.

You can have two different problems with an XML document:

- It might have a syntactic flaw, in which case we say that it is not well formed.

- It might have a semantic problem, in which case we might consider it invalid.

To help illustrate this point, I'll show you two examples. The first is of an XML document that is not well formed, and the second is a document that is invalid. Consider this simple XML document:

```
<Planets>
    <PlaXnet>
      <Name>Mercury</Name>
      <OrbitalPeriod>Unknown</OrbitalPeriod>
      <Moons />
    </Planet>
</Planets>
```

This code is not well formed because the tag `<PlaXnet>` does not match the closing tag `</Planet>`.

The following document is well formed, but we might not consider it valid, because it does not conform to our idea of how the document should look:

```
<Planets>
    <OrbitalBody>
      <Name>Mercury</Name>
      <OrbitalPeriod>Unknown</OrbitalPeriod>
      <Moons />
    </OrbitalBody>
    <Planet>
      <Name>Venus</Name>
      <OrbitalPeriod>Unknown</OrbitalPeriod>
      <Moons />
    </Planet>
</Planets>
```

Syntactically nothing is wrong with this document, but we still might find it dissatisfactory because it refers to Venus as a `Planet` and Mercury as an `OrbitalBody`. This offends our sense of symmetry. Furthermore, it might cause serious problems in a program that expects both Venus and Mercury to be called `Planets`.

We do not need to add anything to an XML document to determine if it is well formed. A good parser can detect with relative ease syntactic errors such as the `PlaXnet` node shown previously. LINQ exposes such a parser. If you called `XDocument.Load` on the `PlaXnet` file, LINQ would throw an exception and complain that the document is not well formed. Visual Studio is also quite helpful when we are working with a document that is not well formed. If we open such a document in the Visual Studio editor, the offending syntax is highlighted in red, and an error message is displayed if you hover the mouse over it, as shown in Figure 15.3.

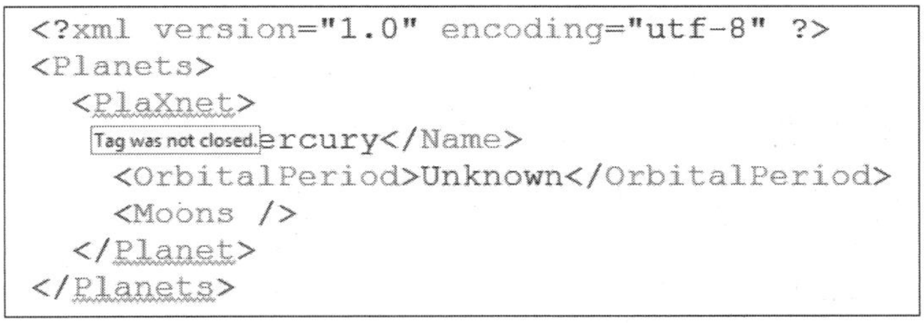

```
<?xml version="1.0" encoding="utf-8" ?>
<Planets>
  <PlaXnet>
    Tag was not closed. ercury</Name>
      <OrbitalPeriod>Unknown</OrbitalPeriod>
      <Moons />
    </Planet>
</Planets>
```

FIGURE 15.3   Problems with documents that are not well formed are clearly visible in Visual Studio.

▪ Visual Studio Has a Built-in XML Editor

To invoke the Visual Studio XML editor, you need do nothing more than open a file that has an XML extension or a proper XML declaration. If you want to start a document from scratch and then open or create a project, choose Project, Add New Item from Visual Studio, and select the XML File template.

As you can see, it is not difficult to find out if a document is well formed. Assuring that it is semantically valid, on the other hand, is more complex.

Unfortunately, there have been a number of different attempts to create a way to validate XML documents. The first attempt was to associate a Document Type Definition (DTD) with an XML file. The DTD could be inserted directly in an XML document, or saved to a file with a DTD extension. Tools were written that made it possible to use the contents of this file to determine whether a document contained the right XML tags in the right places.

The DTD specification, however, was not particularly rigorous. As a result, documents could be validated successfully against a DTD and still be incorrect. In particular, DTDs were not at all rigorous about type checking. The situation was perhaps a bit analogous to what might happen if a

C# developer had to work with a compiler that did not understand the difference between a string and an integer. DTD also knew nothing about namespaces and had other, more esoteric shortcomings. It is true that DTDs are relatively easy to use and have a few other important virtues, but their lack of rigor made them less than appealing in some situations.

To resolve this problem, several new standards were developed. The one most generally accepted as the best solution for schema validation is called XSD. An XSD file is written in XML format. It contains syntax rich enough to define the types of data in an XML file and to define the structure of data in a particular namespace. In short, it can be used to confirm the validity of an XML file.

This is not the place to discuss the details of the XSD standard. Fully understanding it is a chore, but most developers can find their way around such a document with relative ease. Here, for instance, is the syntax for defining the Name node in our FirstFourPlanets.xml file:

```
<xs:element name="Name" type="xs:string" />
```

This code says that a Name node is an element and that its content is of type string. Here is code that states that the Moon element can appear from 0 to *n* times in a document:

```
<xs:sequence minOccurs="0">
  <xs:element maxOccurs="unbounded" name="Moon">
```

Visual Studio can automatically generate an XSD file based on an existing XML file. Suppose you have an XML file that looks like this:

```
<?xml version="1.0" encoding="utf-8" ?>
<Planets>
  <Planet></Planet>
</Planets>
```

Add this document to your project and open it in the Visual Studio editor. Choose Xml, Create Schema from Visual Studio. The following XSD schema is automatically generated:

```
<?xml version="1.0" encoding="utf-8"?>
<xs:schema attributeFormDefault="unqualified" elementFormDefault=
"qualified" xmlns:xs="http://www.w3.org/2001/XMLSchema">
  <xs:element name="Planets">
```

```
    <xs:complexType>
      <xs:sequence>
        <xs:element name="Planet" />
      </xs:sequence>
    </xs:complexType>
  </xs:element>
</xs:schema>
```

In general, if you have a valid XML document, you can create an XSD schema using the technique I describe here. This schema file can be used to validate the structure of your XML files.

Validation

LINQ to XML makes it fairly simple to validate a document. The code shown in Listing 15.9 illustrates how to proceed. These simple lines of code from the ValidateXmlWithSchema program that accompanies this book demonstrate how to validate an XML document against an XML schema.

LISTING 15.9   Validating an XML Document Against an XML Schema

```
bool documentIsValid = true;
System.Collections.IList<string> list = null;

public void ValidationEventHandler(object sender, ValidationEventArgs e)
{
    list.Add(string.Format("Error: {0}", e.Message));
    documentIsValid = false;
}

public bool TestXmlValidation(System.Collections.IList list)
{
    this.list = list;

    XDocument planetXmlDocument = XDocument.Load("NewPlanets.xml");
    XmlSchemaSet schemas = new XmlSchemaSet();
    schemas.Add("", "NewPlanets.xsd");

    // Test 1
    list.Add("Start Test 1");
    planetXmlDocument.Validate(schemas, ValidationEventHandler);
    list.Add(string.Format("Document {0} valid",
      documentIsValid ? "is" : "is not"));

    // Test 2
    list.Add("Start Test 2");
```

continues

LISTING 15.9   Continued

```
        documentIsValid = true;
        ForceDocToFailValidation(planetXmlDocument);
        planetXmlDocument.Validate(schemas, ValidationEventHandler);
        list.Add(string.Format("The document {0} valid",
            documentIsValid ? "is" : "is not"));

        return documentIsValid;
    }

    private static void ForceDocToFailValidation(XDocument planetXmlDocument)
    {
        var planet = new XElement("Planeted",
                        new XElement("Name", "Mercury"));
        planetXmlDocument.Root.Add(planet);
    }
```

The first step is to load your XML document, and then you instantiate an instance of the XmlSchemaSet class. You can then load a schema into the XmlSchemaSet class. For now, you can leave the namespace name as an empty string:

```
XmlSchemaSet schemas = new XmlSchemaSet();
schemas.Add("", "NewPlanets.xsd");
```

Near the end of this section, I will show you how to use the first parameter of the Add method to pass in a namespace.

To validate the document, call the Validate method of your XDocument object. Pass in the XmlSchemaSet class and a callback method designed to handle the results of the validation process:

```
public void ValidationEventHandler(object sender, ValidationEventArgs e)
{
    list.Add(string.Format("Error: {0}", e.Message));
    documentIsValid = false;
}

public bool TestXmlValidation(System.Collections.IList list)
{
    // ... Code omitted here

    planetXmlDocument.Validate(schemas, ValidationEventHandler);

    // ... Code omitted here
}
```

The `ValidationEventHandler` callback is a fairly simple method that takes two parameters. The first is of type `object`, and the second is a simple class called `ValidationEventArgs`. This class contains three properties, the most important of which is a message describing the results of events that occur during validation:

```
public class ValidationEventArgs : EventArgs
{
    public XmlSchemaException Exception { get; }
    public string Message { get; }
    public XmlSeverityType Severity { get; }
}
```

If you look carefully at the code in Listing 15.9, you will see that it calls the `Validate` method twice. The first time it validates a syntactically and semantically correct version of our Planets XML file. The program then inserts an invalid node into the document and attempts to revalidate it. The invalid node looks like this:

```
<Planeted>
    <Name>Mercury</Name>
</Planeted>
```

Note that this is valid XML, but an element called `Planeted` was not expected in this document. As you have seen, the documents in this chapter have elements called `Planets` and elements called `Planet`, but not elements called `Planeted`. As a result, this second attempt to validate the document fails, because it violates the rules defined in our XSD schema. The schema looks for `Planets` elements and `Planet` elements, but it objects if we try to use a `Planeted` element and passes the following error strings to the callback:

```
Error: The element 'Planets' has invalid child element 'Planeted.'
       List of possible elements expected: 'Planet.'
The document is not valid.
```

This error signifies that an element called `Planet` was expected, but instead an element called `Planeted` was found. The code in the document was well formed, but it was semantically incorrect, so the error occurred. Note also that the schema understands that at this location in the document elements of type `Planet` are valid, but elements of type `Planeted` are invalid. It knows what nodes can be used at any particular level in the document.

Namespaces and Validation

You saw a moment ago that the `XmlSchemaSet` class supports namespaces. Consider the following simple XML document:

```
<?xml version="1.0" encoding="utf-8" ?>
<Planets xmlns="http://www.charliecalvert.com/planets">
  <Planet>
    <Name>Mercury</Name>
    <OrbitalPeriod>Unknown</OrbitalPeriod>
    <Moons />
  </Planet>
</Planets>
```

This document contains a namespace called `Planets`. If you create an XSD file based on this document, it will have a header that explicitly mentions this namespace:

```
<?xml version="1.0" encoding="utf-8"?>
<xs:schema attributeFormDefault="unqualified" elementFormDefault=
                                              "qualified"
   targetNamespace="http://www.charliecalvert.com/planets"
xmlns:xs="http://www.w3.org/2001/XMLSchema">
  <xs:element name="Planets">
    <xs:complexType>
      <xs:sequence>
        <xs:element name="Planet">
          <xs:complexType>
            <xs:sequence>
              <xs:element name="Name" type="xs:string" />
              <xs:element name="OrbitalPeriod" type="xs:string" />
              <xs:element name="Moons" />
            </xs:sequence>
          </xs:complexType>
        </xs:element>
      </xs:sequence>
    </xs:complexType>
  </xs:element>
</xs:schema>
```

This call to the schema `Add` method uses the first parameter, called `target-Namespace`. This field was not used in the schema code shown in the previous section. You can use the contents of this field to initialize the XmlSchemaSet class:

```
XmlSchemaSet schemas = new XmlSchemaSet();
schemas.Add("http://www.charliecalvert.com/planets", "PlanetNs.xsd");
```

In this call to the Add method, I use the first parameter to pass in namespace. Otherwise, the code you write is identical to the code in the previous example.

Annotations

Annotations are one of the minor features of LINQ to SQL. They let you add an object to a particular node by decorating it with the class of your choice. This class is usually a custom class that lets you associate data or actions with the node. Listing 15.10 is an example of how to use annotations.

LISTING 15.10   A Simple Example of How to Annotate the Nodes of an XML File

```
public class Details
{
    public int Position { get; set; }

    public Details(int fact)
    {
        this.Position = fact;
    }

    public string GetFirstLetter(XElement element)
    {
        return "First letter is: " + element.Value[0];
    }
}

class Program
{
    static void Main(string[] args)
    {
        XElement planets = new XElement("Planets",
            new XElement("Planet", "Mercury"),
            new XElement("Planet", "Venus"),
            new XElement("Planet", "Earth"),
            new XElement("Planet", "Mars"));
```

continues

LISTING 15.10   Continued

```
        int count = 1;
        foreach (var item in planets.Descendants("Planet"))
        {
            item.AddAnnotation(new Details(count++));
        }


        foreach (var item in planets.Descendants("Planet"))
        {
            Details detail = item.Annotation<Details>();
            Console.WriteLine(detail.Position);
            Console.WriteLine(detail.GetFirstLetter(item));
        }
    }
}
```

The code shown in Listing 15.10 begins by creating a simple XML file that looks like this:

```
<Planets>
  <Planet>Mercury</Planet>
  <Planet>Venus</Planet>
  <Planet>Earth</Planet>
  <Planet>Mars</Planet>
</Planets>
```

It then annotates each `Planet` element in the file:

```
int count = 0;
foreach (var item in planets.Descendants("Planet"))
{
    item.AddAnnotation(new Details(count++));
}
```

The `Details` class is used to track the position of the planet relative to the sun and to associate a simple action with each `Planet` node. This data is not stored in the XML file and is accessible only at runtime. For instance, here is a simple way to access the annotations created by this code:

```
foreach (var item in planets.Descendants("Planet"))
{
    Details detail = item.Annotation<Details>();
    Console.WriteLine(detail.Position);
    Console.WriteLine(detail.GetFirstLetter(item));
}
```

The code uses the `Annotation` method to retrieve the annotation associated with a particular `XElement`. Because the method is generic, you don't need to cast the value it returns.

You probably will have your own reasons to use this feature, or to ignore it if that is your want. It is the kind of feature that suits itself to solving custom problems that none of the developers at Microsoft anticipated.

Should You Use C# or VB?

Before closing this chapter, I should take a moment to discuss a technology you may have heard about called *XML literals*. This technology ships with Visual Basic, but it is not part of the C# language.

The developers of VB decided that LINQ to XML would be simpler if the XML syntax were adopted as part of the Visual Basic language. As a result, VB developers can insert an XML document directly into their code.

Consider this short, but complete, VB console application:

```
Module Module1
    Sub Main()
        Dim xml = <Planet>
                      <Name>Mars</Name>
                      <Moons>
                          <Moon>Phobos</Moon>
                          <Moon>Deimos</Moon>
                      </Moons>
                  </Planet>
        Console.WriteLine(xml)
    End Sub
End Module
```

Here you can see a fragment of valid XML embedded directly in a program. This code compiles and runs smoothly, and you can see that it is even properly syntax-highlighted.

The equivalent C# code would look like this:

```
class Program
{
    static void Main(string[] args)
    {
        var xml = new XElement("Planet",
```

```
            new XElement("Name", "Mars"),
            new XElement("Moons",
                new XElement("Moon", "Phobos"),
                new XElement("Moon", "Deimos")));
    }
}
```

Although the C# code is shorter and more descriptive, there is no question that VB makes working with XML inside your program remarkably intuitive. The Visual Basic team went on to define XML literal syntax for querying XML, for writing transforms, and for all the features you've read about in the last three chapters.

The VB technology is built on top of LINQ to XML. All the VB XML code that you write as XML literals is eventually translated into LINQ to XML code that is essentially indistinguishable from the code you've seen in this chapter. All the same classes and types are used. For instance, the VB code shown in this section is translated at compile time into code similar to the C# code shown in this section. As a result, there is little you can do with LINQ to XML in VB that you can't do in C#, and vice versa.

The future is always open, and it is always possible that the C# team will reverse course and add XML literals into their language. So far, however, that has not been done. Here are some unofficial reasons why the C# team is hesitant to include XML literals in the C# language:

- The C# team feels that mixing C# and XML would be both confusing and risky. In recent years, for instance, a faction has preferred JSON to XML. If XML were to be replaced by JSON, or by some other technology, an XML syntax that was part of C# would become an anomaly, an odd vestigial appendage to the language that no longer served a purpose.

- It is always possible that a standards body will either add new features to XML or make changes to the existing language. If these changes are adopted, should the C# language adopt those changes as well? What if it breaks old code? What if one of the changes is in some way incompatible with C# and cannot easily be adopted into the language?

- Or consider the opposite scenario. What if C# wanted to add an exciting new feature whose syntax conflicted with XML syntax? If XML were part of C#, that feature could not be added, because it might cause an irreconcilable conflict.

The issues involved in incorporating XML into C# are not insignificant. For now, it seems unlikely that the team will change their position, but nothing is written in stone, and change is always possible.

Few people would argue that the C# syntax for LINQ to XML is simpler than the XML literals syntax found in VB. However, the C# syntax is both elegant and powerful. Many consider it a significant improvement over other tools that perform similar tasks. If you find XML literals appealing, remember that you can always add your own custom VB assemblies that contain XML literals into your C# projects.

Summary

In this chapter, you have seen that LINQ to XML provides the tools you need to

- Transform XML documents.
- Move XML data into databases.
- Move relational data into XML documents.
- Work with XML namespaces.
- Work with XML schemas.
- Annotate the nodes of your documents.

LINQ to XML is a very powerful tool that is remarkably easy to use. It is based on modern programming techniques, and it makes quick work of jobs that have traditionally challenged XML developers. By tapping into the elegance of LINQ query expressions and the power of the LINQ query operators, LINQ to XML has quickly established itself as a significant tool in the marketplace.

That's all I'll say about LINQ to XML. It is a big subject, but the fundamentals are not hard to understand. If you use this technology in your own programs, you should find it both easy and enjoyable to work with XML files and to transform them into data that your program can easily consume.

■ 16 ■

Introduction to LINQ Patterns and Practices

W E HAVE COVERED using components of LINQ to access data from databases, XML sources, and collections of objects. These components are great tools to use while building applications. This chapter considers some common usage patterns and effective practices for making the best use of these tools. The patterns provide a blueprint for key parts of applications, and the practices describe how to best address certain scenarios and ensure specific capabilities such as productivity, performance, and security. Not surprisingly, relational data is often a key source or even *the* key source of data in applications. Hence, the discussion in this chapter focuses heavily on LINQ to relational databases.

Before we discuss patterns and practices, it is important to remember this adage (or perhaps cliché): The answer to every question about whether a particular pattern is appropriate is "It depends." Perhaps more important than a pattern is the context in which it is applicable and the trade-offs it entails. In that spirit, this chapter gives you a general framework to start thinking about the key issues with and reasons for the patterns rather than cataloging a large set of patterns. The cataloging is being done more efficiently and comprehensively by the LINQ community on blogs, forums, and web sites. The testing of patterns is best done with real analysis and measurements with your own applications and use cases.

The recommendations in this chapter are to some degree a matter of design philosophy and taste, which can be subjective and personal. Hence, the reasoning behind a recommendation should be more interesting than the recommendation itself.

Using Language Features Judiciously

C# 3.0 (and VB.NET 9.0 as well) provides a set of LINQ-related features to improve programmer productivity. This can be viewed in two ways: the time to get the application built correctly the first time and, more importantly, expressing the intent clearly to reduce maintenance costs over time. The former is often a dominant factor in adoption, and the latter is the real source of productivity. Let's look at the productivity implications of the key language features first.

Declarative queries and query syntax provide a clear and concise way to express your intent. They do not provide anything that you couldn't do yourself with foreach loops and other imperative constructs. But they can make your program more readable during development and much easier for others to understand and maintain. You do cede some control and the ability to tweak the exact implementation, but in most cases, the long-term benefits of readable and maintainable code are well worth it. For example, the following query is certainly very doable with pre-LINQ C# code, but the intent is much more concise and clear in the new form. The query uses `Type.GetMethods()` and organizes the methods alphabetically with overload counts:

```
// Choose your favorite type here
Type type = typeof(string);

var overloadQuery = from m in type.GetMethods()
                    group m by m.Name into g
                    orderby g.Key
                    select new {
                        MethodName=g.Key,
                        Overloads=g.Count()};
```

Extension methods add almost another dimension beyond inheritance and virtual methods. They allow you to create the appearance of having additional methods on classes that you cannot change. You cannot change them either because you do not control the source code, or because the extension is not appropriate in every situation and should be explicitly selected by including the extension namespace with a `using` statement. However, you should use this feature with extreme care. It is very easy to abuse it by extending classes that cannot accommodate the extension method's contract. In particular, resist the temptation to extend .NET framework types such as `Object` and `String`. Liberal use of extension methods can also make your code quite difficult to understand.

The introduction of `var` has been a source of significant controversy—mostly unwarranted. First, it is wrongly thought of as a nonstatic typing feature. It is not. As explained in Chapter 4, "C# 3.0 Technical Overview," it does not compromise static typing. It merely provides the convenience of inferred type based on the initializer. Second, it is considered a sign of laziness and bad for readability of code. It should not be. Explicitly stating complex, nested generic types is not necessary for readability. In Visual Studio, a ToolTip shows the inferred type anyway. It is true that `var` is not really necessary for declaring variables of simple types such as `int` and `string`. But `var` is convenient for fairly complex generic types and is essential for anonymous types, because no type name can be specified. However, there are legitimate concerns about readability where tools other than Visual Studio are used, because without the ToolTip, declaration with `var` can be harder to read.

Anonymous types can be very handy while developing your program. However, they are limited, because they cannot be used as return types of a method. Hence, in most cases, you need to create a nominal (named) type.

In a nutshell:

- Do use queries and query syntax to declare your intent.
- Define extension methods sparingly, if at all, and do not extend basic system classes.
- It is OK to use `var` for complex types, especially for complex types generated on your behalf.
- Anonymous types in the current form are limited to a method scope.

As in the case of language features, it is worth understanding the strengths and limitations of libraries that implement LINQ. Next we will discuss some of the issues developers encounter when using LINQ to query and update relational data.

Going Beyond Stored Procedures: The Dynamic SQL Debate

One of the most tiring debates in the Object Relational space is about using dynamic SQL and stored procedures. Many versions ago, stored procedures provided a performance edge in addition to better access control. Several database versions ago, the edge for specific query execution largely disappeared with better query optimizers. Greater control over who can execute what (or even what queries can be executed) is offset by the corresponding loss of flexibility. So dynamic SQL, views, and table-valued functions (TVFs) provide interesting alternatives to stored procedures.

In most common cases, the queries generated by a component such as LINQ to SQL are as good as handwritten SQL. Occasionally they are even a bit better if the query writer is not a SQL expert. Hence, in those cases, the use of dynamic SQL is not a performance disadvantage compared to handwritten SQL or a stored procedure. However, TVF and stored procedures have a place when you want additional influence over the execution plan, when you want better access control, or when you need to use some procedural logic beyond the capabilities of SQL. But more important, many developers may have no choice but to use stored procedures, because that is all they are allowed to use. Indeed, LINQ to SQL or LINQ to Entities cannot solve this organizational rather than technical problem. Instead, they accommodate it by supporting stored procedures. LINQ to SQL stored procedure support is discussed in Chapter 10, "Using Stored Procedures and Database Functions with LINQ to SQL."

Where stored procedures are not mandated by organizational authorities, it is worth considering the following options in decreasing order of flexibility and increasing order of additional work:

- **Dynamic SQL for CRUD operations:** This option provides maximum flexibility with minimal additional code that needs to be maintained.

- **Views and/or TVFs for queries and stored procedures for CUD operations:** This option provides much of what a pure stored-procedure solution provides but adds composability to further filter the results with efficient execution on the server. See Chapter 10 for some examples of the use of TVFs.
- **Stored procedure-only access:** This is the final fallback when neither dynamic SQL nor TVF can be used. With this option, composability and deferred execution are not available.

Often a combination of the three provides the best trade-off between flexibility and control. In addition to stored procedure support through mapped methods, you can execute arbitrary SQL using the `Execute-Query()`, `Translate()`, and `ExecuteCommand()` methods in the `DataContext` class. These are not the mainline features but are available for interoperability in very specialized cases where generated SQL or stored procedures cannot be used. For example, suppose you cannot add a stored procedure due to access restrictions, and you have special knowledge of the data's statistics. You could use a highly customized and optimized dynamic SQL statement directly for specific queries by using `ExecuteQuery()` or `Translate()` as an excape hatch.

Designing Mid-tier with Persistent Entities and Business Logic

Data entities are CLR objects mapped to rows in the database. Hence, they are very close to the shape of the data in the database. Mapping does provide varying degrees of flexibility in changing the correspondence between columns and properties and altering the types of properties. But by and large, the entities are still structurally and semantically close to the entities in the database. This closeness has two key implications. First, entities are often normalized like the data in the database. Second, they are carriers of data rather than guardians of business logic or business processes. Let's look at what these implications mean for shaping data and separating concerns related to persistence, transferring data, and encapsulating business logic.

Data Shaping

The first implication can actually be positive where data needs to be updated. Normalization eliminates or minimizes duplication of data and thereby avoids inconsistency between multiple copies of the data. Information about a customer is not duplicated in each of the customer's orders. Only the customer's key is used for referential integrity. There are limited cases of denormalization that are useful:

- For data-binding purposes, showing a human-readable field instead of a database ID is advisable, especially where it is not modified. For example, when displaying `Order_Detail`, showing `Product.Name` is more meaningful than showing `Order_Detail.ProductID` mapped to a foreign key.

- A collection `Order.Order_Details` is a denormalized way of showing the relationship between `Orders` and `Order_Details`. It is a natural way to write object models and is, in fact, appropriate for read-write scenarios as well.

- In a few cases, many-to-many relationship may be manageable as collections in two entities. For example, if a product is supplied by multiple suppliers, and each supplier can provide multiple products, thinking about `Supplier.Products` and `Product.Suppliers` can be a good starting point. However, often the "hidden" entity in the middle—`ProductSupplier`—has its own relationship data. For example, a `ProductSupplier` may have its own lead-time requirements or costs. This requires an explicit class—`ProductSupplier`—that contains more than the keys for `Product` and `Supplier`. Hence, it is important to carefully think about the domain objects—`Products` and `Suppliers`—and to not rush into denormalization of many-to-many relationships.

In general, regardless of the mapping capabilities, it is better to avoid radically altering the correspondence in the mapping layer. There are already two powerful and well-understood technologies for changing the shape on either end of the Relational-Object divide. You can write excellent views or TVFs in the database to change the shape (including denormalization). Likewise, on the object side, LINQ `Select` clauses as well as the full power of C# or VB.NET imperative constructs are available to transform one object into another. Cramming more shape changes into mapping can be detrimental, because it introduces a third place to manage shape with considerably inferior power of expression and poorly understood constraints and limitations. It also creates yet another artifact to maintain, with its own skill set needs and its own evolutionary trajectory. That is likely a risk factor for an application's initial productivity and lifecycle.

When the desired shape of a business object with its own encapsulated functionality is significantly different from that of the database entity, two separate classes may be appropriate—one for the business object and another for the data in the database. The latter is then called a Data Transfer Object (DTO). In addition to shaping, aggregating data from multiple sources can also be done better with DTOs. Each DTO can be retrieved and saved by its own `DataContext` or equivalent persistence service provider. Where such a reshaping or aggregation is necessary, you can use LINQ to SQL or LINQ to Entities entity classes as DTOs. However, in most other places, an additional layer of entities is unnecessary and can be expensive in development time, performance, and application lifecycle costs. The entity classes generated by LINQ to SQL or LINQ to Entities often provide a reasonable core for building business objects.

Data shaping may also be necessary in service scenarios where you take the business objects and expose the underlying data for use by clients on another tier through a web service. You may choose to not expose sensitive information or information that is not relevant in the context of a service. For example, you may not expose an employee's date of birth because it is sensitive. You also may choose not to show an employee's hiring date, because it may not be relevant in a service that is used for an organization's address book. You may also choose to denormalize data so that it is more self-contained for clients of your service. For example, a product published through a service may use category name instead of category ID even if `Product` and `Category` are distinct business objects. Thus, you may again need to choose whether to selectively add attributes (such as `DataContract`) to reuse the business object or create a separate class. You have to make the choice based on your application and scenarios. But LINQ offers plenty of capabilities.

It is very easy to filter a collection and project into an appropriate type with a simple LINQ query. In the following code segment, a collection of

Product entities is populated using LINQ to SQL. Then a projection of the Product entity is created. It is augmented with additional information from the Category entity to form a shape that makes sense as a `DataContract`. LINQ is particularly suitable for creating such "object views" in a clear and succinct fashion. Together with database views, such object views provide a powerful and flexible mechanism that can be used in various tiers. In most cases, they are superior to clever but limited tricks in the mapping.

```
// Shaping and filtering from database to mid-tier
// Set up DataContext to eager-load Categories and Suppliers
List<Product> Products = (from p in db.Products
                          where p.Discontinued == false
                          select p).ToList();

// Elsewhere in the application ...
// Shaping and filtering from mid-tier to service boundary
// Class ProductInfo must be declared beforehand with DataContract
IEnumerable<ProductInfo> ProductInfoList =
                from p in Products
                where p.Supplier.Country == "USA"
                select new ProductInfo
                {
                    Id = p.ProductID,
                    Name = p.ProductName,
                    CategoryName = p.Category.CategoryName,
                    UnitPrice = p.UnitPrice.Value
                };
```

Alternatively, you can add attributes to the entity classes. Both LINQ to SQL and Entity Framework designers add the `DataContract` attributes to the entity classes for you—the former through opt-in for all the classes (none by default) and the latter by default. Although the capability exists in the tools, it is important to be cautious about it for two reasons. First, it leads to strong coupling between the shape of the data in the database and the data published in the service. This is undesirable, because the two typically are intended to serve different purposes and should have a business logic layer in between. Second, the all-or-nothing approach is rarely practical; some entity shapes may be substantially similar across tiers, and others may need to be significantly transformed. For example, you may publish category information publicly, whereas product information may be published without inventory details. Except for demo scenarios that show how to publish the database through services and a few simple applications, turning every entity in its entirety into a `DataContract` is more often an antipattern.

Separation of Concerns

The previous chapters looked at the `DataContext` on the one hand and the entities or mapped classes on the other. The distinction is more than a matter of implementation convenience. It represents a separation of concerns that is worth understanding. The `DataContext` provides persistence services; it handles connection, query translation, persistence operations, units of work, and transactions. The entities (and other mapped classes) hold the data related to the concepts in the application domain—`Customer`, `Order`, `Product`, `Supplier`, and so on.

Persistence and Entities

Entities do not themselves have methods for query or persistence and can be serialized to another tier if necessary, because they are not tethered to a database connection or a transaction. This separation is different from the Active Record pattern used for persistence. In the Active Record pattern, you could write the following:

```
Product product = new Product()
product.ProductName = "Great Product";
product.UnitPrice = 123;
product.Save(); //pseudocode showing Active Record pattern
```

In LINQ to SQL, as we have seen in previous chapters, a more natural pattern would be as follows:

```
Product product = new Product()
product.ProductName = "Great Product";
product.UnitPrice = 123;
db.Products.InsertOnSubmit(product);
db.SubmitChanges();
```

Although it is possible to build an Active Record pattern out of LINQ to SQL primitives, it is neither natural nor consistent with the design of LINQ to SQL. A `SubmitChanges()` operation does not save a single entity mapped to a single row or even just an entity hierarchy. It provides a unit of work that encompasses all changed objects in the `DataContext` instance. An operation such as `Save()` should not be mixed with business logic; it is an operation supported by a persistence service provider—DataContext in the case of LINQ to SQL or ObjectContext in the case of LINQ to Entities.

The persistence-related services provided by the DataContext include

- Queries—specifically, language-integrated
- Object identity—ensuring that you don't have to deal with copies of an entity
- Change tracking and computation of all changes for submitting to the database
- Batching of changes as a unit of work and transactional semantics

These are valuable services that should not be confused with the entities in your application domain. These are concerns for the persistence layer, not for the entities or business logic layer.

An object-relational mapper such as LINQ to SQL is great for working with relational data. That is often the key repository of data for an application. But for testing your application, you may want to consider the ability to hide the repository's relational implementation and substitute a "mock" implementation in its place. This is useful for testing your business logic independent of the database semantics, and it also helps with more efficient execution of tests. The details of mocking a DataContext can be quite intricate and hence are out of scope for this introductory discussion. However, that pattern has been covered in various forms on blogs and forums related to LINQ. See Appendix A for a useful post that covers this topic in detail.

Data Entities and Business Logic

The separation of concerns for business logic is more subtle. In some cases, business logic can be easily added to an entity; in others, it may be best handled in a distinct object serving as a "business object." To tease apart these cases and the rationale behind each one, let's consider the example of discount computation as the business logic and how it could relate to entities such as Order, Customer, and Supplier.

Let's start with a basic example of the first case just described—it is a computation that can be nicely encapsulated in the Order class as follows. For our discussion, we will assume a richer data entity than what Northwind's Order table can support. We will assume additional members in the Order class—Discount and SubTotal. The following code checks Order.SubTotal against a threshold amount and returns 10% of the SubTotal as the discount or nothing:

```
partial class Order
{
    public decimal ComputeDiscount()
    {
        // Compute based on state of the Order and business rules
        return (
            this.SubTotal > discount_threshold ? (SubTotal * 0.1M) : 0);
    }
}
```

The generated entity classes are partial classes to enable such extensions. As described in Chapter 11, "Customizing Entity Persistence and Adding Business Logic," you can extend the generated data entities in multiple ways. You can add methods and computed properties; you can add implementations of partial methods to validate individual properties and the entire entity. See Chapter 11 for an example of the Order class with added logic.

This addition of business logic to a data entity is quite simple and powerful. It is applicable where the business logic really belongs to the specific data entity. The rudimentary business logic shown in the preceding example uses only the information in the instance and discount_threshold tied to the business rule. However, a richer discount computation may involve more entities and rules that go well beyond the Order data entity. For example, the discount may be based on a customer's orders in the last three months, or the products ordered, or the shipper used, or the current sale, or some combination of all these factors. As the logic gets richer, the conceptual "business object" Order starts looking a lot different from the Order data entity. Perhaps encapsulating it with the Order entity data may not work as well if the discount computation requires data from multiple entities and possibly multiple sources of data, not just one database. In such a case, you should consider using the Order entity mapped to Northwind's Orders table as a DTO while having a separate business object to handle complex business logic that spans many DTOs—Customer, Order,

Order_Detail, Product, Supplier, and so on. Such a decision should not be taken lightly, because an additional class—or more likely, a whole set of classes—imposes a significant burden. It adds initial complexity but, worse still, it increases the concepts and code for movement of data and synchronization between layers—the DTO layer and the business object layer. That adds to lifecycle costs for the application as it evolves.

DTO and business objects are points on a continuum. Picking the right points on the continuum requires analyzing the data that the business logic touches and whether the functionality directly maps to the persistent entity. A business object is about the logic and the business process it covers. A data entity provides a reasonable initial point for crafting a business object, but it should not artificially restrict the scope of a business object. It is almost always better to consider the business logic and processes before making a decision one way or the other. For some business objects, the data entities may be just fine as the core. For others, a more detailed design and partitioning may be warranted before the data entities start playing a role. For example, in an order-processing application, you may find that order processing is best handled with a composite business object that uses many data entities. Shipper or Supplier data entities may be adequate for business functions and may not need more complex business object counterparts.

LINQ to SQL makes it quite easy to write a business object and then map the persistent members of that object to database tables and columns. Several previous chapters—in particular, Chapter 11—contain examples of how you can write your own class and map it. This is distinct from the database-first approach that the designer supports, in which you can drag and drop tables, stored procedures, and so on. Unfortunately, because tools can generate data entities very efficiently, they may end up becoming the default "business objects." Tools should be a productivity aid rather than the primary driver of the design.

Managing Concurrency

Concurrency management often does not get the priority it deserves during the early development cycle. It is like an insurance policy. There is no immediate payoff in terms of features for the effort you put in, but they are essential when concurrent changes cause trouble. Data access components such as LINQ to SQL give you several tools, but only you know the characteristics of the data in your application and the cost-versus-risk trade-off in assuming that certain operations are safe.

Concurrent changes affect queries, not just inserts, updates, and deletes. When you retrieve a Customer entity and then the Order entities in its Orders collection, you may be using two separate queries that may see data from different *epochs*. In other words, the data may have changed between the two queries due to some intervening concurrent update. As a trivial example, consider retrieving all "premier" customers based on some criterion and then retrieving their orders in a separate query for granting credit approval for the orders. In between the two queries, a premier customer could have lost its premier status due to a concurrent change. In this case, the Customer data for the Order entities is not current, and the user of the application may see inconsistent information. This is particularly common when you use deferred loading based on user input. The "think time" and coffee breaks of the end user of your application can easily create opportunities for a change between the two queries.

In this case, Customer and Orders could have been retrieved in a single transaction with the appropriate isolation level and its attendant cost of reduced throughput in the database. But fortunately, many applications are tolerant of such changes over some period of time. A gap of a few seconds or minutes may be acceptable in your application if the data changes infrequently and if safeguards detect and compensate for the inconsistencies. For example, consider an online bookseller that lets you order the last copy of a book in stock based on somewhat stale inventory information. The last copy may have been sold between the time that the inventory information is queried and when the order is submitted. In this case, it may be cheaper and more efficient for the bookseller to detect the inconsistency and apologize with a discount offer than to lock the database to ensure that the information is always current.

Hence, it is important to understand the business context of your application and the implications of features such as multiple queries or deferred loading. There is no single "right choice" for all data or all applications. It is a business decision informed by the constraints and capabilities of the technology.

Limitations of Optimistic Concurrency Checks

It is important to understand the capabilities and limitations of optimistic concurrency checks in a data access component such as LINQ to SQL or LINQ to Entities. The checks are performed only at an entity's granularity. If your update logic relies on information within the entity, the optimistic concurrency check gives you good protection. However, if your update logic relies on values from multiple entities, there is no built-in support to perform optimistic concurrency checks across multiple entities.

The traditional database concept of optimistic concurrency check relies on checking the entire "read set"—all the rows that are read for a given update. The mid-tier realization of optimistic concurrency check used in LINQ to SQL and prior components such as `DataSet` is a pragmatic and efficient simplification of the database concept. So it is important to understand what it does not cover. For example, if the discount applied to an order depends on having `OrderDetails` that refer to products on sale, a check for just the order's properties may not suffice. A change in a product's "on sale" status could go undetected. As the application developer, you need to think about the semantics of the entity and the application that uses the entity to decide whether optimistic concurrency checks are necessary and sufficient for your purpose. If necessary, you can retrieve and update data in one transaction where stronger guarantees are needed. However, more often than not, the business semantics are quite tolerant of changes. For example, a sale often lasts several days or at least hours, whereas most orders get processed in minutes or even seconds. Plus, for better customer relationships (that is, a business reason rather than a technology reason), a site may want to honor a sale price even if the user interaction straddles the sale's expiration time.

Unit of Work and Reusing a DataContext Instance

A `DataContext` instance is ideally suited for a unit of work in a two-tier application. You can retrieve an object graph through one or more queries and make changes to the graph by changing or deleting retrieved objects and by adding new objects. When all the changes are done, you can submit them all in one shot. This is the basic pattern discussed throughout the last several chapters. It works best when conflicting concurrent updates are not likely for the duration of the unit of work. That is dependent on the application and the data it consumes. In some cases, users' think time running into minutes or even hours may not be a problem. In others, the duration of a unit of work may be best limited to faster computations that can happen in seconds, if not quicker.

The same logic can be extended to the reuse of a `DataContext` instance after the completion of a `SubmitChanges()` call. The instance continues to hold on to the entities retrieved before the `SubmitChanges()` call, and it can be used for additional queries as well. However, the same considerations about the time elapsed and the likelihood of concurrent changes apply. Remember that after an entity is retrieved using a `DataContext` instance, it is insulated from concurrent changes in the database until `SubmitChanges()` is called. A retrieved entity is not overwritten by subsequent query results in the same `DataContext` instance unless you explicitly `Refresh()` the entity. Hence, it is important to consider the maximum duration for which you want to use a `DataContext` instance and if your application can tolerate potentially stale data.

The pattern for using a `DataContext` instance in a stateless mid-tier of an application is quite different from both the patterns just discussed. It is covered in the following section.

Understanding Performance

For higher-level abstractions, a key concern of users is performance. LINQ is no exception. We will discuss the costs and rules of thumb for optimization. But first you need to understand the context.

Defining Context

A common question is whether a specific LINQ component provides the right performance. The only way to get a relevant answer is to measure the performance *in the application scenarios that matter*. Micro-benchmarks can give you insight into the general costs of a technology. But their relevance cannot be decided out of the context of your entire system. For example, if you are using the number of queries per second as a proxy for performance of a data access layer, these could be some sample questions:

- Which queries are performance-critical, and which ones are not?

- How does desired/required user experience translate into specific hot spots in the application?

- How well does a micro-benchmark that assumes no other loads on the system predict the performance of a fully loaded system? How does a choice for a better micro-benchmark result affect other applications using the same database server?

- How often do you load large amounts of data versus small amounts of data?

- Is your system database performance constrained, or do you have scalability issues on the mid-tier?

Such questions let you avoid the biggest trap—premature optimization that can complicate your application without helping with its performance-critical parts. In short, for performance planning, measurement, and tuning, defining the context is the key. Now, in that context, let's look at the benefits and costs of using some LINQ components and solutions to obtain better performance. The following discussion largely focuses on the costs in the mid-tier and in the LINQ components in particular. For an in-depth discussion of the impact that LINQ components have on database performance, refer to Bob Beauchemin's chaper in the book, *The SQL Server 2008 MVP Project*, and his blog posts. Additional resources are listed in Appendix A.

Costs and Optimizations

As discussed in earlier chapters, LINQ is designed for composability and performance. The two are closely related. Deferred execution allows queries to be composed without the overhead of executing intermediate queries. A method can return an `IQueryable<T>`, which allows further queries to be composed against it. Execution occurs only when the results are consumed. On the other hand, a method that uses a string query (such as a SQL command) and that returns a collection cannot provide comparable composability.

LINQ provides a higher level of abstraction whose implementations entail some costs. As in the case of using higher-level languages or managed code, you have to decide if the productivity benefits of the abstraction are worth the costs. The costs vary depending on the operation and the sizes of collections. The following are some aspects of the cost of using LINQ in general and some of the key LINQ components in particular.

First, it is critical to understand the difference between a LINQ query and its results. A LINQ query is the definition of a computation. You can execute it as many times as you like, or you can execute it once and cache the results. The low-hanging fruit for better performance is often avoiding unnecessary re-execution of a query. You can execute the query once and cache the results over a certain period of time if you do not expect the results to change (or if your application can tolerate stale data). This optimization matters most when the basic cost of running a query is high (you have to execute a database query, for example) or when the queried collection is large (for instance, you are going through a large collection to find a few objects in the result) or when the computation itself is very expensive (such as when an expensive predicate is run in the `Where` method or clause). Beyond this general opportunity exist component-specific challenges and opportunities.

LINQ to Objects implementation relies on extension methods for `IEnumerable<T>`. C# or the VB.NET compiler translates a LINQ query from expression syntax into a set of method calls. The translation to method calls and the execution of the method calls typically performs only basic optimizations based on the structure of the code. Unlike in the case of a database, it does not have statistics about the data (such as the size of a collection, indexes, or distribution of values) for doing additional optimizations such as picking hash joins or nested loop joins based on sizes of collections. Hence, there may be more optimal ways to deal with very large sets of data than bringing them all into memory and using LINQ to Objects queries against them. This is exactly why LINQ uses expression trees that are translated more efficiently into query data. LINQ to SQL is one such component that translates expression trees into SQL statements that the database query processor can optimize.

LINQ to SQL provides object abstraction over relational data. This involves the following costs over the use of a `DataReader` (which is not surprising, because LINQ to SQL uses `DataReader` in its implementation). The costs are incurred because services are provided over and above what you get from a DataReader:

- **Query translation:** As shown in Figure 8.1 in Chapter 8, "Reading Objects with LINQ to SQL," a compiler generates an expression tree that is translated into SQL at runtime. This does involve some cost that can be amortized using compiled queries.

- **Object materialization:** Objects need to be constructed and filled with values from rows returned by the database.

- **Identity caching:** Updates require object identity, and object identity is obtained by maintaining a cache to look up an object reference given a key value. Some overhead is associated with hashing the key values. This overhead applies only to queries returning entities. It is not applicable to those returning nonentity objects (projections).

- **Copy of original values:** This overhead is incurred only if you don't use designer/SqlMetal-generated classes and don't implement INotifyPropertyChanging.

If you find that a particular query is on a critical path, you can use the following optimizations:

- Compiled query: As discussed in Chapter 8, a LINQ to SQL query can be parameterized and compiled. This does not eliminate the translation cost, but it amortizes it over multiple executions. Use of a compiled query provides the maximum performance gain in query scenarios. Alternatively, you could also use a stored procedure or a TVF for the performance-sensitive queries. These two options are at very different levels. Compiled query is a choice of an application developer and can be considered specific to an application. Stored procedure or TVF may be controlled by a database administrator (DBA) and should be appropriate for the database.

- Object materialization speed is automatically significantly improved by LINQ to SQL implementation through the use of cached materializers. You don't need to write any code to take advantage of it. In fact, this is one area where hand-rolled code for filling objects using `DataReader` is likely to do worse, not better.

- If you do not plan to modify the entities retrieved from a given `DataContext` instance, you can set `DataContext.ObjectTracking-Enabled` to `false` and eliminate the overhead of hashing materialized objects. This setting is not appropriate for changing entities.

- The overhead of maintaining original values for retrieved entities that are not modified is automatically eliminated by the generated code, as described in Chapter 9, "Modifying Objects with LINQ to SQL." If you are writing your own persistent classes, you can get the same benefit by implementing `INotifyPropertyChanging`, which triggers the "copy before write" optimization in the LINQ to SQL runtime.

Unit of Work and DataContext Lifetime

Simple performance optimizations exist for insert, update, and delete operations as well. `DataContext` provides `SubmitChanges()` for a unit of work. The size of a unit of work can be as small as a single insert, update, or delete operation to thousands of such operations and everything in between. By default, `SubmitChanges()` commands are executed in a single transaction. Hence, both safety and fixed overhead are involved in a `SubmitChanges()` call. If you are performing a number of changes, and if your application does not need to commit them one at a time, avoid making a `Sub-mitChanges()` call for each operation, and consider using a single unit of work for multiple operations. At the other extreme, if you are inserting hundreds of thousands of objects, more optimal alternatives exist, such as using the relational bulk insert API. `DataContext`'s unit of work is a powerful tool when you have a small to moderate number of changes that can be submitted together.

In the case of stateless mid-tier applications such as ASP.NET web applications, the unit of work takes a very different form. Consider a web application for changing the details of an order. A given session has a request for one or more orders and possibly a request to update some of the retrieved orders. Typically, you do not want to hold state related to the query request on the server until the update request is received. This helps improve scalability. Many query requests can be served without growing the state on the server and also because an update request may never be submitted for a given query request if the application's user decides not to change anything. As discussed in Chapter 9, LINQ to SQL lets you use different `DataContext` instances for a query and the corresponding update that is sent some time later. `DataContext` instantiation has been optimized by caching mapping, so you can use a new `DataContext` instance for each request. `DataContext` also implements `IDisposable` to provide easy cleanup. If you compile a set of commonly used queries and cache them for use across multiple `DataContext` instances, you can further optimize your web application. Additionally, the use of the `Attach()` method, described in Chapter 9, cuts down on unnecessary queries to the database for serving an update request.

In a nutshell, there are two common, optimized patterns for `Data Context` usage—a unit of work pattern in which a single instance can be used to retrieve an object graph, and making a set of changes in a single transaction. The second pattern is the lightweight, per-request instance with a set of compiled queries for the stateless web server scenario.

Improving Security

LINQ to SQL and LINQ to Entities make the task of building secure applications easier. They enable safer composition by virtually eliminating SQL injection attacks and encouraging secure practices.

Some applications using relational data relied on string concatenation to build SQL query statements. This enabled UI-driven query composition but also made the application vulnerable to SQL injection. For example, imagine a user interface that lets you see your login name based on your e-mail address, which you can enter. If this is done through a simple (badly designed) mechanism that concatenates the user input from a text box with the following query stub, it is easy to inject SQL for information disclosure, or worse:

```
SELECT LoginName
FROM Accounts
WHERE email = <input text>
```

This query is prone to injection text input such as `SomeUser@live.com' OR name like 'Robert%`. Notice the clever use of a closing quotation mark inside the input text. It lets a malicious user complete the literal and continue with additional probing to discover more information. In this case, I may be able to see the login names of all users whose names start with Robert:

```
SELECT LoginName
FROM Accounts
WHERE email = 'SomeUser@live.com' OR name like 'Robert%'
```

Although databases and relational data access libraries took a number of steps to mitigate the threat, applications still had to grapple with the trade-off between quick and simple query composition on the one hand and injection-proofing on the other. LINQ to SQL queries are not strings. Even when they are translated to SQL, all the user input is treated as SQL parameters. The translated queries shown throughout this book show that parameterization is strictly enforced—even when literals are used in the LINQ query. For example, the following LINQ query and its SQL translation from Chapter 8 show the parameterization of Spain:

```
var CustomerQuery = from c in db.Customers
                    where c.Country == "Spain"
                    select c;
```

```
SELECT [t0].[CustomerID], [t0].[City],[t0].[Country]
FROM [dbo].[Customers] AS [t0]
WHERE [t0].[Country] = @p0
-- @p0: Input NVarChar (Size = 5; Prec = 0; Scale = 0) [Spain]
```

This injection elimination is very doable in plain SQL through disciplined use of parameters and appropriate ways to execute SQL. But LINQ to SQL makes it easier and automatic. You don't have to think about it every time.

You still have to make sure that you handle connection strings with care in a configuration file or equivalent storage. If you do not use integrated security, the connection string likely contains sensitive information such as a database login ID and password. Hence, it needs to be secured. This need to secure secrets such as passwords is not specific to LINQ but is still relevant to applications built using LINQ.

Finally, LINQ components are libraries that are loaded and unloaded as part of the CLR application domain. Unlike a server operating system or database server, they are not owners or guardians of persistent data. LINQ components by themselves do not have any notion of authentication or access control. Hence, data must be secured at the source. For example, relational data must be secured through login and least permissive grants for dynamic SQL and stored procedures and functions.

Summary

This chapter introduced a few key patterns and practices for effectively using LINQ components in an application. The patterns span a broad range of LINQ features, from language extensions to libraries, with special emphasis on LINQ's database access components. We covered concerns from multiple tiers—advantages of dynamic SQL and stored procedures, ensuring correct separation of concerns for the mid-tier of an application, and end-to-end performance and security. The abstractions provided by LINQ components are designed to incorporate some of the common patterns and best practices. Yet, it is important to understand the considerations for their judicious use. The discussion in this chapter was introductory and foundational and meant to be a starting point for more detailed explorations.

■ 17■

LINQ Everywhere

T HIS CHAPTER POINTS to the future, to the ways in which LINQ will be used in the coming years. The primary goal is to give you an overview of several alternative LINQ providers not covered in the previous chapters. You've read about LINQ to Objects, LINQ to SQL, and LINQ to XML. These technologies shipped with Visual Studio 2008 and C# 3.0, but they are only a portion of the larger, still-emerging LINQ story.

The providers covered in this chapter are examples of what LINQ will become in future years. LINQ is not just about the existing providers we have studied in this book. It is about the potential to create providers for many other data sources.

Many of the most important tasks performed on computers involve manipulating data. In fact, it could be argued that computers are really for working with a disparate set of data sources. LINQ is important because it provides a concise, unified, integrated way to work with a wide variety of data sources.

Other Flavors of LINQ

This chapter introduces several variants of the LINQ technology so that you can get a feel for how LINQ is used throughout the industry. LINQ is an extendable technology, and over the years, it will be used in many different ways, for many different purposes. The main goal of this chapter is to give you a sense of the variety of possible LINQ services, in part so that you can be aware of their existence, and in part so that you can begin to imagine the uses to which LINQ can and will be put.

This book has covered LINQ to Objects, LINQ to SQL, and LINQ to XML in considerable depth. The topics covered in this chapter, however, are introduced only briefly. Nearly all of them are currently still under development, and several of them are potentially very large subjects. Nevertheless, I hope that this brief introduction to these technologies will give you a sense of their potential.

Finally, I should point out that I will mention an open-source product called LINQExtender. This tool is designed to help you build your own LINQ extensions. One of the technologies discussed in this chapter, LINQ to Flickr, is built on top of LINQExtender. Even though I will not discuss LINQExtender, that project is a place to start if you want to explore that technology.

Parallel LINQ

The code shown in this section uses a prerelease version of PLINQ called the Microsoft Parallel Extensions to .NET Framework 3.5. When PLINQ finally ships, it will run only on .NET 4.0 or later. The version I'm using that runs on top of 3.5 is for evaluation purposes only. There will never be a shipping version that runs on .NET 3.5.

This LINQ provider is being created at Microsoft by the Parallel Computing team; it is not the work of the C# team that created LINQ to Objects and LINQ to SQL. Here is the web site for the Parallel Computing team:

http://msdn.microsoft.com/en-us/concurrency/

Currently, these extensions are available only in prerelease form. You could download them either as Visual Studio 2008 compatible extensions to .NET 3.5, or as part of the prerelease version of Visual Studio 2010. Because the download sites might change over the coming months, I suggest that you find these resources by going to the Parallel Computing site or the Visual Studio site:

http://msdn.microsoft.com/en-us/vs2008

Parallel LINQ, or PLINQ, is only a small part of the Parallel Extensions to the .NET Framework. It is, however, an important part. Because it is a simple and natural extension of the material covered in this book, I think you will find it easy to use.

Consider this code fragment:

```
var list = Enumerable.Range(1, 10000);

var q = from x in list.AsParallel()
        where x < 3300
        select x;

foreach (var x in q)
{
    Console.WriteLine(x);
}
```

These lines look nearly identical to the code you have seen so often in this book. The only significant difference is the call to `AsParallel` at the end of the second line. Although we have often used type inference to hide the return type of a LINQ query, I'll pause and take a second look at this instance. Rather than returning `IEnumerable<T>`, this version of PLINQ returns `IParallelEnumerable<int>`:

```
IParallelEnumerable<int> q = from x in list.AsParallel() etc...
```

In the near future, PLINQ queries of this type will probably return `ParallelQuery<int>`. Because this product is still evolving, it might be simplest to use `var`, at least during the prerelease phase, and let the compiler choose the type. That way, you can save typing and avoid problems with anonymous types, and you need not concern yourself with changes in the API as the product develops. As was made clear earlier in the book, it is almost always appropriate to use `var` to designate the return type of a LINQ query, and there are generally only special circumstances when you would do otherwise.

Here are the results of this first PLINQ query:

```
2
1
3
4
```

```
6
512
5
7
513
8
12
514
9
13
515
10
14
516
11
15
517
16
72
518
17
```

The numbers shown here are in a relatively random order because they are being returned from different threads. It is important to remember that the sequence of values returned by LINQ is not always guaranteed to be presented in a particular order. If order is important in your code, you can add a call to AsOrdered to the query after the call to AsParallel. Alternatively, you could insert a GroupBy clause to establish the desired ordering. Otherwise, developers should assume that the ordering from a PLINQ query will be random.

Query Data with Parallel LINQ

Now that you understand the basics of Parallel LINQ, let's move on to look at a more interesting example. Improved performance is the main reason to write code that can run in parallel. The program shown in this section uses a timer to demonstrate how PLINQ can improve performance in a program.

Performance improvements become more evident when our code has access to more processors. The code I show here runs faster on a two-processor machine, but it really starts to come into its own on a four-processor machine. Moving up to even more processors yields more powerful results. For instance, the following results show an improvement of

1.44 times when using two processors and almost two times when using four processors:

```
2 Processors = 1.44 x improvement:
Linear: 00:00:13.15
Parallels: 00:00:09.10

4 Processors = 1.96 x improvement:
Linear: 00:00:15.00
Parallel: 00:00:07.68
```

These tests were run against prerelease software, so these numbers are almost certain to change before release, and, of course, different machines yield different results. Furthermore, the degree of improvement you will see is likely to change depending on the type of algorithm you run, the number of cores on your machine, the machine's architecture, how many caches there are, how they're laid out, and so on. Although it is rare, some queries show superlinear performance enhancements. In other words, there is a greater than four-fold speedup on a four-core box. An improvement of two times, such as the one shown, or even a three-time improvement, is common.

The following sample program is called FakeWeatherData, and it is available with the other programs that accompany this book. It features a simple LINQ to XML query run against a file with 10,000 records in it. The data I'm querying is not real. It consists of random dates and temperatures generated by a simple algorithm included in the FakeWeatherData program.

The XML file is structured like this:

```
<?xml version="1.0" encoding="utf-8" ?>
<Samples>
  <Sample>
    <Year>1973</Year>
    <Month>May</Month>
    <Day>15</Day>
    <Temperature>10</Temperature>
  </Sample>
  <Sample>
    <Year>1970</Year>
    <Month>Feb</Month>
    <Day>10</Day>
    <Temperature>14</Temperature>
```

```
    </Sample>
    ... 9,998 records omitted here
</Samples>
```

The program also uses a simple C# class to encapsulate the data from the XML file:

```
class WeatherData
{
    public string Year { get; set; }
    public string Month { get; set; }
    public string Day { get; set; }
    public string Temperature { get; set; }
}
```

The parallel version of the query in the program looks like this:

```
var list = (from x in doc.Root.Elements("Sample").AsParallel()
        where x.Element("Year").Value == "1973" &&
            x.Element("Month").Value == "Apr" &&
            x.Element("Day").Value == "15"
        select new WeatherData
        {
            Day = x.Element("Day").Value,
            Month = x.Element("Month").Value,
            Temperature = x.Element("Temperature").Value,
            Year = x.Element("Year").Value
        }).ToList();
```

Accompanying this code is a similar LINQ query that does not use PLINQ:

```
var list = (from x in doc.Root.Elements("Sample")
        where x.Element("Year").Value == "1973" &&
            x.Element("Month").Value == "Apr" &&
            x.Element("Day").Value == "15"
        select new WeatherData
        {
            Day = x.Element("Day").Value,
            Month = x.Element("Month").Value,
            Temperature = x.Element("Temperature").Value,
            Year = x.Element("Year").Value
        }).ToList();
```

The program queries the data in the XML file first using the parallel code and then using standard LINQ. By comparing the time it takes each block of code to execute, you can get a sense of the relative improvement available through PLINQ. I'll show you how to make such comparisons in a moment. I will also discuss some tools that will become available to help profile code of this type.

You can see that the PLINQ query contains a call to AsParallel, but the other query does not. Other than that, the two queries are identical. The fact that the two queries look so much alike points to a primary strength of PLINQ: Very little specialized knowledge is necessary to begin using it. This does not mean that the subject is utterly trivial—only that the barrier to entry is low. This is not the case with most concurrent programming models.

LINQ queries are designed to be read-only, working with immutable data. This is a good model for parallelism, because it makes it unlikely that data will mutate, thereby setting up the potential for a race condition. You should note, however, that PLINQ does nothing to prevent this from happening; it is simply that LINQ is designed to make it unlikely.

Note also that the declarative LINQ programming style ensures that developers specify what they want done, rather than how it should be done. This leaves PLINQ free to ensure that concurrent LINQ queries run in the safest manner possible. If LINQ had been defined more strictly, such that it had to process each element in a certain order, the PLINQ team would have had a much more difficult task.

The code in both these queries pulls out only the records from the XML file that have their date set to April 15, 1973. Because of deferred execution, the query would not do anything if I did not call ToList(). As a result, I added that call and converted the result into a List<WeatherData>. Although hardly earthshaking in importance, these calls ensure that the code actually does something, and thus give PLINQ scope to take advantage of the multiple processors on your system.

Simple timers are created to measure the difference between the standard LINQ query and the PLINQ query:

```
private static void RunTest()
{
    XDocument doc = XDocument.Load("XMLFile1.xml");

    Stopwatch sw = new Stopwatch();

    sw.Start();
    LinqOrdinarie(doc); // Run the regular LINQ query
```

```
        sw.Stop();
        ShowElapsedTime("Linear", sw.Elapsed);

        sw.Reset();

        sw.Start();
        ParallelLinq(doc); // Run the PLINQ query
        sw.Stop();
        ShowElapsedTime("Parallels", sw.Elapsed);
    }

    // Format and display the TimeSpan value.
    private static TimeSpan ShowElapsedTime(string caption, TimeSpan ts)
    {
        string elapsedTime = String.Format("{0}: {1:00}:{2:00}:{3:00}.{4:00}",
            caption, ts.Hours, ts.Minutes, ts.Seconds,
            ts.Milliseconds / 10);
        Console.WriteLine(elapsedTime, "RunTime");
        return ts;
    }
```

At least with the prerelease version of PLINQ that I've played with, I've found it very useful to set up timers to confirm that PLINQ actually can speed up an operation. My record at guessing which code will benefit from running in parallel is not good, so I find that confirming the code's effectiveness by explicitly measuring it is worthwhile. You can either use the simple StopWatch class from the System.Diagnostics namespace, as shown here, or you can use a profiler. Note that a thread-aware profiler might ship with some versions of Visual Studio 2010.

I've found that the advantages of concurrent LINQ become more obvious the longer the operation I'm timing lasts. As a result, I've placed the query inside a loop and added a variable to the program called NUM_REPS. By setting NUM_REPS to a large number, such as 500, you can clearly see the benefits that can be accrued when you run LINQ queries in parallel on multiple processors. Note that the first time PLINQ is used, its assembly needs to be loaded, the relevant types need to be JIT compiled, new threads need to be spun up, and so on. As a result, many developers see improved performance after they get past the initial warm-up time.

Although it is very easy to get started with PLINQ, you still need to consider complexities that are inherent in the subject. For instance, PLINQ sometimes develops a different partitioning scheme for your data, depending on whether you are working with an enumerable or an array. To learn more about this subject, see the following post from the Parallel Programming team:

http://blogs.msdn.com/pfxteam/archive/2007/12/02/6558579.aspx

The simple PLINQ examples shown in this section should help you get started with this powerful and interesting technology. Parallel LINQ is still in its infancy, but already it provides a way to greatly simplify tasks that normally are not easy to perform.

LINQ to Flicker

LINQ to Flickr allows developers to write queries against the Flickr repository of images hosted by Yahoo!. It also allows you to upload and delete photos from your stream and to create and remove comments. I've elected to show LINQ to Flickr in this chapter because it is reasonably well written and runs against a data resource, Flickr, that nearly all developers can access.

Flickr is a repository for photographs. It is a public site that you can use without charge. It is located at http://www.flickr.com/.

You can create your own free Flickr account and upload pictures to it that can be shared with the public. If you have an existing Yahoo! account, you are already automatically a member of the Flickr community.

Flickr supports an API that allows you to write queries against photos that are hosted on the site. This API forms the foundation on which LINQ to Flickr is built. The documentation for the API is found here:

http://www.flickr.com/services/api/

You can apply for a free API key that allows you to log into Flickr and call the API:

http://www.flickr.com/services/api/keys/

LINQ to Flickr is a LINQ provider that wraps the API and allows you to write traditional LINQ queries against the data in the Flickr repository. From a developer's point of view, LINQ to Flickr is simply another flavor of LINQ, such as LINQ to SQL, LINQ to Objects, or LINQ to XML. Behind the scenes it uses the Flickr API, but that fact is not at all obvious. Nor do you need to understand the API to use LINQ to Flickr. You only need to know LINQ.

Here is the URL for the web site from which you can download LINQ to Flickr:

http://www.codeplex.com/LINQFlickr

LINQ to Flickr (also known as Athena) is built on top of a tool called LINQ-Extender. The DLL that encapsulates LINQExtender comes with LINQ to Flickr, but if you want your own copy of the source for LINQExtender, you can download it here:

http://www.codeplex.com/LinqExtender

■ Other Provider Toolkits

LINQExtender is not the only tool of its kind. See, for instance, the LINQ IQueryable Toolkit (http://www.codeplex.com/IQToolkit). All this technology is quite new. In this chapter I'm simply providing links to these resources; I'm not yet ready to make a judgment as to which tool is best.

The author of LINQ to Flickr, Mehfuz Hossain, has also written an application that demonstrates what can be done with his code. This reference application is called FlickrXplorer, and it can be downloaded here:

http://www.codeplex.com/FlickrXplorer

FlickrXplorer is a web application. You can compile and run it yourself, or you can access a copy of it here:

http://www.flickrmvc.net/

To compile FlickrXplorer, you need a copy of a Microsoft library called MVC installed on your system. You can download MVC here:

http://www.asp.net/mvc/

MVC is an interesting and powerful tool in its own right, but I will not discuss it here. You can use LINQ and MVC in the same application, but there is no direct connection between the two technologies.

To create a LINQ to Flickr application, first create a simple console application. Add an application configuration file to the project by selecting Project, Add New Item in Visual Studio. Select Application Configuration File, and click the Add button. Insert the following contents into the configuration file, and insert your personal Flickr API keys where indicated:

```xml
<?xml version="1.0" encoding="utf-8" ?>
<configuration>
  <configSections>
    <section name="flickr"
        type="Linq.Flickr.Configuration.FlickrSettings, Linq.Flickr"/>
  </configSections>

  <flickr apiKey="INSERT YOUR API KEY"
    secretKey="INSERT YOUR SECRET KEY"
    cacheDirectory="cache" />
</configuration>
```

In the References section of Visual Studio Solution Explorer, add these two DLLs, which are part of the LINQ to Flicker download from CodePlex:

Linq.Flickr.dll

LinqExtender.dll

Note that LinqExtender depends on the `System.Core` namespace.

When you are done, Solution Explorer should show that you have added the libraries to the References section, as shown in Figure 17.1. In the Solution Explorer, you can also locate the App.config file with your API keys.

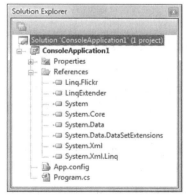

FIGURE 17.1   Linq.Flickr.dll and LinqExtender.dll are visible in the References section of Solution Explorer, along with the application configuration file.

Listing 17.1 shows the code for your program.

LISTING 17.1   The Code for a Simple LINQ to Flickr Application

```
using System;
using System.Linq;
using Linq.Flickr;

namespace LinqToFlickrTest
{
    class Program
    {
        static void Main(string[] args)
        {
            FlickrContext context = new FlickrContext();

            var query = from photo in context.Photos
                        where photo.SearchText == "IMG" &&
                            photo.ViewMode == ViewMode.Owner
                        select photo;


            Console.WriteLine("Pictures found {0}", query.Count());

            foreach (var item in query)
            {

                Console.WriteLine("{0} {1}", "FileName", item.FileName);
                Console.WriteLine("{0} {1}", "Title", item.Title);
                Console.WriteLine("{0} {1}", "WebUrl", item.WebUrl);
                Console.WriteLine("{0} {1}", "Url", item.Url);
            }


        }
    }
}
```

Note that the search term I've chosen may not work for the pictures in your Flickr repository. I've used the string "IMG" here, but you might want to choose some other string used in the title or description of your pictures.

Although it is not absolutely necessary, you will find that things go more smoothly if you are logged into Flickr before running the program. Even though this is a console application, your browser opens the first time you run this application, and you are taken to the Flickr site. It reports that you have "successfully authorized the application." If you are not currently logged in, you are asked to log in before you see this message. Here is the exact text of the message I received from the Flickr site:

```
You have successfully authorized the application.
You can go ahead and close this window now.
If you ever want to revoke authorization, you can do that in your
account.
```

At this stage you should be all set to retrieve results from the site. For instance, the code just shown returns the following data in my case, although it is likely that you will retrieve different information:

```
Pictures found 2

FileName: 3bc8f41b-d921-4ab9-b170-15b544e8e41d
Title: IMG_1852
WebUrl: http://www.flickr.com/photos/53173747@N00/3085317496/
Url: http://farm4.static.flickr.com/3210/3085317496_536df49d80_s.jpg?v=0

FileName: 07fb7451-7395-4584-8f87-5eca6062058e
Title: IMG_1764
WebUrl: http://www.flickr.com/photos/53173747@N00/3084242106/
Url: http://farm4.static.flickr.com/3189/3084242106_938c17c616_s.jpg?v=0
```

That is all I'll say about LINQ to Flickr. Like nearly all the code shown in this chapter, LINQ to Flickr is still under development and is likely to change before it is finished. Hopefully I've given you enough information that you can get up and running using this relatively sophisticated, powerful, easy-to-use tool. Mehfuz has done us all a favor by working so hard to create this well-designed program. I hope you have fun working with it.

LINQ to SharePoint

LINQ to SharePoint is a powerful tool created primarily by Bart De Smet, a talented Microsoft employee who works on the WPF team. It is designed to allow you to run LINQ queries against the data stored in the lists found on a SharePoint site.

Like LINQ to Flickr, LINQ to SharePoint is hosted on CodePlex:

http://www.codeplex.com/LINQtoSharePoint

Go to the Releases tab on CodePlex, and download the MSI. There is also a zip file containing the source for the project, but you need the source only if you want to see how the project is constructed. You don't need the source just to use LINQ to SharePoint.

Microsoft does not support the LINQ to SharePoint download from the CodePlex site, but Bart has done a great job with this technology. Even the early version I worked with for this chapter is quite sophisticated and easy to use.

Users of LINQ to SharePoint need access to a SharePoint site they can query. The official name and current version of SharePoint is Windows SharePoint Services 3.0, SP1. Don't be confused. If you saw a product called Visual Studio *Services*, you would rightfully think it was not Visual Studio itself. And if you saw a product called Windows Vista *Services*, again, you would be right to think it was not Vista itself. But in this case, Windows SharePoint *Services* is SharePoint. (Providing a rational explanation for this naming scheme is beyond the scope of this book!)

There are at least three ways to get access to a SharePoint site:

- You might have access to a SharePoint site through your workplace. If you can sign into a SharePoint site, you will probably have the rights to query it with LINQ to SharePoint.
- You can download and install a free version of SharePoint Services 3.0 if you have control of a machine that runs Windows Server 2003 or Windows Server 2008.
- There is also a one-month trial version of SharePoint called Microsoft Office SharePoint Server 2007 VHD. This and many other useful Virtual PC files are available at http://www.microsoft. com/vhd.

No real setup is involved with the first and third options. Instead, I will focus on option 2, which I believe is the best way to get to know and understand SharePoint, and the best way to experiment with the possibilities inherent in LINQ to SharePoint.

As you have read, SharePoint is a free download, but you must have Windows Server 2003 or 2008 to run it. While writing this book, I used a copy of Windows Server 2008, the 64-bit version. To install SharePoint on that OS, I first used W2K8 Server Manager to add the Web Server (IIS) Role. Then I downloaded the 64-bit version of Windows SharePoint Services 3.0, SP1. I ran the install and chose the Basic setup. This is pretty much a forehead install, which means that it requires very little effort. When I was done, I had a copy of SharePoint up and running on my system, as shown in Figure 17.2.

FIGURE 17.2 A nearly pristine new SharePoint site with the default configuration.

After installing SharePoint, I clicked the Add new announcement button, shown in Figure 17.2. I typed in a new announcement, as shown in Figure 17.3, and then clicked OK.

Now that you have a copy of SharePoint set up, you can go to the Code-Plex link listed earlier in this section and download LINQ to SharePoint. The install for this product is very simple and requires no explanation.

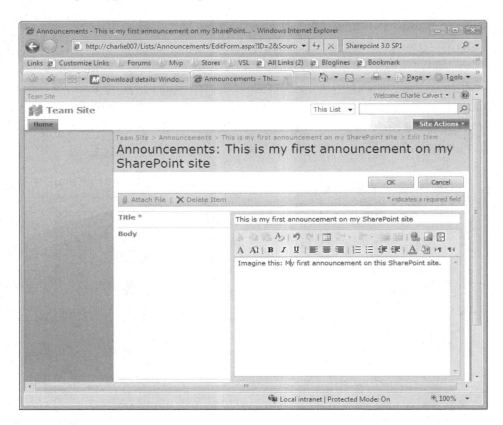

FIGURE 17.3 Adding a new announcement to a SharePoint site.

■ Registering the Assemblies

After I installed LINQ to SharePoint and tried to use the LINQ to SharePoint Wizard inside the IDE, I received an error stating Could not load file or assembly BdsSoft.Sharepoint.Tools.EntityGenerator.dll. This error occurs on the 0.2.4 release of LINQ to SharePoint. It is the result of a failed install into the GAC of the assemblies that are needed to run LINQ to SharePoint. If you encounter this problem, you can fix it as follows:

1. Open a command prompt with Administrator privileges.

2. Locate the BdsSoft assemblies, which are probably in a directory like this one:

   %ProgramFiles%\BdsSoft LINQ to SharePoint

3. Create a text file called GacFiles.txt containing a list of all the DLLs in the BdsSoft directory:

BdsSoft.SharePoint.Linq.dll

BdsSoft.SharePoint.Linq.ObjectModelProvider.dll

BdsSoft.SharePoint.Linq.Tools.DebuggerVisualizer.dll

BdsSoft.SharePoint.Linq.Tools.EntityGenerator.dll

BdsSoft.SharePoint.Linq.Tools.Installer.dll

BdsSoft.SharePoint.Linq.Tools.Spml.dll

4. Make sure that the GacUtil.exe file is in your path. It is probably located here:

C:\Program Files\Microsoft SDKs\Windows\v6.0A\Bin

Alternatively, open the Visual Studio command prompt from the Windows Start menu.

5. Issue this command:

```
Gacutil.exe /il GacFiles.txt
```

After completing the install of LINQ to SharePoint, you are ready to run a sample program. Create a standard console application by selecting File, New Project, Console Application from Visual Studio. Choose Project, Add New Item. Select LINQ to SharePoint File, as shown in Figure 17.4.

After you select the SharePoint template, Visual Studio takes you to the LINQ to SharePoint Entity Wizard, as shown in Figure 17.5. Currently, an options dialog available from the first screen of the wizard allows you to decide how to handle the plural forms of names from a SharePoint database. There is no need to use that dialog when creating this sample.

The second page of the LINQ to SharePoint Wizard lets you enter the name of the SharePoint site to which you want to connect. Enter your URL, as shown in Figure 17.6, and click the Test connection button. If the connection succeeds, the Next button becomes active, allowing you to move to the next page of the wizard.

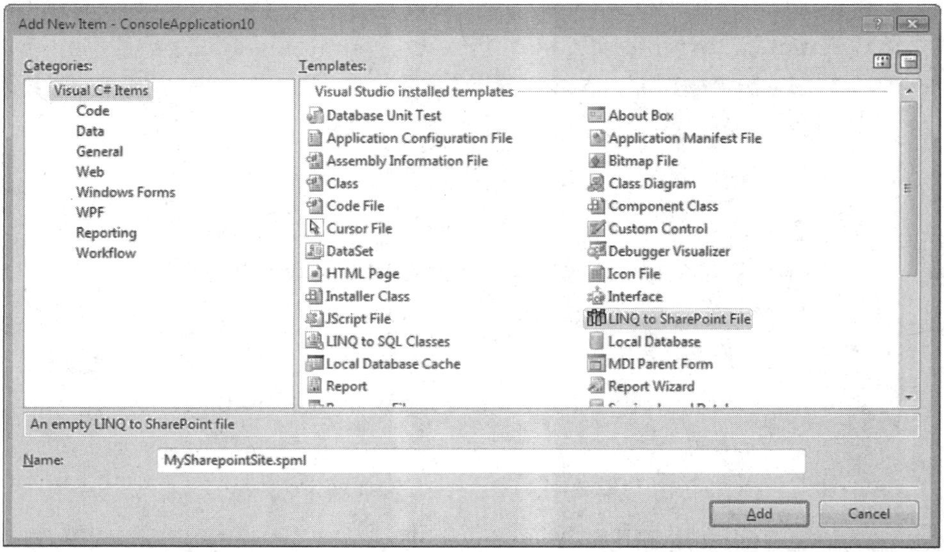

FIGURE 17.4   Selecting the LINQ to SharePoint template from the Add New Item dialog.

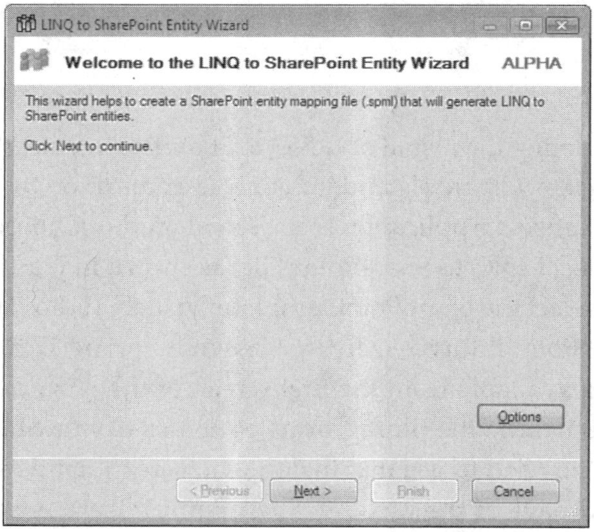

FIGURE 17.5   The first screen of the LINQ to SharePoint Entity Wizard.

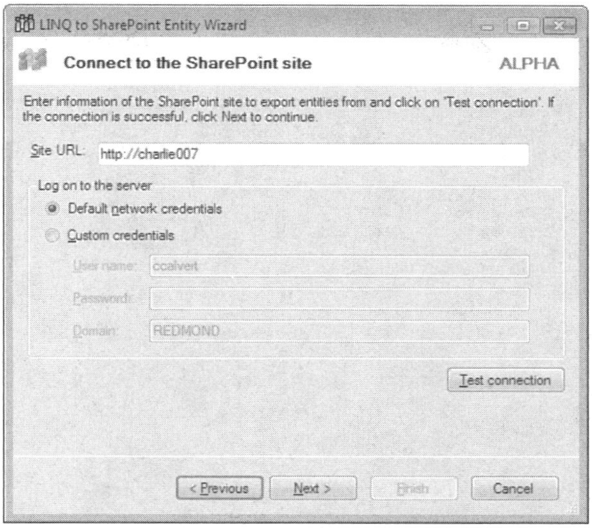

FIGURE 17.6 Connecting to a SharePoint site using the SharePoint Entity Wizard.

The URL shown in Figure 17.6 is the URL of the name of the server on which I developed the applications for this section. The URL will likely differ on your machine; it may take a more standard form, such as http://www.mysite.com.

There are two ways to select the credentials for your site. You can sign in with your default network credentials or sign in with custom credentials. The choice you make depends on how your network and SharePoint instance are configured. If you have questions, find the people who run your SharePoint site, and ask them for details.

The next page in the wizard allows you to choose the lists from the SharePoint site that you want to query in your program, as shown in Figure 17.7. This is roughly the equivalent of choosing the tables from the database that you want to query when using the Object Relational Mapper in a LINQ to SQL application. The default is not to have the Object Model option turned on, because that works only for querying a local machine.

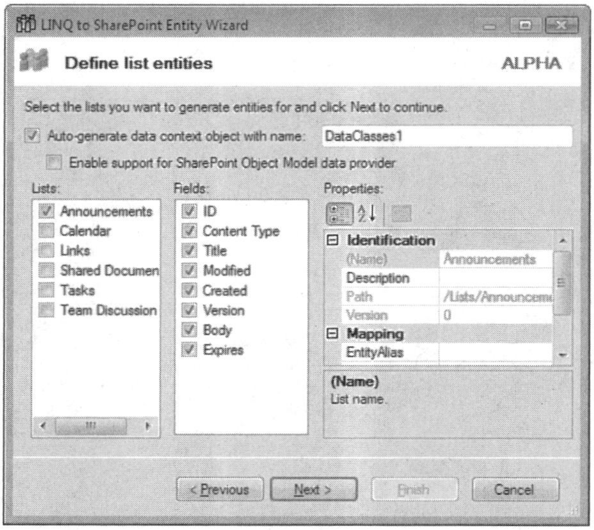

FIGURE 17.7   Choosing the lists from the SharePoint site that you want to query from your program.

The final screen in the wizard allows you to review the choices you made while stepping through the wizard, as shown in Figure 17.8. You can see that we have chosen to create an entity for the list of Announcements on the SharePoint site found on the machine called Charlie007. Our `DataContext` that we can use to gain access to the lists on the site is called `DataClasses1SharePointDataContext`.

If everything looks in order, go ahead and click Finish in the wizard. At this point, code similar to what is produced by the LINQ to SQL Object Relational Designer is added to your project. A new node with a name like MySharePointSite.spml is added to Solution Explorer, and inside that node is a file with a name like MySharePointSite.designer.cs. This file contains a `SharePointDataContext` that is roughly equivalent to the `DataContext` found in a LINQ to SQL project. It contains one class for each entity you opted to import from the SharePoint site. Again, it is easy to draw parallels between the code in this file and the code generated by the Object Relational Designer or SqlMetal in a LINQ to SQL project. Note that LINQ to SharePoint ships with a program called SpMetal, which is roughly equivalent to SqlMetal.

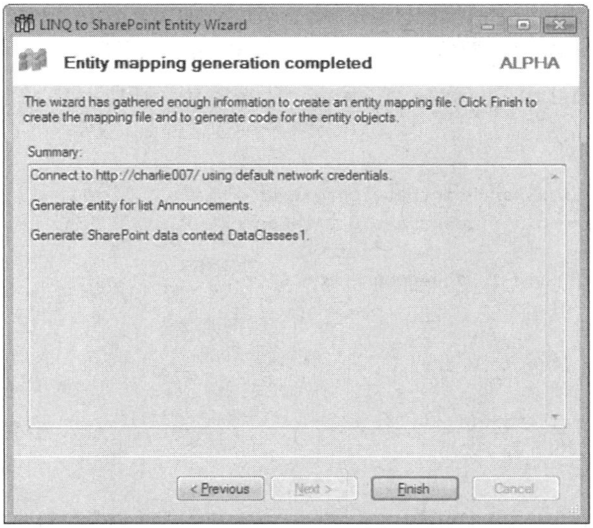

FIGURE 17.8   We are connected to machine charlie007 using the default network credentials, and we have generated an entity for the list of announcements.

When you are done, Solution Explorer looks something like Figure 17.9. Note the presence of the BdsSoft assemblies in the References section. An ObjectModelProvider entry will be present if you selected that option.

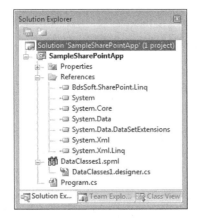

FIGURE 17.9   Solution Explorer after you have imported several SharePoint lists into your project with the LINQ to SharePoint wizard.

After you finish running the wizard, you can begin writing queries against the SharePoint data found on your site. Here, for instance, is a simple query against the common Announcements section that is part of many SharePoint sites:

```
MySharepointSiteSharePointDataContext db =
    new MySharepointSiteSharePointDataContext();

var query = from c in db.Announcements
            select c;

foreach (var item in query)
{
    Console.WriteLine(item.Title);
}
```

Note that we begin by creating a `SharePointDataContext`, just as we begin by creating a `DataContext` when building a LINQ to SQL application. You can then issue a query using the same syntax you would use in a standard LINQ to SQL or LINQ to Objects application.

The simple C# team community site that I'm querying returns the following data, which of course will differ from the data on your site:

```
This is my first announcement on my SharePoint site
Get Started with Windows SharePoint Services!
```

After you get started, it is easy to see the next steps. You can begin adding a `where` clause, for instance:

```
var query = from c in db.Announcements
            where c.Title.StartsWith("T")
            select c;
```

This query would retrieve the first, but not the second, of the two announcements returned by the first version of this query. You can experiment with the other LINQ operators, finding which ones work and which ones might not have been implemented yet. It is unlikely that LINQ to SharePoint will ever implement all 49 operators covered in Chapter 6, "Query Operators." Nevertheless, this tool is still under development, and it will grow in depth over time.

That is really all you need to know to get started using LINQ to Share-Point. As you can perhaps tell, this is quite a sophisticated tool that is well designed and easy to use. Currently LINQ to SharePoint does not support all the query operators available in LINQ to SQL. I should add that the author of LINQ to SharePoint has no plans to implement all the operators, but he is busy adding new ones, such as the `join` operator.

Overall, LINQ to SharePoint is an excellent example of what can be done to extend LINQ. It is also a very useful tool that should be valuable to many developers. If you use SharePoint regularly, you will find this tool an excellent resource.

Working with Processes

I want to close this chapter with a simple example that I hope will serve as a cautionary note for LINQ developers. When I first started working with LINQ, I was not fully aware of the power of LINQ to Objects. Unfortunately, I have seen developers do a great deal of work to create a LINQ provider for a technology that LINQ to Objects already fully supports. Remember that any data source that produces an `IEnumerable<T>` or `IEnumerable` can be queried by LINQ to Objects without any extra work on your part. If you want to use LINQ with a particular technology, check to see if it already supports LINQ to Objects or if it would be possible to quickly convert your data source into an array of some kind that fully supports LINQ queries. If you can do so without paying too great a price in terms of performance, don't worry about the need to create your own provider.

To illustrate the point, I ask you to recall material covered in earlier chapters on using LINQ with the C# Reflection API. The code shown in those samples is commonly called LINQ to Reflection, but it's really just LINQ to Objects run against the collections produced by the Reflection API. The code may appear to magically pull data from the Reflection API, but, in fact, it just uses LINQ's capability to work with methods that return `IEnumerable` or `IEnumerable<T>`.

Listing 17.2 shows an example of a query that you might be tempted to think is part of something called LINQ to Diagnostics. In fact, this is just another example of the power inherent in LINQ to Objects. Listing 17.3 shows the output.

Listing 17.2 contains a query that retrieves and filters the processes running on your machine. To write such code, you need do no special work. Instead, you can write a LINQ to Objects query directly against a class found in the System.Diagnostics namespace.

LISTING 17.2   By Using the System.Diagnostics Namespace, You Can Write Queries Against the Processes Currently Running on Your System

```
static void Main(string[] args)
{
    var query = from p in Process.GetProcesses()
                orderby p.VirtualMemorySize64 descending
                select p;

    foreach (var item in query.Take(5))
    {
        ShowProcess(item);
    }
}

public static void Write(string caption, string data)
{
    Console.WriteLine("{0}: {1}", caption, data);
}

public static void Write(string caption, long data)
{
    Write(caption, string.Format("{0:N0}", data));
}

public static void ShowProcess(Process process)
{
    ShowTitle(process.ProcessName);
    Write("MainWindowTitle", process.MainWindowTitle);
    Write("VirtualMemorySize64", process.VirtualMemorySize64);
}
```

LISTING 17.3   The Output from the Code Shown in Listing 17.2

```
==================
sqlservr
==================
MainWindowTitle:
VirtualMemorySize64: 1,630,756,864
==================
```

```
WINWORD
=================
MainWindowTitle: Chapter16 Advanced LINQ0.docx - Microsoft Word
VirtualMemorySize64: 473,960,448
=================
VCSExpress
=================
MainWindowTitle: ProcessScan - Microsoft Visual C# 2008 Express Edition
VirtualMemorySize64: 438,231,040
=================
explorer
=================
MainWindowTitle:
VirtualMemorySize64: 420,114,432
=================
Zune
=================
MainWindowTitle: Zune
VirtualMemorySize64: 412,151,808
```

The query shown in this example is very simple:

```
var query = from p in Process.GetProcesses()
            orderby p.VirtualMemorySize64 descending
            select p;
```

The `Process` class supports a method called `GetProcesses` that retrieves all the programs running on your system. You can see the same list of programs in the Windows Task Manager.

In our query, the LINQ `OrderBy` operator is used to sort the items retrieved in descending order by the amount of memory they take up. The resulting list is quite interesting, because it gives you a sense of which programs are using the most memory on your system.

Here is the declaration for `System.Diagnostics.Process.GetProcesses`:

```
public static Process[] GetProcesses();
```

This method returns an array of `Processes`. As mentioned in Chapter 4, "C# 3.0 Technical Overview," the developers of C# and .NET ensured that arrays are fully queryable by LINQ. The Base Class Library (BCL) has no array type called `Process[]` or `int[]`. Instead, the CLR improvises, so to speak, and spins up a new type for you at runtime. These types appear to implement the following set of interfaces:

```
System.ICloneable
System.Collections.IList
System.Collections.ICollection
System.Collections.IEnumerable
System.Collections.Generic.IList<T>
System.Collections.Generic.ICollection<T>
System.Collections.Generic.IEnumerable<T>
```

These types also inherit from `System.Array`. As you can see, `IEnumerable` and `IEnumerable<T>` are supported. As a result, you can query such an array with LINQ.

There really isn't much else to say about this example. I've included it here just as a reminder that sometimes we don't need to create a fancy LINQ provider just to access a particular data source. Please don't spend hours trying to create your own LINQ provider when a few simple calls to LINQ to Objects will solve your problem. On the other hand, if you see a real need for a new LINQ provider, and you think you have the time and ability to create it, please get to work as soon as possible, and share your efforts with the community. When you are done, visit the "Links to LINQ" section of my blog, and let me know about your creation so that I can help tell the community about your contribution:

http://blogs.msdn.com/charlie/archive/2006/10/05/Links-to-LINQ.aspx

Summary

In this chapter you have had a look at several different flavors of LINQ. If you look in Appendix A, or follow the URL to my "Links to LINQ" blog post, you will find that there are many other flavors of LINQ that I did not cover in this chapter. Some of them are at least potentially quite important and sophisticated, and others are small projects that have never received much attention put together by a single person. Nevertheless, the extensions to LINQ are a vitally important part of the LINQ story. Hopefully you have found the few examples shown here sufficiently illustrative to encourage you to explore the matter in more depth and perhaps also write your own provider.

Let me wrap up this chapter by taking a moment to stress the importance of this topic. The LINQ providers I've described in this chapter are still in prerelease form. Even when they are released, it will probably take several iterations to bring them to maturity. Nevertheless, even as they are now, they are remarkably easy to use, and they show the promise of great power.

The providers described in this chapter extend LINQ so that it can become

- An ideal way to perform concurrent programming by removing many of the impediments that have prevented developers from working with multithreaded applications.
- An easy means of querying a site such as Flickr.
- An easy to use tool for working with the lists found on a SharePoint site.
- An excellent way to perform concurrent programming without having to encounter many of the impediments that have prevented developers from working with multithreaded applications.

We are still at the dawn of the LINQ era. When object-oriented programming first emerged, it was not obvious how important it would become. The same was true of the Web, of multimedia technology, and of many other tools. LINQ came into the world remarkably fully formed, but this chapter only hints at the many ways LINQ can be extended to solve myriad problems. The future of LINQ is bound up with the future of LINQ providers such as the ones described in this chapter. As we witness the development of increasingly powerful and sophisticated LINQ providers for an increasingly large range of data sources, we will see the emergence of an important new technology that will have a significant capability to simplify and improve how we write and maintain our code.

18

Conclusion

THE LINQ PROJECT started with the observation that bringing queries into a modern programming language would simplify the task of programming. A deeper examination of the problem of integration revealed a few key differences between the world of queries and the pre-LINQ mainstream programming languages:

- Queries in strings are begging to be integrated into the host language. A developer is deprived of programming language benefits such as compile-time type checking, IDE support for autocompletion, unified syntax, and common object model if queries remain in strings.

- Queries are declarative, whereas much of the code in a language such as C# is imperative. A SQL query defines the set without specifying the minute details of implementation.

- Multiple, domain-specific query languages exist—SQL for relational data and XQuery for XML, to cite a couple. Other domains have their own variants. Queries are also interesting in the domain of collections and objects.

- SQL deals with rectangular results, whereas the natural fit for objects is object hierarchies and graphs.

- Efficient execution of queries often requires specialized processors and execution at the source of data. Bringing all the data into a program's CLR application domain is not an effective strategy. As a corollary, the following point is also true:

- Efficient integration of query into programming language requires an efficient composition mechanism.

- Transformations are closely related to queries. Projection using the SELECT clause in SQL and the RETURN clause in XQuery are two examples.

LINQ in the present form was born after many iterations and experiments with the building blocks, syntax, components, and tools. As built, it has the essential qualities described in Chapter 3, "The Essence of LINQ." Now that we have looked at some key LINQ components in detail, it is worth revisiting the foundational qualities and tying them back to the differences just mentioned:

- **Integrated:** Queries are first-class citizens of C#, VB.NET, and other LINQ-enabled languages. Developers can now use all the standard programming language facilities and tools for queries.

- **Declarative:** Query expressions declare the intent, and LINQ libraries provide the implementations.

- **Unitive:** LINQ provides a unified mechanism across domains—relational, XML, and object, to name a few. Data can flow between these domains in a LINQ query without the developer having to do plumbing work.

- **Hierarchical:** Results of a LINQ query are not limited to tabular structure. Object hierarchies and graphs are just as easy to get. This capability takes LINQ beyond SQL in power of expression.

- **Extensible:** LINQ allows efficient providers such as LINQ to SQL to be plugged in using expression trees to represent code as data.

- **Composable:** LINQ operators speak the common language of `IEnumerable` and `IQueryable`, and deferred execution allows query expressions to be composed with very little cost.
- **Transformative:** LINQ provides a powerful set of capabilities to transform data within and across domains. This nicely complements the core query capabilities.

These qualities provide a strong foundation for LINQ to grow in a number of domains beyond the traditional object, relational, and XML domains. Chapter 17, "LINQ Everywhere," covered some of the interesting domains where LINQ has already started blossoming. It is particularly important to look at LINQ from the point of view of the current and potential breadth of implementations. Traditionally, many developers equate query with SQL. Hence, it is easy to focus on relational LINQ implementations such as LINQ to SQL or LINQ to Entities and to see them as the main LINQ story. But doing so misses the point that LINQ provides a common language for a number of domains and a common language for flowing data across domains.

LINQ technologies are built on the foundation of simple but powerful building blocks. These building blocks not only help integrate queries into the language but also enrich the programming experience in C# and VB.NET beyond queries. Lambda functions enable and encourage a functional and declarative style of programming. Expression trees open a whole gamut of possibilities by representing code as data. Object initializers provide a much more concise notation. Partial methods make generated code even more customizable. Such are the additional benefits of the building blocks over and above their role in the core LINQ story.

This book has described the first release of LINQ. Like object-oriented programming and .NET, the first release is only a beginning. We expect LINQ to evolve and mature in future releases to become a key tool for developers in the years to come. The current richness described in this book and the even bigger future it enables is the essence of LINQ.

A

Tips for Developers

Accessing the Source Code

Most of the source code shown in this book is drawn from sample programs that are available for download. The sample programs are stored in a zip file that you can download and decompress to a directory where you have rights to compile and run programs. If you are uncertain where to place the files you download, we recommend putting them in your Documents directory.

Most of the chapters in this book have source code associated with them. The code is divided by chapter. For example, all the programs associated with Chapter 2, "Getting Started," are in a directory called Chapter02. Many of the individual programs containing the source are mentioned by name in the text. You might also find it helpful to run each of the sample programs to become familiar with the contents, or to use the Windows built-in search facilities to find sample programs that cover a particular feature. For instance, after downloading the source, you might type a few words from the book's source code into Windows Search. The search facility could then take you directly to the program that contains that code.

You can access the source code from the following URL:

www.informit.com/register

Go to this URL, sign in, and enter the ISBN. After you register the product, a link to the source content will be listed on your Account page, under Registered Products.

Northwind and the Visual Studio Samples

The sample programs just mentioned are the primary reference code for this book. However, you might find other samples useful.

The C# team created a series of LINQ samples that ship with Visual Studio 2008. To access these samples, choose Help, Samples from Visual Studio. From the samples link, you will find instructions to access a local copy of the samples and to download a copy from the Web. The samples come in a zip file. You should decompress the contents of this file to a directory over which you have complete control. For instance, you might place it in your Documents or My Documents directory. The projects included with the samples contain Visual Studio solution files that can be opened and run by selecting the F5 key, or by choosing Start Debugging from the Visual Studio Debug menu.

Dinesh helped oversee the creation and development of the samples, and Charlie drove the actual release of the samples. As a result, you should find that many of the samples that ship with Visual Studio make an excellent companion to the material found in this book. In particular, you should explore the excellent SampleQueries project, which contains more than 500 examples of how to write LINQ queries. The SampleQueries project was originally developed by C# Compiler PM Alex Turner, and the code in that sample has been reviewed by many developers on the C# development and documentation team. Other important projects, such as the ObjectDumper sample, are included in this group of samples.

The C# Visual Studio samples ship with all copies of Visual Studio 2008 except for the Express version. Updated copies of the samples are also available online. Because the online versions have been updated, they are the preferred versions of the samples. However, most of the changes in the online version are minor, and you will find the versions that ship with Visual Studio to be very useful.

Included with the samples is a custom version of the Northwind database. This database is used by both the C# team's samples and the LINQ to SQL samples used in this book.

You can download the C# team's samples from Code Gallery at http://code.msdn.microsoft.com/csharpsamples.

The copy of the Northwind database that is included with the C# samples has extra data and metadata designed to illustrate some of the features of LINQ. Because there are some 50 LINQ operators, it was not possible to illustrate them all using the standard release of Northwind. Therefore, the database was modified slightly to allow Alex and other team members to write queries that illustrated how to use all the LINQ operators.

You should be able to download the original, unmodified version of Northwind from either of these URLs:

http://www.microsoft.com/downloads/details.aspx?FamilyID=06616212-0356-46A0-8DA2-EEBC53A68034&displaylang=en
http://tinyurl.com/yzx6lz

Version Numbers

The version numbers of the releases of the .NET Framework and C# that have appeared in recent years are somewhat confusing. The following list can help you disambiguate these version numbers:

* Visual Studio 2005 includes C# 2.0 and the .NET Framework 2.0.
* The release of Windows Vista was accompanied by .NET Framework 3.0.
* Visual Studio 2008 includes C# 3.0 and .NET Framework 3.5.

Essential Downloads

Everyone who reads this book should have several essential programs installed on this system. Without these programs you will not be able to run some or all of the sample programs described in this text.

Installing Visual Studio Express

If you do not already have a copy of Visual Studio installed, you can download a free copy of the Express version from Microsoft's web site. All the programs in this text can be compiled with Visual Studio Express. Most of the sample programs used in the book were developed with Visual Studio Express for C#. You can download this product here:

http://www.microsoft.com/express/

Installing the .NET Framework

If you have Visual Studio on your system, the .NET Framework will have been installed automatically. The .NET Framework includes all the tools and libraries needed to compile the programs found in this book.

The Framework is free. The current version of the Framework is 3.5, Service Pack 1. Most of the code in this book was developed against the .NET Framework Version 3.5 and tested with Service Pack 1. Thus, you should be able to run the samples against 3.5 or 3.5 Service Pack 1. The .NET Framework Version 4.0 will ship at the same time as the next version of Visual Studio, and it and other, future versions of the Framework can also be used to compile all the programs in this book. Early versions of the Framework are not LINQ-aware and cannot be used to compile most of the programs shown in this text.

Here is the home page for the .NET Framework:

http://msdn.microsoft.com/en-us/netframework/default.aspx

On this page you can find links to the current and previous versions of the .NET Framework..

By default, the .NET Framework is installed into your Windows directory:

C:\Windows\Microsoft.NET\Framework\v3.5

At the command prompt, you can type the following to move to your Windows directory:

```
cd %windir%
```

You should then be able to change into the .NET Framework directory by typing this:

```
cd Microsoft.NET\Framework
```

From there, you can type DIR to see the list of installed frameworks, or type cd v3.5 to enter the .NET Framework 3.5 directory.

Although I don't recommend it, you can compile the samples discussed in this book from the command line. The compiler is called CSC.exe and it is found in that directory. MSBuild.exe, and the other tools you need to develop LINQ applications, are also available in the v3.5 directory. As a result, if you want to compile from the command line, you need to either work from inside that directory or ensure that the directory is on your path.

Visual Studio makes it much easier for you to develop the programs found in this book, and I strongly recommend that you use it unless you have some specific reason for avoiding it. However, all the code and sample programs shown in this book can be developed and run from the command line using the .NET Framework. The steps for compiling a LINQ program from the command line will be outlined later in the section "Compiling from the Command Line" of this appendix. Please note that you can use the tool called SqlMetal.exe instead of the Object Relational Designer.

Installing SQL Server Express

Database technology plays a key role in this book, primarily in Chapters 7 through 10. Microsoft ships a free database called SQL Server Express. Although it isn't designed for deployment as part of an enterprise database application, SQL Server Express nevertheless supports the APIs and functionality found in the full version of Microsoft SQL Server. It provides a good test platform for you to run LINQ queries against while you are learning about LINQ or other database APIs. All the queries you write should work unchanged in the regular version of Microsoft SQL Server if you decide to upgrade to that product. You can find links to download the free SQL Server Express from the Express home page:

http://www.microsoft.com/express/

Compiling C# Programs

The simplest way to compile and run a C# program is from inside Visual Studio. All the programs in this book will compile with the free version of Visual Studio called Visual Studio Express. I developed almost all the sample programs for this book using Express. As mentioned previously, you can download this small, light version of Visual Studio from this URL:

http://www.microsoft.com/Express/

You can build two primary types of programs in Visual Studio. The first is a console application that displays output at the command line, and the second is a Windows Forms application that runs inside the Windows GUI. Most of the programs in this book are command-line applications, but I've rewritten some as Windows Forms applications because that format offers a simpler way to help you sort out a large number of small samples.

To create a console application in Visual Studio, follow these steps:

1. Choose File, New Project. The dialog shown in Figure A.1 appears.

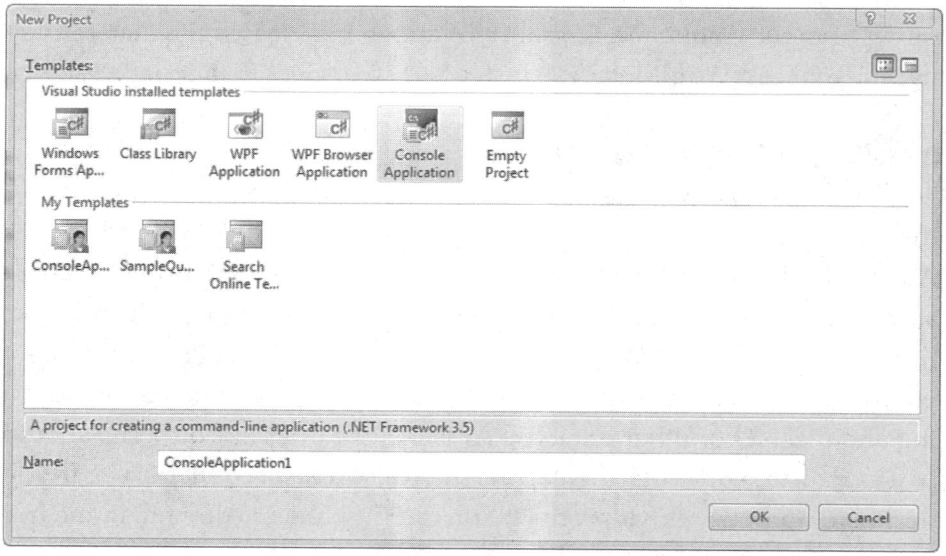

FIGURE A.1   The New Project dialog in Visual Studio Express.

2. Click OK to select the default name and location for the project.

After you complete these two steps, the Visual Studio editor should open with the following code visible and ready to edit:

```csharp
using System;
using System.Collections.Generic;
using System.Linq;
using System.Text;

namespace ConsoleApplication1
{
    class Program
    {
        static void Main(string[] args)
        {
        }
    }
}
```

You can start typing code directly into the Main method:

```csharp
static void Main(string[] args)
{
    var list = new List<int> { 1, 2, 3 };

    var query = from n in list
                select n;

    foreach (var item in query)
    {
        Console.WriteLine(item);
    }
}
```

To run the program, select Debug, Start Without Debugging. The default key binding for this command is Ctrl-F5. You can also run a program by choosing Debug, Start Debugging. The key binding for this command is F5. When working with console applications, I prefer the first of these two options because it leaves the console window open so that you can view the results of your work.

You can create a Windows Forms application in Visual Studio by choosing File, New Project and selecting Windows Forms Application. Choose View, Toolbox from Visual Studio. From the Common Controls section of the Toolbox, drag a Button and TextBox onto the main form for your project, as shown in Figure A.2.

FIGURE A.2 Creating a simple Windows Forms application.

Double-click the Button to create an event handler where you can write your code:

```
private void button1_Click(object sender, EventArgs e)
{
    var list = new List<int> { 1, 2, 3};

    var query = from n in list
                where n % 2 == 0
                select n;

    textBox1.Text = query.Single().ToString();
}
```

If you want to display multiple items in the form, drop down a ListBox rather than a TextBox. Click the Button to create a method, just as you did before, but this time write code that looks like this:

```
private void button1_Click(object sender, EventArgs e)
{
    var list = new List<int> { 1, 2, 3};
```

```
    var query = from n in list
                select n;

    foreach (var item in query)
    {
        listBox1.Items.Add(item.ToString());
    }
}
```

Compiling from the Command Line

If you use Visual Studio as your development environment, you will rarely encounter difficulties compiling and running simple programs of the type covered in this book. Because the Express version of Visual Studio is both free and an excellent, high-quality development tool, most people can use it or other versions of Visual Studio to work with the programs in this book. However, sometimes you might need to compile from the command line. The next few paragraphs outline some examples demonstrating how to proceed.

To compile LINQ programs from the command line, you need a copy of the .NET Framework 3.5 or greater installed on your system. The Framework is installed automatically if you install Visual Studio. You can also download it separately, as explained earlier.

Here is a simple batch file for compiling and running a console application called SimpleNumericQuery that consists of a single source file called Program.cs:

```
PATH=%PATH%;%windir%\Microsoft.NET\Framework\v3.5\
csc.exe /out:SimpleNumericQuery.exe /target:exe Program.cs
SimpleNumericQuery.exe
```

This code is designed to be run from the command prompt. You can launch the Windows command prompt by clicking the Vista Start button and typing CMD. This launches a command window where you can enter the code for compiling your program.

The first line of this batch file sets up the path. The second line compiles the program, and the third runs the program.

Here is how to compile a Windows Forms application:

```
PATH=%PATH%;%windir%\Microsoft.NET\Framework\v3.5\
csc.exe /out:MyProg.exe /target:exe Program.cs Form1.cs Form1.Designer.cs
MyProg.exe
```

You can learn more about the command-line compiler by opening a command prompt, setting the path as shown in the sample batch files in this section of the text, and typing the following:

```
csc /?
```

There are advanced tools for compiling C# applications from the command line. These include the MSBuild.exe program that ships with the .NET Framework and the open-source NANT project available from http://nant.sourceforge.net/. MSBuild can be very easy to use. For instance, if you create a project in Visual Studio, in many cases you can compile that project from the command line by simply setting up the path and typing MSBuild.exe from the directory where the source for your project is stored.

Connecting to a Database

To learn how to connect to a database, read this post from Charlie's blog:

http://blogs.msdn.com/charlie/archive/2007/11/19/connect-to-a-sql-database-and-use-the-sql-designer.aspx

I will maintain this post on my blog, but the following is the text in case you don't have access to online materials.

To begin working with LINQ to SQL in Visual Studio 2008, you need a database that you can query and a copy of Microsoft SQL Server or SQL Express. In this post, I'll focus on SQL Express because it is free and because it gets installed by default when you install all versions of Visual Studio except for some forms of Visual Studio Express.

Follow these steps to install and access the copy of the Northwind database that accompanies the samples that ship with Visual Studio 2008:

1. From Visual Studio, choose Help, Samples.

2. Follow the directions to install the Visual Studio 2008 C# Samples to a subfolder of your Documents directory. Note that the latest copies of the samples are always available online at http://go.microsoft.com/fwlink/?LinkID=85559.

3. After installation, the Northwnd.mdf database file is found in a directory called CSharpSamples\LinqSamples\Data, where CSharpSamples is a subdirectory created when you installed the samples.

Choose File, New Project (or press Ctrl-Shift-N) and create a new console application:

1. In Project types, select Windows, as shown in Figure A.3.

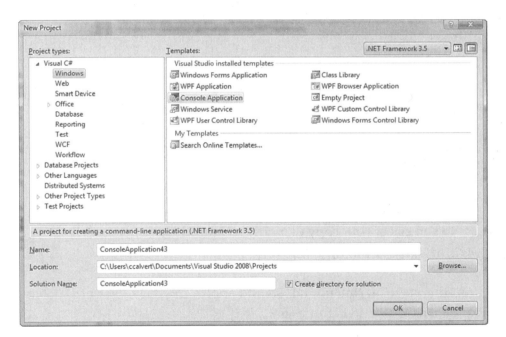

FIGURE A.3 Creating a new console application.

2. In Templates, select Console Application, as shown in Figure A.3.

Create a connection to the Northwind database:

1. Choose View, Server Explorer (or press Ctrl-W, L). In Express editions of Visual Studio, this tool is called Database Explorer.

2. Right-click the Data Connections node, and choose Add Connection. This brings up the Add Connection dialog, shown in Figure A.4.

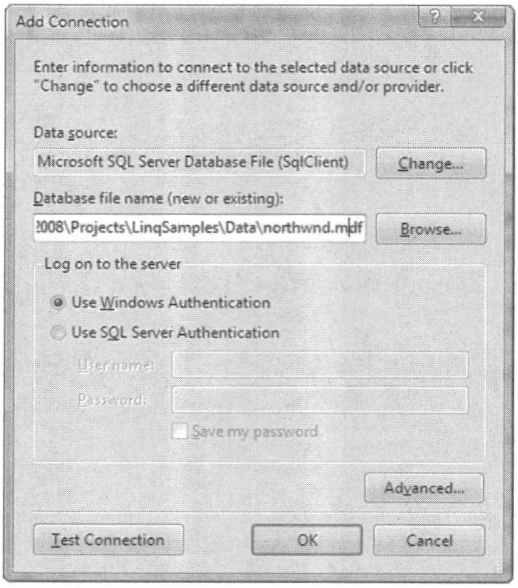

FIGURE A.4 Click the Browse button in the Add Connection dialog and locate your copy of Northwnd.mdf.

3. In the Add Connection dialog, click the Browse button and navigate to and select your copy of Northwnd.mdf.

4. Click the OK button.

At this stage Northwnd.mdf should appear in your server or Database Explorer, as shown in Figure A.5.

FIGURE A.5   The Server Explorer provides a view of the Northwind database.

Using the Object Relational Designer

The Object Relational Designer, (LINQ to SQL Designer) is explained in some depth in Chapter 8, "Reading Objects with LINQ to SQL," and it is occasionally referenced in the other chapters on LINQ to SQL. We have also included a short getting started guide in this appendix.

The Object Relational Designer allows you to configure and view the metadata of the database tables you want to query. There is a command-line version of this tool called SqlMetal that is not covered in this document. By default, SqlMetal is part of the Visual Studio and .NET Framework 3.5 install and is stored in %ProgramFiles%\Microsoft SDKs\Windows\ v6.0A\bin.

Select Project, Add New Item (or press Ctrl-Shift-A). This command brings up the Add New Item dialog. Select LINQ to SQL Classes from the list of Visual Studio Installed Templates, as shown in Figure A.6.

Drag the Customer table from the Server Explorer onto the Designer, as shown in Figure A.7.

In Figure A.7 the Customer table has been dragged from the Server Explorer onto the SQL Designer. Stored procedures can be dragged onto the area where you see the text that begins "Create methods by dragging items...."

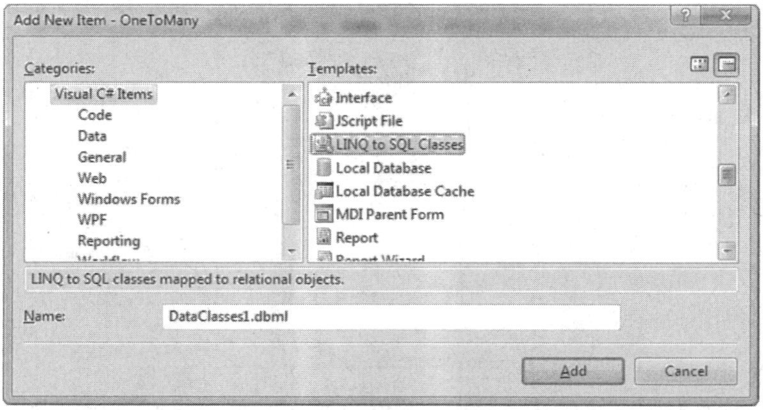

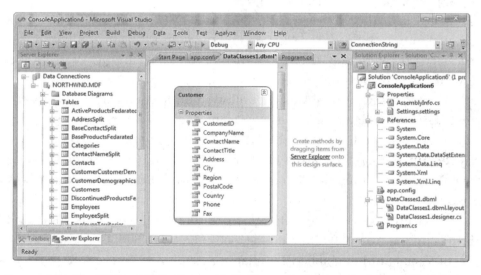

Figure A.6 Choose the LINQ to SQL Designer from the list of available templates available in the Add New Item dialog.

Figure A.7 The LINQ to SQL Designer with the Server Explorer on the left and the Solution Explorer on the right.

Several things happened as you completed the preceding steps:

1. When you added the SQL Designer to your project, a new node in the Solution Explorer called DataClasses1.dbml was added to your project. As shown in Figure A.7, it contains two files, DataClasses1.dbml.layout and DataClasses1.designer.cs.

2. When you dragged the `Customer` table onto the designer, an Object Relational Mapping (ORM) was created between the `Customer` table in the database and a `Customer` class generated by the SQL Designer. The result of this mapping was the production of a class called Customer that was placed in DataClasses1.designer.cs. This class is called an entity class, and it allows you to access the data and fields of the `Customer` table.

3. A second class, called a `DataContext`, was also created in Data-Classes1.designer.cs. You can use this class to automatically connect to your database and easily access the data and fields in the `Customer` table.

4. A file called app.config was added to your project. It contains an automatically generated connection string for your database.

This is not the place to fully explore the O/R Designer and the code it generates. However, the preceding steps give you two key benefits:

- They ensure that you can automatically connect to the database.
- They let you access the `Customer` table in the database via an object in your program.

After you drag items from the Server Explorer onto the SQL Designer, you can modify the view that your program will have of the data. For instance, you can delete some of the fields from the `Customer` table, as shown in Figure A.8. This operation modifies the classes generated, not the actual table on the server.

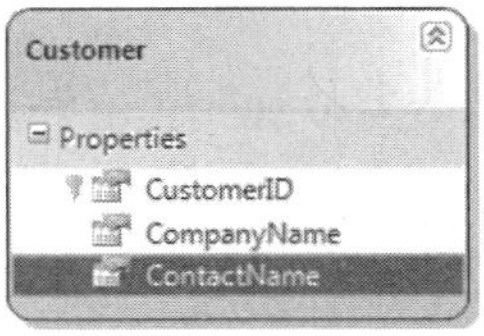

FIGURE A.8   A modified view of the `Customer` table with only three fields visible and other fields deleted.

You can now test your work by opening Program.cs in the Visual Studio editor and typing in the following code:

```
using System;
using System.Linq;

namespace ConsoleApplication41
{
    class Program
    {
        static void Main(string[] args)
        {
            DataClasses1DataContext db = new DataClasses1DataContext();

            var query = from c in db.Customers
                        where c.City == "London"
                        select c.City;

            foreach (var q in query)
            {
                Console.WriteLine(q);
            }
        }
    }
}
```

Summary

In this brief introduction to the Object Relational Designer, you have seen how to

- Download and install the Northwind database from the samples that ship with Visual Studio.
- Access the database through the SQL Designer.

You can learn more about LINQ by running the SampleQueries project that ships with Visual Studio samples referenced in this article.

Important Resources

Here are a few of the most valuable blog posts that have been written about LINQ:

Mocking DataContext for testability

- http://andrewtokeley.net/archive/2008/07/06/mocking-linq-to-sql-datacontext.aspx
- http://blogs.msdn.com/mattwar/archive/2008/05/04/mocks-nix-an-extensible-linq-to-sql-datacontext.aspx

Performance related blog posts:

- http://blogs.msdn.com/ricom/archive/2007/06/22/dlinq-linq-to-sql-performance-part-1.aspx
- http://blogs.msdn.com/ricom/archive/2008/01/14/performance-quiz-13-linq-to-sql-compiled-query-cost-solution.aspx
- http://www.sqlskills.com/BLOGS/BOBB/post/MHO-LINQ-to-SQL-and-Entity-Framework-Panacea-or-evil-incarnate-Part-6.aspx

Entity Framework Mapping Scenarios:

- http://weblogs.asp.net/zeeshanhirani/archive/2008/12/08/my-christmas-present-to-the-entity-framework-community.aspx

Reference Materials: Getting Help

This book is not primarily a reference. Instead, it is meant to explain how LINQ works, the structure of its architecture, and best practices for its use. However, a good reference can help supplement the materials found in this book and can help answer many common questions about LINQ.

The LINQ documentation created by Microsoft is primarily a reference document. It is available both inside Visual Studio and for free via the MSDN library found on the web. Here are some important pages that can help you navigate through the online LINQ documentation:

- The Root MSDN Library Page: http://msdn.microsoft.com/en-us/library/default.aspx
- .NET Development: http://msdn.microsoft.com/en-us/library/aa139615.aspx

- .NET Framework 3.5: http://msdn.microsoft.com/en-us/library/ w0x726c2.aspx
- System.Linq: http://msdn.microsoft.com/en-us/library/system. linq.aspx
- System.Data.Linq: http://msdn.microsoft.com/en-us/library/ system.data.linq.aspx
- System.Xml.Linq: http://msdn.microsoft.com/en-us/library/ system.xml.linq.aspx
- Code generation: http://msdn.microsoft.com/en-us/library/ bb399400.aspx
- More on joins: http://msdn.microsoft.com/en-us/library/ bb311040.aspx
- For more information on the operators, see the section of the online help called "The .NET Standard Query Operators." It was written by Anders Hejlsberg and Mads Torgersen. The URL is http://msdn. microsoft.com/en-us/library/bb394939.aspx.

I do not suggest using these references materials as a primary means of learning LINQ. However, these pages can be a useful addendum to this text. If you understand in a general way how LINQ works, but you need answers to detailed questions, the links provided here may sometimes help you find answers.

Finding LINQ Providers

I maintain a list of links to LINQ providers on my blog. Here is the address of the relevant article:

http://blogs.msdn.com/charlie/archive/2006/10/05/Links-to-LINQ.aspx

Including Data Files in Your Project

When you're working in Visual Studio, defining the path to a document can be a chore. You face two primary problems:

- The path to your project may be long and complex.
- Projects can easily be moved from one location to another, which causes the path to change.

Both of these problems can be solved easily when you are working inside the IDE. If you are working with an XML file that you want your program to load, do these three things:

1. Place the file in the directory where your main project file resides.
2. Add the file to your project.
3. Set the Copy to Output Directory property of your XML file to Copy if Newer.

This ensures that the XML file is in the same directory as the project executable. Hence, it can be loaded directly into the project without your having to consider the path to the file: doc.Load("MyFile.xml");

C# Keywords and Contextual Keywords

C# has a wide variety of keywords and contextual keywords. Keywords are reserved words and may not be used by developers as variable names. Contextual keywords are reserved words in certain circumstances but may be used as variable names.

Consider the contextual keyword var. If it's used to designate that type inference should be used as part of a type definition, it is a keyword:

```
var myInteger = 3;
```

It is the context in which this word is used that makes var a reserved word in this case. If it's used in a different context, it is not a keyword. For instance, here var is simply a variable name:

```
int var = 3;
```

The C# team developed this policy because they did not want to break existing code. They knew that some developers might have used var as a variable name, and they did not want to force them to modify their code.

Instead, they developed contextual keywords so that they could add new features to the language without breaking existing code.

Most LINQ keywords are contextual, because they were added to the language in version 3.0, after C# had been out for several years. The following are the existing C# keywords and contextual keywords as of C# 3.0.

C# Keywords

abstract	event	new	struct
as	explicit	null	switch
base	extern	object	this
bool	FALSE	operator	throw
break	finally	out	TRUE
byte	fixed	override	try
case	float	params	typeof
catch	for	private	uint
char	foreach	protected	ulong
checked	goto	public	unchecked
class	if	readonly	unsafe
const	implicit	ref	ushort
continue	in	return	using
decimal	int	sbyte	virtual
default	interface	sealed	void
delegate	internal	short	volatile
do	is	sizeof	while
double	lock	stackalloc	
else	long	static	
enum	namespace	string	

Contextual Keywords

from	join	partial (method)	var
get	let	select	where (generic type constraint)
group	orderby	set	where (query clause)
into	partial (type)	value	yield

Visual C# 2008 Key Bindings

The developers of Visual Studio put a considerable amount of effort into defining a set of key bindings that can make it easy to navigate through the component parts of a C# project. Table A.1 is an overview of the default key bindings for C# developers.

The C# Express edition of Visual Studio has only one possible set of key bindings; it corresponds to the settings shown in Table A.1. Other versions of Visual Studio, however, have multiple key bindings available, including those for C# developers, VB developers, general developers, Team Test developers, and web developers. Here is how to change the settings so that the key bindings are set to the default values for C# developers:

1. Select Tools, Import and Export Settings.
2. Choose Reset All Settings, and click Next.
3. You can optionally save your current settings or select to overwrite your existing settings. Click Next.
4. Select the Visual C# Development Settings, and click Finish.

The items shown in Table A.1 are broken into different categories. For instance, the first items are part of the Edit category, the File category is second, and so on.

TABLE A.1   The Visual C# Key Bindings

Command	Key Binding
Edit	
Edit.CollapseTo-Definitions	Ctrl-M, O
Edit.ToggleAllOutlining	Ctrl-M, L
Edit.ToggleOutliningExpansion	Ctrl-M, M
Edit.StopOutlining	Ctrl-M, P
Edit.CommentSelection	Ctrl-K, C or Ctrl-E, C
Edit.UncommentSelection	Ctrl-K, U or Ctrl-E, U
Edit.FormatDocument	Ctrl-K, D or Ctrl-E, D
Edit.FormatSelection	Ctrl-K, F, or Ctrl-E, F
Edit.InsertSnippet	Ctrl-K, X
Edit.SurroundWith	Ctrl-K, S
Edit.InvokeSnippetFromShortcut	Tab
Edit.CycleClipboardRing	Ctrl-Shift-V
Edit.Replace	Ctrl-H
Edit.ReplaceInFiles	Ctrl-Shift-H
View.ShowSmartTag	Ctrl-. or Shift-Alt-F10
File	
File.NewProject	Ctrl-Shift-N
File.OpenProject	Ctrl-Shift-O
Project.AddClass	Shift-Alt-C
Project.AddExistingItem	Shift-Alt-A
Project.AddNewItem	Ctrl-Shift-A
Window.ShowEzMDIFileList	Ctrl-Alt-down arrow

Command	Key Binding
Edit.OpenFile	Ctrl-O
IntelliSense	
Edit.CompleteWord	Ctrl-Space
Ctrl-K, W	
Edit.ListMembers	Ctrl-J
Ctrl-K, L	
Edit.QuickInfo	Ctrl-K, I
Edit.ParameterInfo	Ctrl-Shift-Space or Ctrl K, P
Make Completion List Transparent	Ctrl
Navigation	
Edit.FindAllReferences	Shift-F12 or Ctrl-K, R
Edit.GoToBrace	Ctrl-]
Edit.GoToDefinition	F12
Edit.GoToNextLocation	F8
Edit.IncrementalSearch	Ctrl-I
View.ClassViewGo-ToSearch, Combo	Ctrl-K or Ctrl-V
View.ForwardBrowseContext	Ctrl-Shift-7
View.PopBrowseContext	Ctrl-Shift-8
View.NavigateBackward	Ctrl-minus sign (-)
View.NavigateForward	Ctrl-Shift-minus sign (-)
Edit.FindInFiles	Ctrl-Shift-F
Edit.FindSymbol	Alt-F12
View.ViewCode	F7

continues

TABLE A.1   Continued

Command	Key Binding
View.ViewDesigner	Shift-F7
View.ViewMarkup	Shift-F7
Window.MoveToNavigationBar	Ctrl-F2
Edit.Find	Ctrl-F
Edit.GoTo	Ctrl-G
Edit.GoToFindCombo	Ctrl-/
Window	
View.ClassView	Ctrl-W, C
View.CodeDefinitionWindow	Ctrl-W, D
View.Command-Window	Ctrl-W, A
View.ErrorList	Ctrl-W, E
View.ObjectBrowser	Ctrl-W, J
View.Output	Ctrl-W, O
View.PropertiesWindow	Ctrl-W, P
View.SolutionExplorer	Ctrl-W, S
View.TaskList	Ctrl-W, T
View.Toolbox	Ctrl-W, X
View.ServerExplorer	Ctrl-W, L
Window.CloseToolWindow	Shift-Esc
Data.ShowDataSources	Shift-Alt-D
Window.CloseDocument, Window	Ctrl-F4
Window.NextDocument, WindowNav	Ctrl-Tab

Command	Key Binding
Refactor	
Refactor.EncapsulateField	Ctrl-R, E
Refactor.ExtractInterface	Ctrl-R, I
Refactor.ExtractMethod	Ctrl-R, M
Refactor.PromoteLocalVariabletoParameter	Ctrl-R, P
Refactor.RemoveParameters	Ctrl-R, V
Refactor.Rename	Ctrl-R, R or F2
Refactor.ReorderParameters	Ctrl-R, O
Debugging	
Debug.Autos	Ctrl-D, A
Debug.CallStack	Ctrl-D, C
Debug.Immediate	Ctrl-D, I
Debug.Locals	Ctrl-D, L
Debug.QuickWatch	Ctrl-D, Q
Debug.Start	F5
Debug.StartWithoutDebugging	Ctrl-F5
Debug.StepInto	F11
Debug.StepOut	Shift-F11
Debug.StepOver	F10
Debug.StopDebugging	Shift-F5
Debug.ToggleBreakpoint	F9
Debug.Watch	Ctrl-D, W
Debug.EnableBreakpoint	Ctrl-F9

continues

TABLE A.1   Continued

Command	Key Binding
Make Datatip Transparent	Ctrl
Build	
Build.BuildSolution	F6 or Ctrl-Shift-B
Build.BuildSelection	Shift-F6

Answers to Chapter 4 Exercises

Here are the answers to the exercises found in Chapter 4, "C# 3.0 Technical Overview." The exercises are found in the section "Generic Methods, Delegates, and Lambdas"—more specifically, in the subsection "Lambdas."

1. `Action<string> display = (a) => Console.WriteLine(a);`

2. `Func<int, int> multiply = (a) => (a * 5);`

3. `Action displayWarning = () => Console.WriteLine("Warning");`

4. `Func<int, int, int, decimal> calculate = (a, b, c) => (a + b) / c`

5. `Func<int, int, long> add = (a, b) => ((long)a + b);`

6. `Func<int, int, long> add = (a, b) => ((long)a + b);`

```csharp
using System;
using System.Collections.Generic;
using System.Linq;
using System.Text;

namespace ConsoleApplication1
{
    class Program
    {
        public static void Display(string value)
        {
            Console.WriteLine(value);
        }
```

```csharp
public static int Multiply(int a)
{
    return a * 5;
}

public static void DisplayWarning()
{
    Console.WriteLine("Warning");
}

public static decimal Calculate(int a, int b, int c)
{
    return (a + b) / c;
}

public static long Add(int a, int b)
{
    return a + (long)b;
}

public static string ShowMe(string a, int b, int c)
{
    return string.Format(a, b, c, (b + c));
}

static void Main(string[] args)
{
    Action<string> display = (a) => Console.WriteLine(a);

    Display("Some Text");
    display("Some text");

    Func<int, int> multiply = (a) => (a * 5);

    Console.WriteLine(Multiply(3));
    Console.WriteLine(multiply(3));

    Action displayWarning = () => Console.WriteLine("Warning");

    DisplayWarning();
    displayWarning();

    Func<int, int, int, decimal> calculate =
        (a, b, c) => (a + b) / c;

    Console.WriteLine(Calculate(5, 4, 3));
    Console.WriteLine(calculate(5, 4, 3));

    Func<int, int, long> add = (a, b) => ((long)a + b);
```

```
        Console.WriteLine(Add(Int32.MaxValue, Int32.MaxValue));
        Console.WriteLine(add(Int32.MaxValue, Int32.MaxValue));

        Func<string, int, int, string> showMe =
            (a, b, c) => string.Format(a, b, c, (b + c));

        Console.WriteLine(ShowMe("{0} + {1} = {2}", 3, 5));
        Console.WriteLine(showMe("{0} + {1} = {2}", 3, 5));


    }
  }
}
```

Index

Microsoft .NET Development Series

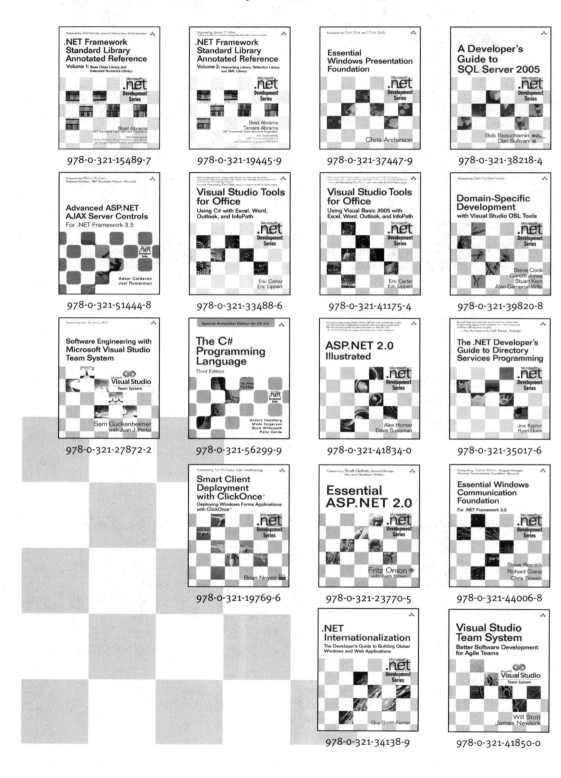

.NET Framework Standard Library Annotated Reference
Volume 1: Base Class Library and Extended Numerics Library
Brad Abrams
978-0-321-15489-7

.NET Framework Standard Library Annotated Reference
Volume 2: Networking Library, Reflection Library and XML Library
Brad Abrams
Tamara Abrams
978-0-321-19445-9

Essential Windows Presentation Foundation
Chris Anderson
978-0-321-37447-9

A Developer's Guide to SQL Server 2005
Bob Beauchemin
Dan Sullivan
978-0-321-38218-4

Advanced ASP.NET AJAX Server Controls
For .NET Framework 3.5
Adam Calderon
Joel Rumerman
978-0-321-51444-8

Visual Studio Tools for Office
Using C# with Excel, Word, Outlook, and InfoPath
Eric Carter
Eric Lippert
978-0-321-33488-6

Visual Studio Tools for Office
Using Visual Basic 2005 with Excel, Word, Outlook, and InfoPath
Eric Carter
Eric Lippert
978-0-321-41175-4

Domain-Specific Development
with Visual Studio DSL Tools
Steve Cook
Gareth Jones
Stuart Kent
Alan Cameron Wills
978-0-321-39820-8

Software Engineering with Microsoft Visual Studio Team System
Sam Guckenheimer
with Juan J. Perez
978-0-321-27872-2

The C# Programming Language
Third Edition
Special Annotated Edition for C# 3.0
Anders Hejlsberg
Mads Torgersen
Scott Wiltamuth
Peter Golde
978-0-321-56299-9

ASP.NET 2.0 Illustrated
Alex Homer
Dave Sussman
978-0-321-41834-0

The .NET Developer's Guide to Directory Services Programming
Joe Kaplan
Ryan Dunn
978-0-321-35017-6

Smart Client Deployment with ClickOnce
Deploying Windows Forms Applications with ClickOnce
Brian Noyes
978-0-321-19769-6

Essential ASP.NET 2.0
Fritz Onion
with Keith Brown
978-0-321-23770-5

Essential Windows Communication Foundation
For .NET Framework 3.5
Steve Resnick
Richard Crane
Chris Bowen
978-0-321-44006-8

.NET Internationalization
The Developer's Guide to Building Global Windows and Web Applications
Guy Smith-Ferrier
978-0-321-34138-9

Visual Studio Team System
Better Software Development for Agile Teams
Will Stott
James Newkirk
978-0-321-41850-0

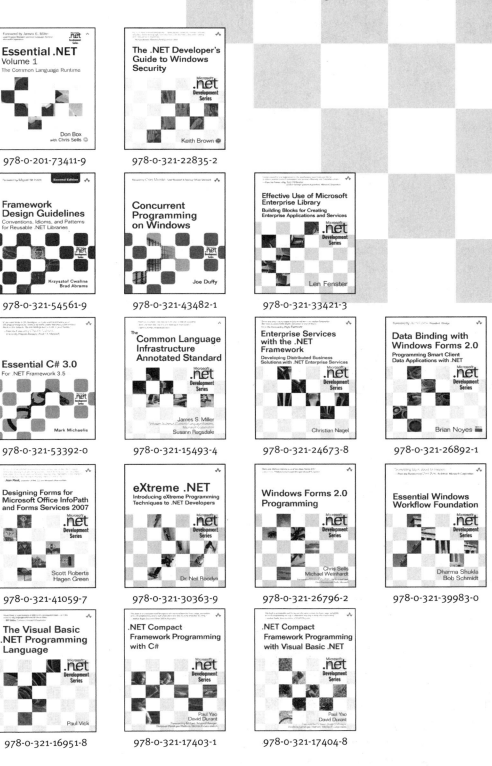

For more information go to informit.com/msdotnetseries/

Essential .NET Volume 1 — The Common Language Runtime — Don Box with Chris Sells
978-0-201-73411-9

The .NET Developer's Guide to Windows Security — Keith Brown
978-0-321-22835-2

Framework Design Guidelines Conventions, Idioms, and Patterns for Reusable .NET Libraries — Krzysztof Cwalina, Brad Abrams
978-0-321-54561-9

Concurrent Programming on Windows — Joe Duffy
978-0-321-43482-1

Effective Use of Microsoft Enterprise Library Building Blocks for Creating Enterprise Applications and Services — Len Fenster
978-0-321-33421-3

Essential C# 3.0 For .NET Framework 3.5 — Mark Michaelis
978-0-321-53392-0

The Common Language Infrastructure Annotated Standard — James S. Miller, Susann Ragsdale
978-0-321-15493-4

Enterprise Services with the .NET Framework Developing Distributed Business Solutions with .NET Enterprise Services — Christian Nagel
978-0-321-24673-8

Data Binding with Windows Forms 2.0 Programming Smart Client Data Applications with .NET — Brian Noyes
978-0-321-26892-1

Designing Forms for Microsoft Office InfoPath and Forms Services 2007 — Scott Roberts, Hagen Green
978-0-321-41059-7

eXtreme .NET Introducing eXtreme Programming Techniques to .NET Developers — Dr. Neil Roodyn
978-0-321-30363-9

Windows Forms 2.0 Programming — Chris Sells, Michael Weinhardt
978-0-321-26796-2

Essential Windows Workflow Foundation — Dharma Shukla, Bob Schmidt
978-0-321-39983-0

The Visual Basic .NET Programming Language — Paul Vick
978-0-321-16951-8

.NET Compact Framework Programming with C# — Paul Yao, David Durant
978-0-321-17403-1

.NET Compact Framework Programming with Visual Basic .NET — Paul Yao, David Durant
978-0-321-17404-8

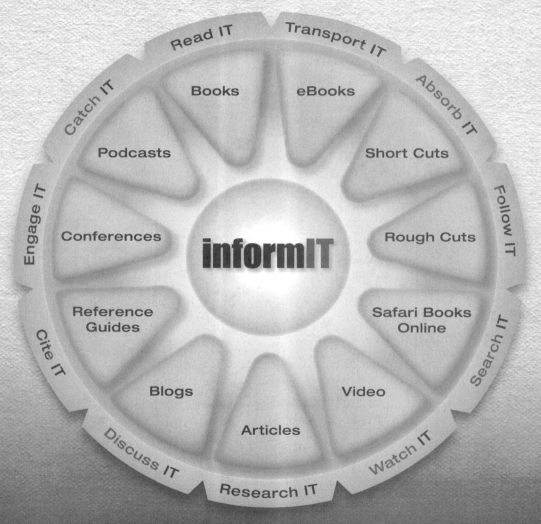